ALSO BY MARK JONES LORENZO

Affront to Meritocracy: Stories of Overlooked Talents, Ignored Abilities, and Hidden Truths

Not Ok: A Requiem for GW-BASIC

Apophenia's Antidote: A Probability and Statistics Primer

Its Wildness Lies in Wait: Mathematical Fallacies, Cognitive Traps, and Debunking the Myths of the Lottery

The Paper Computer Unfolded: A Twenty-First Century Guide to the Bell Labs CARDIAC (CARDboard Illustrative Aid to Computation), the LMC (Little Man Computer), and the IPC (Instructo Paper Computer)

Ok: The Resurrection of GW-BASIC

Endless Loop: The History of the BASIC Programming Language (Beginner's All-purpose Symbolic Instruction Code)

Adventures of a Statistician: The Biography of John W. Tukey

ABSTRACTING AWAY THE MACHINE
◇◇◇

ABSTRACTING AWAY THE MACHINE
◊◊◊
The History of the FORTRAN Programming Language
(FORmula TRANslation)

Mark Jones Lorenzo

SE BOOKS
Philadelphia | Pittsburgh

Ψ
SE BOOKS
5307 West Tyson Street
Philadelphia, Pennsylvania 19107
www.sebooks.com

Copyright © 2019 by Mark Jones Lorenzo

All rights reserved. Printed in the United States of America. No part of this book may be reproduced in any manner whatsoever without written permission except in the case of brief quotations embodied in critical articles and reviews. For information, contact SE BOOKS.

References to websites (URLs) were accurate at the time of writing. Neither the author nor SE BOOKS is responsible for URLs that may have expired or changed since the manuscript was prepared.

Published in full-throated defiance of Yog's Law.

Library cataloging information is as follows:

Lorenzo, Mark Jones
 Abstracting away the machine : the history of the FORTRAN programming language (FORmula TRANslation) / Mark Jones Lorenzo.
 p. ; cm.
  Includes bibliographical references.
  I. Title
1. Fortran (computer programming language). 2. History (computers).
  QA76.73.F25 BT22 2019
  005.1337'53120—js22

ISBN: 978-1-082-39594-9

10   9   8   7   6   5   4   3   2   1

Dedicated to John W. Backus:
A pioneer who proved that laziness is the father of invention

History is the long process of outsourcing human ability in order to leverage more of it.

—RICHARD POWERS

FORTRAN. It sounds like something spelled backwards.

—HARLAN HERRICK

CONTENTS

◊◊◊

	INTRODUCTION	13
1	The Two Births of 1924	17
2	A Stroll Down Madison Avenue	27
3	Hand-to-Hand Combat with the Machine	39
4	The UNIVAC and the IBM 701	43
5	Speedcoding	49
6	Building the IBM 704	55
7	The Automatic Programming Proposal	59
8	Assembling the Team	73
9	The Language Takes Shape	85
10	Punching a Shared Place in History	93
11	A Motley Crew	105
12	Making a Statement	111
13	The Symbolic/SHARE Assembly Program	127
14	Building the First FORTRAN Compiler	133
15	FORTRAN I, Accidently Distributed	147
16	The (Short) History of FOR TRANSIT	161
17	FORTRAN, the Sequel	167
18	Great Optimism and Little Discipline	173
19	The Need for Some Standards	177
20	Knocking Down the Tower of Babel	191
21	Coloring Outside the Lines	199
22	Setting the Standards, Again	211
23	FORTRAN the Foil: Rise of the Competition	227
24	Implicit None	263
25	In the Shadow of John von Neumann	277
26	High Performance and Beyond	283
27	Too Afraid to Fail	293

IN THE BEGINNING...	297
RESOURCES	301
ACKNOWLEDGMENTS	323
ABOUT THE AUTHOR	325

INTRODUCTION
◊◊◊

A high-level computer language *abstracts away the machine* because the programmer need not be an expert in the machinations of computer hardware components, nor understand the blizzard of zeros and ones that comprise a machine language, nor even juggle the mnemonics of an assembler in order to successfully program a computer. High-level languages (HLLs) automate, hide, or otherwise abstract away the underlying operations of the machine, allowing the programmer to focus on the coding problem at hand rather than having to worry about managing memory or conforming to the operations of a particular kind of processor. All of those details are hidden from view. Instead, programming in a form of natural language, rather than an unreadable machine code, becomes the order of the day, with low-level numeric coding giving way to high-level symbolic, algebraic-style manipulation.

Innumerable high-level languages were developed over the past six decades, including ALGOL, BASIC, C/C++, COBOL, Java, LISP, LOGO, Pascal, PL/I, Python, and Visual Basic. These languages succeeded in opening up the field of computer programming to the masses. No longer was coding the province of a small band of technical experts—a "priesthood"—who knew the ins and outs of the hardware cold. First scientists, then engineers and businesspeople, and, eventually, precocious young folks and home consumers stormed the gates. Now practically anyone could learn how to tell a computer what to do, and the computer would do it.

But all HLLs owe a huge debt of gratitude to FORTRAN, a contraction of FORmula TRANslation (or, less commonly, FORMula TRANslator), which was the first mature high-level programming language to achieve widespread adoption. Many programming practices that we take for granted now came about as a result of FORTRAN. Created over a three-year period at IBM by an elite development team led by a brilliant but wayward mathematician named John W. Backus, FORTRAN was implemented initially on the IBM 704 Data Processing System mainframe computer in the mid-1950s, with dialects of the language rapidly spreading thereafter to other platforms. FORTRAN was simultaneously breathtakingly original and yet also a product of its time, since in creating the language the development team leveraged the available hardware at least as much as designing optimal software routines; in fact, the 704 hardware was expressly co-designed by Backus with the requirements of his nascent programming language firmly in mind.

FORTRAN's powerful compiler, which translated human-readable code into code a computer could understand, produced incredibly clean and optimized standalone executable programs, all of which could be run independently of the compiler, setting the standard for decades to come. In the 1960s the language was standardized, with machine-dependent commands excised, and many platform-independent implementations followed. With the language now portable, able to run on any computer (at least in theory), FORTRAN, almost by accident, secured a stranglehold in the fields of science and engineering. The language also came to dominate in the supercomputing industry.

But FORTRAN, a blue-collar workhorse more concerned with results than with style, was a victim of its own success—the language sowed the seeds of its own demise. New high-level languages sprouted up, stealing the good bits from FORTRAN while simultaneously defining themselves in opposition to it. FORTRAN had become the foil. As these new languages pierced the cutting edge of the programming landscape, they redefined computing paradigms (e.g., with structured programming, object-oriented programming, and the like), and FORTRAN—though eventually (and repeatedly) modernized and formally renamed Fortran—struggled to keep up through multiple standardization efforts, finally ceding significant ground to its successors as it slowly withdrew from the spotlight. To add insult to injury, even John Backus eventually turned against his creation.

This is not a book on how to program in any implementation of FORTRAN, nor is it a technical manual; although there are passages that are technical in nature, they serve strictly to further the narrative. (Sometimes, full programs or program snippets are used to illustrate technical ideas. When these lines of code appear, they are displayed using one of several fonts: **Century Schoolbook** for pre-Fortran 90, and `Courier New` for Fortran 90 and beyond as well as for assembly language. Note that code from languages other than FORTRAN, as well as from "FORTRAN 0," is typically printed in Garamond, the same font used in the body text.) Rather, the focus in ABSTRACTING AWAY THE MACHINE, which chronicles the complete history and development of the FORTRAN programming language, is set squarely on telling three interlocking stories: (1) How an elite group of computing trailblazers built FORTRAN, (2) Why the conditions at the time were ripe for them to succeed, and (3) What happened after they did.

Tracing the long arc of FORTRAN's development and maturation serves as more than merely an interesting academic exercise—it is integral to understanding not only the history of programming but also the state of computer science today. The birth of FORTRAN planted a seed that led to the full flowering of high-level languages, since FORTRAN overcame initial skepticism by demonstrating to the world that a well-made HLL really could abstract away the machine.

ABSTRACTING AWAY THE MACHINE
◇◇◇

CHAPTER 1

The Two Births of 1924

If not for two births in 1924—that of IBM, and also of John W. Backus—FORTRAN would not exist.

International Business Machines, or IBM, officially began as a merger of multiple tabulating and timekeeping device businesses in the early twentieth century. But the success of the corporation came about because of the increasing demand for data processing that began in the nineteenth century in the United States. At the forefront of that demand was efficient tabulation of the census, conducted by the Bureau of the Census. Constitutionally required once per decade in order to properly apportion members of the House of Representatives, the first federal census was conducted in 1790 with little difficulty, since the young nation's population was relatively small and—besides—not all human beings were counted equally (or at all). Relatively few clerks were needed by the Bureau to handle the workload.

After the Civil War, however, conducting the decennial census spiraled into a logistical nightmare. The 1880 census required around 1,500 clerks, engaging frantically in a crude form of manual data processing consisting of transcribing check marks and compiling demographic information on endless stacks of tally sheets. Taking more than seven years to complete, the continued population growth of the U.S. threatened to make the next census require longer than a decade to complete—surely leading to an untenable situation of having to compile data from two censuses simultaneously.

The solution to speeding up the manual data processing came from a brilliant engineer named Herman Hollerith. Born in Buffalo, New York, in 1860, Hollerith, the son of German immigrants, attended Columbia University and graduated with an Engineer of Mines degree. Thanks to the influence of one of his professors at Columbia, he landed a job at the Census Bureau on the eve of the 1880 census. Over dinner one evening at the home of John Shaw Billings, an overseer of the census, the conversation turned to the intractable difficulties of compiling masses of data. If only there were a way to mechanize the process, Billings said to Hollerith, data processing could be much quicker and more accurate.

Hollerith readily took to the idea. Five years later, in 1889, inspired by a railroad conductor's ticket punch, Hollerith filed a patent for an electromechanical tabulating machine, whereby a person's demographic information could be recorded by the presence (or absence) of holes on punched cards (also referred to simply as punch cards). "I was traveling in the West and I had a ticket with what I think was called a punch photograph," he recalled. "[T]he conductor…punched out a description of the individual, as light hair, dark eyes, large nose, etc. So you see, I only made a punch photograph of each person."

Also in 1889, Hollerith penned a comprehensive article proposing a punched card size for the upcoming 1890 census: "For the work of a census, a card 3" × 5½" would be sufficient to answer all ordinary purposes. The cards are preferably made of as thin [manila] stock as will be convenient to handle." When the census arrived, Hollerith's punched cards had twelve rows and ten columns and utilized round holes, with each hole representing a single piece of data, or bit. The next several censuses saw punched cards evolve, containing more columns, more rows, and a bigger size overall: 3¼ by 7⅜, which were not arbitrary dimensions—the cards were the same size as U.S. paper currency at the time, which served as a convenience for Hollerith, since he used U.S. Treasury Department boxes to store the cards. By 1927, punched cards with round holes would reach their maximum density: forty-five columns. And by the 1930s, with punched cards proliferating beyond mere census use—some of which contained workaday computer programs, others of which served as encoded social security checks (starting in 1940)—the fragility of the precious cards became a cause for concern. Warnings were printed on the cards, directed to a public only slowly warming to the technology: "Do not fold or bend this card," "Do not fold, tear, or mutilate this card," "Do not fold, tear or destroy," and, most famously, "Do not fold, spindle, or mutilate." The latter warning was coopted in the 1960s by radical left student groups. Steven Lubar, author of "'Do Not Fold, Spindle or Mutilate': A Cultural History of the Punch Card," explains why:

> Punch cards became not only a symbol for the computer…, but a symbol of alienation. They stood for abstraction, oversimplification and dehumanization. The cards were, it seemed, a two-dimensional portrait of people, people abstracted into numbers that machines could use. The cards came to represent a society where it seemed that machines had become more important than people, where people had to change their ways to suit the machines. People weren't dealing with each other face-to-face, but rather through the medium of the punch card.

The Free Speech Movement student protests of the mid-1960s at the University of California-Berkeley latched onto the phrase "Do not fold, spindle, or mutilate" because university administration employed punched cards for class registration, with Berkeley's student newspaper explaining, "The incoming freshman has much to learn…perhaps lesson number one is not to fold, spindle, or mutilate his IBM card." As Lubar concludes, "The punch card stood for the university, and, of course, students had begun to fold, spindle and mutilate them." (Even today, variants of the phrase appear above detachable portions of bill payments. For instance, the current Pennsylvania Department of Transportation vehicle title and registration paper renewal form warns, "PLEASE DO NOT STAPLE, BEND, FOLD, OR MUTILATE.")

In the 1920s, though, punched cards were not yet ubiquitous enough to achieve notoriety. Near the end of the decade, the cards would receive a major upgrade. In 1928, Hollerith cards were increased in storage density but not in size (changing the size of the card would render all of IBM's equipment useless): upgraded to twelve rows by eighty columns with more structurally-sound rectangular holes rather than circular ones, they became the standard-sized, corner-cut IBM eighty-column punched cards, which were referred to as IBM computer cards or simply IBM cards.

By the 1960s, IBM cards had reached their zenith as a storage medium. These late-model punched cards had two unlabeled rows at the top of the cards, typically referred to as the 11 and 12 rows (or the Y and X rows, respectively), and, underneath them, the remaining ten rows, labeled with a string of eighty 0s, eighty 1s, eighty 2s, all the way to the bottom of the card, containing a row of eighty 9s. A card's top three rows—the two blank rows and the zero row—were called the "zone" rows. Since the 12-row was at the top, the top of the card was referred to as the "12-edge"; likewise, the bottom of the card was called the "9-edge."

Encoding digits was straightforward: punch a hole in the appropriate digit row. Encoding uppercase alphabetical characters and symbols was slightly trickier, requiring at least two holes: one in the zone row, and at least one hole in the remaining digit rows. Punctuation characters, including #, @, $, and &, ultimately brought the total to forty-eight punch combinations that were together referred to as the IBM 029 Code, informally called the Hollerith code. The following diagram relays how the IBM 026 Printing Card Punch translated characters into hole punches:

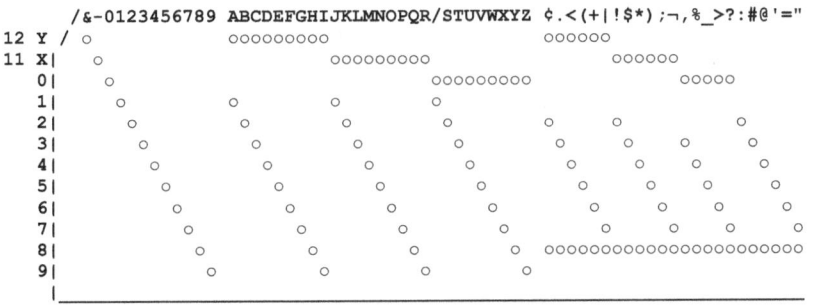

For instance, an A was represented by two punches in a single column: on the 12-row and the 1-row. A dollar sign ($) was represented by three punches in a single column: on the 11-row, the 3-row, and the 8-row. As the characters were typed, the 026 Card Punch would print the characters just above the 12-row (e.g., if an A was punched, the letter A would appear at the very top of the card, with the correct punches in the same column below the letter).

The cards were fragile; one had to be especially careful not to punch too many holes into a single card. Although 2^{12}, or 4,096, possible characters technically *could* be have been encoded into any particular column—meaning that, theoretically, punched cards could have been encoded in binary—in practice the cards would weaken to a considerable degree with too many punches, so much so that feeding punched-up cards into card-reading machines would jam the equipment and destroy the cards. Thus, the Hollerith code restricted each column to a maximum of three punches in order to maintain the structural integrity of the cards. But regardless of the physical constraints, substantial creativity resulted in IBM cards becoming quite versatile as they evolved, with techniques such as the "multi-punch-mode" and swapping special character sets depending on different needs (e.g., with computer programming).

The IBM eighty-column-by-twelve-row punched card, with eighty bits of data stored in each row (eighty bits since each of the eighty holes of a row could be either punched or not punched), came about as a result of a competition between two inventors at IBM: J. Royden Peirce and Clair D. Lake. Peirce proposed keeping the round holes, but permitting each hole to represent more than one character. Lake proposed rectangular holes, which could be more easily read by the machines but would require redesigning the equipment. IBM ran with Lake's idea, and the IBM card was born.

The first generation of punched cards, which were used for the 1890 census with the mass-produced Hollerith Census Tabulators, had round holes with very few columns. Hollerith's early tabulating machines had three parts: a Pantographic punch; a sorting box; and a card-reading station, or press. Unpunched cards were first fed into the "punch station" of the Pantographic punch, whereby a punch operator gripped a stylus hovering over a card template—which decoded the various demographic options on a card—and pressed downward overtop the appropriate holes, thereby punching holes in the card locked in the punch station. Completed punched cards were placed into a sorting box and then fed into the card-reading station for tabulation. For each data point represented on a particular punched card, a metal pin made contact with a miniscule cup of mercury by passing through a punched hole (there were 288 pins and cups), thus closing an electronic circuit—and electromagnetically advancing a counting dial by a single digit. There were forty such dials, each keeping track of demographic data, as card after card was fed through the card-reading station. After each card was read completely, the machine would ring a bell automatically.

In 1887, Hollerith took his machine to Baltimore, Maryland, which served as a proving ground. A year later, the new superintendent of the census, Robert Porter, recognizing the need for a better means of conducting the census, devised a competition: it would be Hollerith pitted against two other inventors, Charles F. Pidgin and William C. Hunt, both of whom had invented tabulating systems of their own. However, Pidgin's and Hunt's approaches still relied on manual tabulation, optimizing the process via color-coding the inks or the cards themselves. Because Superintendent Porter was a public proponent of Hollerith's system, he recused himself as a competition judge. Regardless, Hollerith's tabulating machine proved itself to be much faster in tests than his competitors', and preparations began in earnest for the 1890 census. Western Electric was contracted to build Hollerith Census Tabulators, and paper manufacturers geared up to produce the more than sixty million punched cards that would be needed. In 1890, with more than two thousand clerks standing ready at the Census Bureau, forty-five thousand census enumerators compiled data from around the country. Several months later, the population of the United States was publicly announced: roughly sixty-three million people. Controversy immediately ensued, since the number sounded too small to a public eager to hear that the country was growing without bound. The *Boston Herald* and the *New York Herald* both blamed the new machines for the supposed "undercount," but the machines performed as promised—though there was much tabulating yet to be done.

Punching clerks, an occupation typically staffed by women, punched between five hundred and seven hundred cards per day; when the process wrapped up, nearly sixty-three million cards had been punched, but significantly less time had been needed for data compilation than in the previous census.

The use of punched cards eventually spread from the government to commercial industry, but it spread slowly, in part because of the high cost of the Hollerith machines but also due to their specialized nature: they were built for the census, and nothing more. Which left Hollerith's machines collecting dust in between censuses and Herman Hollerith without a steady income stream. So he looked to the business sector, establishing a company called the Tabulating Machine Company, or TMC, to market and sell his machines, but by then preparations were in order for the upcoming 1900 census. Although the machines performed admirably again for the census work, with the assassination of President William McKinley, a new census superintendent was appointed—one who was dissatisfied with the soaring costs of the equipment Hollerith provided the government. In 1905, the Census Bureau demanded two things from Hollerith: cut costs and improve the tabulating machines. He balked at both of their requests, leading the Census Bureau to employ engineer James Powers to revamp the Hollerith machines (which he did, enabling data printouts).

Hollerith, now free from the shackles of the Census Bureau, devoted most of his attention to building TMC and gearing his machines toward business uses. (He also sued the government for patent infringement but lost.) His newer, more automatic, machines employed a larger punched card: twelve rows by forty-five columns. TMC grew at a rapid clip over the next decade, acquiring about one hundred loyal customers for its products. But Hollerith, in poor health, decided to sell TMC.

In 1911, the "Father of Trusts" and master merger of businesses Charles Ranlett Flint had an idea. Through the acquisition of stocks, he would merge TMC with three other companies: the International Time Recording Company (which made employee-clocking equipment), the Computing Scale Company of America (which produced commercial scales), and the Bundy Manufacturing Company (which made timekeeping equipment; a portion of Bundy had already been folded into International Time Recording). Together, these four companies would become the Computing-Tabulating-Recording Company, or CTR, a conglomerate with headquarters in Endicott, New York.

The Tabulating Machine Company was sold for $2.3 million. Hollerith received $1.2 million for the sale. He took a step back from day-to-day operations but stayed on as chief consulting engineer of CTR. Hollerith had to make way for a larger-than-life personality who would come to dominate and lead the conglomerate: Thomas J. Watson.

Thomas John Watson, born in 1874 in Campbell, New York, hated working in an office, so he found himself, after college, traveling the country selling pianos and organs. Eventually, after obtaining an NCR Corporation cash register, he visited the company and repeatedly petitioned them for a sales job; eventually they relented, at which point he landed as a sales apprentice under John J. Range in Buffalo.

At the time, NCR was struggling to fend off competitors selling second-hand cash registers on the cheap. Promoted to sales manager in his early thirties, Watson was placed in charge of an NCR operation in Rochester, New York, by John Patterson, head of the company. The operation, however, was clandestine, since Patterson instructed Watson to do all he could to send the second-hand dealers to the cleaners—courtesy of illegal tactics like buying up all their stock and then flooding the market with it at much lower cost. Although Patterson, Watson, and a number of other NCR employees were ultimately convicted of violating the Sherman Antitrust Act and each sentenced to a suspended term of one year in prison, Watson's success at implementing Patterson's illegal scheme led him to rise even further in the company. He would train NCR sales forces and, during this period, arrive at what would become a famous slogan:

> The trouble with every one of us is that we don't think enough. We don't get paid for working with our feet; we get paid for working with our heads…. Thought has been the father of every advance since time began…. 'I didn't think' has cost the world millions of dollars.

A one-word summary of his disquisition could be found posted throughout NCR offices and plants: THINK.

Watson's ascendance at NCR was stopped dead in its tracks by Patterson, who fired him in 1911. Watson, unperturbed, petitioned Charles Flint for leadership of the newly formed 1,300-employee Computing-Tabulating-Recording Company, which Watson secured once legal troubles following him from NCR were dismissed. Unlike Hollerith, who felt that the machines should be able to sell themselves, Watson took charge of the sales force and gave them a mission: "Sell applications, new applications…. Sell aggressively. Sell results. And sell honestly." THINK placards were hung everywhere. CTR products spread internationally.

The business model for punch-card machines was mostly rent-based, thus securing relatively stable revenue streams during both good and bad economic conditions; the machines paid for themselves after only several years of being rented out. CTR was also the main supplier for the punched cards, guaranteeing itself even more steady revenue. With a three-fold increase in income by the early 1920s validating his radical change to the company's culture, in 1924 Watson changed the name of CTR to the International Business Machines Corporation (IBM). John Backus was born that same year.

John Warner Backus grew up in Wilmington, New Castle, Delaware. He was the middle child, with an older sister and a younger brother. His father, Cecil F. Backus, was born in Virginia in 1886 to a family living in poverty; making it to college, but not finishing, Cecil gained expertise in chemistry, rising to the position of chief chemist for the Atlas Powder Company, which specialized in the manufacture of nitroglycerine. There was a recurring critical problem at the company, though: some of Atlas's plants were exploding. Even those plants that didn't explode were producing yields well below expectations. Cecil took charge, investigating the issue and discovering that the temperature was the culprit: the German thermometers Atlas employed to regulate yields were faulty. So he traveled to Germany, studied how the thermometers were constructed, and returned to Atlas with a much-improved product. Needless to say, "their plants stopped blowing up so much," his son recalled.

Cecil's successes at Atlas garnered attention outside of the company—enough that the DuPont company, based in Wilmington, asked him to join their operations. But World War I intervened, and Cecil had to put his work at DuPont on hold in order to serve as a munitions officer. Although DuPont promised that his job would be held for him until he returned from the war, the elder Backus came back only to discover it was a promise not kept. So Cecil—not a very nice man, but certainly a smart one, as his son remembered—instead studied the market and became a stockbroker. And he became very rich, rich enough so that his children didn't want for anything material.

Maternal care and love were another story, however. John Backus's memory of his mother was very faint for many years—she died shortly before he turned nine years old, and he could really only recall her plugging in a light which had short-circuited—but in his mid-sixties, with the help of LSD, he remembered that she had sexually abused him. After her death, Cecil remarried, but young John wouldn't find maternal salvation with his stepmother, either, describing her as a neurotic alcoholic, a "really horrible woman" who "would sort of hang out the window yelling tirades at people, and stuff like that."

Perhaps as a reaction to his dysfunctional upbringing, Backus, a self-described "sadistic" child, would lure kids into the shed at the rear of his family home and "sort of mess around with them in some nasty, humiliating way." Until eighth grade he attended Tower Hill School in Wilmington and then was shipped off to the Hill School, a preparatory boarding school, in Pottstown, Pennsylvania. "The delight of that place was all the rules you could break," he said later.

> I flunked out every year. I never studied. I hated studying. I was just goofing around. It had the delightful consequence that every year I went to summer school in New Hampshire where I spent the summer sailing and having a nice time.

He rarely returned to his family in Wilmington.

After successfully graduating from the Hill School in 1942 despite low grades and spotty attendance, Backus enrolled at the University of Virginia. His father encouraged him to study chemistry there, but Backus was not keen on completing the lab work. By the second semester, the poor academic habits that he had developed at the Hill School returned—he rarely showed up to classes (going to only one class per week: music appreciation), attended many parties, and eventually got himself expelled.

In 1943, Backus was drafted into the U.S. Army. He was stationed at Fort Stewart in Georgia, set to be corporal of an antiaircraft crew. After several months, his exceptional performance on an Army aptitude test earned him selection for specialized training—first in Alabama, then at the University of Pittsburgh in a pre-engineering program. He already knew much of what he was studying there, but he enjoyed himself nonetheless (especially at the Pittsburgh Playhouse, a local bar and hangout). Backus's "checkered educational career" had begun to turn a corner.

The Battle of the Bulge resulted in the drafting of most of the young, eligible men in Pittsburgh, but Backus escaped being shipped overseas because of his stellar performance on yet another aptitude test; he was sent to Haverford College in Haverford, Pennsylvania, to study medicine instead. And he flourished there.

To prepare for medical school, Backus interned at an Atlantic City hospital. He worked there for twelve hours a day and lived at the Traymore Hotel on the Boardwalk. His health became a concern, though, when one day, while working in the neurosurgery ward, doctors examined a large bump on his head, which turned out to be a slow-growing bone tumor. They excised the tumor and inserted a metal plate constructed of numerous flat triangles atop his skull. Backus spent his remaining time in Atlantic city as a patient in the hospital, wandering the city streets at night no longer bearing any responsibilities as an intern.

Before the end of the World War II, Backus enrolled in medical school at Flower and Fifth Avenue Medical Hospital in New York (which became New York Medical College). Why New York? Partly to get away from his family. "I had visions of right away doing research on the functions of the brain," he said. "But at medical school, all they wanted you to do was memorize, memorize, memorize…that's all they want you to do. You must not think." He didn't last a year there. During that time, he was very self-conscious and insecure about the "squishy plate" in his forehead. He wanted it replaced with something better, so he traveled to a veteran's hospital on Staten Island for a series of procedures involving casting a smooth new plate with a hydrologic press; at one point, he had to walk around town with his skin exposed and no plates while waiting for the finished product (which he helped to design) to be installed.

When he moved to New York, Backus procured a small apartment in a "ratty apartment building" on East 71st Street for eighteen dollars a month. The residence was situated in a Czech neighborhood, with a Czech restaurant right down the street. Some of his friends from the Army lived close by: one was a composer who lived with his wife one floor down; another, a singer, lived right across the street. (Backus lived there until he married his first wife, Marjorie Jamison, whom he met through a mutual friend from the University of Virginia; as their marriage was winding down, his first wife introduced Backus to the woman who would become his second wife: Barbara Stannard. He had two daughters: Karen and Paula.)

In 1946, after being discharged from the Army, Backus's life was directionless. When he was in grade school and high school, he had no idea what he wanted to be; afterward, for a time, he envisioned himself as a doctor, but that didn't work out—leaving him back where he started. But there was one goal he still had: "By the time I got out of the Army, my one ambition was to build a good hi-fi set," Backus recalled. Such sets weren't readily available then. "I got this huge chassis, that had these gigantic transformers and stuff. Didn't work very well, I must say, because I wasn't an electrical engineer. But I tried." Figuring he needed professional experience to proceed, Backus leveraged the G.I. Bill in order to enroll at a radio technician school. There, he assisted an instructor—"a very nice teacher—the first good teacher I ever had"—with some amplifier-curve calculations and realized he was intensely interested in mathematics and good at it, too. "The fact that it [mathematics] had an application—that interested me." So, he enrolled as a graduate student at Columbia University to study mathematics, despite never thinking of himself as a "scholar" as well as having a distaste for studying.

Both John Backus and IBM were born in 1924. But it took a quarter of a century for their destinies to intersect.

CHAPTER 2

◊◊◊

A Stroll Down Madison Avenue

While studying for his master's degree in mathematics at Columbia University in the late 1940s, John Backus received a tip from a classmate: check out "an interesting thing" on Madison Avenue and 57th Street. That interesting thing turned out to be the IBM Selective Sequence Electronic Calculator, or SSEC.

Columbia University astronomy professor Wallace Eckert led the charge to build the SSEC. Wallace John Eckert, born in 1902 in Pittsburgh, Pennsylvania, snagged degrees from Oberlin and Amherst before earning a doctorate from Yale in 1931. Shortly thereafter, Eckert landed at Columbia and began fiddling around with the tabulating equipment in the Columbia Statistical Bureau, all in an effort to perform more exacting astronomical research, in between his trips to Columbia's Rutherford observatory atop Pupin Hall.

Astronomy, like many other disciplines, was in upheaval thanks to the technology wrought by punched cards. Ernest W. Brown, a professor at Yale, had taken many years to compile his *Tables of the Motion of the Moon* (1919) by hand, but punch-card machines made mincemeat out of such time-consuming and error-filled hand calculations as well as the more primitive methods of mechanical devices, as the British astronomer Leslie J. Comrie demonstrated by improving upon Brown's lunar tables.

The equipment at the Statistical Bureau was stocked only several years prior to Eckert's arrival by the president of IBM, Thomas J. Watson, Sr., after a request was made by professor Benjamin D. Wood. But Eckert was dissatisfied with the selection—he needed more tools. So he asked Wood to again contact Watson, this time requesting machines like the 601 Multiplying Punch (which multiplied punch-calculated products of numbers without repeatedly adding the numbers together, and stored programs as notches on phenolic strips), which Eckert would later modify to perform numerical interpolation. "[T]here now [would be] available all the necessary units for a laboratory which would automatically perform the most laborious calculations encountered in science," Eckert realized. Watson agreed to send the items.

After the new equipment arrived several weeks later, it was stockpiled in the attic of the Columbia Astronomy Department in Pupin Hall; in 1937, the attic, called the Astronomical Hollerith-Computing Bureau, was rechristened the Thomas J. Watson Astronomical Computing Bureau, available to astronomers both within and outside of the university. Eckert was installed as the acting director, and a board was organized. Ernest Brown was installed on the board, as were professors from Harvard and Princeton. Most notable, however, were the formal ties established between Columbia and IBM. Not only was C. H. Tomkinson, manager of the IBM Commercial Research Department and the person who originally suggested establishing the Computing Bureau, appointed as a Computing Bureau board member, but Thomas Watson was made a trustee of the university while the president of Columbia was simultaneously appointed a member of the IBM Board of Directors.

Using the new IBM equipment, Eckert built a flexible control system of mechanical relays—which snapped open and shut courtesy of an electrical current passing through a control wire—and a plugboard that could quickly switch between batch processing and numerical integration, with the solutions to complex differential equations available at the touch of a finger. Eckert, who would later write the *American Air Almanac* while stationed at the Naval Observatory during World War II, even prepared a book, *Punched Card Methods in Scientific Computation* (1940), bound with an orange cover and thus usually referred to as the "orange book," which detailed how to use the new punched card equipment, in place of the ubiquitous mechanical desk calculators, to the astronomers and other scientists who dropped by Pupin Hall—which included future luminaries like J. Presper Eckert (no relation to Wallace), Vannevar Bush, and even Howard Hathaway Aiken, a doctoral candidate at Harvard who had big plans to build a computer to solve differential equations for his thesis.

Eckert, pleased with his own dealings at IBM, told Aiken to contact the company for help. Aiken had earlier approached George Chase, the chief engineer of the Monroe Calculating Machine Company, which, like IBM, manufactured calculating machines; Monroe refused to build Aiken's machine, so Chase also told Aiken to seek IBM's assistance. Around the same time, a technician from the Harvard physics department, hearing of Aiken's desire to build a computer, directed him to the only partially built calculating engines of Charles Babbage, a professor of mathematics at Cambridge University in nineteenth century England who sketched out detailed plans for programmable mechanical calculators.

Although mechanical calculators were invented nearly two centuries before Babbage was born—the Stepped Reckoner, which was a kind of automated abacus that could handle all four arithmetic operations, built by the mathematician Gottfried Leibniz is probably the most famous example; Leibniz wrote, "…it is beneath the dignity of excellent men to waste their time in calculation when any peasant could do the work just as accurately with the aid of a machine"—what made Babbage's machines unique was their programmability.

Babbage's son Henry had donated a small portion of one of his father's calculating engines to Harvard. Aiken was fascinated by Babbage's ideas and sufficiently inspired after carefully examining the donated machine which, when he first uncovered it, was still in mothballs. Aiken "consciously saw himself as Babbage's twentieth-century successor," according to Martin Campbell-Kelly and William Aspray in *Computer: A History of the Information Machine* (1996).

So Aiken drew up a proposal for IBM, justifying the need for computational power from a scientific perspective, rather than a business one:

> The intensive development of the mathematical and physical sciences in recent years has included the definition of many new and useful functions nearly all of which are defined by infinite series or other infinite processes. Most of these are inadequately tabulated and their application to scientific problems is thereby retarded.
>
> The increased accuracy of physical measurement has made necessary more accurate computation in physical theory, and experience has shown that small differences between computed theoretical and experimental results may lead to the discovery of a new physical effect, sometimes of the greatest scientific and industrial importance.

But Aiken had more in mind than the automation of mere arithmetic operations; rather, he believed that a machine could be built to handle powers, logarithms, multiple bases, signed numbers, grouping symbols, trigonometric functions (such as sine, cosine, and tangent), hyperbolic functions, transcendentals, as well as being able to compute finite and infinite series, calculate real-valued roots of equations, find solutions to differential equations (including for his thesis), and numerically integrate and differentiate functions.

James Bryce, IBM's chief engineer, was taken by Aiken's proposal, and spoke about it to Watson, who agreed to fund the construction of the computer to the tune of many thousands of dollars (its budget would balloon over the coming years). But Aiken didn't specify precisely *how* IBM should build the machine; rather, he mostly left it up to the company's engineers, although Aiken did suggest the punched card system of the state-of-the-art Jacquard loom mechanical loom (developed by Joseph Marie Jacquard in the early 1800s), which Babbage had first viewed as the *sine qua non* of a programmable computer like the Analytical Engine.

In 1938, after being exposed to the operations of IBM machines, Aiken traveled to the IBM Endicott Laboratory, where he assisted and consulted with company engineers over the next several years, although most of details of the construction were passed off to IBM. It took years of work before the machine could run through a test problem, but, by 1943, the electromechanical Harvard Mark I Computer, or Automatic Sequence Controlled Calculator (ASCC), was completed at IBM's Endicott plant in New York. Although during its construction Aiken had to leave campus to serve in the war, by 1944 he had returned stateside and was assigned the responsibility of running the Mark I by the U.S. Navy Bureau of Ships, which delivered the computer to Harvard.

The ASCC was a leviathan, more than four dozen feet long, weighing over 10,000 pounds, containing around 750,000 parts, and using paper tape (containing program instructions) and card punch on electric typewriters for input/output and registers for stored memory. Multiple additions and subtractions took mere seconds, with more complex arithmetic and trigonometric operations requiring over a minute to perform. Sometimes the ends of the three-inch-wide paper tape would be pasted together, forming a literal programming loop of instructions for the machine to execute. But implementing a conditional branch while a program was running was impossible; in order words, programs could only be run in a strictly linear fashion, from start to finish with no rerouting midstream.

At the tail end of the war, the ASCC was put to pragmatic use, calculating ballistics trajectories and atomic bomb parameters—although those operating the massive machine didn't quite realize what they were calculating or why.

Thanks to a mistake of Aiken's, IBM shifted gears to pursue the mainframe computer business with a vengeance. Before the public unveiling of the ASCC, Thomas Watson decided to dress it up, hiding its electromechanical parts in a sleek glass and stainless-steel enclosure designed by Norman Bel Geddes. Aiken strongly disapproved of the move, believing it harder to expand and maintain the machine with such accoutrements. At the dedication ceremony, which Watson attended, Aiken not only announced to the world that he was the sole inventor of the ASCC, but didn't even bother to mention IBM's massive (and nearly total) financial contribution to the project. Watson was furious at Aiken, and he put that fury to constructive use by directing his engineers to build an electronic calculator to surpass the Harvard Mark I.

It wouldn't take much to top it, since the Harvard Mark I was slow, burdened by its many moving parts despite being the first fully automatic computer. In addition, as Campbell-Kelly and Aspray observe, the machine was "fertile training ground for early computer pioneers." Take Grace Hopper, for example, who had earned a Ph.D. from Yale in mathematics a decade prior. Grace Brewster Murray Hopper, born in 1906 in New York City, New York, would eventually earn the rank of rear admiral. While programming the Mark II, Hopper once had to remove a dead moth that was blocking the computer tape and a relay—thus "debugging" the program, as she later famously put it.

Even before the final bombs of World War II were dropped, IBM began making moves to employ scientists to develop their computers. Like many corporations with worldwide interests at the time, IBM was opportunistic and transactional; although their base of operations was firmly planted in the United States during the war, IBM helped Nazi Germany's trains run on time. As journalist Edwin Black, author of *IBM and the Holocaust: The Strategic Alliance Between Nazi Germany and America's Most Powerful Corporation* (2001), devastatingly describes it,

> IBM Germany, known in those days as Deutsche Hollerith Maschinen Gesellschaft, or Dehomag, did not simply sell the Reich [Hollerith] machines and then walk away. IBM's subsidiary, with the knowledge of its New York headquarters, enthusiastically custom-designed the complex devices and specialized applications as an official corporate undertaking. Dehomag's top management was comprised of openly rabid Nazis who were arrested after the war for their Party affiliation. IBM NY always understood—from the outset in 1933—that it was courting and doing business with the upper echelon of the Nazi Party. The company leveraged its Nazi Party connections to continuously enhance its business relationship with Hitler's Reich, in Germany and throughout Nazi-dominated Europe.

Thomas Watson visited Nazi Germany more than once, not hesitating to dine with der Führer himself. Watson even oversaw the building of a school to train Hollerith machine technicians. The Hollerith machines were used to compile census data of Jews throughout the continent as well as performing other tabulating functions that aided in the functioning of the totalitarian regime. More than fifty years later, IBM released a single terse statement of apology, acknowledging the relationship between the company and the Third Reich while also noting that "Thomas J. Watson, Sr., received and subsequently repudiated and returned a medal presented to him by the German government for his role in global economic relations" and "IBM and its employees around the world find the atrocities committed by the Nazi regime abhorrent and categorically condemn any actions which aided their unspeakable acts."

Post-World War II, IBM pivoted away from any involvement with Nazi atrocities by engaging in an unmatched run of computing innovation. They began this historic run by, for the first time in their history, hiring a scientist with a doctorate: Wallace Eckert. He would now work in his own building, first on 116th Street (a former five-story fraternity house), and then later in a larger building on 115th Street (a former Julliard School residence) christened the Watson Scientific Computing Laboratory. Eckert thought of the laboratory as just that—a scientific laboratory, not a computing center, and therefore prime real estate for experts to discuss and solve complex problems while waiting around for the machines, relegated to the background, to spit out results. In 1946, Eckert, while still retaining his IBM appointment, was hired as Professor of Celestial Mechanics at Columbia. That same year, IBM began construction of a machine that would serve as Thomas Watson's revenge for Aiken's Mark I slight: the IBM Selective Sequence Electronic Calculator.

Like the ASCC, the SSEC was constructed at IBM's Endicott plant; Eckert and the members of the Watson Scientific Computing Laboratory assumed the responsibility of designing and building the machine. Also like the ASCC, the SSEC was massive: over 21,000 relays, 12,500 vacuum tubes, and dozens of paper tape readers, with paper tape much bigger and bulkier than the ASCC (similar to the ASCC, however, were the tape programming loops of routines). Arithmetic operations such as multiplication were orders of magnitude quicker than the Harvard Mark I; the machine proved its mettle by compiling lunar positions, data which eventually assisted in the moon landing a decade later. Programming the SSEC involved turning standard IBM punched cards into input tapes that the machine could read by using "The Prancing Stallion" punch machine. Only one SSEC was built. If sold, which it never was, the SSEC would have cost its buyer a tidy sum: one million dollars in 1940s money.

Let us pause for a moment to discuss vacuum tubes, which were rapidly becoming a mainstay of computing as they replaced mechanical and electromechanical components in computers. A machine with relays could only be considered electromechanical at best, but a machine with no moving parts used for computation—and stocked with vacuum tubes instead—would be considered electronic. Vacuum tubes' function mirrored that of electromechanical relays, but with the added advantage of having no moving parts; such parts were a drag on computation and would also wear down and break over time.

The vacuum tube was invented by English physicist John Ambrose Fleming, who developed the thermionic valve, an airtight glass bulb containing two electrodes, one of which, when heat was applied, would emit electrons. All that was needed to make such a device useful was a "switch" to control the flow of electrons; the American inventor Lee de Forest, the "Father of Radio," fashioned that switch by adding a third electrode to the design—creating the triode vacuum tube, the Swiss Army Knife of electronic components without which radios, long-distance telephone, talking movies, and, of course, early computers, would not have been possible.

But vacuum tubes were expensive, fragile, and burned out rather quickly, like light bulbs. Considering that computers required hundreds or even thousands of the tubes, much downtime with these early machines was spent replacing burned out vacuum tubes.

Vacuum tubes eventually were retired in favor of transistors, which accomplished the same function but much more reliably and compactly. Invented in 1947 by John Bardeen, William Shockley, and Walter Brattain at Bell Telephone Laboratories, transistors consisted of two electrodes separated by a semiconductor material (usually silicon or germanium); the semiconductor would be controlled by a switch, allowing electrons to pass through it (closing the circuit), or not. Transistors could flip between on/off states thousands of times faster than vacuum tubes, which were already much, much faster than relays (which were limited by the physical mass of the relays themselves; purely electronic components experienced no such limitations). Better yet, transistors weren't anywhere near as fragile as vacuum tubes, because they were constructed of solid material—hence transistors were termed *solid-state components*.

In January 1948, about two years after construction began, the electromechanical SSEC was dedicated at a ceremony attended by Watson, Eckert, chief architect and co-inventor Robert Rex Seeber, chief engineer Frank E. Hamilton, and operator Betsy Stewart. The ceremony took place at the IBM World Headquarters building at 590 Madison Avenue in Manhattan, New York City, where the SSEC was situated in a U-shape within an open space roughly sixty feet long by thirty feet wide; numerous fifteen-foot-high black circular columns littered the space. Watson wasn't impressed with the aesthetics, urging that the columns be removed before the dedication ceremony. Although they weren't—the building would have collapsed if they had been—all traces of the ungainly columns were excised from the brochure photo of the SSEC disseminated during the ceremony. Watson also avoided calling the SSEC a computer, but rather an automatic calculator or super-calculator, since at the time the term "computer" was typically a reference to a human being, usually a woman, who performed hand calculations, and IBM employed quite a few of these computers, as did many other organizations—both prior to World War II, when computers (and tabulating machine operators) were in high demand, and for a time after the war, despite the advent and proliferation of electronic mainframe computers rendering manual labor-intensive calculation work redundant. (The term *computer* was coined in 1613 by Richard Braithwaite, a British author. In the book *The Yong Mans Gleanings*, he wrote, "I have read the truest computer of Times, and the best Arithmetician that ever breathed, and he reduced the days into a short number." Braithwaite could never have conceived that the best Arithmetician wouldn't have the need to breathe.) Quite simply, Watson didn't want to scare people into thinking that his company was positioning technology to someday replace human workers. "[N]o machine can take the place of the scientist; this machine only leaves him more time for creative thinking," he said.

Watson didn't approve the building of the SSEC as part of a strategy to produce very many electromechanical computers (or calculators); in fact, by the late 1940s Watson went on record to say that there existed no demand for anything more than a handful of computers, and IBM wasn't interested in competing in that new market regardless. To underscore the point that the SSEC was not the opening salvo of a commercial project, Watson affixed a plaque, with his signature, on the frame of the SSEC. The plaque read as follows: "This machine will assist the scientist in institutions of learning, in government, and in industry to explore the consequences of man's thought to the outermost reaches of time, space, and physical conditions." Notice the singular: *This machine*, meaning the particular assemblage at IBM headquarters. Watson sounding more like a philosopher king than the head of a large national corporation was intentional: he had donated equipment to Columbia because he recognized the importance of education and science for its own sake, rather than for commercial interests. "Our motto down through the years has been and will continue to be 'There is no saturation point in education.' We have always placed special emphasis on this in our scientific development," he said. Once, when chided for investing in a paper-and-pencil test-scoring machine, Watson remarked, "Who wants to make money out of education?" Columbia even offered science courses such as Astronomy 111 (Machine methods of scientific calculation I) and 112 (Machine methods of scientific calculation II) taught by "Dr. Eckert and assists" as well as "Mr. Seeber," respectively, that involved "laboratory work" with the SSEC.

The company's strategy, when it came to electronics, was "evolution not revolution," whereby electronics would be slowly integrated into existing products to improve them, to speed them up, so the products would evolve. Improving upon the 601 Multiplying Punch, which Eckert had requested from IBM after arriving at Columbia, was an early example of this evolution-not-revolution philosophy, with multiplications courtesy of electromechanical means in the 601 sped up considerably with pure electronics and several hundred vacuum tubes running the show in the IBM model 603 Electronic Multiplier (developed by Byron Phelps), which was quickly replaced by the best-selling 604, a (slightly) programmable model housing over one thousand vacuum tubes. (Programs were stored as complicated placements of wires on plugboards, although the plugboards were typically "unwired" to make way for different programs.) The programmability came courtesy of the Card Programmed Calculator (CPC), which allowed for independence of program code—on a deck of cards, rather than hardwired into the components themselves—and came about as a result of a makeshift marriage of the model 603 and a 405 accounting machine by IBM and Northrop Aircraft. Northrop required precision equipment for the calculation of missile trajectories and found that the model 603 Multiplying Punch needed some turbocharging in speed and flexibility, so they hooked up some extra equipment to the base model to allow for control of the apparatus through program cards. By 1948 IBM, seeing the popularity of Northrop's "poor man's ENIAC," codified and packaged the setup into the CPC.

But the CPC was not a *stored-program computer*, which treated program instructions and data the same way in memory with the instructions themselves able to be dynamically altered by the machine while a program was running (and programs could self-generate other programs). It didn't matter how a program was loaded into the computer's memory: via paper tape, punched cards, magnetic cores, magnetic tape. Once instructions were stored in electronic memory, however, they could be delivered, quite literally, at light speed to the rest of the apparatus. (Hence the imperative for continued miniaturization in the computer industry: while the speed of transmission couldn't be increased—the laws of physics were immutable—the distances between electronic components could be shrunk. Grace Hopper illustrated this idea with her 11.8-inch-long educational aids called "nanoseconds," colorful plastic-coated wires that visually represented the distance electricity travels in one billionth of a second.)

The CPC worked like an old-fashioned player piano: each instruction was executed as printed on the punched cards, with none stored in any sort of memory. The SSEC was only debatably a stored-program computer: on the one hand, electromagnetic relays could store programs that were read in from paper tape, which then could be run from memory; on the other hand, there wasn't much relay storage to speak of. The Harvard Mark I was not a stored-program design, since instructions and data were dealt with separately in memory (this set up is typically called a *Harvard architecture*).

The ENIAC—or Electronic Numerical Integrator and Computer—was developed in the mid-1940s by John W. Mauchly and J. Presper Eckert but didn't completely conform to the stored-program design, either, despite it being one of the first truly reprogrammable, digital, entirely electronic (as opposed to electromechanical) computers built, largely because its storage capacity was minimal despite it being burdened with 18,000 vacuum tubes as well as an inefficient means of programming and reprogramming the machine: via the physically taxing process of plugboard programming, which involved tangling and untangling wires and flipping lots of switches. (Eventually, with the help of physicist Nicholas Metropolis and computer scientist Richard Clippinger, the machine could be programmed using ballistic tables, or sets of countless nobs enclosing zero-to-nine decimal dials.) Plus, the ENIAC's vacuum tubes would blow out left and right, meaning the machine worked for around a half a day at a time before at least one tube needed replacing.

The term "stored-program computer" is usually used synonymously with *von Neumann architecture*, named for the mathematician John von Neumann, born in Budapest, Hungary, in 1903. Von Neumann was a child prodigy who thought it fun to memorize the *Cambridge History of the Ancient World*. After landing at the Institute for Advanced Study at Princeton, von Neumann was invited to join the Manhattan Project, America's classified World War II program assigned the task of building the first atomic bomb—a project that von Neumann realized would necessitate working with both very large and very small numbers, something he thought an electronic calculator, like the one being constructed at the Moore School of Electrical Engineering at the University of Pennsylvania (more on this later), could do well.

After World War II ended, von Neumann became a consultant on the construction of the ENIAC. He believed that the nascent electronic computer, though endlessly fascinating to him, had some serious issues, so he began drawing up plans for a completely new design—a stored-program computer—that would address them. The Electronic Discrete Variable Automatic Computer, or EDVAC, was the result. Von Neumann understood that the computer was unlike other mechanical devices; rather, the computer was what the historian Michael S. Mahoney has called a "protean machine":

> [W]hereas other technologies may be said to have a nature of their own and thus to exercise some agency in their design, the computer has no such nature. Or, rather, its nature is protean; the computer is—or certainly was at the beginning—what we make of it (or now have made of it) through the tasks we set for it and the programs we write for it.

The upshot, writes Mahoney, is that "[w]hat kinds of computers we have designed since 1945, and what kinds of programs we have written for them, reflect not so much the nature of the computer as the purposes and aspirations of the communities who guided those designs and wrote those programs."

"Von Neumann played a leading role in the launching of electronic computers," wrote mathematician Stanislaw Ulam, who worked closely with von Neumann. "His unique combination of gifts, his interests, and traits of character suited him for that role…. It was his feeling for and knowledge of the details of mathematical logic systems and the theoretical structure of formal systems that enabled him to conceive of flexible programming." Although there is no doubt that von Neumann was a key force who guided the early development of computers, he was far from the only one.

The limited memory of the ENIAC was a technical problem partially solved by J. Presper Eckert for the EDVAC through the use of mercury delay-line storage (written with electronic pulses), with many times greater capacity than the electronic tubes of the ENIAC. ("Only in the next iteration of its design, the EDVAC, could it do things no earlier machine had been able to do, namely make logical decisions based on the calculations it was carrying out and modify its own instructions," Mahoney explained.) That, coupled with shifting to binary (base 2), instead of decimal (base 10), dramatically increased the quantity of *words* (a computer-context term for pieces of data or information; the SSEC was limited to 150-word storage) that could be stored using the same amount of memory.

The EDVAC contained five overarching components: a memory, to store program instructions and data; a control unit, to process instructions; an arithmetic unit, to perform calculations; an input unit, to read in data and programs; and an output unit, to report results to the user. In 1945, von Neumann typed up all these ideas into a document called *A First Draft Report on the EDVAC*, which was the first written and disseminated description of the stored-program computer. But the EDVAC's creation was far from a solo effort, despite von Neumann's affixing his name—and *only* his name—atop the *EDVAC Report*, ultimately leading to the stored-program design being deemed unpatentable because the report had been distributed far and wide, against Mauchly and Eckert's better judgment (they would attempt to profit off of computer construction by establishing the Electronic Control Company in 1946, with orders from the Census Bureau and others for their UNIVAC and BINAC machines, but the company failed only several years later) as well as inadvertently granting von Neumann the singular, albeit false, public distinction of being the inventor of the computer. (In fact, there is evidence, such as from computer designer Harry Huskey, that the notion of internal programming was informally broached prior to von Neumann's arrival as an EDVAC consultant.)

The ENIAC wasn't quite completed in time to help the Allies with the war effort against Germany, Japan, and Italy. During the Second World War, though, the U.S. government did make limited use of the Harvard Mark I to solve problems related to atomic weaponry. After the war, the IBM SSEC was employed to slog through thermonuclear weapon calculations originating at Los Alamos National Laboratory in New Mexico. The American physicist Robert D. Richtmyer was busy investigating fission explosions in work that came to be known as the "Hippo Problem." In February 1950, the "Hippo was checked out on the IBM Company's SSEC in New York," according to an internal document circulated much later by the U.S. Atomic Energy Commission. "To calculate this [thermonuclear] problem in noticeably more realistic (though still far from complete) detail was probably physically, and certainly psychologically, impossible without the aid of computing devices such as the (now obsolete) SSEC which only began to appear about 1948." Around the same time as the Hippo Problem, the Adjutant General's office submitted a proposal to design a program formulating the best questions to put to military recruits in order to predict their future military-related success; but analyzing the inputs of such a program would have kept the SSEC busy for more than a century and a half.

So, the SSEC was a dinosaur in both senses of the term: not only was the machine vastly oversized and ponderous, but the technology was also effectively outdated by the time of its construction, despite the calculator being the most technologically advanced machine available at the time. The dismantling of the SSEC four years later heralded the extinction of the electromechanical computer. Yet despite computer engineers discarding the electromechanical framework in favor of the more reliable and faster electronic paradigm, the SSEC gave IBM's engineers experience designing, building, and working with computers.

The SSEC also imprinted itself on popular culture for some time to come—in large part because the computer, situated on the ground floor of the building, was visible through the windows of IBM headquarters to passersby walking along Madison Avenue and 57th Street. The sight of thousands of neon flashes and tape relays and processions of switches had pedestrians referring to the SSEC as "Poppa." The visual kinetics also enhanced the reputation of IBM among the general populace, a conscious goal of Watson's since the facilities were opened to the public for inspection and tours.

In 1950, writers from *The New Yorker* were even offered a guided tour by SSEC co-inventor Rex Seeber. In the resultant article, titled "Never Stumped," the functioning of the machine is described in terms mirroring the human brain, with

> cerebral parts…[like] tubes and wires behind glass panels, covering three walls of the room. Two hoppers, looking rather like oversized mailboxes, stand near the middle of the room. One is the "in" hopper, into which questions are inserted on punched cards

or tapes; the other is the "out" hopper, from which, if all goes well, the answer emerges.

Conceptualizing computers as human brains was all the rage, but there was nothing new about cutting-edge technologies being turned into metaphor to explain body and mind. Here, also from 1950, is a snippet of *The Saturday Evening Post*'s "You're Not Very Smart After All" by John Kobler:

> In appearance, a digital calculator—SECC, for instance—is a large chamber or more whose sides are glass enclosed panels of electronic tubes. When SSEC is at work, the panels blink furiously with a click-clacking sound, a galaxy of noisy glass stars in a glass sky. Standing in this chamber with the IBM motto, THINK, emblazoned over the doorway, visitors sometimes remark that they feel not like a man with a brain inside him, but like a brain with a man inside it.

Kobler took the metaphor too far, however, when he wrote that these "mechanical brains" are "human enough to play gin rummy, even have nervous breakdowns." An unnamed scientist told Kobler that "We think of it [the machine] as having temperament...a woman's temperament." The piece even broached the issue of computers descending into insanity (a speculation of MIT's Norbert Wiener, the "Father of Cybernetics"). Howard Aiken, quoted in the article, wouldn't go along with all the anthropomorphizing: "They can't think any more than a stone.... They're timesaving tools, pure and simple. There is no substitute for the mathematician, and there never will be." (We still live with these machine-as-human metaphors today with preferred terms like "memory," rather than "storage.")

In 1952, the year it was dismantled, the SSEC appeared in a key scene of the anticommunist thriller *Walk East on Beacon*. Based on a *Reader's Digest* article by J. Edgar Hoover, the film shows the SSEC in action, clinking and clanking, mysteriously calculating variables and spitting out reams of computer paper containing endless rows of digits, with on-screen characters hurriedly shuffling from control panels with blinking lights to physical outputs, making perfect sense of the opacities by shouting out numbers and placing critical-to-plot telephone calls. There are also not-so-subtle hints of the SSEC in the design of the EMERAC, featured in the Katherine Hepburn vehicle *Dark Set* (1954). Seven years later, an SSEC clone appeared on the cover of an issue of *The New Yorker* illustrated by cartoonist Charles Addams (who created the Addams Family): a lone elderly woman, operating the machine in near darkness with only the light of a small overhead desk lamp to guide her, looks pleased as a Valentine's Day card is printed out (the issue was dated February 11, 1961). The NYU doctoral candidate Anne Pasek perfectly captures the scene: "The computer secretary, now wizened with age, receives a token of affection back from the machine that she has attended to for so long." This "Robot Brain," as some reporters referred to the SSEC, proved to be the paradigmatic massive mainframe, the first thing that might spring to the mind of an American public that revered the power of computers in a *Sputnik* age—even if they didn't quite know what purpose they served or precisely how they worked.

John Backus was in the same boat. Yes, he was a graduate-level expert in mathematics (having appreciated algebra but not calculus), but he had little experience with computers. The tip from his classmate led him to Madison Avenue and 57th Street to visit the IBM Computer Center in the spring of 1949. According to a profile from the July/August 1979 issue of IBM's *THINK* magazine—of course named for the company's slogan, which Watson had conjured up when he worked at NCR—Backus hadn't even finished his master's before stumbling upon the SSEC. But in an interview conducted three decades later, Backus recalled that "I had just graduated. I had just gotten my master's degree from Columbia. But I hadn't even begun to look for a job, but I just found this place and I walked in and it looked so interesting." He then flashed a Cheshire Cat grin and said, "I asked if they would give me a job."

He hadn't yet even turned thirty years old.

CHAPTER 3

◊◊◊

Hand-to-Hand Combat with the Machine

Programming on the SSEC presented John Backus a life-changing opportunity, one that he was not about to let slip through his fingers.

Backus, nearly finished his master's in mathematics from Columbia, had not yet begun job hunting. But once the IBM systems services representative who was showing Backus around the SSEC was asked if a job was available, she told Backus to interview with the co-inventor of the machine, Rex Seeber, immediately. "I had holes in the sleeves of my jacket and my shoes needed shining.... I looked sloppy and disheveled," Backus recalled. "I have to look respectable," he protested to her—but she set up the interview anyway and took Backus upstairs to meet Seeber. After solving a puzzle, or some sort of "homemade test," or mathematics "brainteasers" consisting of informal oral questions (there are numerous conflicting accounts), Backus was hired then and there—as an SSEC programmer—despite the fact that Backus "did not know what that meant." "That was the way it was done in those days," Backus explained. As the old adage goes, chance favors the prepared mind.

Rex Seeber's history with computers started with the Harvard Mark I. Born in Detroit, Michigan, in 1910, Robert Rex Seeber earned an undergraduate degree from Harvard in 1932; from there, he was hired by the John Hancock Mutual Life Insurance Company to work in their actuarial department. Actuarial gave him experience with IBM punch-card machines and desk calculators. Ten years later, he joined the U.S. Navy as a civilian researcher, where he made innovative use of IBM machines. In 1944, Seeber read about the unveiling of the ASCC, and asked the Navy to transfer him to the Harvard Computation Laboratory so he could assist with its operation. Howard Aiken and Rex Seeber's working relationship got off to a poor start, though, when Seeber asked Aiken if he could use vacation time (which he had earned) before starting on the project. Aiken refused the request, forcing Seeber to start working immediately. And work he did—upwards of eighty to ninety hours per week; most of that time was spent programming the machine. Aiken had plans to build a bigger and better computer, the Mark II. Before he left the laboratory, Seeber offered suggestions to Aiken for its design, but Aiken disregarded them. Seeber came to resent his boss, especially Aiken's reticence to give credit to IBM for the design or construction of the ASCC. Seeber resolved to get hired by IBM after the war, so he could "help them build a bigger and better computer than the Mark I…that IBM could have for its own use." Of course, his plans became a reality. In a report he wrote for the 25th anniversary of his Harvard graduation, Seeber bragged that he had a "major part in all phases of conception, invention, design, constructing, and testing (and naming!) of the IBM selective sequence electronic calculator," as well as being in charge of its operation throughout its life.

Backus was indeed hired to program, but programming a machine like the SSEC was more akin to "hand-to-hand combat" than what we think of today as programming, he said. Even putting aside the how abstract the work was—there were no "programming languages" to speak of, and no translators or compilers, so the programs had to be written at a low level so the machine could understand and run them directly—it was intensely physical work, work that required running back and forth between many electromechanical parts (such as toggle switches and relays) in the large, open space that was the ground floor of the IBM headquarters; air conditioning helped to keep the premises chilled, a standard practice to reduce the chances that the vacuum tubes would overheat and subsequently burn out. Reflecting on the early days of computing, the Dutch computer programmer Edsger W. Dijkstra wrote, "For fantastic pieces of equipment they were: in retrospect one can only wonder that those first machines worked at all, at least sometimes. The overwhelming problem was to get and keep the machine in working order."

Indeed, Backus remembered that "behind glass cases around the walls were tape units and relays, some of which would fall out as it was operating because they were heavily used." It was all frustrating work that Backus, who had joined the ranks of the starched-white button-down shirt, dark blue pinstriped suit IBM men, nevertheless loved. "You had the machine for two weeks all to yourself, just to check your tapes and plugboards and things like that," he recalled. "And then, of course, you had to be there the entire time the program was running, because it would stop every three minutes, and only the people who programmed it could see how to get it running again." In spite of all that, "[p]rogramming in the early 1950s was really fun," with a "vital frontier enthusiasm" that has since dissipated. He continued:

> Much of its pleasure resulted from the absurd difficulties that "automatic calculators" [like the SSEC] created for their would-be users and the challenge this presented. The programmer had to be a resourceful inventor to adapt his problem to the idiosyncrasies of the computer: He had to fit his program and data into a tiny store, and overcome bizarre difficulties in getting information in and out of it, all while using a limited and often peculiar set of instructions. He had to employ every trick he could think of to make a program run at a speed that would justify the large cost of running it. And he had to do all of this by his own ingenuity, for the only information he had was a problem and a machine manual….

> [To program the SSEC,] [y]ou just read the manual and got the list of instructions and that was all you knew about programming. Everybody had to figure out how to accomplish something and there were of course a zillion different ways of doing it and people would do it in a zillion different ways.

His first programming assignment on the SSEC was the compilation of lunar tables using Fourier series, which were later utilized by the Apollo space program. (A table of moon positions is called a "lunar ephemeris." Before compact calculators and computers were ubiquitous, volumes of such books of precomputed tables for mathematical functions of every stripe were mainstays in universities, businesses, libraries, and government offices.) Coding using machine language instructions, as Backus had to do, was "like eating with a toothpick," as Charles Petzold, the author of *Code: The Hidden Language of Computer Hardware and Software* (2000), observed. "The bites are so small and the process so laborious that dinner takes forever." The punched cards or paper tape that contained the programs were printed in binary code; to repeat a sequence of code required gluing together the tape in a loop and mounting it into a tape-reading station to be run ad infinitum. Backus describes a strange, and unintended, consequence of this: at least once during his time there, the loop was no ordinary loop, but a Möbius strip, a one-sided surface in three-dimensional space made by giving the paper tape a half-twist before joining the ends together. Numbers were read in reverse order every second revolution of the tape through the tape-reading station. It took quite a while before the technicians realized what was causing the issue. No wonder Backus termed programming those early machines a "black art."

Richard W. Hamming, who earned a doctorate in mathematics from the University of Illinois and then used primitive computers at Los Alamos during the Manhattan Project, agreed with Backus. "Paper tapes are a curse when doing one-shot problems—they are messy, and gluing them to make corrections, as well as loops, is troublesome (because, among other things, the glue tends to get into the reading fingers of the machine!)" But Hamming recognized the necessity of using paper tape. "With very little internal storage in the early days," he said, "the programs could not be economically stored in the machines (though I am inclined to believe the designers considered it)."

More than two years of experience with the SSEC made a Backus a programmer. It also, in his mind, settled any debate about whether or not the SSEC was a stored-program computer. True, the machine's electromagnetic relays were able to store programs that were read in from paper tape and then proceed to run them from memory, but there was little such memory to speak of. (The SSEC could also punch data into tapes as an intermediate step while a program was running.) "I think it's an extreme stretch to consider [the SSEC] the first 'stored program' computer," Backus concluded, "even though one of the programs...used some specially prepared storage cells as the source of an instruction after some data was stored in it."

In 1952 the SSEC was decommissioned in favor of the IBM 701. Named the "Defense Calculator," the 701 was expressly built to (profitably) assist the United States in the Korean War. Shedding moving parts in favor of an all-electronic setup, it was the company's first true stored-program and mass-produced, general-purpose large computer. One observer noted that the 701 changed the "balance between user and machine," because "[o]ne man at the RAND Corporation took two years to program a problem that ran in two minutes" on the 701.

But while John Backus found the two years programming the SSEC "delightful," after using the newly installed 701 to calculate missile trajectories, he was beginning to become restless from the interminable tedium of coding.

CHAPTER 4

◊◊◊

The UNIVAC and the IBM 701

As the UNIVAC of Eckert and Mauchly rose to fame by correctly predicting election results, IBM took advantage of the sudden demand for computers by quickly developing and mass-producing the 701 and the 650.

John William Mauchly, born in 1907 in Cincinnati, Ohio, became interested in science and electricity as a teenager. He studied engineering and physics at Johns Hopkins, earning a doctorate in 1932. The next year, he traveled to Ursinus College in Collegeville, Pennsylvania, to head the physics department—of which he was the only member. He gained a reputation there for "irreverent Professor Ho-Hum lectures he used to deliver on the last day of class before Christmas," according to his biographer. Fascinated with weather data, he sought automated ways of generating it—which led him to the Atanasoff-Berry Computer (ABC), a quasi-electronic vacuum tube machine built by John V. Atanasoff at Iowa State University. Intrigued by the technology, Mauchly took the Defense Training Course for Electronics at the University of Pennsylvania's Moore School in the summer of 1941. The lab instructor was J. Presper Eckert. And Mauchly and Eckert, despite their different backgrounds, immediately hit it off.

John Adam Presper Eckert was born in 1919 in Philadelphia, Pennsylvania. Eckert had a privileged upbringing: he was chauffeured to elementary school each day and, in high school, had the opportunity to work with Philo Taylor Farnsworth, one of the inventors of the television. His parents sent him to Wharton, but he was bored with business classes, so Eckert transferred to the Moore School to study electrical engineering. By 1940, he had already applied for his first patent; he had also become infamous on campus by constructing his "Osculometer," a machine which supposedly relayed the intensity of a couple's kiss by lighting up a series of bulbs. Eckert, not the best student but an outstanding engineer, earned an undergrad degree in electrical engineering in 1941 and a master's in 1943.

The University of Pennsylvania, impressed by what they saw during that summer class in 1941, hired John Mauchly as an instructor of electrical engineering; two years later, he was promoted to assistant professor. In 1943, the United States Army Ordnance Department contracted the Moore School to build a computer to automate the construction of artillery firing tables. It was then that Mauchly and Eckert began their first large-scale computing project together: the ENIAC.

In 1944, John Mauchly, fresh off of building the ENIAC with J. Presper Eckert, met with officials at the Bureau of the Census in Washington, D.C., as well as with members of the military, to gauge potential interest for the governmental use of computers. Convinced that there was a market for their products, but not especially possessing the best business acumen, Mauchly and Eckert founded the Electronic Control Company in March of 1946 after refusing a deal from the University of Pennsylvania: sign patent releases on their future technology in exchange for tenured positions. Renamed the Eckert-Mauchly Computer Corporation (EMCC) a year later, the company, though short-lived, would pioneer a vision of computer use for business applications rather than simply building souped-up scientific instruments.

Eckert and Mauchly signed a contract with the Census Bureau to develop a new machine tailored to the government's data-processing needs. The contract had the Bureau agreeing to an advancement payment to the company of $300,000, but the computer ended up costing nearly a million dollars to plan and build. Eckert and Mauchly set up shop in a men's clothing store in downtown Philadelphia, and they lured engineers from the Moore School at the University of Pennsylvania to join the company. By late 1947, a dozen engineers were hard at work constructing the successor to the EDVAC: the UNIVersal Automatic Computer, or UNIVAC.

The engineers had to overcome heretofore-unseen computing challenges, such as with memory storage. The breakthrough came with the use of magnetic-tape storage rather than traditional punched cards. The use of magnetic tape for digital, rather than analog, applications necessitated the development of new digital recording apparatuses and chemical coating on the tape itself.

Eckert and Mauchly could hardly keep the lights on without more advance orders for the UNIVAC. A side project helped them secure some additional revenue, with Northrop Aircraft commissioning Eckert and Mauchly to build them a missile-guidance computer. Called the BINary Automatic Computer, or BINAC, the machine was a small, stripped down version of the UNIVAC; it took several years to build. But cash flow was still a major concern.

By the late 1940s, after initially balking at the prospect of purchasing a UNIVAC, the Prudential Insurance Company of America expressed interest in retaining the services of EMCC, if not in purchasing a computer outright. Much of this interest can be traced to the efforts of a single employee at Prudential, Edmund Berkeley, who saw the unlimited potential of computers earlier than most.

Born in New York City, New York, in 1909, Edmund Callis Berkeley earned a degree in mathematics and logic at Harvard before landing a job as an actuary. There, he made use of punch-card machines, eventually working with Howard Aiken during World War II; Berkeley would help Aiken build the Harvard Mark II after the war. He would also write the first book popularizing the possibilities of computers to the lay public: *Giant Brains, Or Machines that Think* (1949), another contribution to the zeitgeist of computers-as-brains that was beginning to take hold as an *idée fixe*. In *Giant Brains*, he proposed the first personal computer, called the Simon, a "very simple machine that will think," built on a Harvard, not von Neumann, architecture. Berkeley dedicated the remainder of his life to the abolishment of nuclear weapons.

In 1947, Berkeley helped convince a skeptical Prudential board of directors that Eckert and Mauchly's ideas could benefit the insurance company. In 1948, Prudential put down only $150,000 for the purchase of a UNIVAC, which EMCC accepted. For the same price, EMCC also sold a UNIVAC to the marketing research firm AC Nielson, based in Chicago.

Despite a serious cash flow problem, EMCC expanded its operations, hired more people, and moved to a larger site in Philadelphia. In addition, more capital was secured courtesy of the American Totalisator Company, whose vice president, the inventor Henry Strauss, was friends with EMCC's patent attorney. Strauss had invented a totalisator, an electronic automated system for calculating betting odds and dispensing tickets for horse races, and he saw the threat that a machine like the UNIVAC might pose to totalisator machines. So, he orchestrated a half-million dollar cash infusion that secured forty percent ownership of EMCC. Strauss also became EMCC's board president.

EMCC moved yet again, staying within the Philadelphia city limits in a building the company's more than one hundred employees had all to themselves. A short time after the move, the BINAC was completed. Proving itself to be unreliable, it was nonetheless delivered to Northrop in 1949; the BINAC, a stored-program computer, caused enough of a stir that IBM and Remington Rand sent employees to attend the unveiling of the machine. With the company's fortunes seemingly having turned, and its reputation sky-high, Eckert and Mauchly continued building and promoting the UNIVAC. But the sudden death of Henry Strauss in a plane crash caused American Totalisator to withdraw their investment in EMCC, leaving the company yet again in a state of financial turmoil. Which led Eckert and Mauchly to make a difficult decision: they would sell the company. And their first choice to buy it was IBM.

In 1949, the IBM SSEC was no threat to the UNIVAC, which had not quite yet been completed, so IBM hurriedly developed two new computers: the Magnetic Drum Calculator (MDC) and the Tape Processing Machine (TPM). The MDC was a stored-program computer that utilized a slow but reliable magnetic-drum memory. Development of the TPM, a true competitor to the UNIVAC, came about as a reaction to the success that Eckert and Mauchly were finding with the BINAC and the magnetic-tape storage design of the UNIVAC. Both the MDC and the TPM were beset by delays of one sort of another, including the opening hostilities of the Korean War. But the biggest reason for the TPM's delay was due to a decision by thirty-five-year-old Thomas Watson, Jr., the scion of the septuagenarian head of IBM, who was one step away from taking over the corporation from his father. The younger Watson saw a short-term opportunity with the outbreak of the Korean War: build a series of "Defense Calculators" for the government geared toward scientific, rather than commercial, purposes, machines that could help with the design of aircraft and nuclear weapons. Satisfying this demand for Defense Calculators—something the government had more or less requested from Watson Senior, after the patriarch had asked the government what Big Blue could do to help the war effort—effectively put the development of the TPM on hold, leaving the UNIVAC as the only computer being constructed for a non-scientific, commercial market.

Eckert and Mauchly figured that, in this environment, IBM would be anxious to purchase EMCC. They were proven mistaken, however, when a meeting with the Watsons went south. In recalling the meeting years later, the younger Watson noted that "our lawyers had told him [Eckert] that buying their company was out of the question. UNIVAC was one of the few competitors we had, and antitrust law said we couldn't take them over." The elder Watson wasn't impressed with the magnetic tape concept, either. "Having built his career on punch cards, Dad distrusted magnetic tape instinctively," Watson Junior said. "On a punch card, you had a piece of information that was permanent.... But with magnetic tape, your data were stored invisibly on a medium that was designed to be erased and reused."

Mauchly, who had assumed a relaxed pose, putting his feet up on the table, left the meeting without having ever even opened his mouth. Eckert and Mauchly next shopped their company to Remington Rand, a manufacturer of office equipment. The duo interviewed with James Rand, the president of Remington Rand, on his yacht. Rand made them an offer: a buyback of stock and the controlling interest of the company that American Totalisator vacated, as well as retaining Eckert and Mauchly as salaried employees. They accepted. General Leslie R. Groves, who was the director of the Manhattan Project, was charged with overseeing EMCC, a new subsidiary of Remington Rand; he took a hands-off approach.

But Remington Rand wasn't satisfied with the existing contracts for the UNIVAC, and they tried to renegotiate them. The Census Bureau dug their heels in: the agreement was for $300,000, and not a penny more. Acquiescing on that order, Remington Rand next went after AC Nielson and Prudential, demanding a half a million dollars instead of the sale price of $150,000. Both companies canceled their orders.

Work on the UNIVAC continued unabated. Testing of the machine commenced in the summer of 1950. The building was not air conditioned, and the five thousand vacuum tubes produced an unbearable heat for the engineers, who, dressed only in shorts and undershirts, would frequently have to douse themselves with bottles of water.

Before the machine was shipped off to the Census Bureau, software had to be written and acceptance tests had to be run. At first, Mauchly was put in charge of the software programming team, but later Grace Hopper, who had worked with Howard Aiken at the Harvard Computation Laboratory, took over. (By 1952, she had finished writing the machine's first *compiler*, which converted programming instructions to machine code for execution by the computer.) In March of 1951, after passing its acceptance tests without fault, the first UNIVAC was delivered to the Census Bureau. Business began picking up, as the government ordered several more UNIVACs.

The UNIVAC gained worldwide fame after being featured on CBS's presidential election night coverage in 1952. With the help of some statisticians, Mauchly wrote a program that would predict incoming election results based on voting data from the two prior presidential elections. With coverage anchored by Walter Cronkite in New York City, and a fake panel powered by Christmas lights blinking in the background, a

UNIVAC in Philadelphia (cameras and a CBS correspondent were stationed there as well) spit out its first prediction at 8:30 PM: based on early returns, Dwight D. Eisenhower was poised to beat Adlai Stevenson in a landslide. Fearful that the computer's output, if publicized, would prove itself embarrassingly wrong—after all, opinion polling during the week before the election consistently showed that the race was likely to be tight—the UNIVAC's prediction was not reported on-air. Instead, technicians adjusted the prediction model to churn out a more conservative output. The machine still had Ike winning, but not with quite the same spread. Nonetheless, the final Electoral College tally was very close to what the UNIVAC had initially predicted at 8:30 PM, leading the engineers to regret their reticence to stand by the machine's analysis. Nonetheless, the UNIVAC was now famous, with tens of millions of people having seen the machine—or at least a cheap mockup of the machine—in action. It was famous enough to shift the public's notion of a computer: from IBM's SSEC to Eckert and Mauchly's UNIVAC. (The demonstration was also impressive enough to cause other companies to poach EMCC's programmers and engineers.)

IBM was feeling the pressure; even before election night, they realized that they had ceded ground to EMCC by focusing all their energies on constructing the Defense Calculator for the military, while there still existed commercial demand for computers that the UNIVAC was filling. But all hope was not lost: recall that besides the Defense Calculator, which became the IBM 701 Electronic Data Processing Machines (plural because of the numerous connected units of the computer; it would be renamed the 701 Data Processing System), Big Blue had two other computers in the developmental pipeline: the Magnetic Drum Calculator, which became the IBM 650, and the Tape Processing Machine, which became the IBM 702. The TPM was poised to compete with the UNIVAC, but the 701 was completed first, in December of 1952 after a two-year development cycle, and the rental orders—the monthly cost was $8,100—came pouring in. The SSEC was disassembled, and the first assembled 701 assumed pride of place at IBM world headquarters in New York City for the public to gawk at.

The IBM 702 Electronic Data Processing Machine took an additional four years to develop and build before it was finally released. In the meantime, those who wanted to use the most advanced computing technology on offer at IBM had to be satisfied with the 701, units of which were rolling off the assembly line in Poughkeepsie, New York, at a relatively rapid clip. The 701, a true stored-program computer (in which programs and data were both stored in electronic memory; the SSEC, recall, was only debatably a stored-program computer), was the very first IBM mass-produced large computer.

An IBM press release from March 1953 relayed to the public some of the potential uses of the new machine:

> The calculators, which will rent for $11,900 monthly or more, depending upon storage capacity, will be used for the calculation of radiation effects in atomic energy; for aerodynamic computations for planes and guided missiles, including vibration and stress analysis, design and performance computations for jet and rocket engines, propellers, landing gear, radomes, etc.; on studies related to the effectiveness of various weapons; and on steam and gas turbine design calculations. A company which has pioneered the use of high-speed digital computers for cost accounting with the IBM Card-Programmed Electronic Calculator, will use the 701 to speed and simplify the immense

task of assembling and interpreting production cost data from its several plants. In government agencies the 701 will be used principally on classified problems.

As "the machine that carried us into the electronics business," according to Watson Junior, the IBM 701 was twenty-five times faster than the SSEC but only took up twenty-five percent of the space. Using a mix of cathode-ray tubes, magnetic drums, and magnetic tapes for electronic storage, the computer processed operations in binary, though initial and final results could be in decimal. More than 16,000 addition or subtraction operations could be performed each second. Electronic pulses, as many as a million a second, directed the action of the arithmetic components and the control section of the massive machine.

Besides at IBM headquarters, the 701 was installed at eighteen sites, such as Los Alamos, New Mexico, for the University of California; Santa Monica, California, for the Rand Corporation; Washington, D.C., for the U.S. Weather Bureau; and Seattle, Washington, for the Boeing Corporation, which was the last such installation of the computer (it was made from leftover spare parts). Lockheed Aircraft Company procured two IBM 701s: one was assigned to the Mathematics Analysis Department for aircraft design calculations, while the other was given to the Factory Data Processing Group for parts inventory and labor-time management.

In 1954, with the advent of MIT's Jay Forrester's core memory, replacing the unreliable Williams tube memories of the UNIVAC and the 701, the 701's and 702's successors were announced: the 704 scientific computer and the 705 EDPM, respectively. By 1955, orders for the 700 series surpassed those of the UNIVACs, though it was the "workhorse" 650—the rock-solid reliable but fairly primitive Magnetic Drum Data Processing Machine—that dominated the market, with over three hundred machines delivered and installed by 1956. The 650s were performing electronic data processing in government, industry, and universities; in short, they had proliferated and indeed become "a vital factor in familiarizing business and industry with the stored program principles," as IBM predicted. Though Remington Rand was still producing the UNIVAC, including a scientific version called the UNIVAC 1103—after acquiring Engineering Research Associates and merging with Sperry Gyroscope to form Sperry Rand—the company was faltering. It wasn't just that Big Blue had the edge in advertising; they had also secured the Semi-Automatic Ground Environment (SAGE) government contract bid, which called for the company to construct fifty Whirlwind computers (based on Jay Forrester's memory design) that would detect bomber activity at the borders of the United States. Though models of the UNIVAC continued to be churned out, the computer never posed a serious threat to IBM's dominance again.

Meanwhile, still stationed at IBM headquarters and busy programming the 701, John Backus had an inspired idea.

CHAPTER 5

Speedcoding

Although necessity is often pegged as the mother of invention, John Backus proved that laziness is the father—and can spur a fair number of groundbreaking ideas.

As the novelist L. P. Hartley put it, "The past is a foreign country; they do things differently there." Indeed, back in the early 1950s, there wasn't yet the rigid distinction between the hardware components and software of a computer; they were fuzzy, nebulous concepts. In fact, the term *software* would not be used in print until 1958, in the article "The Teaching of Concrete Mathematics" (appearing in *The American Mathematical Monthly*) by the Princeton statistician John W. Tukey. After writing about the "mechanics of computation, numerical and algebraic," that, without the help of electronic assistance, consumes a large proportion of students' time, Tukey proceeds to explain the distinction between computing hardware and software:

> Numerical computation, through the centuries, has often faced up to reality and made things easier. The use of logarithmic tables, even by those who do not know how to recompute them, and of desk calculators and, now, electronic calculators, even by those who cannot repair them, has been a commonplace. Today the "software" comprising the carefully planned interpretive routines, compilers, and other aspects of automative programming are at least as important to the modern electronic calculator [computer] as its "hardware" of tubes, transistors, wires, tapes, and the like.

The main takeaway from the passage is this: efficient software makes understanding the inner workings of computers unnecessary. Though there is evidence of the use of the term "software" prior to 1958, Tukey's piece is the first usage of the term as we take it to mean today.

In addition, "software packages," though they did exist, were not offered for sale. They were included with the hardware or distributed free of charge. Plugboards for the

CPC, as well as IBM 650 packages as detailed in IBM Technical Newsletters from the 1950s, are examples. Instead of calling them software packages, they were sometimes referred to as "abstractions," as in "matrix abstraction"—a software routine for working with mathematical matrices.

Like software, the term *programmer* was also ill defined in the 1950s. When the Dutch computer scientist Edsger Dijkstra wrote "programmer" as his occupation on his marriage license in 1957, he was ordered to change it—since there was no such profession in the Netherlands. He penciled in "theoretical physicist" instead.

Though numerous computing terms weren't yet pinned down, by the early 1950s computers were starting to come into their own. "Computing machines came about through the confluence of scientific and technological developments," wrote the mathematician Stanislaw Ulam in *Adventures of a Mathematician* (1976). The effective use of computers continued to increase through a kind of feedback loop:

> On one side was the work in mathematical logic, in the foundations of mathematics, in the detailed study of formal systems, in which von Neumann played such an important role; on the other was the rapid progress of technological discoveries in electronics which made it possible to construct electronic computers. They, in turn, provided such a quantitative increase in the speed of operation so much greater than the mechanical relay machines that it produced a qualitative change and vastly improved and enlarged the use of the tool.

But none of that theoretical stuff much impressed John Backus. Stuck in front of an IBM 701 day after day, coding missile trajectories, he became restless. "I didn't like writing programs" for the machine, he reflected years later. He admitted to being "lazy"—"[m]uch of my work has come from being lazy," he added—so "I started work on a programming system to make it easier to write programs for the 701. And that wound up as something called Speedcoding."

As authors Dennis Shasha and Cathy Lazere explain in *Out of Their Minds: The Lives and Discoveries of 15 Great Computer Scientists*, Speedcoding was "born of the pain of computing with large numbers on a small machine": it would cast off the yoke of oppression by the machine upon the user. Speedcoding solved a problem that started with von Neumann's observation, while he was working on the Manhattan Project, that atomic bomb calculations involved working with really large numbers and really small numbers. Von Neumann figured that while mathematicians—who were likely doing the programming, after all—wouldn't necessarily know the results of the calculations before they were fed into a machine, they could at least predict their scale; thus, the idea of *scaling factors* was born. As Shasha and Lazere explain,

> The idea is simple enough. Suppose that a computer word can store only three digits. To represent the number 517, you write 517 into that computer word and specify the scale as 0. To represent 51.7, you write 517 into the word and specify the scale to be −1; for 5170, you write 517 into the word and specify a scale of 1; for 5,170,000, you specify a scale of 4; and so on. A positive scaling factor is the number of 0s following

the number, and a negative scaling factor is the number of digits to the right of the decimal point.

But was it really reasonable for von Neumann to believe that those who programmed the machines would be able to juggle all these scaling factors and calculations in their heads? Backus, for one, thought it wasn't even remotely realistic. "You had to know so much about the problem," remembered Backus, "it had all these scale factors—you had to keep the numbers from overflowing or sorting big round off errors. So programming was very complicated because of the nature of the machine." Even though the 701 offered programmers a slightly higher degree of abstraction to work with than earlier computers—namely, a very primitive assembly language, where the memory management of the zeros and ones took place behind the scenes—Backus still found solving the scaling factor problem worthy of his time. "Well, programming in machine code was a pretty lousy business to engage in, trying to figure out how to do stuff," Backus told an interviewer fifty years later. "I mean, all that was available was a sort of a very crude assembly program. So I figured, well, let's make it a little easier. I mean it was a rotten design, if I may say so, but it was better than coding in machine language."

The solution to the scaling factor problem? The use of so-called *floating-point numbers*, where each number would drag along its scaling factor. An IBM 701 press release from March 1953, after Speedcoding was released, detailed the use of floating-point arithmetic: "Using a 'floating point' technique, the machine notes the position of the decimal point in the input numbers, keeps track of the point, and finally reports the position of the decimal point as the results are printed." The decimal point can, effectively, "float," with no set number of digits in front of or behind it. (The opposite is called *fixed-point*, in which the number of digits before and after the decimal are constant. Integers are a type of fixed-point number, since all integers have precisely zero digits after the decimal. Von Neumann was a proponent of fixed-point, since he believed that the associated scaling factors could be easily predicted by programmers. Plus, floating-point, with a variable number of digits before and after the decimal, is slower for a machine to process.)

Think of floating-point numbers as a form of scientific notation—but a scientific notation easily digestible to a computer in binary (base 2). Especially when performing scientific calculations, numbers often have really large magnitudes (e.g., the number of atoms in the universe) and really small magnitudes (e.g., the length of an atom's nucleus measured in meters, where there would be a cavalcade of zeros after the decimal point). Imagine setting aside storage space in a computer for such massive numbers: because of the quantity of digits, most of the memory of these early machines would have been gobbled up after storing only a few numbers (let alone how complex and slow the arithmetic using these memory-crushing numbers would be).

So, calculating with such numbers directly really wasn't an option. Instead, real numbers in decimal (base 10) were typically chopped into three sections when working with them as floating-point numbers in binary: a *sign bit* (relaying whether the number is positive or negative), an *exponent*, and a *mantissa*. The problem came with the conversion of some decimal numbers into binary (such as 0.1 in base 10 to base 2), where the exact value in decimal resulted in a nonterminating (repeating) expansion of digits in binary—

forcing the computer to chop off all binary digits of the number past a certain point, since there wasn't infinite memory available in which to store a single massive number. (To illustrate this same effect with our everyday lived experience in base 10, we often truncate repeating decimals, such as writing 2/3 as 0.666.) But truncation results in a loss of precision and can occasionally lead to floating-point round-off errors, which can in turn result in strange arithmetic effects such as adding the decimal number 0.1 to itself only to obtain a sum of 0.200000000001 rather than 0.2. (Again, to illustrate this same effect in base 10, if we add 2/3 to itself in fractional form, we obtain 4/3, but if we add 0.666 to itself, we obtain 1.332—except 4/3 = 1.333 rounded to three digits, so converting 2/3 to 0.666 *prior* to the addition results in a loss of precision *starting* at the thousandths place.) And it wasn't just the prehistoric computers of the 1940s and '50s that had this issue with floating-point arithmetic; modern computers have it too, since the amount of memory available to store any particular number is of a finite, not an infinite, quantity, but there are workarounds involving variable types in today's computer languages.

As the IBM Speedcoding System manual (released in September 1953) makes clear, for several key reasons the user should not expect a perfect correspondence between decimal and binary numbers.

> As has been pointed out above, the necessary conversions between the decimal information read into and printed by the machine and the binary information used inside the machine are performed automatically by [the Speedcoding System]. Note, however, that [the Speedcoding System] permits the binary quantities inside the machine a much greater magnitude range than is permitted those quantities to be converted to decimal and printed. In this connection the programmer should not attempt to print any quantity whose decimal exponent is larger, in absolute value, than 236.
>
> It is important to note that because of the intrinsic error involved in conversion from the decimal floating-point form to the binary floating-point form, the programmer should not expect an exact correspondence between his decimal input and the resulting binary numbers stored in the machine. For example, the floating-decimal number with fractional part +.1 and exponent part +1 (which is a floating-decimal representation of the integer 1) happens to result in the stored binary number $1 + 2^{-34}$.

The Speedcoding System was in effect an emulator, one of the world's first "virtual machines," and was called, at the time, an "interpretive program." (In fact, Richard Hamming has characterized the entire history of software as one of progressing from absolute to virtual machines.) Speedcoding came to be considered an *interpreted language*—the Speedcoding system was an *interpreter*, not a compiler—meaning that any source code written via Speedcoding had to be run through an intermediary program, line by line, rather than compiled to the native machine language of the hardware in order to be executed directly. Other interpretive systems at the time included DUAL and SHACO, both developed at Los Alamos, which emulated the CPC on the 701.

Instructions of Speedcoding, running on an IBM 701, caused the machine to behave, in effect, akin to a three-address floating-point calculator with *index registers* (called R_A, R_B, and R_C, which hold data and/or instructions and reduced the "number of instructions in a loop by a factor of 1/2"), despite the fact that the fixed-point 701 had but a single address and no index registers. Speedcoding didn't treat data and instructions in the same way. Each Speedcoding instruction had two *operation codes* (*opcodes*), which were machine language instructions directing the processor on how, precisely, to proceed. The first opcode (called OP_1), which could be either an arithmetic operation or an input-output operation, was assigned three addresses (called A, B, and C; addresses are locations pointing to where data is stored), while the second opcode (called OP_2), which was a logical operation (including conditional or unconditional control; the incrementing of data stored in registers; and comparisons between accumulator contents and an address), was assigned only one address (called D) and was always executed immediately after the first operation code in an instruction. Arithmetic operations beyond mere addition, subtraction, multiplication, and division were possible; instructions for calculating square roots, exponentials, logarithms, and trigonometric functions were also available. Thus, the "operations were not part of the hardware and were selected for their utility to the mathematician," explained historian Jean Sammet. She offered this example of a single line of Speedcoding:

```
523 SUBAB 100 200 300 TRPL 500
```

which, she writes, "shows an instruction in location 523 which causes the computer to subtract the absolute value of the contents of location 200 from the value in 100 and to put the result in 300; then the computer tests the sign of the result in 300 and transfer control to 500 if it is positive."

Speedcoding input-output operations handled information transfers between magnetic drums or tape, printers, and electrostatic storage (i.e., a set of cathode-ray tubes of internal memory, which could hold roughly 700 words; a word consisted of 72 binary digits). In fact, the 701 was the first computer with electrostatic storage. Instructions were key punched onto cards and then read into the 701 by placing the cards into the card reader's hopper; programs could also be saved for posterity by recording them on magnetic tape.

The IBM 701 Speedcoding System traded memory for functionality. In using 310 words of storage, roughly a third of the memory of the 701 was dedicated to Speedcoding. Speedcoding also traded speed, rather ironically, for functionality. In a presentation to the Association for Computing Machinery (ACM) in 1953, Backus asked his audience a question: "Since this floating point Speedcoding calculator is slower than the 701, despite the conveniences that it offers, you might ask: Why go to a lot of trouble to make an extremely fast calculator like the 701 behave like a slower one?" The answer, of course, was that the programming itself was made easier—and "programming and testing cost often comprise between 50 and 75% of the total cost of operating a computing installation. Since Speedcoding reduces coding and testing time considerably, and is fairly fast in operation, it will often be the more economical way of solving a problem."

In addition to floating-point operations, Speedcoding also offered programmers "automatic address modification, flexible tracing, convenient use of auxiliary storage, and built-in checking." Programs that might have required two weeks to code in 701's built-in but bare-bones assembly language could be programmed using the Speedcoding System in mere hours, bragged Backus. "For example, a matrix multiplication program requires about twelve instructions. There are only two instructions in the principal loop." Speedcoding was an abstraction layer, a "synthetic computer," affixed atop a mass of hardware.

Putting aside Backus's admissions of persistent laziness—"It was pure laziness. Writing programs was a big drag—you had to have enormous detail and deal with things you shouldn't have to. So I wanted to make it easier"—the idea for Speedcoding was also inspired by the programmable functionality of the IBM Card Programmed Calculator (CPC).

By the time the 701 was released, a meeting among IBM's New York Scientific Computing Service, which took place in Poughkeepsie in August of 1952, resulted in many "useful and provocative ideas in this area…[in terms of reducing] the amount of time spent in problem preparation," according to the Foreword of the IBM Speedcoding System manual. At this Poughkeepsie meeting, members of the IBM development team met with scientists from Los Alamos and United Aircraft. Development of the Speedcoding System, referred to as SPEEDCO I, began in January 1953, with Backus supervising the development team: Harlan Herrick, Donald Quarles, Sherwood Skillman, John Pulos, and Lucy Siegel. John Sheldon also contributed, as well as loosely supervising the effort. Of these team members, only one—Harlan Herrick—would remain with Backus as he shifted his attention toward solving a much more complicated problem.

CHAPTER 6

◊◊◊

Building the IBM 704

The IBM 704 was built for more than just speed—it was designed to run the most abstract computer language the world had ever seen.

Like the IBM 701, the IBM 704 Data Processing System was built for scientific and engineering applications. But the machine improved on its predecessor in a number of key ways, besides simply being faster. For example, the electrostatic storage via cathode-ray tube was ditched in favor of high-speed magnetic core storage, whereby thousands of tiny pinhead-sized cores were arranged on wires; electronic pulses changed the cores' magnetic states. The high-speed memory was complemented by magnetic-drum storage and bulk storage, courtesy of magnetic tapes. Programs were fed into the machine either through magnetic tape or punched cards; output was obtained from punched cards, magnetic tape, or a line printer.

But the game-changing improvement was transforming the floating-point "interpretive program" from software (Speedcoding) into hardware. (John Backus realized that with indexing and floating-point abilities now built-in, any "gross inefficiencies" hiding in software would be exposed—suboptimal software could no longer be excused on account of its hogging processing power to simulate floating-point operations. If code wasn't optimal, it would now solely be the fault of incompetent programmers, not underpowered machines.) Both fixed-point and floating-point arithmetic were available, interchangeable, and automatic, making the 704 the first mass-produced computer with such arithmetic capabilities; a general-purpose accumulator and a multiplier-quotient register would do the arithmetic heavy lifting. In addition, three index registers, called A, B, and C—or, alternatively, 1, 2, and 4 (in octal, or base 8)—which could store portions of programs for repeated execution, came built-in; each register had a capacity of twelve, thirteen, or fifteen bits, which equated to 4,096, 8,192, or 32,768 words, respectively. The machine was announced publicly in May of 1954, and IBM took preorders.

John Backus had some involvement in planning out the 704, but Gene Amdahl was responsible for most of the design. Gene Myron Amdahl was born in 1922 on a farm lacking electricity in Flandreau, South Dakota. His mother was a teacher who worried that her children had copious intellectual stimulation, so she purchased a full encyclopedia set for them, which the family devoured. Although he didn't initially want to attend college after finishing high school, a year working on the family farm changed his mind. During the gap year, Amdahl developed an interest in mechanical engineering and science, discovering himself be a "whiz" at mathematical disciplines such as geometry and trigonometry.

During the Second World War, Amdahl served in the Navy, finishing an engineering physics degree at South Dakota State College of Agriculture and Mechanical Arts (now South Dakota State University) several years after the war. From there, he gained admission to the University of Wisconsin-Madison to study theoretical physics; one of the leading theoretical physicists in the world, a man by the name of Robert G. Sacks, was the head of the theoretical physics department. "I still remember the opening lecture in quantum mechanics," Amdahl recalled, "where my major professor explained to us that theoretical physics was really very much like a religion in that it really was based on faith. Faith that there would ultimately be a simple description of nature. Somehow or another that stuck with me through all of those years."

Like Backus, Amdahl saw a need for computers to perform intense calculations. After spending thirty days working through a particular set of physics calculations using nothing but desks calculators and slide rules, Amdahl "decided that there had to be a better way to do it. So I began to invent computers." Yes—*invent*. "There was nothing," he claimed. "There were no computers around. We had an analog computer over at the electrical engineering department." He dropped by the department, investigating the capabilities of the computer by auditing a class. Even the mathematics department was no better: the most advanced computing technology there consisted of only a single multiplier.

He started wondering: Perhaps I could create a digital differential analyzer? (He would successfully write a program simulating an analog differential analyzer years later on the digital IBM 704.) That summer, in 1950, he worked at the Aberdeen Proving Ground, where they were building the EDVAC; the ENIAC was there, too, and Amdahl took it all in, formulating ideas for his Wisconsin Integrally Synchronized Computer (WISC).

> Well, I designed my own computer while I was there, you know, planning the ideas for it, which was very different from what they had at Aberdeen. You know, it was floating point. Aberdeen was all fixed point and there was a four-address thing; I had a three-address one. I had overlap, which didn't occur in any of the others. So I had four instructions in [the] course of execution concurrently, including figuring out a way to divide at the same rate, generating one bit of quotient at a time by either adding or subtracting the next time. And I was going to patent that and found out that it had been patented earlier by von Neumann....

Amdahl earned his doctorate in 1952, of which the design for the WISC was a critical part. He joined IBM immediately after graduating; company execs scoped him out the year before, after a newspaper article describing the work he was doing at the University of Wisconsin brought him public renown, and had offered him a lucrative position, though they didn't have any interest in acquiring the WISC.

IBM put Amdahl to work mimicking a neural network on the 701; one thousand "neurons" were being simulated using a simple model formulated by the Canadian psychologist Donald Olding Hebb. After six months of working on the project, and another year spent on character recognition, Amdahl was pulled into several meetings centering on building a next generation 701. During this time, completely on his own and not because of any directive from a superior, Amdahl "wrote an emulator program, which allowed me to write a program which would use 701 instructions," he said. "In it I could call for floating point operations and do floating point computations. I could call for integrations and operate like a digital differential analyzer including a curve for getting variables in effectively by averaging four-point interpolation." His approach to simulating floating-point, of which he gained the requisite experience by building the WISC, was markedly different than Backus's Speedcoding System (which, as we've seen, did more than merely simulate floating-point arithmetic). Regardless, Amdahl's creation remained in the laboratory for his use only.

Before the 704, though, came the 701A, with modest improvements to the 701. First thing's first, Amdahl realized: add as little hardware as possible yet still imbue the new 701A with floating-point capabilities. Except for a "pot full of diodes and wires," Amdahl succeeded—until magnetic core memory was added, and some more vacuum tubes were used for the obligatory three index registers. After roughly a year of working on the 701A, the concept was dropped in favor of the 704, of which Amdahl was appointed chief designer. He shared an office, and worked with, two talented engineers: Elaine Boehm, a Radcliffe alumna and the first woman to work in the engineering department (Amdahl hired her), and Jacob Johnson, who worked on the character recognition project. Boehm was an exceptional programmer, constantly debating possible features of the 701A (and then the 704) with Amdahl.

During this time, Amdahl met Backus at IBM, who by now had grander visions than simply Speedcoding. For starters, Backus had discovered he wasn't the only programmer focusing on simulating floating-point operations. David J. Wheeler designed a floating-point emulator for the vacuum tube ILLInois Automatic Computer, or ILLIAC I, while working at the University of Illinois. When Wheeler's floating-point system was presented at the same symposium in which Speedcoding was unveiled, Backus was disappointed with the "curious jumble of compromises" of his effort as compared to the "spare, elegant, and powerful" Wheeler design.

More pressingly, it wasn't just arithmetical calculations that were the problem with the computers on hand, Backus realized; the *programming itself* was the issue, costing more money than the machines themselves. "Programming was expensive because you had to hire many programmers to write in 'assembly' or second generation languages, which were only one step removed from the binary or machine code of 0s and 1s," Backus said. "Assembly language was time-consuming; it was an arduous task to write commands that were specific to a particular machine and then to have to debug the multitude of errors that resulted. As a consequence, the ultimate goal of the program was often lost in the shuffle." So Backus set out to create a new, user-friendly programming language.

Backus became involved in the gestation of the 704 because he needed to make sure the new computer could serve the needs of his rapidly evolving programming language concept. To that end, he met with Amdahl at least six times during the design of the 704. What were their discussions like? "We'd go over what I was putting in the machine," recalled Amdahl, who would later arrive at "Amdahl's law," which is still widely used to model the speed of programs run in machines employing parallel processing. "[Backus] would comment on some of it. A few changes were made because of him. On the whole, though, some of the things went in the way I wanted to put them in. For instance, the indexing started with the maximum number and went down to zero—my way of doing it. That gave me an automatic determination of when you'd completed the count." But what did Backus want in the 704 with respect to indexing? "He wanted it all to be additive. And we made it so you could get his too."

For his part, Backus remembers his frustrations centering on hardware—specifically, magnetic drums. "[T]he designers were just totally preoccupied in getting a drum unit designed," he said. "You know, one of these crazy magnetic drums" which would be able to store between one thousand and ten thousand words. To hear Backus tell it, the "designers" of the 704 were so fixated on the drum design that floating-point arithmetic and index registers weren't even on their radar.

> Actually, I kept sort of suggesting that they do this [putting in floating point hardware and inserting index registers], and they kept talking about this damn drum. In the design meetings, I kept bringing this up and bringing it up. They kept talking about the drum. Finally, I decided, well, there's only one way to get their attention. So I spent an hour just deriving some cockamamie scheme for designing it.... It would have taken about a ton of hardware to implement what I had described and Amdahl said, "Oh, you don't need to do that. It's just easy to do it [with] just this. It doesn't take hardly any more hardware."

"In fact, I sort of credit myself with getting index registers and stuff and floating point built into the 704," Backus added.

However it happened—whether through the expertise of Amdahl or the needling of Backus (or both)—the massive IBM 704 was primed and ready to run the most abstract programming language in history. But that language would need to be written first.

CHAPTER 7

❖❖❖

The Automatic Programming Proposal

A short memo John Backus shot off to his boss at IBM, Cuthbert Hurd, sowed the seeds of the first successful high-level programming language.

Cuthbert Corwin Hurd was born in 1911 in Estherville, Iowa. He earned three degrees in mathematics from three different colleges: a bachelor's from Drake University in 1932, a master's from Iowa State University in 1934, and a doctorate from the University of Illinois in 1936. Hurd completed post-doctorate work at Columbia and MIT, and then traveled to the Atomic Energy Commission laboratory in Oak Ridge, Tennessee, where he served as a resident mathematician. IBM hired Hurd in 1949, installing him as the director of the Applied Science Division. He helped with the installation of an IBM 602 at Oak Ridge.

When the Korean War broke out a year later, he and James Birkenstock, who had joined IBM in 1935 and since then served in many roles, were assigned but a single task: Determine how IBM could assist the Allies in the war effort. Their answer was simple: build the IBM 701, also known as the Defense Calculator. Hurd served as an advisor to Thomas Watson during the assembly and development of the 701. Two years and three million dollars later, the 701 supplanted the SSEC, replacing the older machine in the showroom at Madison Avenue and 57th Street.

As IBM moved on from the 701 to the 701A and then the 704, Backus started to worry because the expenses pendulum had swung from hardware costs to programming costs. "[W]hat can we do for the poor programmer now?" he asked. "You see, programming and debugging were the largest parts of the computer budget, and it was easy to see that, with machines like the 704 getting faster and cheaper, the situation was going to get far worse." The rental costs of a 704 ran to the millions of dollars; computing time landed at about four hundred dollars per hour. Backus knew that the issues went far beyond simulating floating-point operations, which would be built into the 704 regardless. They went to the heart of programming itself.

In writing Speedcoding, Backus had been influenced by books such as *The Preparation of Programs for an Electronic Digital Computer* (1951) by Maurice V. Wilkes, David J. Wheeler, and Stanley Gill, which detailed efforts to code the stored-program EDSAC (Electronic Delay Storage Automatic Calculator) using a type of symbolic notion. The *subroutine*, which grouped together programming instructions or commands, was created by Wheeler, who was a computer scientist working at the University of Cambridge, as well as Wilkes, a British computer scientist. As Wheeler explained in a 1952 article,

> A sub-routine may perhaps best be described as a self-contained part of a programme, which is capable of being used in different programmes. It is an entity of its own within a programme. There is no necessity to compose a programme of a set of distinct sub-routines; for the programme can be written as a complete unit, with no divisions into smaller parts. However it is usually advantageous to arrange that a programme is comprised of a set of sub-routines, some of which have been made specially for the particular programme while others are available from a 'library' of standard sub-routines....
>
> One next considers the methods by which subroutines can be used. There are a number of different ways of transferring control to subroutines and arranging that control is returned to the appropriate point to which it is required. One of the simpler methods was that used for the closed sub-routines of the EDSAC in which it was arranged that when the sub-routine had performed its part of the computation then control was returned to a point in the main programme immediately after the orders which had called it into use.

The importance of subroutines to development of modern programming cannot be overstated. "In the beginning there was the EDSAC in Cambridge, England, and I think it quite impressive that right from the start the notion of a subroutine library played a central role in the design of that machine and of the way in which it should be used," declared Edsger Dijksta in a famous lecture from 1972. "It is now nearly 25 years later and the computing scene has changed dramatically, but the notion of basic software is still with us, and the notion of the closed subroutine is still one of the key concepts in programming."

Although *The Preparation of Programs for an Electronic Digital Computer* laid out some of the foundations of *structured programming*—in which independent modules like subroutines and a ban on unconditional jump statements were employed to ensure the readability and reusability of the code—the basic ideas for subroutines and compilers predated even Wheeler and Wilkes' work. As Frances Allen, a longtime employee of IBM, noted,

> Libraries of subroutines and the use of combining routines ("compilers") had been proposed by [Herman Heine] Goldstine and von Neumann…and existed in several systems. A book on programming [i.e., *The Preparation of Programs for an Electronic Digital Computer*] published in 1951 describes a system having open and closed subroutines and preset and program parameters. Preset parameters were incorporated into the subroutine when it was read into the system and remained fixed for all executions; program parameters were passed with the call to the subroutine. The programmer's task was to

write a combining routine which would take the proper subroutines from tape and modify them appropriately. *The motivation for these facilities was to reduce programming time; they were the first step in the direction of using a computer to help prepare programs for itself.* [emphasis added]

With these proto-compilers, the programmer would write a series of "pseudo-codes to refer to subroutines, and the compiler performed the combining function," Allen added. The compiler, such as it was, would reference the appropriate prefabricated subroutines (based on the pseudo-codes) and cobble them together into a working program. Such compilers were not robust—at least, compared to what was to come—and lacked flexibility.

By 1954 there were also compiler projects in the works for the 701 and the 704, independent of what Backus was poised to do at IBM, called PACT I and PACT IA. These efforts, which had been undertaken by a group of IBM customers and employees—specifically, aerospace companies in and around Los Angeles—were among the first to leverage a technique involving the indexing of variables in a table that came to known as *hashing*. (Hashing, which organized data efficiently to permit quick searches, was born almost entirely at IBM. Big Blue engineer Hans Peter Luhn wrote a memo in 1953 suggesting the idea. Independently around the same time, Gene Amdahl and other IBM employees teamed up to write a hashing algorithm for a 701 assembly program.) Backus dismissed any suggestion that PACT influenced his ideas (or the ideas of those who ended up working with him), since his design was already "frozen" by the time the PACT project began.

Backus was restless, because he was aware of how much more could be done. He had his finger on the pulse of the zeitgeist. "I mean, you've got to make it easier to program this thing [the 704]," he said. His experience had led him to see the full scope of the problem.

It wasn't just the difficulties in programming that were creating inefficiencies in how computers were being used—there were inefficiencies in the programs themselves and in how the machines were being utilized to run them. Mainframe machines remained idle as data and programs were loaded sequentially, and applications programs were being written on an ad hoc basis with few standards adhered to. Systems programs—those that handled the "business" of keeping the computer functional and operational, such as with I/O routines—were beginning to be standardized, eventually leading to operating systems (OS). Operating systems evolved from batch processing systems, in which a central control program, called an "automatic operator," could manage and monitor systems programs and the like, cutting down on time inefficiencies between jobs that left machines idle. Assemblers were written to package together common manually coded routines for quick accessibility by the programmer, but even the best of them were time-consuming, difficult to use, and relatively impenetrable to everyone but the experts. Backus had larger ambitions than simply writing a better assembler; rather, he was interested in automating and routinizing algorithms at a higher level of abstraction than mere systems programming. He wanted to, in the words of Richard Hamming, "buffer…the user from the machine itself."

So, in December 1953, Backus penned a memorandum to Cuthbert Hurd, who was his boss at IBM (Hurd became Backus's boss when Backus was still programming the SSEC), suggesting the development of an "automatic programming" or "automatic coding" system. In the memo to Hurd, "I kind of laid out the fact that half the cost of running this thing was programming it. I mean, in counting the machine costs and everything," Backus recalled. After all, "The salaries of programmers generally equaled or exceeded the rental [costs]." Essentially, implementing the Backus proposal "would just mean getting programming done a lot faster. I had no idea that it [automatic programming] would be used on other machines. There were hardly any other machines." Backus figured that the project would take six months to complete, tops.

We can get a good sense of the contents of Backus's memorandum by examining the first paragraph of an Introduction to an early manual for the automatic coding system eventually assembled by Backus and his newly formed development team.

> [The purpose of the automatic coding system] was to reduce by a large factor the task of preparing scientific problems for IBM's next large computer, the 704. If it were possible for the 704 to code problems for itself and produce as good programs as human coders (but without the errors), it was clear that large benefits could be achieved. For it was known that about 2/3 of the cost of solving most scientific and engineering problems on large computers was that of problem preparation. Furthermore, more than 90% of the elapsed time for a problem was usually devoted to planning, writing, and debugging the program. In many cases the development of a general plan for solving a problem was a small job in comparison to the task of devising and coding machine procedures to carry out the plan. The goal of [this] project [is] to enable the programmer to specify a numerical procedure using a concise language like that of mathematics and obtain automatically from this specification an efficient 704 program to carry out the procedure. It was expected that such a system would reduce the coding and debugging task to less than one-fifth of the job it had been.

A paper released in the fall of 1954, co-written by Backus, also serves as a guide to his thinking at the time of the memo—especially regarding his proclivity for selling the advantages of the automatic coding system by wrestling with the time-cost tradeoffs:

> It seems to be quite generally true that the personnel costs of a computing installation are at least as great as the machine cost. Furthermore, it is reasonable to assume that personnel cost for coding and debugging constitute considerably more than half the total personnel cost. Finally, at installations which have relatively few long term problems, as much as 1/2 of the machine cost is devoted to debugging. Therefore, in a crude fashion one can say that out of every dollar spent to solve an average problem on a high speed computer, less than 25 cents is spent for analysis and programming, more than 25 cents is spent for personnel coding and debugging cost, about 25 cents for machine debugging cost, and about 25 cents for machine running cost.

Notice that Backus wasn't coming at the coding problem from a theoretical point of view, claiming that he could "prove correctness," or that programming in the proposed language would be "structured," or that the language would be "Turing complete." Instead, his argument was entirely an applied one, a pragmatic one. It certainly wasn't about the "beauty of programming in mathematical notation." Backus's interest in the theoretical would come much later.

Cuthbert Hurd would later place John Backus among the first rank of thinkers he ever encountered. "They've [the top minds] gotta think tops-down and bottoms-up," he said. "There are very few people like that." Hurd considered John von Neumann one such person; Backus was another.

Yet despite the persuasive arguments he had relayed to his boss, at first Hurd didn't give the green light for Backus's automatic programming proposal—because of von Neumann. In 1951 when Hurd was still at Oak Ridge, he helped to lure von Neumann, who was already working as a government consultant, to consult for IBM. Which led to some awkward moments, as Hurd described years later:

> After [von Neumann] became a consultant he'd spend two and a half days a month and he'd drive usually from Princeton and then get on the west side highway and go up to Poughkeepsie and he'd drive fast, and I think he believed that I had some magic, so when he got tickets I would pay them. Because he'd hand me [a] ticket, no way to fix them.... I'd take that ticket and give it [to] the downtown manager in New York, where the Police court was, and he would go around and pay the fine.

It turned out to be von Neumann, not Hurd, who objected to Backus's proposal. "He [von Neumann] didn't see programming as a big problem," recalled Backus. "I think one of his major objections was you wouldn't know what you were getting with floating point calculations. You at least knew where trouble was with fixed point if there was trouble. But he wasn't sensitive to the issue of the cost of programming. He really felt that [it] was a wasted effort." Apparently, when hearing of the automatic programming system, von Neumann exclaimed, "Why would you want more than machine language?", although this quote may be apocryphal. According an anecdotal sketch provided by J.A.N. Lee of the Virginia Polytechnic Institute,

> One of von Neumann's students at Princeton recalled that graduate students were being used to hand assemble programs into binary for their early machine. This student took time out to build an assembler, but when von Neumann found out about it he was very angry, saying that it was a waste of a valuable scientific computing instrument to use it to do clerical work.

An attendee of the meeting in which Hurd presented Backus's idea to von Neumann described the scene this way: von Neumann "seemed...to be somewhat bored by the proceedings and, yes, he did at the end acquiesce in a recommendation that the project be pursued but, on theoretical grounds, seemed to dismiss the whole development as but an application of the idea of Turing's 'shortcode.'" Von Neumann was not "unduly negative" but more "apathetic," largely because he could perform the manipulations mentally that these programming aids performed automatically.

Von Neumann wasn't the only person skeptical of Backus's proposed automatic programming system. Others, both inside and outside of IBM, were not sold on the idea (including J.A.N. Lee). One skeptic, expressing the consensus opinion at the time, told John Greenstadt, who had attended the meeting with Hurd and von Neumann, that "Backus has bitten off more than he can chew!" And once the project started, an IBM executive, who had kept close tabs on Backus's progress, asked Greenstadt what he thought of the whole "fiasco."

"This [skeptical] belief came from their experience in coding for small, badly designed computers—this was truly a difficult task—and their experience with clumsy and slow automatic programming systems, of which there [were] quite a few," explained Backus. He even took responsibility for one of those "slow" systems: Speedcoding.

In fairness, though, skepticism of automatic programming also stemmed from the complexities of the new 704 hardware. According to an article from the February 8, 1999, issue of *Computerworld* magazine entitled "Born of Frustration,"

> Built-in floating-point coprocessors and index registers would let the 704 use automatic mathematical statements, which would eliminate the need to write repetitive instruction code. The improvements meant that the programming techniques had to be a lot more clever [Backus said], because "you couldn't mask inefficiencies."

Indeed, the IBM 704 was a complex piece of machinery. In 1962 at Bell Telephone Laboratories, John L. Kelly, Jr., along with Max Mathews, would create a recording of a computer-synthetized voice singing a song: "Daisy Bell (Bicycle Built for Two)," written in 1892 by British songwriter Harry Dacre. Which proved inspirational to Arthur C. Clarke, who saw a demonstration of the 704 "singing" and integrated the idea into the novelization and the movie script of *2001: A Space Odyssey* (1968). As the HAL 9000 computer is disconnected in *2001*, he sings "Daisy Bell" with a sad resignation.

The 704 could also play chess, as illustrated by the 1959 IBM short film *"Thinking" Machines*. The mathematician and IBM employee Alex Bernstein, along with several colleagues, wrote the Bernstein Chess Program for the 704 in 1957. As shown in the film, the chess program is first loaded onto a reel of magnetic tape; meanwhile, a standard chess board, with all the pieces, is set up next to the computer. The human being playing against the computer physically moves the pieces on the board for both players, human and computer. When the human takes his turn, he relays the move to the machine by depressing some combination of the gray and cream switches on the front panel of the 704; the machine, well versed in the rules of the game, flags and rejects any illegal moves. Then, using a line printer, the 704 prints out on paper the positions of all the pieces on the board. Finally, after running through possible moves and narrowing them down to about seven, the computer prints out its decision of where to move. "It can defeat an inexperienced player, but can be outwitted by a good one," explains the narrator of the film. Furthermore, the machine doesn't learn from its mistakes, since it will make the same moves in a deterministic way if presented with the same set of circumstances.

But the larger problem, and perhaps the main reason for the skepticism about automatic programming systems in general, was that Backus's idea had been tried before by others, and—because of how much these systems slowed down the hardware they ran on, the difficulties of coding with them, their lack of efficiency at handling "housekeeping" operations, the promise of their capabilities not matching the reality, and the lack of agreement in the early 1950s about what "automatic programming" meant, among a myriad of other reasons—automatic programming had only met with modest success at best.

For example, there was Glennie's AUTOCODE, developed in the early 1950s by Alick Glennie for the Manchester Mark 1 at the University of Manchester in England. The Mark 1, unrelated to Howard Aiken's Harvard Mark I, was a stored-program computer containing index registers and built after World War II. This first iteration of AUTOCODE, which was strictly fixed-point, permitted various mathematical operations but was especially cumbersome to use (replete with an abundance of machine-dependent commands), although it made use of the first working compiler, translating source code into machine language.

A second, "cleaner" iteration of AUTOCODE appeared several years later (but before Backus sent off his memo to Hurd). Developed by R. A. "Tony" Brooker, who succeeded Alan Turing at the Computing Machine Laboratory at Cambridge, this AUTOCODE was able to perform the tasks of a relatively complex scientific calculator on a level of abstraction above that of an assembler.

There are more examples. Consider Short Code. In the late 1940s, John Mauchly developed Short Code (originally called Brief Code), an algebraic interpreter, which first ran on the BINAC and then on the UNIVAC by the early 1950s. Short Code could read in algebraic equations, including parentheses and equals signs (for expression assignments), as input—using two-digits groupings to represent memory locations, variables, symbols, and arithmetic and mathematical operations—and then output the intended results. William Schmitt implemented Short Code for the BINAC, and then, with Robert Logan's help, implemented Short Code for the UNIVAC as well. (The program was later ported to the Univac II.) Of course, programs written in Short Code ran much slower than equivalent programs written in machine code.

There were automatic programming systems being developed independently in Russia during the early 1950s as well. Though the programming notation, developed by the mathematician Alexey Andreevich Lyapunov, was exceedingly complicated, these systems employed cutting-edge optimization methods. Andrey Petrovych Ershov, who wrote a book about compiler design, was also a key player in Soviet computing.

The Eckert-Mauchly Computer Corporation (EMCC) proved fertile ground for the creation of the first modern complier. Before proceeding, though, we should keep in mind the sage words of John Backus. "There is an obstacle to understanding, now, developments in programming in the early 1950s," he writes. "There was a rapid change in the meaning of some important terms during the 1950s. We tend to assume that the modern meaning of a word is the same one it had in an early paper, but this is sometimes not the case." Specifically, the term "compiler," Backus notes, meant different things to different people at the time. For example, at the Office of Naval Research (ONR) Symposium in May of 1954, Backus counted at least a half-dozen different uses of the word compiler by attendees presenting papers. There was the compiler method of Nora B. Moser, the New York University compiler system of Roy Goldfinger, and the LMO edit compiler of Merritt Elmore, all of which did not treat the notions of "compilers" and "compiled code" in quite the same way.

Years after the symposium, the computer scientist and historian Jean Sammet would offer a concise definition of a compiler: "a compiler must perform at least the following functions: Analysis of the source code, retrieval of appropriate routines from a library, storage allocation, and creation of actual machine code." All the "compilers" described at the ONR Symposium fell short, in one way or another, of Sammet's standard.

There was one compiler in particular that Backus found distasteful: the single-pass A-0 for the UNIVAC I, which was written by Grace Hopper and her team at Remington Rand between late 1951 and mid-1952. The term "compiler" was coined by the team to describe the A-0's functionality: it translated symbolic code into machine language. "All I had to do was to write down a set of call numbers, let the computer find them on the tape, bring them over and do the additions. This was the first compiler. We could start writing mathematical equations and let the computer do the work," Hopper recalled. Each word, during compilation of code, had at least three addresses of memory locations, resulting in difficulties involving so-called forward jumps (with unknown locations) through the program that Hopper was able to solve by analogizing the compilation process to her time playing undergraduate women's basketball:

> Therefore, if you got the ball and you wanted to get down there under the basket, you used what we called a "forward pass." You looked for a member of your team, threw the ball over, ran like the dickens up ahead, and she threw the ball back to you. So it seemed to me that this was an appropriate way of solving the problem I was facing of the forward jumps! I tucked a little section down at the end of the memory which I called the "neutral corner." At the time I wanted to jump forward from the routine I was working on, I jumped to a spot in the "neutral corner." I then set up a flag for the [forward jump] which said, "I've got a message for you." This meant that each routine, as I processed it, had to look and see if it had a flag; if it did, it put a second jump from the neutral corner to the beginning of the routine, and it was possible to make a single-pass compiler and the concept did come from playing basketball.

Hopper presented the fruits of her team's labors at an ACM conference in Pittsburgh in May 1952—she was frequently delivering public talks about the latest in computing technology—but interest in the A-0 proved tepid. People had trouble wrapping their heads around one simple fact: that computers could do more than arithmetic. Which left Hopper to do just as much innovating as selling over the next several years, since people were "allergic to change." She followed up the A-0 with the improved A-1 and A-2 (in 1955), which finally gained widespread currency.

In a talk presented to the High Speed Computer Conference at Louisiana State University in February 1955, Hopper bragged about her floating-point A-2 compiler:

> The A-2 compiler, as it stands at the moment, commands a library of mathematical and logical subroutines of floating decimal operations. It has been successfully applied to many different mathematical problems. In some cases, it has produced finished, checked, and debugged programs in three minutes. Some problems have taken as long as eighteen minutes to code.

The era of the compiler had begun—though some have argued that the A-2 was really a *macro expander*, rather than a full-fledged compiler.

The A-2 was followed by the B-0, renamed the FLOW-MATIC, released in 1958 (preliminary specifications were done in 1955), which was designed to appeal to customers for whom mathematics was not a second language. "I decided there were two kinds of people in the world who were trying to use these things," she said. "One was people who liked using symbols—mathematicians and people like that. There was another bunch of people who were in data processing who hated symbols, and wanted words, word-oriented people very definitely. And that was the reason I thought we needed two languages." FLOW-MATIC, especially suited for writing business applications for billing and payroll, would be a word-oriented data-processing language for word-oriented people; programs could be written using English-style sentences, if not English grammar. FLOW-MATIC introduced long identifiers, like PAYROLLREPORT; the use of verbs for operations like ADD; more options with data types beyond merely fixed- and floating-point; and a clear separation between the data description and the data processing sections of a program. By the end of the decade, Hopper and others were calling for greater standardization of business computing, which resulted in the Conference/Committee on Data Systems Languages (CODASYL). FLOW-MATIC, in large part, evolved into COBOL, the Common Business Oriented Language.

But all that lay in the future. Let's rewind the story back to the creation the first compiler, the A-0 system (Arithmetic Language version 0). For her part, Hopper agreed that the A-0 was limited. "It wasn't what you'd call [a compiler] today, and it wasn't what you'd call a 'language' today," she said. "It was a series of specifications. For each subroutine you wrote some specs. The reason it got called a compiler was that each subroutine was given a 'call word,' because the subroutines were in a library, and when you pull stuff out of a library you compile things. It's as simple as that."

Maybe, but Backus hated it. The A-0 compiler was "clumsy and ran slowly and was difficult to use," he said. In a later interview, he was even harsher: "her ideas were just [such] cockamamie stuff. Her scheme for this—I forget the name of her proposed compiler—but it was part machine code, part this, part that.... [It was a] [c]ompletely unworkable thing." In his seminal paper submitted for the proceedings of the ACM SIGPLAN History of Programming Languages (HOPL) conference, Backus also has little good to say about the early A-2 compiler, what he termed a "synthetic computer": "instead of 'pseudo-instructions' its input was then a complex sequence of 'compiling instructions' that could take a variety of forms ranging from machine code itself to lengthy groups of words constituting rather clumsy calling sequences for the desired floating point subroutine, to 'abbreviated form' instructions that were converted by a 'Translator' into ordinary 'compiling instructions.'" But in that same paper, he calls an automatic programming system developed by J. Halcombe "Hal" Laning and Neal Zierler of MIT both "elegant," "simple," and demonstrably "algebraic"—certainly much more recognizably "algebraic" than either Glennie's AUTOCODE or Hopper's A-2.

☼☼☼

The Laning and Zierler system is the most important automatic programming development to precede Backus's memo to Hurd. Designed for the MIT Whirlwind I vacuum-tube computer, the system was based on an earlier algebraic compiler called "George" that Hal Laning developed. A colleague of Laning's at MIT, Richard H. Battin, recalled the genesis of George:

> In the summer of 1952, following about six months experience as a user of Whirlwind, Hal felt computers should be capable of accepting conventional mathematical language directly, without having to recast engineering problems in an awkward manner using logic that was too far removed from the engineer's daily experience. Over the next few months he personally brought this idea to fruition with the development of the first algebraic compiler called "George"—from the old saw *"Let George do it."*

By the spring of 1953, George was functional. "The first nontrivial program executed by George was a set of six nonlinear differential equations describing the lead-pursuit dynamics of an air-to-air fire-control problem," Battin recalled. After taking less than an hour to program in the equations for the problem, George successfully executed the program on the first try.

A short time later, the Whirlwind's hardware was upgraded with magnetic drum memory. Laning brought Neal Zierler on as a collaborator to help optimize George for the new hardware as well as to produce documentation for the system.

The Laning and Zierler system, which handled floating-point operations, could process algebraic notation and nested parentheses as part of a simple algebraic language; it could work with single-letter variables and subscripts; and it had available a rich catalog of mathematical functions, implemented by typing the letter "F" along with an integer superscript indicating the desired function; these functions—including for sine, cosine, tangent, logarithms, and square roots—ranged from F^1 to F^{23}. For example, the following line of code would set the variable x equal to the expression $3(\sqrt{y} \sin z)$:

$$x=3(F^1(y)F^2(z))$$

The Laning and Zierler system could also calculate solutions to differential equations, with the letter "D" signifying d/dt. Input came via punched paper tape generated by a Friden Flexowriter teleprinter (to the uninitiated the machine looked like a run-of-the-mill electric typewriter, but it punched holes into paper tape), while the system compiled (although the term wasn't invented yet) the algebraic expressions into executable machine code that the 1024-storage-cell Whirlwind could run—thereby slowing down the machine tenfold (although speeds would improve later on). Laning and Zierler even offered a user manual. As Jean Sammet noted, the system

> appear[ed] to be the first…in the United States to permit the user to write expressions in a notation resembling normal mathematical format, *e.g.*,

$c = 0.0052 \ (a-y)/2ay,$
$y = 5y,$

Although conditional transfers of control (using the CP instruction) and unconditional transfers of control (using the SP instruction) were possible, Laning and Zierler did not include a looping statement. There was, however, a PRINT instruction available to generate program output, and the STOP instruction terminated a program.

Evidence suggests that Laning had a proof of concept as early as 1952, according to Backus, who laments that it took the priesthood generation—the elitist programmers who came of age in the 1940s and '50s—much too long to recognize the brilliance of the Laning and Zierler system, with virtually no mention of the elegant breakthrough in the computing literature of the time. "Dr. Laning was the first person to conceive of and implement what we would now call a true compiler," Backus wrote in 1991, "a program that converts *a description of a computer program* into a real machine-language program that a computer can then execute whenever desired." He continued:

> Before Laning, no one had conceived of and implemented an elegant and powerful language for expressing a computation (although there were examples of *very* much less sophisticated schemes to aid the programmer). His concepts of a programming language and a compiler were completely original at the time. They were the beginning of the entire programming language and compiler business, which in turn made computers accessible to large numbers of users.

Yet Backus, in the midst of launching his own rebellion against the priesthood, also managed to miss Laning's breakthrough. Finished in mid-1953, the Laning and Zierler system was described (although not demonstrated) publicly at an Office of Naval Research (ONR) Symposium on automatic programming in 1954.

Two years after its public release, Grace Hopper sang the praises of the Laning and Zierler system at another ONR symposium, documenting its wide-ranging impact on the computing milieu.

> A description of Laning and Zierler's system of algebraic pseudocoding for the Whirlwind computer led to the development of Boeing's BACAIC for the 701, …AT-3 for the UNIVAC, and the Purdue System for the Datatron and indicated the need for far more effort in the area of algebraic translators.

In her speech at the 1956 ONR Symposium on Automatic Programming for Digital Computers, which she organized, Hopper pointed to one more automatic programming system that was inspired by Laning and Zierler's: John Backus's sequel to Speedcoding, which was in the latter stages of its development at IBM at the time. But how much was Backus influenced by the Laning and Zierler system?

The system's influence on Backus is "a question which has been muddled by many misstatements on my part. For many years I believed that we had gotten the idea for using algebraic notation…from seeing a demonstration of the Laning and Zierler system at MIT." Upon deeper reflection, however, Backus remembered that

> …we were already considering algebraic input considerably more sophisticated than that of Laning and Zierler's system when we first heard of their pioneering work. Thus, although Laning and Zierler had already produced the world's first algebraic compiler, our basic ideas for [an automatic programming system beyond Speedcoding] had been

developed independently; thus it is difficult to know what, if any, new ideas we got from seeing the demonstration of their system.

Here is the backstory for Backus's dismissal of Laning and Zierler's influence. On May 21, 1954, Backus sent a letter to Hal Laning, asking if he (Backus) could see the system be put through its paces, after hearing about the Laning and Zierler system—but not seeing it in action—at the ONR Symposium held earlier that month. "Last week I attended a session in Washington at which [MIT] Professor Charles Adams described the system for translating algebraic formulae into computer programs which you and your associates have developed," Backus wrote to Laning.

> After the meeting he gave us a copy of the description by you and Mr. Zierler.
>
> My programming research group here is beginning work on such a system for IBM's newly announced 704 calculator. We would very much appreciate the opportunity to benefit from your work in this area. Our formulation of the problem is very similar to yours: however, we have done no programming or even detailed planning. Therefore, detailed discussions with you and some of your associates in this work would perhaps save us much time and duplicated effort.

Note that the "copy of the description" that Backus was given by Adams was the twenty-five page Laning and Zierler system manual *A Program for Translation of Mathematical Equations for Whirlwind I*, containing numerous example programs and detailed programming descriptions. Several weeks later, in early June of 1954, Backus, Harlan Herrick, and Irving Ziller of IBM traveled to MIT for a demonstration.

Backus and Herrick had presented a paper at the same ONR Symposium (held on May 13-14, 1954) where they first heard about the Laning and Zierler system. In that paper, they pointedly ask: "[C]an a machine translate a sufficiently rich mathematical language into a sufficiently economical program at a sufficiently low cost to make the whole affair feasible?" The paper, which explains Speedcoding, first lays out the differences between an "interpretive system," which translates nonmachine code line-by-line during runtime, and runs very slowly as a result, with a "compiling system," which translates all of the nonmachine code into machine code prior to the program's execution. Backus and Herrick then justify the tradeoff of efficiency and speed of operation with user friendliness by listing the objectives that they believe Speedcoding satisfied:

1. As few instructions as possible should be required to specify a program. Programming time should be minimized.
2. Programs should be easy to check out [i.e., debug].
3. Scaling [factors] should be unnecessary [by using floating-point arithmetic].
4. Address modification should be made very convenient.
5. Transfer of arbitrary blocks of information to and from high-speed storage should be easy to specify.
6. Common functions should be readily available.
7. Optional automatic checking of calculations should be provided.

Of course, these objectives carried over to Backus's new automatic programming project, the successor to Speedcoding, that he had begun working on at IBM. Perhaps the clearest indication that Backus and Herrick had indeed arrived at programming in an algebra-style code prior to seeing the Laning and Zierler system demonstrated at MIT comes from these lines in their paper:

> Obviously the programmer would like to write "X" instead of some specific address, and if he wants to add X and Y he would like to write "X + Y" instead of, perhaps,
>
> ```
> CLEAR AND ADD   100
> ADD             106
> ```
>
> or some such gibberish. To go a step further he would like to write $\Sigma\ a_{ij} \cdot b_{jk}$ instead of the fairly involved set of instructions corresponding to this expression.

Backus and Herrick conclude their paper by noting that a Speedcoding program, as written for the IBM 701, is a waste of time for the 704, which already has the program's features built in to the hardware *ab initio*. So, automatic programming had to evolve, allowing users to write programs utilizing some sort of "natural mathematical language."

"Whether such an elaborate automatic-programming system is possible or feasible," they conclude, "has yet to be determined." As Donald Knuth and Luis Trabb Pardo observe in their paper "The Early Development of Programming Languages" (1976), the Laning and Zierler system proved that an automatic programming system like Backus and Herrick described was indeed possible. (Together, Knuth and Pardo are perhaps best known for their Trabb Pardo-Knuth algorithm, or TPK, a concise algorithm involving many programming concepts that they wrote in numerous languages with the express purpose of illustrating how programming languages evolved.)

That summer, after Cuthbert Hurd green-lighted Backus's proposal—"He [Hurd] said, 'Fine, do it!'... He really understood," Backus said; "[h]e agreed, even without an argument"—John Backus, Harlan Herrick, and several other people at IBM were well on their way to finding out if such a system was feasible as well.

CHAPTER 8

Assembling the Team

After Cuthbert Hurd approved John Backus's proposal to develop an automatic programming system, Backus assembled a team of talented individuals that kept a single idea firmly in mind: the design of the computer language was secondary to building an efficient compiler.

When Backus reminisced about programming in the 1950s, he was most struck by "a vital frontier enthusiasm virtually untainted by either the scholarship or the stuffiness of academia," adding: "Action, progress, and outdoing one's rivals were more important than mere authorship of a paper." This "frontier enthusiasm" would repeat in the computer industry a generation later courtesy of computer hobbyist groups such as Silicon Valley's Homebrew Computer Club, which had as members future luminaries like Steve Wozniak.

Backus first recruited Irving Ziller. He had been hired by IBM to work in their computing service bureau two years earlier after graduating from Brooklyn College. Ziller's initial assignment at the company involved transferring over customer applications from the Card Programmed Calculator (CPC) to the IBM 701. To complete the task, Ziller "made use of the similarity between CPC programming and Speedcoding," according to Emerson W. Pugh in *Building IBM: Shaping an Industry and Its Technology* (1995). But Ziller was also stuck programming electronic calculator plugboards, electrical switchboards housing masses of sockets and wires that were staples of the earliest days of programming. "This, as you can imagine, was a fairly tedious job," Ziller recalled years later. "Anyone doing plug boards understood the emerging need to simplify the programming process."

Cuthbert Hurd was in charge of the Applied Sciences Department; once Backus pitched his automatic programming idea to him, Rex Seeber shifted Backus over to Hurd's department. Also working under Hurd was Ziller. Backus recalled that "it was easy to persuade [Hurd] to let me get Irv to work with me. It just sort of went like that—one by one." Ziller had joined the team by January 1954.

Next to come on board was Harlan L. Herrick, the third member of the team (he joined in May 1954), who had already worked with Backus on Speedcoding. A math major at Iowa State University who went on to snag a master's degree in mathematics from the University of Iowa, Herrick then earned a scholarship to Yale for additional graduate studies. While in New Haven, though, he spotted an article about the SSEC and, because of his dissatisfaction at the university, applied for a programming job at IBM. (Herrick had spent a total of eight years at Yale, where he also taught mathematics.) The company hired Herrick, immediately putting him to work programming the SSEC. Herrick, a preternaturally gifted chess player who had racked up several tournament wins, was the most experienced programmer on the team; because he knew the seemingly insurmountable challenges facing them, he thought their chances of success were low. "I said, 'John, we can't possibly simulate a human programmer with a language—this language—that would produce machine code that would even approach the efficiency of a human programmer like me, for example.' I'm a great programmer, don't you know?"

Reminiscing on programming in that era, Backus tellingly wrote, "Just as freewheeling westerners developed a chauvinistic pride in their frontiersmanship and a corresponding conservatism, so many programmers of the freewheeling 1950s began to regard themselves as members of a priesthood guarding skills and mysteries far too complex for ordinary mortals." Perhaps Herrick was defensive because he was worried: Could a computer *really* replace a human being at something that required the talent, intuition, and skill of programming? In this way, Herrick was a pioneer of another sort: among the first people employed in a white-collar job who feared automation; of course, if Backus's team completely succeeded in their task, Herrick would have contributed to his own demise as a programmer (or, at least, as a machine language programmer).

The fourth member of the team, Robert A. "Bob" Nelson, had only recently been hired by IBM to complete technical typing assignments. His background was in cryptography, having worked for the U.S. State Department in Vienna, Austria. Nelson was brought on board at the same time as Herrick. He was there at the first team meeting: "There were four of us on that day," remembered Nelson. Going forward with the project was "an act of faith. There were no benchmarks to compare the work to. There was only the group of us working together and seeing what each other was doing and having faith in ourselves." When working in a new area, Nelson added, "I really think it helps if you are something of a science fiction writer. Because you have to construct scenarios for how to get from here to there, where there is someplace no one has ever been before."

In early 1954, Backus and Ziller began their project in a small office in the Jay Thorpe building on Fifth Avenue, which was nearby IBM headquarters at 590 Madison Avenue. By the time the full team was assembled, the operation had moved to the 19th floor of the annex of 590 Madison Avenue. Stationed there, they were adjacent to the elevator machinery. On the ground level was a 701, accessible by IBM employee and customer alike. Every morning when they arrived to work, they took the elevator—and it traveled very, very slowly. But they still had to walk up one flight of stairs because the elevator couldn't reach the annex on the top floor. Whenever Herrick and Ziller would step into the elevator, the elevator man, who was named Lou, would tease them: "Oh, there they are! Bring the men in the white coats!" Lou's point? "We were sort of irregular IBMers," lacking the polish and the formal dress style of cookie-cutter IBM men—with their pinstriped suits and starched white shirts—who appeared to walk and talk in lockstep.

Backus noticed that their productivity was widely variable, partly because the team was moved to different locations multiple times. After 590 Madison Avenue, their next move was to the fifth floor of a small building on 56th Street. IBM employees always had to punch in by 9:15 AM. Most people punched in a minute before, and Backus, commuting by train, was lucky to arrive on time. But after a while, Backus noticed something unusual: that no matter when he arrived, the rest of his team was already present. Finally, he was privately told why:

> Someone confided in me that across the street from our building was an empty lot and behind that was the back of an apartment building. In one of the apartments lived a young woman who slept without any clothes on. She used to get up in the morning and dance very exuberantly for a while before going to work. So that was a period of great productivity because everyone came in very early and the show was over after a while, and everybody settled down to work long before starting time.

Backus never got to watch "Dancer Nus," as they called her, since he never arrived on the train early enough to see her "water her flowers before getting dressed." Shortly thereafter, the team's site was relocated again, this time to a spot overlooking the dressing rooms of the Jay Thorpe department store. And then once again, to a location with the dressing rooms of Bonwit Teller, a luxury department store, clearly visible. Their productivity declined since "[f]or some peculiar reason, people spent an awful lot of time at the windows," Backus joked. Finally, they were moved to a building without a view. With their productivity again sky high, the team wrapped up the project, and not a moment too soon. Because of all the delays in finishing the work, along with the relentless criticism that was arriving at his doorstep (recall that one IBM executive called the project a "fiasco"), Backus had contemplated handing over the reins to someone else to see the project through to its completion—a move which, luckily, never materialized.

No matter the location, the team members were invariably stuck in an open room with many desks, all pushed up against each other, but lacking dividers. It was a terribly claustrophobic environment. "We were all in each other's pockets," as one development team member described it. "When I first got there, I noticed that IBM used the closed-shop technique," said another, who joined the team later on. "You programmed, but you didn't have to see a computer. If you had a problem to run, you would submit your deck and take your turn. You'd come back in the morning and the listings would be on your desk. And that's the way you worked." He continued:

> Everybody had a specific task. And they knew that I was unfamiliar with their schemes, so they would just hand me the code listings. They'd say "Herrick has this problem and

we need a flow chart for that." I would read his machine language code and turn it into a flow chart. Then we could see errors and we could make changes to the program. So, now he has something that will serve him as a programming aid without wasting his time chasing around randomly.

"They were the nicest group of people you've ever met," he added, "all of them."

Recall that in June 1954, Backus, Ziller, and Herrick visited MIT to see a demo of the Laning and Zierler system. According to Ziller, "It was pretty good, very nicely done conceptually. But they took an academic approach. They couldn't care less about efficiency." (After writing the algebraic compiler at MIT, Hal Laning turned his attention to other interests, first working on a guidance systems for missiles and a Mars satellite and then, most famously, helping to write the software for the Apollo Guidance Computer. Because of Laning's thoughtful programming, last-minute errors in the LM Eagle's guidance computer that cropped up during Neil Armstrong and Buzz Aldrin's descent to the lunar surface triggered a software reboot, retaining the critical navigational data rather than slipping into an endless loop—thereby allowing the two Americans a safe landing on the moon.) In the months before and the months that followed, the team developed a nascent computer language on paper with efficiency as their primary goal. "As far as we were aware," Backus said, "we simply made up the language as we went along." Nelson expanded his role from technical typing to programming, "quickly [becoming] an outstanding programmer, absolutely critical to…the project," remembered Backus.

Their scope, initially, was narrow. Although they expected the language to revolutionize the 704, they didn't necessarily think it would be written to run on many IBM computers, let alone computers built by other companies; they certainly could not have fathomed that the language would dominate the computer industry for decades to come and spawn countless successor languages.

Backus's team realized that the real challenge wasn't in the design specifications of the language per se, but in building a compiler that could read and understand English-style programs and translate them into efficient, clean, executable 704 machine code. Unlike with Laning and Zierler's approach, the development team realized that *efficiency* was of paramount importance: the compiler had to be as close to perfect as they could muster. "At that time, most programmers wrote symbolic machine instructions exclusively (some even used absolute octal [base 8] or decimal machine instructions)," Backus (and a coauthor) explained.

> Almost to a man, they firmly believed that any mechanical coding method would fail to apply that versatile ingenuity which each programmer felt he possessed and constantly needed in his work. Therefore, it was agreed, compilers could only turn out code which would be tolerably less efficient than human coding (intolerable, that is, unless that inefficiency could be buried under larger, but desirable, inefficiencies such as the programmed floating-point arithmetic usually required then)….
>
> [The development team] had one primary fear. After working long and hard to produce a good translator program, an important application might promptly turn up which would confirm the views of the [skeptics]:…its object program would run at half

the speed of a hand-coded version. It was felt that such an occurrence, or several of them, would almost completely block acceptance of the system.

Above all, as Ziller explained, "Our primary objective, or focus, was to permit people to concentrate on the essence of their problems and eliminate preoccupation of the mechanics of the computer per se," adding, "We were in completely uncharted waters. We were trying to do something that, basically, no one had ever tried to do before and nobody had ever succeeded in doing."

Essentially, he was saying, the language the team was developing would abstract away the machine, "enabl[ing] the programmer to write a program in some high-level programming code, which was easy for humans to write since it looked like English or algebra, but which the computer could convert into binary machine instructions," as authors Martin Campbell-Kelly and William Aspray write in *Computer: A History of the Information Machine*. But what, precisely, was high-level programming?

An Interlude on Computer Languages, High and Low

Before we continue our story, we need to pause to look at how high-level languages (HLLs) differ from low-level languages. In the book *Bitwise: A Life in Code* (2018), author David Auerbach suggests that "[c]omputers are best understood as a series of *abstraction layers*, one on top of the other. Each new top layer assembles the previous layer's pieces into more complex, high-level structures." He then goes on to discuss how these layers of abstraction are akin to a restaurant, where the *diner* represents a program in a high-level computer language:

> Diners read the menu and know just enough about the dishes to decide what they want to eat. They don't have to worry about how much salt to put in the soup, how long dishes need to cook, or how to lay out the food on the plate. They have only high-level control over the end result, their meal. Without knowledge of what goes on in the kitchen, diners take into account their taste preferences, allergies, recommendations, and such, and order a meal off the menu. The chef, who knows how to translate the dishes on the menu into actual recipes, is the compiler or interpreter, who translates high-level instructions (the diner's order) into far more specific low-level instructions (the exact ingredients list and instructions for cooking). The kitchen cooks are the actual computing hardware, who have the expertise to perform a variety of precise cooking skills reliably without error. They make the dishes based on the exact instructions given to them by the chef. The diners remain ignorant of the details.

The computer scientist Jean Sammet, who, in the early 1960s, led the development of the symbolic mathematics programming language called FORMAC (FORmula MAnipulation Compiler), an add-on to the language that Backus's team would create, proffered four characteristics that all HLLs share:

1. Knowledge of machine code is unnecessary.
2. There is a good potential for converting a program written in high level language for one computer to run on another computer with minimal difficulty.

3. There is an instruction expansion, *i.e.*, a single statement in a high level language will produce many machine code instructions.
4. The notation for the language is problem oriented, *i.e.*, it is closer to the original conceptual statement of the problem than are machine instructions.

Sammet excluded "assembly languages (even with macros), languages for doing microprogramming, command languages, and text editors" from being classified as HLLs.

Let's look at an example of a modern high-level programming language running on an Intel 64-bit x86 instruction set. Suppose that we want to write a program to do the following: assign numerical data into two variables, called i and j, and perform an arithmetic operation on them, storing the result in a third variable, called k. Here is a possible implementation:

program highlevel

```
    i = 13
    j = 40
    k = i + j
```

end program highlevel

Our highlevel program is far removed from the machine level. The same program, written in an assembler (but edited here for space constraints), looks much less mathematical:

```
    mov     DWORD PTR [rbp-4], 13
    mov     DWORD PTR [rbp-8], 40
    mov     edx, DWORD PTR [rbp-4]
    mov     eax, DWORD PTR [rbp-8]
    add     eax, edx
    mov     DWORD PTR [rbp-12], eax
```

The mov stands for move; a mov instruction moves or copies data from the source operand (located after the comma) to the destination operand (before the comma). (An *operand* describes the data to be operated on in some fashion by the computer.) The eax and edx are called general-purpose registers, which function as temporary holding pens for data. The variables i and j are assigned the values 13 and 40 (that's not quite what is happening here, but let's keep things as simple as possible), respectively:

```
    mov     DWORD PTR [rbp-4], 13
    mov     DWORD PTR [rbp-8], 40
```

Then these two values, 13 and 40, are copied into the general-purpose registers eax and edx:

```
    mov     edx, DWORD PTR [rbp-4]
    mov     eax, DWORD PTR [rbp-8]
```

Next, using the `add` instruction, the data point stored in the `edx` register is added to the `eax` register, with the result held in the `eax` register:

```
add     eax, edx
```

And, finally, the result of the addition is stored into the variable k.

```
mov     DWORD PTR [rbp-12], eax
```

"A programming language is low level when its programs require attention to the irrelevant," quipped the computer scientist Alan Perlis. Writing programs in assembly language, unlike in an HLL, forces the programmer to be cognizant of low-level operations, like storing and retrieving data from memory and making sure to properly load quantities into registers before performing even the simplest of arithmetic operations.

The *mnemonics* of an assembler's instruction set—instructions like `add` and `mov`—are an abstracted form of machine code because these mnemonics are easily readable by human beings. Peel away even more of these abstractions, and the same six lines of assembly code might look something like this in hexadecimal (base 16) machine code, with the addresses shown in bold and the contents of the addresses not bolded:

```
40074dc7     45 fc 0d 00 00
400754c7     45 f8 28 00 00
40075b8b     55 fc
40075e8b     45 f8
40076101     d0
40076389     45 f4
```

For an even more abstract taste of this programming stew, consider that the hexadecimal machine code could be turned into *binary* machine code. For instance, the hexadecimal fc is 11111100 in binary. Now imagine the entire program written in ones and zeros, making the code completely impenetrable to nearly everyone but the most insanely patient programmer—and the computer, of course. This is called programming in *absolute binary*—where the addresses and instructions of the machine code are all written in binary.

Programming in octal (base 8) groups binary digits into blocks of three, making things simpler. Counting with octal proceeds like this: 0, 1, 2, 3, 4, 5, 6, 7, 10, 11, 12, and so on. The decimal number 5 converted to binary is 101. But 101 converted to octal is 5. Here's another example: the number 378 in decimal is 101111010 in binary but a compact 572 in octal.

If we can group binary digits into threes, then why not group them into fours? That's what hexadecimal (base 16) does. Counting with hexadecimal proceeds like this: 0, 1, 2, 3, 4, 5, 6, 7, 8, 9, A, B, C, D, E, F, 10, 11, 12, and so on. The decimal number 15 converted to binary is 1111. But 1111 converted to hex is F. Here is another example: the number 163 in decimal is 10100011 in binary but a very compact A3 in hex.

If we can have our computer understand more compact forms of binary like octal or hex, which the computer can then automatically convert into binary form, then why not take things a step further—and permit users to program using symbolic names, called mnemonics (like `add` or `mov`), which could in turn be translated to binary? These English-style words would make programming easier and more accessible. And, while we're at it, why not also allow for symbolic addresses as well? With this, we now have an assembly language.

According to Richard Hamming, who worked at Bell Labs in the 1950s, the use of symbolic addresses was "a real heresy for the old time programmers." But he knew how painful programming in absolute binary could be. "I once spent a full year," Hamming recounted, "with the help of a lady programmer from Bell Telephone Laboratories, on one big problem coding in absolute binary for the IBM 701, which used all the 32K registers then available. After that experience I vowed never again would I ask anyone to do such labor." Once he realized that IBM had available a symbolic coding system for the 701, he requested it, and he and the "lady programmer" (no word on her name) found the programming process to be significantly streamlined. Tellingly, though, there was resistance to the innovation.

> [W]e told everyone about the new [symbolic] method [of programming the 701], meaning about 100 people, who were also eating at the IBM cafeteria near where the machine was. About half were IBM people and half were, like us, outsiders renting time [on the machine]. To my knowledge only one person—yes, only one—of all the 100 showed any interest!"

The resistance that Hamming encountered presaged the initial reluctance of programmers to adopt Backus's team's HLL.

Clearly, programming in an HLL or even in assembly language is more intuitive than in hexadecimal or octal machine code, let alone absolute binary: the further away from the zeros and ones (or other types of numbers) we get, the more understandable programming becomes for a human being. For a computer, though, the reverse is true: the less abstract, the closer to the zeros and ones, the easier it is for the machine to "understand" the code.

Recognize, however, that no HLL abstracts away the machine completely; programmers still need to adjust to the symbolic logic ruling the computer. Programming using nothing more than natural language commands is still a distant dream. As Alan Perlis also said, "When someone says 'I want a programming language in which I need only say what I wish done,' give him a lollipop."

In order to successfully build a high-level programming language, abstracted away from the instruction symbols of an assembler, Backus's team realized early on that assignment statements and subscripted variables had to be included. (Essentially, subscripted variables were the equivalent of *arrays*, or data structures housing an indexed collection of elements; but there are subtle differences between subscripted variables and modern arrays, which will be touched upon later.) To relieve some of the tedium of the bookkeeping and the repetition of hand coding, Herrick suggested the **DO** statement, which would loop blocks of code. The problem of implementing the looping mechanism, though, centered on the index registers, of which the 704 had three available—three more than the old 701. "Harlan invented this **DO** statement and so we knew we would have problems there—how to do it," explained Backus. (The DO statement would be initially termed a DO-formula.)

> We had three index registers and all these subscripts. It was very very difficult to figure out which index registers to use given the information in the program. You would get terrible code if you tried to do it in a general way. We knew that we would have to analyze code for its frequency and all kinds of stuff.

Of course, Harlan Herrick didn't invent programming loops. In 1833, Augusta Ada, the daughter of poet Lord Byron, met Charles Babbage. Deep in the throes of conceptualizing his programmable Analytical Engine, Babbage, a professor at Cambridge, and Ada, a precocious teenager, struck up an epistolary correspondence. She contributed a *Notes* addendum to an article describing the Analytical Engine by Louis Menabrea; it is in her *Notes* that the methods for programming Babbage's device, including with loops, are spelled out. "Both for brevity and for distinctness," she wrote, "a *recurring group* is called a *cycle*. A *cycle* of operations, then, must be understood to signify any *set of operations* which is repeated *more than once*. It is equally a *cycle*, whether it be repeated *twice* only, or an indefinite number of times...."

Even among programming languages in the twentieth century, Backus's team didn't arrive at loops first. Contemporaneous to Speedcoding, Heinz Rutishauser, a Swiss mathematician, along with Ambros Speiser, developed the Superplan language on the ERMETH, a Swiss-designed computer. Although rudimentary, Superplan used arrays and also had a looping mechanism (including nested loops, or loops within loops), called the *Für* loop—which evolved into the "for" loop of numerous programming languages thanks to the statement appearing in the influential ALGOL programming language, which Rutishauser—as well as Backus and other computer scientists—wrote in the late 1950s.

Rutishauser was, by his own admission, influenced by the complex Plankalkül (Plan Calculus) programming language, developed in the early 1940s by Konrad Zuse, a German engineer who had built the primitive programmable binary digital Z1 computer in his parents' apartment. Plankalkül, though having no means of input/output, was highly innovative, perhaps being the first programming language with assignment statements, which were denoted with arrows:

> *Take some calculated value on the left-hand side of a statement* → *and store it on the right-hand side.*

Most early algebraic languages would follow suit by placing the computation-storing variable on the right-hand side of an assignment statement rather than on the left. (The Laning and Zierler system is one of the few to place the variable on the left-hand side.)

Because of Backus's team's "unscholarly attitude" (Backus's words), they only briefly considered Rutishauser's work, concluding that it didn't bring anything new to the table. It should be underscored, however, that the development team, and especially Backus, recognized that what they were trying to accomplish wasn't wholly new or original, but was rather the next logical step in the evolution of programming. Contrast that sense of humility with Darwin's and Newton's attitudes toward their discoveries. Explained Oliver Sacks,

Darwin was at pains to say that he had no forerunners, that the idea of evolution was not in the air. Newton, despite his famous comment about "standing on the shoulders of giants," also denied any forerunners. The "anxiety of influence" (which Harold Bloom has discussed powerfully in regard to the history of poetry) is a potent force in the history of science as well. In order to successfully develop and unfold one's own ideas, one may have to believe that others are wrong; one may have to, as Bloom insists, misunderstand others and (perhaps unconsciously) react against them. ("Every talent," Nietzsche writes, "must unfold itself in fighting.)

Backus, remember, was reacting against Grace Hopper's A-0 compiler, among other translators in circulation. Just as the idea for automatic coding was floating in the ether several years earlier, so were many of the other ideas that coalesced into what Backus and his team would create. But it took a number of fortuitous events to bring it all together.

Even though there were many early stresses and challenges to contend with, the workplace atmosphere among the development team was very relaxed, informal, and congenial. Besides the site relocations, the team was mostly left alone by IBM brass—for months on end—largely because the company didn't consider the development team to be engaging in anything more than an open-ended research project. Every so often, people would ask them: "When are you guys going to be done?" The team would always reply: "Six months. Come back in six months." The budget "kept being extended by six months every time somebody asked," Backus said, but he never drew up or submitted a formal budget as the months turned into years. Backus was proud of IBM management, who were publicly unwavering in their support for the development team despite the delays. He contrasted Remington Rand's management, which Grace Hopper toiled under, with IBM's.

Backus recalled that "we had a great deal of fun. It was a very nice group of people. My main job was to break up chess games at lunchtime because they would go on and on." (Backus would later claim that he received too much credit for the team's work, since each member contributed so much to the effort.) Herrick was the chess master—he was a "chess freak," in fact—and there were many games of regular chess and some of blindfold chess, where players were blindfolded and thus not privy visually to the positions of the pieces, running continuously. Besides chess, the wintertime brought snowball fights as a means of distraction. The small development team got along famously, with perpetual discussions and conversations the order of the day. There was palpable sense of excitement in the air. They were all relatively young, either from the Greatest Generation (born 1910 to 1924) or the Silent Generation (born 1925 to 1945); Backus was still shy of thirty. They were young enough to work all day but also subject themselves to sleepless nights in order to take advantage of computer time during the less-than-busy nightshift (they would sleep at the Langdon Hotel on 56th Street, which was across the street from IBM headquarters, if they had to, during daylight hours; the Langdon disappeared long ago). They were certainly too young to heed the words of their contemporaries, their elders, and their critics: That what they had set out to do could not be done. So, they had a willingness to fail.

Although the development team was largely left alone by mostly indifferent IBM higher-ups, at least one Big Blue employee was positively bullish behind the scenes. In 1956, a thirty-year-old doctoral student named Edward Feigenbaum landed a summer job at IBM in New York City after taking a course with the political scientist Herbert Simon at Carnegie Mellon; Feigenbaum figured that the rudiments of programming might help him solve logic problems he was grappling with. "We young kids were down on the ground floor of a brownstone right around the corner from IBM's main building," recalled Feigenbaum. "They set us up with desks and everything and we were working away."

> One day that summer, a guy comes down from the fourth floor of this building to tell us students about a marvelous new development that was happening. "You know how you students are sitting there writing codes called 'clear and add,' 'store,' and all that? You're not going to have to do that anymore. We're doing a thing [with the computer] that allows you to write [and program] formulas…." By the fall it had come out. The person was John Backus.

Feigenbaum would later achieve his own small measure of fame by building several expert systems.

Despite the fact that their task was effectively impossible, with few at IBM giving them a chance of succeeding, four things happened by the fall of 1954, a little less than one year since Backus delivered his memorandum to Cuthbert Hurd, that turned the tide.

First, the development team was formally christened the "Programming Research Group," with Backus installed as its manager.

Second, in November 1954, the Programming Research Group released their Preliminary Report—a thirty-page paper specifying their new language's preliminary design and ostensible features, including the subscripted variables and the DO loops.

Third, a name was settled on for the language. "We would continuously invent very trite names for the system," Backus said in a documentary film released by IBM in 1982. "And, I would come in with today's name, and try it out on my friends. And they would all say, 'Ugh, God, Backus—no, not that!'"

Herrick: "And one day he [Backus] came in and he said, 'I've got it! FORMula TRANslation—*FORTRAN*.' And I went, 'Ewwwch!'"

Nelson: "But it was the only thing we had, so FORTRAN it became."

Herrick: "FORTRAN. It sounds like something spelled backwards."

And fourth, in September 1954, despite lacking a functional compiler, Harlan Herrick successfully ran the first FORTRAN program.

CHAPTER 9

The Language Takes Shape

Before they wrote the language, the small Programming Research Group penned a detailed paper blueprinting FORTRAN.

At first, FORTRAN wasn't technically a contraction of FORMula TRANlation; rather, it stood for the ungainly IBM Mathematical FORmula TRANslating System. On November 10, 1954, Irving Ziller, Harlan Herrick, and John Backus released a paper on FORTRAN. Called "Preliminary Report, Specifications for the IBM Mathematical FORmula TRANslating System, FORTRAN," the document presents specifications for the new language. From the very first paragraph, the team's unbridled enthusiasm is apparent.

> The IBM Mathematical Formula Translating System or briefly, FORTRAN, will comprise a large set of programs to enable the IBM 704 to accept a concise formulation of a problem in terms of a mathematical notation and to produce automatically a high speed 704 program for the solution of the problem. The logic of the 704 is such that, for the first time, programming techniques have been devised which can be applied by an automatic coding system in such a way that an automatically coded problem, which has been concisely stated in a language which does not resemble a machine language, will be executed in about the same time that would be required had the problem been laboriously hand coded. Heretofore, systems which have sought to reduce the job of coding and debugging problems have offered the choice of easy coding and slow execution or laborious coding and fast execution.

But was their enthusiasm clouding their vision? Reflecting on the matter years later, Backus thought so. He describes various portions of the Report as alternatively "hopelessly optimistic" and based "more of faith than of knowledge." Furthermore, a number of the Report's claims seem built on shaky foundations. For instance, consider these two assertions, both offered without any support or citation (italics present in original):

> *Studies have indicated that a hand coded program for a problem will usually contain at least 5 times as many characters and sometimes 20 times as many characters as the problem statement in FORTRAN language.*
>
> *[A]fter an hour course in FORTRAN notation, the average programmer can fully understand the steps of a procedure stated in FORTRAN language without any additional comments.*

The authors of the Report even venture into the absurd, with this outlandish claim early on:

> *Since FORTRAN should virtually eliminate coding and debugging, it should be possible to solve problems for less than half the cost that would be required without such a system.*

Near the end of the Report, they expand their prognostications. Once "some experience has been gained in use of the system," the authors claim, "it will be possible to write a program to locate the most common of the frequently occurring errors" in a FORTRAN program. Furthermore, they go on to say, if a program doesn't run correctly (or at all), "it should be relatively simple for an operator experienced with FORTRAN-written programs to determine what has happened in a program after a machine failure." But the FORTRAN team was quite a ways away from building any sort of robust error-checking mechanism into the language, despite the confident-sounding prose. Plus, more than half a century removed from FORTRAN's birth, has *any* programming language managed to "virtually eliminate coding and debugging"?

But the team was realistically forward-thinking when it came to considering the possibility of platform independence: far from being a one-off language designed exclusively for the 704, the Report's authors conceive of FORTRAN-like languages built for "future IBM calculators," noting that the time and money spent turning the plans for FORTRAN into a reality would pay dividends for IBM later on. At the time, companies that built their businesses on highly technical pursuits, such as Boeing (who had developed their own algebraic language, BACAIC, for the 701), General Electric, Lockheed, and IBM itself, needed programmers who were skilled at highly technical computer work; it was the province of an elite, expert class of individuals. With few technical standards applying to the variety of machines in use, and no training programs to speak of, companies that utilized the big IBM mainframes or even the hardware of Sperry Rand had nowhere to go to procure functional or experienced "programmers" per se, leading to ongoing programmer shortages, with men and women being snatched up from non-programming disciplines to fill the need, à la IBM's hiring of mathematician John Backus. But after the hiring came the learning curve: programming these machines wasn't easy, and the costs of renting the mainframes were quickly coming to dwarf the costs of programming them. Hence, the benefits of a language like FORTRAN to abstract away the machinations of these massive electronic calculators. Vast knowledge of the hardware of the IBM 704 wasn't necessary, nor was any understanding of the optimization routines or "subprograms" or other direct (machine language) coding techniques. Instead, since programming in FORTRAN resembles manipulating mathematical expressions, the untrained programmer can lean on his understanding of math to help him code. A little machine efficiency would be traded away in favor of ease of use, which would lead to programming becoming a bit more accessible, thus opening the doors wider to talent and thereby addressing the industry-wide programmer shortage.

Economics and cost-benefit analyses aside, when it came to the proposing features of the new language, the Preliminary Report proves that the FORTRAN team was thinking big—and breaking the mold—right from the start. They didn't quite have agreed-upon terms for certain programming concepts yet, so the authors of the Report occasionally fumble around with the verbiage, awkwardly describing a process or operation in print for the first time; these were amorphous concepts that had yet to take on a more concrete form. Some of the ideas the team describes hadn't been implemented on a live machine, a clear case of putting the proverbial cart before the horse. So, unsurprisingly, a mix of quasi-mathematical notation and unformed pseudocode litters the thirty-page Report. Reading it, one is reminded of the nonstandard elevator shaft in the Foundation Building of Cooper Union in New York's East Village: the shaft, and therefore the elevator that services the nine-story building, is cylindrical in shape. Peter Cooper, who founded the school, designed the shaft more than two decades before the first public elevator was built by Elisha Otis. Cooper knew elevators were coming, but he didn't quite know what form they would take. Neither did the FORTRAN team when it came to a number of programming constructs we now, well over half a century later, take for granted.

Obviously aware of the importance of working with fixed- and floating-point numbers in a seamless way, and wanting to take advantage of the built-in arithmetic functionality of the 704's hardware, the FORTRAN team proposed a robust set of possible constants: fixed-point numbers, specifically integers, which could be one to five digits in length (with an optional plus or minus sign); and floating-point numbers, which could be between 10^{-38} and 10^{38} decimal digits in length (with an optional plus or minus sign), complete with the power to place a decimal point between any two digits (or at the end of a sequence of digits—e.g., 53.0).

Variables could be one or two characters in length, but they were subject to certain constraints. If storing an integer, the variable's first character (or only character) had to be an i, j, k, l, m, or n. But if storing a floating-point decimal, the variable's first character (or only character) could *not* be an i, j, k, l, m, or n. So, for example, the variables j, mm, and k1 could only be assigned to integer values, whereas the variables a and xj could only store floating-point decimals. As Donald Knuth notes, "It was the first time in history that someone had considered having a variable name with two letters, so there could be more than twenty-six variables." Although the term is not mentioned in the Report, FORTRAN's variable naming conventions would become known as *implicit typing*, meaning that the language implicitly (indirectly, through implication) assigned newly declared variables a type (integer or floating-point) based simply on the first letter of the variable names. (Later versions of FORTRAN would offer flexibility with implicit typing, courtesy of the **IMPLICIT** statement.)

Both unary operations—which would either take the value of the constant or variable, or the additive inverse (negative) of the constant or variable—and binary operations—in which addition (+), subtraction (-), multiplication (×), division (/), exponentiation (××), or some combination thereof would be applied to multiple constants and/or variables—were available. In theory, an unlimited number of mathematical functions were also available to the programmer—functions such as sin(a), sqrt(a+b), and sqrt(sin(a××2)), which calculated the sine of a quantity, the square root of the sum of two quantities, and the square root of the sine of a quantity squared, respectively. But functions, like variables, also had some constraints, namely that their names had to be at least three characters in length, where the first character had to be alphabetic. More than one parameter (note that in the Report, parameters are called "arguments," and what we conventionally now think of as arguments—i.e., the actual values inserted into a function when it is called—are likewise called arguments) can be written into a function. For example, max(a,b,c), which finds the maximum value among the three quantities within the parentheses.

FORTRAN would allow as much flexibility as possible with the writing of mathematical expressions (*expression*: "Any sequence of variables and functions separated by operation symbols and parentheses which forms a meaningful mathematical expression in a normal way"), as long as they were fewer than 750 characters in length. Examples include a/(b+c)×d, 1.53×10××-14, and E××F (where E and F stand for expressions), but not the adjacent pair ab where a and b are constants, variables, or functions; any adjacent pair like ab must be separated by a binary operation, e.g., a+b. The mathematical order of operations, usually referred to as PEMDAS (parentheses, exponentiation, multiplication and division, and addition and subtraction), was always in force. Parentheses in mathematical expressions could be applied liberally, but the authors of the Report warn programmers to be careful to make sure that all closing parentheses match up correctly with opening parentheses (even offering a counting strategy to help ensure no missing parentheses). So-called redundant parentheses might be needed, the authors caution, to avoid the evaluation of intermediate results in calculations which are less than 10^{-38} or exceed 10^{38}.

Expressions involving only integer constants and variables would always result in integer answers that were unrounded (i.e., truncated after the decimal). For instance, although 6 divided by 3 would output 2, 6 divided by 4 wouldn't output 1.5, but 1. Purely floating-point expressions would be processed using floating-point arithmetic—meaning 6.0 divided by 4.0 would output 1.5. For *mixed expressions*, or expressions involving a combination of fixed- and floating-point arithmetic, the output depended on the type of variable to the left of equals sign: if the variable was of the integer variety, then the expression to the right of the equals sign would result in a truncated integral answer, but if the variable was floating-point, then the expression to the right of the equals sign would result in a decimal answer.

The Preliminary Report also devotes some space to a discussion of subscripts and subscripted variables. In mathematics, subscripts are (typically) integers set slightly below the main text that are utilized to differentiate between like terms in a series, such as $a_1, a_2, a_3, \ldots, a_n$. But subscripts have many other uses in math. The FORTRAN team wanted to capture that same mathematical spirit, albeit in computer code, so they introduced the notion of subscripts—which they wrote were "any fixed point variable or constant"—but put several restrictions of their use, namely that subscripts must always be greater than zero (in addition to being integers) and that expressions involving subscripts cannot exceed three terms in length (e.g., i+n×j is acceptable but i+n×j-j×k is not) or contain parentheses. Subscript expressions were also subject to something called "relative constants," essentially meaning that the values of all but one of the variables in a subscript expression had to be relatively consistent (i.e., change infrequently); the remaining fixed-point variable could change without limit (e.g., in the subscript expression i+n×j, the variables n and j are, let's say, relative constants whereas the variable i does not have to be).

Just like in mathematics, subscripts were not isolated but adjoined to something: in the case of FORTRAN, subscripted variables, which we now typically call arrays. An array stores a collection of items, such as integers, at contiguous memory locations: so, for example, the elements 22, 12, 7, 47, and 53 can be stored, in that order, as a group into a single array; these elements are indexed based on their location in this array, with 22 having the lowest index and 53 the highest index. (Arrays are referred to as subscripted variables in the Report, but also might refer to what are termed *vectors*, or one-dimensional arrays, as well as *matrices*, or two-dimensional arrays; in addition, subscripted variables are presented very generally in the Report, apart from any pseudocode. The intended audience of the paper swings wildly, page by page, between pure mathematicians and programmers, so it is sometimes tough to pin down precisely what the team was intending to do in this preliminary stage.) Subscripted variables could be fixed- or floating-point (recall that the subscripts themselves had to be fixed-point, with values always greater than zero), with one, two, or three subscripts or subscript expressions, all separated by commas enclosed in parentheses, and subscripts could even be nested inside other subscripts, up to a point. Some examples include a(i), a(i,j,k), i(j(k)), a(n(i,j),2×i(j)), and a(5,3,7).

When the authors of the Report write of "arithmetic formulas," they have to spell out for an audience of mid-twentieth century readers what is obvious (to the point of being unstated) to even the most neophyte programmer of today: that an equals sign in a program doesn't have the same meaning as in an algebraic statement. For example, to a mathematician (or anyone else with a basic understanding of algebra), the statement $x = 8 - 3x$ reads as follows: the value of some unknown number is *equivalent* to the quantity of the product of three and the unknown subtracted from eight. To find that unknown, of course, requires several algebraic operations (the unknown is equal to two). But the $x = 8 - 3x$ has a very different meaning in computer code, since the equals sign does not imply *equivalence* but rather *assignment* (or, as Backus and company write, "replace"). Whatever quantity is stored in x, take the product of three and that quantity and subtract this product from eight—and then store this difference back into the variable x, replacing what was previously stored there. Or, as the authors of the Report put it more generally, "Evaluate the expression on the right and substitute this value as the value of the variable on the left." The variable was allowed to have a subscript.

Although the FORTRAN team did not invent the convention of arithmetic formulas, they would popularize it for a wide audience, which included not only other programmers but mathematicians, engineers, and scientists as well. Though it went against the grain, programming languages since have adhered to FORTRAN's arithmetic formula structure—what had once seemed novel came to be natural. Backus and company put the variable on the left of the equals sign because they thought programs would appear more readable that way. "If you put them on the right," Backus said, "the variable being assigned to would be a little hard to find, whereas, they're easy to find if they're on the left."

The FORTRAN team knew that if their nascent language was to have a chance of replacing hand coding, then access to control statements—referred to in the Report as "control formulas"—were de rigueur. Obviously, Backus wasn't about to glue paper tape together to loop code, as he had done while operating the SSEC; he was spared this indignity by Harlan Herrick, who conjured up the DO statement, which was called the DO-formula in the Report. (In the programming milieu at the time, the term "formula" meant what "statement" would later mean.) The DO-formula offered quite a bit of flexibility but, as described in the Report, was especially tricky to understand and use well. The authors of the report offer this example:

$$\text{do } 10, 14, 50 \ i=4, 20, 2$$

Much of the opacity of the DO-formula lies with its use of what are termed "formula numbers"—unique numerical labels that lie to the left of formulas—for example, consider the statement 12 a=b, where 12 is the formula number—and serve as bookmarks for FORTRAN to reference while executing a control formula. These formula numbers could only be integers less than 100,000 in value. In the DO-formula example above, all formulas numbered between 10 and 14 are executed nine times: first with i=4, then i=6, then i=8, ... , then i=20. Therefore, the 4 represents the initial value of the subscript, the 20 represents the upper bound, and the 2 represents the "increment" value. (If the increment is 1, then including a 1 at the end of the sequence was optional.) After the looping sequence was complete, formula 50 would execute once, and control would resume from there. Various permutations of the DO-formula—sans the first two formula numbers, for instance—were possible.

Another of the control formulas, called the IF-formula, was less opaque than the DO-formula. The IF-formula permitted conditional branching, but also relied on formula numbers. To determine which formula to branch to, a single condition was tested: if quantity A was equal to/greater than/greater than or equal to quantity B, then execute the first formula; otherwise, execute the second formula. The authors of the Report offer the example

$$\text{if } (n \times i >= k+1) \ 3, 9$$

meaning that if the product of the quantities stored in the variables n and i is greater than or equal to one unit more than the quantity stored in the variable k, then execute formula 3; otherwise, execute formula 9. Note that only =, >, and >= were available.

There were other control formulas besides loops and conditionals. An unconditional formula jump, called a GO TO-formula, was proffered (e.g., Go to 10—which would, when encountered, unconditionally execute formula 10), as was a STOP-formula—which stopped the machine cold. Pressing the START button on the machine would have FORTRAN pick off right where it left off in the program.

More interesting is the RELABEL-formula, proposed in the Report but never seeing the light of day in the finalized first version of FORTRAN. Thinking that flexibility and nimbleness with matrices (rectangular arrangements of numbers in rows and columns) would be of the highest importance for mathematicians and engineers using the programming language, the authors of the Report describe the mechanics of the RELABEL-formula, which "enable the programmer to cyclically relabel the elements n in a vector, the rows or column of a matrix, the rows or columns or planes of a three dimensional array." (Recall that a vector can be thought of as a one-dimensional array: i.e., a variable containing a single subscript; a matrix can be thought of as a two-dimensional array: i.e., a variable containing two subscripts; and a three-dimensional array, of course, is a variable containing three subscripts.) For instance, suppose the variable b is a vector (a one-dimensional array) containing seven elements, subscripted from 1 to 7. The command

$$\text{Relabel b(3)}$$

will systematically bump back, by two elements, each of the element subscript references. So, for example, if b(3) stored the number 100 before the execution of the RELABEL-formula, afterward, b(1) now stored 100. Likewise, if b(4) stored the number 200 before execution, then b(2) stored 200 after execution. Essentially, the RELABEL-formula resets the referenced subscript to the first subscript of the list of elements, dragging the remaining (higher subscripted) elements along with it. The authors of the Report describe a number of useful mathematical manipulations possible with the RELABEL-formula, especially with matrices. Describing the power of the RELABEL-formula years later, Backus lamented that it had to be deleted from the final product. "[T]his was one facility which we felt would have been really difficult to implement," he wrote, adding that of the proposed features in the Report that were ultimately cut, only the removal of the RELABEL-formula led to "a real sacrifice in [the] convenience or power" of FORTRAN.

The Report details a variety of input-output formulas. Input could arrive via cards or input tapes; data could be "printed or punched or written" on output tapes (in other words, output could be produced on punched cards, from a line printer onto paper, or stored onto magnetic tape). Complicated syntax involving statements such as read (which stored values from a card reader into arrays), read tape, read input tape, read drum, punch, write tape, write output tape, and write drum permitted the user to store and output information to a variety of media using peripherals. Additional commands were set aside for working with tape—namely end file, rewind, and backspace. Notably, the **FORMAT** statement, which would become a mainstay of FORTRAN for years to come, was nowhere to be found in the Report, though something like it was hinted at.

The Report also details four kinds of "specification sentences," or manual entry points that potentially increase the efficiency of a program. The first of these, called "dimension sentences," mandate that the programmer provide the dimensions (the maximum number of subscripts) of an array (i.e., arrays had to be declared explicitly). The second, "equivalence sentences," permits some flexibility with respect to the assignment of storage locations to variables; under certain conditions, the same storage location could be used for different variables. The third, "frequency sentences," allows the programmer to provide FORTRAN with estimates of the number of times he anticipates that blocks of code will be executed during runtime. For example, the programmer may expect "the condition specified by an IF-formula to be satisfied 10,000 times and that the condition will not be satisfied 400 times during the execution of the program." Such estimates will conceivably assist the FORTRAN system in optimizing the program. The fourth type of specification sentence, called "relative constant sentences," lets the programmer identify which subscripted variables don't change their values often. (Recall that relative constants were discussed earlier in this chapter.) Optimization, down to the level of shaving off even a single instruction whenever possible, was the name of the game. To that end, the authors caution against using a construction like the following:

$$i = i + 1$$
$$\text{if } (i > n) \, n1, n2$$

A DO-formula could be written instead to run through the same loop by using one instruction instead of two. The authors of the Preliminary Report sidestep explaining precisely how to do so, thus leaving a proto-FORTRAN programming exercise for the curious reader.

It was J.A.N. Lee, in a 1982 piece for *Annals of the History of Computing* celebrating Pioneer Day, the twenty-fifth anniversary of the release of FORTRAN, who fingered the probable authors of the Preliminary Report: Backus, Herrick, and Ziller. The Report is a landmark document, Lee argues:

> This is the first formal proposal for the language FORTRAN. It lists the elements of the language that are proposed to be included in the eventual implementation, together with some suggestions for future extensions. It is interesting to match this proposal with the Programmer's Reference Manual (1957) and to note that many of the ideas of later FORTRANs as well as Algol [another programming language] appear to have been given birth in this document.

CHAPTER 10

◇◇◇

Punching a Shared Place in History

Building the FORTRAN system as the Programming Research Group envisioned it in the Preliminary Report proved to be anything but simple; luckily, the team stumbled upon a (reluctant) ally.

Before being able to use the FORTRAN system for automatic coding—i.e., before writing a FORTRAN program—preparation was required. By the time the Preliminary Report was finalized, the development team realized how extensive those preparations needed to be, since even the IBM 704, one of the most (if not *the* most) advanced mainframe computer in the world at the time of its release, wasn't simple to use by any means. The paragraphs that follow discursively sketch out the complexities and challenges inherent in using the FORTRAN system to write and execute a program, at least as the team envisioned the language in the mid-1950s. It is important to get a feel for what the process was like. The sheer number of steps and items to consider won't strike modern readers as anything remotely resembling user-friendly, but, to even then-young programmers like John Backus, who cut his teeth on the SSEC, the 704 running the FORTRAN system was a revelation, despite the machine's many limitations.

As the FORTRAN team rightly noted, the symbols used in the Preliminary Report (for instance, the × for multiplication or the / for division) were arbitrary, since as long as the correct Hollerith code was punched in the formula card the aesthetics wouldn't make any difference—FORTRAN would be able to correctly interpret the programmer's intention.

In the late 1800s, Herman Hollerith created the first set of Hollerith codes, which laid out a basic correspondence between alphanumeric characters and the holes of punched cards. Hollerith codes evolved through the coming decades, eventually being standardized by ANSI (American National Standards Institute) X3.26-1980—even as early as 1969, with the standardization of the punches for 128 characters—but were first proposed as a forty-character BCDIC (Binary-Coded Decimal) code by IBM in 1931 and then expanded to 256 characters by IBM in a set of Extended BCDIC codes.

Note that the 128- and 256-character standards originated with ASCII (American Standard Code for Information Interchange) codes, a character set designed in the early 1960s in order to facilitate the exchange of data between different machines. ASCII, containing 7-bit codes with a total of $2^7 = 128$ characters, was itself a product of a proto-ANSI committee, the American Standards Association (ASA). The original 128 characters were expanded to 8-bit codes with a total of $2^8 = 256$ characters, although the history of ASCII is byzantine due to the proliferation of proprietary extended character encodings that included alphabets other than English's and graphics symbols (readers of a certain age may be familiar with these extended ASCII sets from early home computers like the Commodore 64, with its PETSCII character set). ANSI ensured the standardization of Hollerith codes with ASCII, as described in an Appendix of an ANSI report called the *American National Standard Hollerith Punched Card Codes*:

> The standard Hollerith representation was designed to provide for representation of the full ASCII character set in punched cards, in a code which incorporates and extends commonly used Hollerith practices. Such a code thus permits continued use in many applications of existing equipment, files, tabulating procedures, and data code structures based on a subset of the full ASCII. The potential benefits of a capability for full interchange of cards and data from users of the subset to the full set, and limited interchange in the reverse direction, are thus extended to the large body of producers and users of current card equipment.

More relevant to our discussion here is the "Commonly Used Hollerith Codes" detailed in the ANSI report:

> The majority of punched-card equipment, and hence the applications employing them, have a set of 48 characters. This set provides:
>
> Blank or space – 1 character
> Digits 0-9 – 10 characters
> Letters A-Z – 26 characters
>
> for a total of 37 characters, leaving 11 character positions for assignment to punctuation or other special symbols. For the basic 37 characters there is almost complete uniformity in the hole pattern assigned to each graphic.

The hole patterns on punched cards were shown in a diagram in the first chapter.

When the authors of the Preliminary Report mentioned Hollerith codes, they were referring to the BCDIC of the IBM 704, which, slightly modified for the machine, was termed the IBM 704 BCD code; these 6-bit character codes, which mapped alphanumeric and special characters and were adapted from the Hollerith codes of punched cards, were not standardized between manufacturers, unlike ASCII. Yet like the history of ASCII, the timeline of punched card codes from Herman Hollerith to the IBM 704 six decades later is dizzying in its complexity, requiring a book-length study of its own. As Douglas W. Jones of the University of Iowa aptly summarizes it,

The original punched card coding used by Hollerith allowed coding of only a limited alphabet; over the years, this was extended in many ways, but while many of these extensions were upward compatible from the original code, no attempt to standardize the extensions was successful until the end of the punched card era. As a result, keypunch users got quite used to learning, for example, that ¢ was to be typed when [was intended.

The standard punched card had 80 columns, numbered 1 to 80 from left to right. Each column could hold one character, encoded as some combination of punches in the 12 rows of the card.

Furthermore, "IBM's BCD codes were all more complex, partly because of a desire to represent the numeral zero with the 6-bit numeric code 000000 (in the IBM 704, 709, 7040 and 7090) or with 001010 (in the IBM 705, 7080, 1401, 1410 and 1414)." So, not only were the BCD codes not standardized between manufacturers, they also weren't standardized between models from the *same* manufacturer.

With six bits available to represent any BCD character, a total of sixty-four possible characters were available, since $2^6 = 64$. (A 6-bit representation of A, for example, is 010001, and a percentage sign is represented by 111100.) Even more dizzyingly, there were variants of so-called common character sets: some that focused on commercial applications, and others that were designed for FORTRAN users.

Once the specifications for a FORTRAN program were written, making sure to utilize the correct Hollerith codes as well as to properly explicitly dimension any and all arrays, next came the data preparation step, where the programmer would write up the program on a coding form (or coding sheet) to be keypunched into a deck of punched cards. Lower-case letters were not permitted, despite the inconsistent mix of upper- and lower-case statements littering the Preliminary Report.

The FORTRAN Coding Form, as it came to be formally known, contained twenty-four lines and eighty columns, all divvied up into a grid. General information about the program would be written in at the top of the form—things like the program name, the programmer's name, the date, the page number, and any special punching instructions. Underneath resided the grid: here was where, character by character, FORTRAN statements would be penciled in. The first five columns on each eighty-character line were reserved for the statement numbers of formulas that would be referenced somewhere else in the program; a character present in column six, the column labeled "CONT.," meant that the card continued work begun on the previous card (lengthy formulas might require multiple cards); columns seven to seventy-two had space for one FORTRAN programming statement; and columns seventy-three to eighty were left for an identification sequence (which was optional). Each line on a FORTRAN Coding Form corresponded to one punched card. Completed coding forms were typically handed off to data entry clerks, who keypunched the programs onto cards—but, of course, this transfer required much manual labor and was thus far from instantaneous, and an error in the keypunch or in the program itself necessitated the re-keypunching of at least some program statements. (Handwriting a program on coding forms in order to pass off to keypunching clerks did, however, offer the programmer two distinct advantages that would mostly disappear within a decade after the release of the initial version of FORTRAN, as punched cards faded away: the programmer now had to type the source code him- or herself, and the programmer could no longer literally *hold* and *feel* the heft of the computer program—that tactile element of programming was forever gone.)

Note that the previous paragraph detailed the final step in the evolution of coding sheets for FORTRAN. Early FORTRAN coding sheets, loosely featured in the first batch of user manuals released for the FORTRAN system, had space for seventy-two individual characters per line, with a heading above columns one to five reading "STATEMENT NUMBER," which could be any whole number less than 2^{15}, or 32,768, and "C ← FOR COMMENT," meaning that simply by penciling in a "C" on the coding sheet, a programming comment or remark, which is an annotation meant for human beings that the computer would ignore, could be transcribed on lines seven to seventy-two (successive implementations of FORTRAN that utilized coding sheets had this commenting option as well). Computer scientist Donald Knuth noted, "No programming language designer had thought to do this [comments] before: Assembly languages had comment cards, but programs in high-level languages were generally felt to be self-explanatory."

A "CONTINUATION" label was above column six, instructing the compiler to continue work begun on the previous punched card if a character appeared in the column; the programmer could opt for a total of nine "continuation cards," meaning that a single FORTRAN statement could span the length of ten punched cards (with coding sheets having space for sixty-six characters per line, the maximum length of a FORTRAN statement, therefore, was 10×66 = 660 characters). Finally, FORTRAN ignored anything punched into columns seventy-three to eighty, atop which was the label "IDENTIFICATION." The basic layout of an early FORTRAN coding sheet, complete with a short program (which will be explained later on), is shown below.

C ← FOR COMMENT / STATEMENT NUMBER	CONTINUATION	FORTRAN STATEMENT	IDENTI- FICATION
1 5	6	7 72	73 80
C		PROGRAM TO TRAVERSE ARRAY	
		DIMENSION L(10)	
	10	DO 12 K = 1 , 10	
	11	J = J + K	
	12	L(K) = J	
	13		

The coding sheet(s) would be passed off to a keypunch operator, who would use a keypunch machine to type out a *source deck*, which contained all the lines of the source program, one punched card per line. (So, in the example program above, the source deck would consist of six cards.) Each source deck card resembled the FORTRAN coding sheet shown above, with identical headings, but, instead of containing blank lines in which to pencil in FORTRAN statements, had the typical accouterments of IBM cards (e.g., the 0-row, the 1-row, and so on). The keypunch machine would typically relay the FORTRAN statement (as is) on the top of the punched card while underneath would lie the many punched holes that translated the statement's alphanumeric characters and/or symbols into the Hollerith code.

Once the entire FORTRAN program was punched into a source deck and the deck was arranged in the correct order, it was ready to be fed into the input hopper of the card reader, with the 9-edge, located at the bottom of the first card, placed directly toward the feeder. From there, the FORTRAN compiler would run through each source deck card, and then—only if the program had completely compiled without any errors—print out a much smaller second deck of cards, called the *program deck* or *object deck* (containing the object program, written in 704 machine language), which was punched using a binary code. If there were compilation errors, they would be detailed on a computer printout. Then the program could be run by feeding the program deck into the hopper—at which point debugging began, which could be a long and laborious process since each change in the program required the source deck be recompiled; debugging would be facilitated by examining the core dumps and diagnostics printed on the attached line printer. Run the source deck through the card reader too many times, and the wear and tear might necessitate a new source deck be punched. Luckily, there were IBM punched card duplicator machines that could automatically generate a new source deck, such as the IBM 519 Document-Originating Machine.

The authors of the Report proposed two options for the FORTRAN system programmer: press the START button on the 704 to either run the source deck through the machine to generate the binary program deck written in 704 machine language, or forgo the intermediate steps and execute the program instructions immediately. Regardless of which option was selected by the programmer, the cards of the source deck always had to be sorted correctly—in order, from the first program statement to the last.

Recall that with each pass, the FORTRAN compiler would only read the first seventy-two of the eighty columns of a card, ignoring columns seventy-three to eighty. The 704 ignored the columns because of its hardware: possessing two 36-bit machine registers for arithmetic, only seventy-two bits were available to store the data on each row of the cards into the 704's memory. The 704 manipulated 36-bit words in memory, with each character being six bits in length, as shown below. The "S" below refers to the sign bit, which relayed whether the numerical value was positive or negative.

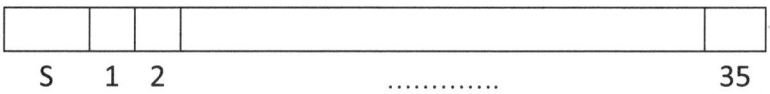

But why was each character six bits long? Recall that the Hollerith code had forty-eight punch combinations for forty-eight possible characters. If, let's say, five bits were used to represent each character instead of six, not all forty-eight characters would make the cut, since $2^5 = 32$—we would be shy by sixteen characters. But at six bits, $2^6 = 64$, covering our bases with room to spare. (Seven or eight bits might have worked as well, but six had the advantage of dividing evenly into thirty-six.) The first implementation of FORTRAN, as we shall see, put a six-character maximum on identifiers like variables names not for some arbitrary reason, but to conform to the limits of the 704's memory. There was another limitation, mentioned above: the range for statement numbers—namely any integer up to 2^{15}, or 32,768. The 704's addresses, or locations pointing to where data was stored, were fifteen bits in length, leading to the 2^{15} restriction. These addresses were usually referenced in octal (base 8) for convenience. (Despite the 15-bit addresses, not every 704 came with 2^{15} 36-bit words of memory. More realistically, $2^{12} = 4,096$, or sometimes even double that amount, was on hand.)

So, if FORTRAN ignored columns seventy-three to eighty by design, then what was their use? (Technically, the 704 could ignore *any* set of eight columns, courtesy of a so-called standard plugboard configuring the precise columns that the card reader would read in. Typically, thirty-six contiguous bits at a time would be read from each row, with rows one to thirty-six called the "left" half of the row, and rows thirty-seven to seventy-two the "right" half of the row; each of these halves were termed "half-rows.") These remaining columns could be utilized for sequencing the cards in order, perhaps using an IBM card sorter, which sorted decks of cards using sequence numbers printed in the ignored columns.

Another common, albeit imprecise, technique of sorting the cards involved drawing a diagonal line across the top edges of a deck. Needless to say, working regularly with punched cards required a preternatural level of precision and dexterity.

The IBM 704 was one of the last commercial mainframe computers to come packaged without an operating system. When FORTRAN ran, it took over control of the entire machine, and only one program could be dealt with at a time. From start to finish—translation of the source deck into a binary object deck, removal of the object deck from the punch, placing of the object deck into the reader, running the program, and then waiting for the printed output and the card decks to emerge—the process took at least fifteen minutes, though usually more time. There were so many places for things to go awry, from the hardware to the punched cards to the moving parts of the hopper to errors in the code itself.

The development team realized that for the FORTRAN system to work smoothly they were depending on more than just the 704 hardware to function as advertised; they were also reliant upon the precision of the (human) keypunch operators. If there were a way to introduce some keypunching leeway, some margin for error, they would gladly take it.

The solution came courtesy of the IBM SHARE user group, established in California in 1955 shortly after IBM released the 701. SHARE, which didn't stand for anything—"It's not an acronym, it's what we do," their modern tagline reads—was the first computer user group; people convened to pool together their knowledge of the 701. SHARE's birth came in response to the massive technical computing needs of the aviation industry in California, which was overflowing with human computers prior to World War II, but transitioned to electromechanical machines during the war thanks to the so-called IBM methods of scientific computation developed by Wallace Eckert.

SHARE's first meeting was at the RAND Corporation in Santa Monica on August 22, 1955. The idea was simple: bring together the 701 mainframe customers, who were individually writing programs and creating resources, to discuss, share, learn, generate insights, and prepare for the imminent arrival of the 704, which would not be compatible with the 701. (In 1953, some computing center directors in California loosely collaborated pre-SHARE to correct what was seen as a major problem: programs written by IBM for the 701—specifically, the assembler—were deemed inefficient and ineffective. These meetings helped set the stage for the later founding of SHARE.) Since the aviation industry had a long history of wartime cooperation, informal voluntary cooperation during peacetime wasn't anathema. Indeed, the founding members of SHARE came from competing companies like Boeing, General Electric, Lockheed, and United Aircraft, among many others in the burgeoning aerospace industry. There were nineteen organizations in all: seventeen companies and two government agencies. As Atsushi Akera, author of "Voluntarism and the Fruits of Collaboration: The IBM User Group, Share," describes it,

> The idea to create the first nationwide computer user group originated with a group of computing center directors intent on improving the operations of their own facilities. They envisioned an organization that could set technical standards, and much more: among their concerns were a shortage of skilled programmers, high labor costs, and, most important, the inefficiency inherent in the fact that firms that had purchased an IBM mainframe still had to write their own programs to perform basic computing functions, a situation that resulted in a massive duplication of programming effort.

"Share's most important work took place between 1955 and 1958, at a time when scientific and engineering installations still made up the majority of customers for IBM's new computers," Akera adds.

From that very first SHARE meeting, technical computing standards called "SHARE Standards" (e.g., common printer configurations, punched-card formats, and assemblers, with a standardized set of mnemonic codes), in terms of hardware configurations and the like, were agreed upon. One of the original members of SHARE, an engineer at North American Aviation named Frank Wagner, recalled, "We committed to distribute any programs that would be of value to others." Also coming from North American Aviation was Fletcher Jones, the SHARE secretary who would become the group's national spokesman. A 1956 statement released by the group, called "SHARE Membership and What It Entails," codified their philosophy: "The principal obligation of a member is to have a cooperative spirit." To some extent, it should be noted, SHARE's transcorporate cooperation was a bit of a shell game, with "volunteerism" held up as a convenient guiding philosophy when in reality the collaborating companies feared antitrust legislation by the U.S. government. But, regardless of the reason, the environment was ripe for significant sharing and collaboration. When it came to software, this communal ethos, this spirit of voluntarism and cooperation, even amongst and between workers of competing corporations, would reemerge in the computer industry in the 1970s with the computer hobbyist groups that formed in the wake of the release of small computers like the MITS Altair 8800. Such groups thrived until the status quo was challenged by entrepreneurs like Bill Gates. (Although SHARE users, unlike the hobbyists, never freely shared application programs, only systems programs and mathematical subroutines expressly designed to increase the efficiency of the hardware.)

Recall that the term "software" as we now understand it would not appear in print until 1958, in an *American Mathematical Monthly* article called "The Teaching of Concrete Mathematics" written by the statistician John W. Tukey; use of the term predates Tukey's article, but typically with respect to people-as-"software" who operated hardware, rather than as in the modern usage. Over the next decade, use of the term would increase slowly; an analysis of the paper content of Joint Computer Conferences ("the only continuing national meetings of that era," according to Bob Bemer, who worked at IBM at the time) from 1951 until immediately prior to the public introduction of FORTRAN found only fourteen indirect references to software.

In the mid-1950s, IBM wasn't invested or particularly interested in the software market; their mainframes didn't come prepackaged with bundles of software like computers do today, but rather a limited assembler and some utilities. The first symbolic assembler for the 701 was called the NR9003, written by Nathaniel Rochester, an MIT-educated engineer who had helped build the Whirlwind I computer. NR9003 was designed to help with diagnostics of the 701, of which Rochester was the engineering manager. Later came the IBM S02, a symbolic assembler created by both William McLelland and Rochester; S02 used a library called the Regional Assembly, thus the assembler was referred to as the Regional Assembly Language. The S02 was of a piece with "regional programming," with storage split into different regions.

Yet IBM's customers desperately needed useful software for their mainframes, even if IBM didn't realize it at first. Part of the problem was that although IBM's programmers might have been well-versed in the engineering requirements within the company, they had little knowledge of outside needs. IBM's business was centered on hardware, including the production of punched cards which represented nearly a quarter of their annual revenue. Therefore, to correct the blind spot, Big Blue formed a symbiotic relationship with SHARE, with the user group becoming a sort of middleman between IBM and its customers. "For a customer that had never owned a computer before, IBM could say, 'You can join SHARE, with literally hundreds of experts and get all the support you need.' It turned out to be best marketing tool that anyone could have invented," remembered Morton Bernstein, a mathematician at RAND and original SHARE member.

During the development phase of FORTRAN, Backus gave talks at numerous SHARE meetings, which were held around four to five times per year in cities like Chicago and Denver, updating members on his team's progress. A theme emerged: Backus would detail the number of man-years the compiler had taken to write, the number of instructions necessary to write it as well as some other specs, such as the quantity of machine language instructions generated for every FORTRAN statement, and would promise completion of the project soon. Invariably, at meeting after meeting, the man-years logged would increase, as would the instruction counts; the compiler's release date would always be pushed back, yet still be right around the corner.

Several months before the compiler's actual release date, David Sayre, who joined the team later in FORTRAN's development, presented at a SHARE meeting, this one in New York City. He introduced and explained FORTRAN's library routines and subroutines. One SHARE member who was there recalled that Sayre

> also talked about how the program would be distributed; it looked like a deck of 1000 binary cards that, when loaded on-line, would write itself on tape and produce compiler tapes. Symbolic cards would not be provided, although several symbolic tapes would be on loan for duplicating, printing, or whatever else would be needed.

"The FORTRAN system," this SHARE member explained, "consisted of a compiler that was loaded for each program (one at a time), compiled, and the output punched onto cards." There was no "monitor system," no operating system, no load-and-go system. Distressingly, the SHARE members learned, FORTRAN would have to take over the whole 704 to run a single program.

SHARE ended up influencing FORTRAN in two ways: in a key aspect of its design, and in its distribution. Recall that the FORTRAN team was looking for a way to allow some leeway when it came to keypunching, rife as it could be with human error. They decided to go with space independence, meaning that spaces (i.e., blank columns on the punched cards) would be ignored by the FORTRAN compiler. "This means that, if desired, the key puncher can space between symbols in exactly the way they are written, or not, without disturbing the meaning of the formula," the Report read. As Backus wrote later on, the space independence "choice was partly in recognition of a problem widely known in SHARE, the 704 users' association. There was a common problem with keypunchers not recognizing or properly counting blanks in handwritten data, and this caused many errors." Backus also believed that a programmer should be able to style his program in as readable and cogent of a form as possible, and a FORTRAN compiler that ignored spaces would further that aim. (A reference manual for a non-IBM FORTRAN implementation later made this joke: "Consistently separating words by spaces became a general custom about the tenth century A.D., and lasted until about 1957, when FORTRAN abandoned the practice.")

Of course, there were other handwriting-to-keypunch translation issues beyond mere spacing for keypunchers to contend with. For example, differentiating between the letter "O" ("oh") and the number 0 (zero) proved thorny. By the time the first version of FORTRAN was released to the public, a slash was placed through the letter "O" to avoid confusion, like this: Ø. The slashed "oh" may have started as an early mathematical convention to avoid confusing letters with digits. But the slashed zero predated electronic computers by centuries, and within several decades of FORTRAN's release, there was an industry-wide shift in convention: from slashed "oh" to slashed zero, which may have been due to the influence of SHARE. Beyond "O" and 0, confusion also reigned with "I" and 1, "B" and 8, and "Z" and 2.

SHARE also later helped with the distribution of the nascent computer language. By the October 1957 SHARE meeting in San Diego, numerous people attending had used FORTRAN, which was released several months prior. A FORTRAN ad hoc standards committee was organized at the meeting, with Don Breheim of North American Rocketdyne appointed chairman. David Sayre stopped by the meeting, speaking to the concerns of many when assuring the crowd that subroutines for separately compiled programs were in the works for the next version of FORTRAN.

"We had dozens of committees on various technical matters. These were very influential in directing IBM as to how they should behave in the technical world," Frank Wagner boasted. "We had a tremendous influence on the use of FORTRAN. It turned out that 90% of the engineering [and] scientific programs were written in FORTRAN. Without SHARE's backing, that wouldn't have happened." True enough, but SHARE's backing of FORTRAN came as a kind of capitulation. Though SHARE users shared resources, collaborating on and coordinating the development of an operating system for the IBM 709 (the successor to the 704) in the late 1950s proved to be too much for the SHARE organization to handle. Shortly after IBM announced that they were developing the 709, SHARE, given full backing and approval by IBM, got to work on systems programs. Although the SHARE 709 System (SOS), an operating system for the 709 built off of the first OS for the 704 (called the GM-NAA I/O), was indeed completed in 1958, it was very difficult for a non-expert to use. SOS came complete with a complex programming language called SCAT, standing for SHARE Compiler Assembler Translator—consisting, of course, of a compiler, assembler, and translator; minor changes to SCAT programs would result in partial retranslations of programs on "SQUOZE" decks—which had hundreds of commands at its disposal, unlike FORTRAN, which had few commands by comparison and was thus appealing to non-programmers like engineers and scientists. As FORTRAN grew in popularity, a subgroup of SHARE was formed: the FORTRAN Standards Committee (replacing the ad hoc standards committee), which attempted to integrate FORTRAN within SOS. Which ultimately proved a futile effort, leaving IBM to write a new operating system for the 709 that would interface with FORTRAN. SOS was, effectively, DOA.

Even if an intrepid FORTRAN programmer managed to overcome all of the handwriting-to-keypunch translation issues, there was still another problem: limited available memory. Any program of instructions read into memory couldn't exceed the available data storage space. For instance, the storage space available in a computer with 4,096 words would be roughly "3,000 units," as stated in the Preliminary Report. (The need to conserve memory underscored how important using "specification sentences," such as with dimensioning arrays, were to writing program instructions.) The 704 was not restricted to 4,096 words; rather, a machine with 4,096 words of core storage was termed a "small 704"; as described in the 704 manual,

> A group of 36 cores constitutes one register in storage. Magnetic core storage units are available with capacities of either 4,096 or 32,768 core storage registers; or two magnetic core storage units, each with a capacity of 4,096 core storage registers, may be used.

Thus, magnetic core storage units are available to give the calculator [the 704] a capacity of 4,096, 8,192, or 32,768 core storage registers.

Note that the 704 had a magnetic drum storage unit as well as high-speed magnetic core storage; the drum memory could hold program instructions as well but was much slower to read or write words than the core storage. Also note that the 704 and later data processing systems were able to accept input from more than just punched cards: the machine could also read magnetic input tapes, which housed information originally stored on punched cards regardless. There were typically at least four tape units available as well.

The development team envisioned many upgrades to FORTRAN since, despite the profusion of detail proffered, the Preliminary Report was only the most basic sketch of a still-nascent programming language. There was much that could be expanded upon and improved. Take built-in mathematical functions, for instance. Backus and company proposed advanced mathematics formulas for summation (summing up the terms of an expression) and even integration (definite integrals only, with numerical answers and which could be found using numerical methods, rather than indefinite integrals, which would have required symbolic manipulation); specifically, a "summation operator" was proposed, but ultimately didn't make the cut. Also recall that books of precomputed tables for mathematical functions were ubiquitous in universities, businesses, and libraries at the time. With that in mind, the team proposed a FORTRAN "table lookup" function that would automate the process—with the programmer simply having to input a table number and argument(s) for the function—although the Report is deliberately vague on whether the 704 would calculate the resultant value via numerical methods (calculation-based) or by searching through premade and stored function values (search-based). Needless to say, it would take until FORTRAN II to realize these mathematical aims.

More intriguingly, the authors of the Preliminary Report suggested the possibility of additional control formulas—beyond IF-formulas and DO-formulas—that were all narrowly geared toward the unique requirements of mathematicians, physicists, and engineers. Proposals of control formulas for complex arithmetic (calculations containing real and imaginary numbers), matrix arithmetic, and linear programming (routines to solve multiple simultaneous equations) didn't make the cut, in part because of their complexity (which is also why the RELABEL-formula didn't survive the Report) but also due to the fact that such specialized algorithms could be programmed using the more general (and basic) set of tools proposed regardless.

Proposed future additions extended into the realm of input-output formulas as well as provisions for the creation of "general formulas," which were abstracted even further from concrete mathematical functions (like sine or cosine).

Around the time that the Preliminary Report was published, several other groups began developing their own algebraic translators, namely individuals at Sperry Rand and at the Purdue University Computing Laboratory. These proto-HLLs were of a much more limited scope than FORTRAN; specifically, unlike the other teams building translators, the goal of Backus's group was to write a compiler that produced optimized object programs. Purdue was busy building the IT, or Internal Translator, for the IBM 650, while Sperry Rand was hard at work developing MATH-MATIC (originally called

AT-3), for the UNIVAC I and II, which ended up being released in 1957, the same year as FORTRAN; the MATH-MATIC project's head was the computer scientist Charles Katz, who worked with Grace Hopper. Boeing managed to release their BACIAC compiler, or Boeing Airplane Company Algebraic Interpretive Coding system, in 1954. Backus believed that the FORTRAN team's free dissemination of the Report gave these groups and others an added urgency to bring their ideas to fruition as quickly as possible. In fact, he recalled specifically sending the Sperry Rand team the Report; though the Report was distributed prior to any MATH-MATIC documents describing the language, and despite the common elements between MATH-MATIC and FORTRAN, it remains an open question just how much, if at all, Backus's team influenced Sperry Rand's.

Impressively, almost everything in the FORTRAN Preliminary Report would make the final cut. But successfully translating those blueprints into a working programming language didn't involve traversing a mere gap—it required negotiating a chasm.

CHAPTER 11

A Motley Crew

The FORTRAN team grew larger as the problems they confronted became more difficult to solve.

After they polished off the Preliminary Report in the fall of 1954, Ziller, Herrick, and Backus spent the next several months presenting their ideas to IBM customers who had placed orders for the 704. They gave talks in around half a dozen cities between late 1954 and early 1955, including Los Angeles, Pittsburgh, Washington, D.C., and Albuquerque. They told audiences that they anticipated the FORTRAN compiler would be completed in roughly six months—which turned out to be overoptimistic, since the system was not finalized until April 1957.

The biggest problem with the talks, though, was that their audiences simply didn't believe them. Perhaps accustomed to being sold a bill of goods, since prior automatic programming systems had promised so much and delivered so little, the development team was offered very little feedback from the people who heard them speak—disappointing from Backus's perspective, since he wanted suggestions and criticism to help spur the team's efforts. But the team was met with mostly silence.

There was one notable exception to this wave of quiet skepticism, coming after a January 1955 talk at United Aircraft Corporation of East Hartford, Connecticut. The development team secured a deal with UA's Walter Ramshaw (who had advised IBM on the Speedcoding project) to permit Roy Nutt, one of their best programmers, to travel to New York multiple times per week on a regular basis to assist in FORTRAN's development. "Basically, the guy was so good—he was humiliating to be around," Ramshaw reflected. He was so good, in fact, that the National Security Agency (NSA) once tried to recruit him as a cryptologist, but to no avail, since Nutt had bigger plans in the private sector.

The oldest of four children, Roy Nutt was born in 1930 in Marlborough, Massachusetts, but was raised in Glastonbury, Connecticut, after his family uprooted. Fittingly, Nutt would come to love gardening since, during the Second World War, he helped tend a victory garden. In addition to growing vegetables, his family also raised chickens, which led the young Roy to mistakenly think himself an expert at sexing chickens, much to the family's amusement.

High school found Nutt intensely focused on typing—quickly and efficiently. After taking a typing class, he could pound out more than one hundred words per minute. Nutt also assumed yearbook activities and was a manager of his school's varsity basketball team. By graduation, the sixteen-year-old Nutt was awarded the Rensselaer medal, presented to the senior with the highest average in mathematics and science.

But the next academic year would not be as uneventful as the previous four. After enrolling at the Worcester Polytechnic Institute—he had been awarded a full scholarship—Nutt struggled, and he failed the first semester. Nutt's father, who had attended Harvard, was furious. "I place the responsibility for this term failure squarely upon your childish philosophy," he wrote to his son. "You want to have a good time. You devote weekends and vacations to that purpose, and for all we know part of your week-days wasting time. If you fail a second term your college opportunity is gone. We cannot send you anywhere else." Part of the problem was that Nutt was repeatedly late for his morning classes because he couldn't afford to buy an alarm clock. Another issue was his age: Nutt had graduated high school two years early, and the students he attended classes with were returning World War II veterans financing their education courtesy of the G.I. Bill, making the contrast in life experience all the more apparent. Although Nutt squeaked by with passing grades in the second semester, he failed the third—and was expelled. He then tried his luck at Boston University, but didn't do well enough to continue there, either.

Returning home to Connecticut, a family friend and professor at nearby Trinity College in Hartford suggested Nutt apply there, with the eventual intent to reapply to Boston University. However, Trinity, which accepted him in 1951, proved to be a fit for Nutt, who spent his free time playing bridge, earning enough at the game to purchase a 1941 Buick. It was a utilitarian purchase, since Nutt—unlike most Trinity students—commuted to campus.

Nutt studied mathematics at Trinity; he figured he would eventually teach the subject. After enrolling in an experimental yearlong course Trinity offered called "Numerical Mathematical Analysis and Machine Methods," however, he shifted his career path to applied computational mathematics. The class was taught by two visiting faculty members—one of whom was Walter Ramshaw from United Aircraft. By taking the class, Nutt was exposed to the latest in computing technology, including visits to the hardware stored at the UA laboratory, which included the Card Programmed Calculator.

The next summer saw Nutt working at UA's research lab, becoming so comfortable with punched cards that he learned how to decode them by sight alone. Through the rest of his time at Trinity, he juggled a taxing schedule: working full time at UA during the summer, and scaling down to the night shift during the academic year. The continuity at UA paid off, because by graduation he had been promoted to night shift supervisor, with more than a half-dozen Trinity students serving as his direct reports.

Nutt earned his bachelor's degree in mathematics from Trinity in 1953, but it was a rocky road to the finish line. At the beginning of his final semester, he was put on academic probation—for spending most of his time computing instead of studying. Regardless, he was hired by United Aircraft as a systems analyst immediately after graduating and assigned to work in the research department headed by his old professor, Walter Ramshaw. By then, Nutt had garnered a reputation as a master programmer. "Roy was known to just sit down at a keypunch machine and keypunch in a program that would run," Backus recalled. Although flowcharting programs and coding them by hand first before keypunching was standard operating procedure in those days, Nutt usually circumvented the preliminary steps, believing them to be superfluous. When it came to programming, Roy Nutt was adept at simultaneously seeing the big and small pictures quite clearly in his mind's eye alone. If he had been born a generation later—the generation of Bill Gates and Steve Wozniak, who came of age in the late 1960s and early 1970s, just in time for the personal computer revolution—Nutt, a programmer and thinker of the highest rank, might have ended up a household name.

Just how much Nutt lived and breathed programming is best illustrated with an anecdote. Back in 1951, while still at Trinity, Nutt asked Ruth Heagle, whom he had known since childhood (their families were friendly), to the winter formal. At their wedding four years later, "[i]nstead of rice, the bride and groom were showered with chads from computer punch cards," according to their son Micah Nutt. "The oily bits of cardboard could never be completely removed from the interior of his car." Perhaps even more tellingly, "his United Aircraft coworkers placed bets as to whether or not the work-obsessed programmer would take his briefcase on the couple's Bermuda honeymoon." Very reluctantly, he left his briefcase at home.

In 1955, Nutt helped to found IBM SHARE, the mainframe computer user group, as UA's company representative. UA had given him the freedom to develop the Symbolic Assembly Program (SAP), a top-notch assembler for the 701, and when SHARE members decided to distribute a 701 assembler, it came down to a decision between five possibilities: GE's "Compiled & Assembled at General Electric," Los Alamos Scientific Laboratories' "Symbolic Regional" assembler, two IBM-developed assemblers, and UA-SAP. Nutt's UA-SAP was chosen; he rewrote it for the 704 and renamed it the SHARE Assembly Program. (Numerous 701s were still in use years after the 704 was released, so Nutt wrote a 704 emulator for the 701 that could run 704 SAP code.) A sardonic commentary on programming bugs appears in the SAP user manual: "the probability that undetected bugs remain in this program differs from unity by the reciprocal of a googolplex." In other words, chances are overwhelmingly likely—virtually one hundred percent ("unity")—that there are undetected bugs, although Nutt holds out hope, by the slimmest of margins (1/googolplex), that all bugs have in fact been stamped out. (We will examine Roy Nutt's SAP assembler later in the book.)

Widely distributed by SHARE starting in 1956, the success and influence of SAP, along with Nutt's Speedcoding work at UA, led to Backus urging Nutt to join the FORTRAN team, at least for several days a week. He did, commuting back and forth from Hartford; as part of the arrangement, Nutt agreed to maintain the same responsibilities and workload at UA, as if he were still working there on a full-time basis. Nutt would remain employed at UA throughout the development of FORTRAN, and for some time thereafter; although IBM tried to snag him, he eventually left UA to cofound Computer Sciences Corporation, a software services company, with Fletcher Jones,

SHARE's spokesman. Interestingly, in 1953 UA had designs on building a compiler of their own, after Nutt (and perhaps several other UA employees) visited staff at MIT, who were hard at work developing an interpreted language. But UA nixed the plan to build a compiler—it was too complex a project. "By the time John Backus suggested cooperation on FORTRAN," recalled Nutt, "we had begun to realize how big a job it would be, and folded our own embryonic effort."

It was Roy Nutt who "was responsible for the whole input-output system" of FORTRAN; consultations with Nutt, before he officially joined the team, led the authors of the Preliminary Report to suggest additional input-output formulas. Nutt would, most notably, create FORTRAN's **FORMAT** statement, which facilitated formatted output.

Nutt was unhappy, though, with the option of inserting parentheses in algebraic expressions in FORTRAN, which he called a "dubious technique…concocted" by Backus and Ziller. Nutt probably objected to an optimization strategy proposed in the Preliminary Report: programmers could alert the FORTRAN system to repeated expressions embedded within the same formula statement by enclosing them in parentheses so the compiler would avoid calculating these expressions repeatedly. So, an expression like this:

$$a \times b \times c \times (a \times b \times c + \cos(a)) + \mathrm{sqrt}(a \times b + h \times \cos(a))$$

could be rewritten using additional parentheses to avoid any duplicate calculations like this:

$$(a \times b) \times c \times ((a \times b) \times c + \cos(a)) + \mathrm{sqrt}((a \times b) + h \times \cos(a))$$

But, instead, Nutt may have disliked the FORTRAN compiler's processing of arithmetic expressions by automatically inserting extra pairs of parentheses depending on operation precedence (we will examine this technique in a later chapter).

Like Roy Nutt, Sheldon Best was not employed at IBM but nonetheless joined the Programming Research Group. Best worked at the Digital Computing Laboratory at MIT; he was loaned out by Charles W. Adams, who employed him at the university. Unlike Nutt, Best's time with the development team was continuous and he was thus granted temporary employee status at IBM. "Almost everyone was there already when I came," recalled Best. He developed and programmed empirically optimal register allocations, critical to the compiler's operation.

Peter B. Sheridan also joined the development team. "I was tickled pink when John decided to take me aboard," but he was under no illusions regarding the difficulty of the task that lay before them: "So we had to discover all the technology that we needed ourselves." Sheridan was hired at IBM in 1952, having earned a BS at City College of New York and an MS at Fordham University. Working with Herrick, Sheridan wrote compiler code to handle the algebraic expressions. Although perhaps *invented*, rather than wrote, is the better term. According to Backus, "When I say that somebody 'wrote a section of the compiler,' it is important to remember that what I really mean is that they *invented* it—they developed all the groundbreaking techniques used in it. It is a great understatement to say only 'somebody wrote a section.'"

At about the same time as Sheridan, David Sayre came aboard as well. Like Backus, Sayre was born in 1924—but in New York, New York, not Philadelphia. Earning a bachelor's in physics from Yale, he completed his doctoral studies in crystallography under the British chemist Dorothy Hodgkin. He then took a job as a senior mathematician at the Johnson Research Foundation, located at the University of Pennsylvania. In 1955, realizing that the future of crystallography would be best served by exploiting computing power—he had already utilized computers for biophysics research—Sayre joined IBM's Thomas J. Watson Research Center as a mathematician. He eventually transitioned to assistant manager of the Programming Research Group. Writing the FORTRAN *Manual* was one of his most important responsibilities. Sayre viewed computers with a hint of whimsy: "You entered a world that kind of ran the way it was supposed to, a world made for working out the logic of something."

After Lois Mitchell Haibt graduated from Vassar College as a mathematics major, demonstrating a superior aptitude in math and science (but less so in the "fuzzy subjects, like English," she recalled), IBM offered her a job programming computers with a starting salary of $5,100, double was she was offered from Bell Laboratories. "I only had a vague idea what that [programming] was. But I figured it must be something interesting and challenging, if they were going to pay me all that money," she said. She took the job, and by the fall of 1955 had joined the development team. "They took anyone who seemed to have an aptitude for problem-solving skills—bridge players, chess players, even women." She would build the arithmetic expression analyzer of the compiler, despite the fact that "none of this theory existed. Nothing was known about *parsing*"—essentially taking a sentence of high-level code and chopping it up into constitute pieces of data that could be easily identified—"it was all invented at the time."

Richard "Dick" Goldberg earned a BA at Swarthmore College in 1948 and a Ph.D. in mathematics from New York University in 1954, spending the years 1954 and 1955 as a postgraduate fellow at NYU's Courant Institute. He then accepted a teaching position at Dartmouth College before decamping, after only a single semester, to work at IBM's Watson Research Center, joining the development team in November 1955. Before arriving at IBM, Goldberg "didn't know anything about computing," he said. "Well, it was very exciting. It was completely outside of my experience." The work was so "out of the ordinary" that he had never done anything like it before in academia. "We were the hackers of those days."

There were several more people who supported the team's efforts. Robert A. "Bob" Hughes, an African American World War II veteran who had been hired at the Lawrence Livermore National Laboratory (LLNL) after finishing his master's at the University of Michigan, was loaned out to IBM by Sidney Fernbach, head of the Computation Department, but only for a spell; he spent the summer of 1956 helping the team with system documentation. (Fernbach sent Bob Hughes to IBM to gather "firsthand information" about FORTRAN; the labs were stocked with modern IBM computers and equipment and Fernbach was interested in FORTRAN's "potential as a programming aid," recalled Hughes.) Harry Cantrell, who worked at General Electric in Schenectady, New York, was a great cheerleader for the team. And Backus's bosses at IBM—Hurd, and then Charles DeCarlo and John McPherson—gave the team a maximum amount of flexibility and a minimum of fuss.

So, by the end of 1955 the development team was in place. "We were this kind of small family," recalled Peter Sheridan. The cantankerous Harlan Herrick described the team as a group of "very unusual people" who, "as a matter of fate, came to join us because they had certain abilities that without them, we probably would have never been able to do what we did." In Herrick's telling, the Programming Research Group attained a sort of mythical status once everyone joined and all the chess pieces were in place—as if each person were imbued with a certain superpower but, only by working together, would they be able to save the world, à la the Fantastic Four or the Justice League.

And indeed, John Backus—the man who exhibited a quiet leadership that permitted the team to work in a "little pool of silence," in the words of David Sayre—would need his motley crew to stretch their powers to the limit in order to solve their biggest challenge to date: coding an efficient compiler.

But before we explore at how they did it, let us first jump ahead to late 1956 and take a detailed look at the nearly finished product. Then, knowing the full scope of the destination (FORTRAN I), we will examine the journey (building the compiler) in detail, with a brief stop to look at SAP as well.

CHAPTER 12

Making a Statement

After successfully building the compiler, the team polished off their new language with a short but comprehensive and eminently readable user manual.

By the summer of 1956, with the compiler design completed and debugging well underway, the development team realized they had a problem: there was no documentation for the end user. It was assistant manager David Sayre, whom Backus affectionately referred to as his "second-in-command" of the Programming Research Department (originally called the Programming Research Group, but by 1956 renamed), who took on the challenge.

The *Programmer's Reference Manual*, a slim volume wrapped in a glossy cover (with a cover design that's since become famous, complete with the word "Fortran," uncapitalized unlike throughout the body text of the *Manual*, plastered proudly across the front cover in Clarendon font) published in October of 1956, opens with a bold declaration: "This manual supersedes all earlier information about the FORTRAN system. It describes the system which will be made available during late 1956, and is intended to permit planning and FORTRAN coding in advance of that time." Late 1956 was supposed to be October 1956, but was in fact was "a euphemism for April 1957," Backus humorously recalls, when FORTRAN, beset by delays, was finally released. (An *Addenda* to the *Manual* was distributed by IBM, offering a number of corrections. The first of these: "Title page. For 'late 1956' read 'early 1957.'") Why? Because, remembered Backus, "As we began to solve one problem, it split up into others we hadn't foreseen. In January 1955, we said we would have it in less than a year. Finally, we did it in 1957." Sayre summarized the long, drawn-out process succinctly: "Little by little, it didn't make mistakes, and then, when it stopped making mistakes—or almost stopped making mistakes—then we could finally issue FORTRAN."

In the *Manual*, Sayre is quite direct: the Programming Research Department believed that FORTRAN was the 704's killer app (of course, he didn't use those words), and they weren't afraid to boast about it. FORTRAN, he writes, "in effect transforms the

704 into a machine with which communication can be made in a language more concise and more familiar than the 704 language itself"—"closely resembling the ordinary language of mathematics"—and the "result should be a considerable reduction in the training required to program, as well as in the time consumed in writing programs and eliminating their errors."

The *Manual* is a breezy read, written with prose that never gets too technical as it describes a "programming language that resembled a combination of pidgin English and algebra," as the technology writer Steve Lohr put it. Subdivided into short chapters that detail constants, variables, and subscripts; functions, expressions, and arithmetic formulas; control statements; input-output statements; specification statements; and example programs, the *Manual* reads like a polished, expanded version of the Preliminary Report, replete with cleanly formatted tables conveying key information and more consistent, modern terminology (e.g., the DO-formula became the **DO** statement). The "FORTRAN 0" of the Preliminary Report, as computer scientist Donald Knuth termed the proto-language, had evolved into FORTRAN I. What follows are descriptions of some of the key sections of the *Manual*.

Right off the bat, Sayre issues a warning to the reader. Yes, FORTRAN will take a source program and turn it into an object program, but there were limits: if the object program was too large for the 704 to run, the programmer had to chop up his or her code into multiple programs—far from a trivial task, since there was no easy way to connect any of these programs together. (Modularity would be a feature of a future FORTRAN implementation.) So, instead, the programmer would be wise to make sure that before translating the source program into the object program, the source program itself isn't too large. Information on these size constraints—in terms of the number of statements, fixed- and floating-point constants, and even the maximum number of allowable **DO** statements (maximum = 150)—are detailed near the end of the *Manual*.

FORTRAN source programs were, of course, composed entirely of FORTRAN statements, which the programmer would sequentially string together. Backus recalled that "statements arose from just writing test programs and finding we didn't have enough statements to write the programs, so we'd make up one and add it to the language." To that end, thirty-two different such statements were at the programmer's disposal. Out of these, fifteen were control statements, determining the flow of program execution.

A caution to the modern reader: FORTRAN had no *keywords*, or reserved words that the compiler would recognize as being set aside for a special purpose; in addition, the FORTRAN compiler completely ignored blanks. So, for instance, consider this looping statement:

$$\text{DO } 11 \text{ K} = 1, 10$$

Reading from left to right *prior* to encountering the comma, the compiler would believe that the following set of characters (ignoring blanks) represent a floating-point variable assignment statement:

$$\text{DO11K=1}$$

The "variable" DO11K, which did not need declaration, is set equal to the value of 1. Thus, it is important to note that the word DO, by itself, signified nothing special to the compiler. But once the comma was encountered, the compiler would be clued in to the fact that this statement was, in fact, a DO statement denoting a loop.

Also, before reading through the list of control statements below, recall FORTRAN's implicit typing rules as described in the Preliminary Report: variables beginning with the letters I, J, K, L, M, and N are automatically set to an integer data type, while any other first letter sets the variable to floating-point (real values). As Backus later pointed out, this rule clearly created barriers to cogent code, with the name COUNT unavailable for an integer counting variable—so a name that was less obviously descriptive like NCOUNT had to be employed. So why did the development team settle on the letters I to N, then? Decades later, Backus explained the decision this way: "Well, it just seemed for a while that people always used *I*, *J*, and *K* for subscripts, and we thought we'd be generous and add a few more."

Variable names could be up to six alphanumeric characters in length with no special characters allowed (this six-character limit was not specified in the Report), thereby conforming to the 36-bit-word architecture of the 704, with fixed-point variables restricted to a magnitude of less than 2^{15} and floating-point variables any value between 10^{-38} and 10^{38}. Scientific notation, with an E standing in as 10, could be utilized with floating-point numbers; for instance, a hardcoded 3.0E+7 meant 3.0×10^7. What's more, values of both variable types could be optionally preceded by a minus sign (-) or a plus sign (+), with any positive integers serving as statement numbers (although statement numbers couldn't be repeated within the same program, otherwise the compiler wouldn't know where to transfer control to).

Also recall the Preliminary Report's extensive proposals centering on subscripts and subscripted variables, or arrays, which mostly made it into the final product. The subscripts themselves, of course, had to be fixed-point quantities (even if they were represented by expressions rather than hardcoded values), but the data stored in the subscripted variables could be either of the fixed- or floating-point variety. Subscripted variables could be one dimensional, such as A(J), N(5), or I(J(KPL+1)); or two dimensional, such as SHI(NA, 53) or N(MU+2, NU+7); or even three dimensional. Subscripted variables, no matter their dimensions, were stored sequentially in memory, albeit in descending order. Any time a subscripted variable was introduced into a program, its use had to be preceded by a DIMENSION statement—one of three specification statements—that set aside the proper amount of storage in the object program for the array. For example, DIMENSION A(500) allowed the programmer to store five hundred real-valued quantities (i.e., numbers with decimals) into the subscripted variable A, from subscript 1 to subscript 500; arrays were not zero-indexed. So, A(22) = 3.14159 set the twenty-second index of the array A equal to an approximation for π (pi). Setting the dimensions of a two- or three-dimensional subscripted variable was self-explanatory, and more than one subscripted variable could be dimensioned using the same **DIMENSION** statement.

What follows is a rundown of the available control statements.

- **GO TO**, for an unconditional jump to another statement; there were variants of **GO TO**: the unconditional **GO TO**, with the statement number hardcoded, as in, say, **GO TO 5**; or the assigned **GO TO**, with the statement number encoded as an integer variable courtesy of an **ASSIGN** statement; or even the computed **GO TO**, with the possible statement numbers arranged in a list—for instance **GO TO (40, 50, 60), I**, where if **I** is assigned to 2, then FORTRAN will jump to statement 50.
- **IF**, for transferring control to another statement, made a decision by comparing a quantity to zero; for example, **IF (B − A) 10, 20, 30** would transfer control to statement 10 if $B - A < 0$, statement 20 if $B - A = 0$, or statement 30 if $B - A > 0$. Although the Report had promised sophisticated conditional statements, complete with inequality symbols, like

    if (nxi >= k+1) 3, 9

    successfully procuring a > symbol to work as advertised proved infeasible. The **IF** statement of FORTRAN I would later be called an arithmetic **IF**.
- **DO**, which was a rather malleable loop statement for its time, permitted the user several looping options; the **DO** statement, which modern readers, perhaps despite having a familiarity with programming loops, might find somewhat confusing, is best illustrated by several examples.

```
10      DO 11 K = 1, 10
11      J = J + K
12      STOP
```

When the compiler reaches statement 10 above, the *range* of the **DO** statement—meaning the block of code that will be looped—includes *only* statement 11; the integer control variable **K** is called an *index*, and it increments by one unit with each iteration. Thus, the **DO** statement executes statement 11 ten times before passing control to statement 12. (The 11 in the statement **DO 11 K = 1, 10** is called a *statement label*.) By the time control passes from the **DO** statement to statement 12, 55 units have been added to the value stored in integer variable **J**.

We could rewrite the **DO** statement to step through the loop by, say, 2's, by appending a number at the end of the **DO** statement; the 2 shown below is called the *step-size*.

```
10      DO 11 K = 1, 10, 2
```

```
          11        J = J + K
          12        STOP
```

Now, once control passes from the DO statement (after the DO statement has been satisfied, meaning that the range has been executed for the final time), J has added only 25 units to its value since only iterations with K equaling 1, 3, 5, 7, and 9 were executed.

Nested DO statements, or DO statements embedded within other DO statements like Russian nesting dolls, were permitted as well. Even a temporary exit out of the range of a DO statement to a (loosely defined) subroutine was permitted—with a well-placed GO TO shuttling control from the subroutine back inside the range of the DO. Absolutely forbidden, however, was fiddling with any of the indexes, either with code in the range or in a subroutine; the indexing of the DO statement could not be altered once it was set (e.g., in the above example, the loop *must* iterate five times, from index 1 to 10 by 2's; no changes could be made). No matter how the DO statement was defined, however, the loop had to iterate at least once.

The power of DO statements was apparent when working with subscripted variables, since DOs permitted traversing arrays with ease. For instance,

```
C                   TRAVERSE ARRAY PGRM
                    DIMENSION L(10)
          10        DO 12 K = 1, 10
          11        J = J + K
          12        L(K) = J
          13        STOP
```

Notice that the range of the DO statement in the example continues through statement 12. (Also notice the presence of unnamed numerical constants, like the 10 in the DO statement, called *magic numbers*—which referred to the hardcoding of constants, rather than using descriptive variables, in source code. The use of magic numbers would proliferate for decades in languages such as FORTRAN and COBOL.)

More sophisticated indexing with arrays, such as triangular indexing, could be facilitated with the DO statement. For example, the following code structure would execute without a hitch:

```
          DO <some range> J = 1 , 20
          DO <some range> K = 1 , J
```

In addition, an array's diagonal elements could be set equal to the value of some expression (in the example below, 1) this way:

```
          DO <some range> J = 1 , 20
          B(J, J, J) = 1
```

Finally, note that the DO statement is a simplified version of the DO-formula. The DO-formula example

do 10, 14, 50 i=4, 20, 2

was detailed in the Preliminary Report. Backus justified the change this way: "I believe the simplification of the original DO statement resulted from the realization that (a) it would be hard to describe precisely, (b) it was awkward to compile, and (c) it provided little power beyond that of the final version."

Regardless of the simplification, upon reflection Backus concluded that the way FORTRAN handled loops was significant. Although most knowledgeable people, if pressed, would conclude that "FORTRAN's main contribution was to enable the programmer to write programs in algebraic formulas instead of machine language," Backus said, they would be mistaken. "What FORTRAN did primarily was to mechanize the organization of loops," since loops were of the utmost importance in writing software for mathematics, science, and engineering applications.

- CONTINUE, which serves as a "dummy" statement marking the end of the range of a DO statement or, in more general terms, a label where control of a program could be passed to; although CONTINUE doesn't do anything per se, sometimes its presence is required. Take the following program, for instance, which checks to see if a particular value (stored in variable B) is stored in a one-dimensional array of floating-point numbers:

```
              DIMENSION A(10)
              B = 3.14
       10     DO 12 K = 1, 10
       11     IF (B – A(K)) 12, 13, 12
       12     CONTINUE
       13     STOP
```

Not only will FORTRAN exit out of the loop if the value stored in B is present in the array, but K will also retain its iterated value—allowing the programmer to pinpoint which index, in fact, contained the value of B. Although it seems like the following program, which avoids using a CONTINUE, is equivalent,

```
              DIMENSION A(10)
              B = 3.14
       10     DO 11 K = 1, 10
       11     IF (B – A(K)) 10, 12, 10
       12     STOP
```

it is not, since if the *final* statement in the range of a DO sequence involves a control transfer (an IF or a GOTO), then the loop will not function as expected.

Backus later surmised that the CONTINUE statement was merely a way to supplement the DO statement, keeping its basic looping structure intact while simultaneously providing it with enhanced functionality: the team wanted to be able to "[skip] to the end of a DO loop without skipping the indexing instructions there: this gave rise to the CONTINUE statement." Backus called such supplementation a "trivial" problem of language design, secondary once the big three design elements were squared away: assignment statements, subscripted variables, and the DO statement—all three ideas which came to the team early in the process. (He would add that language design considerations like type declarations and conditional expressions, considered of obvious importance today, were not even on the development team's radar.) Also considered "trivial" problems by Backus? Machine dependent commands like reading input data. Donald Knuth disagreed, calling both the CONTINUE statement and I/O commands some of FORTRAN's "key innovations." The problem, Knuth noted, was that since "FORTRAN 0" didn't have a CONTINUE statement, a GO TO statement, directed to the line containing a DO-formula, was needed to continue processing the loop in any situation involving a transfer; it would be as if the compiler "forgot" that it was in the midst of a loop if any intra-loop transfer, conditional or unconditional, occurred. Encountering a CONTINUE statement solved the problem—by kind of "reminding" the compiler that it should run another iteration of the loop.

A number of the control statements were machine dependent, meaning that they tapped directly into the idiosyncratic hardware of the 704. There was SENSE LIGHT, which controlled the four sense lights on the front panel of the machine; along with the statement IF (SENSE LIGHT), turning the lights on or off could be utilized creatively as program flags by reading which light was turned on or off and directing program traffic accordingly. Better yet were the sense switches, also located on the front panel of the 704. These switches could be used for runtime user input courtesy of the IF (SENSE SWITCH) statement, which would relay which one of six switches had been depressed while the program was running; this could be a boon to debugging efforts. There were so many switches and lights on the 704's front panel, in fact, that the machine would have hardly looked out of place if featured on an episode of the original *Star Trek* television series.

Understanding the next several FORTRAN statements requires that we delve into a little additional background on the 704 hardware. The machine had a single general-purpose register, called an accumulator (AC), which took care of the intermediate results of arithmetic operations and logical comparisons. The accumulator, part of the 704's Electronic Analytical Control Unit, had a magnitude (absolute value) of 35-bits, along with a sign bit, which relayed the sign, positive (bit = 0) or negative (bit = 1), of a stored signed number. Although nearly all modern computers represent negative integers in binary using a two's complement scheme, which inverts the bits of a positive integer represented in binary and then adds one, the IBM 704 used a "sign-magnitude" convention for its accumulator, meaning that the only way to tell if a binary integer was positive or negative was to glance at its sign bit. Although simpler to use than two's complement, there was a key disadvantage to this scheme: there were two types of zeros possible, the positive zero and the negative zero, and, as a 704 user's manual prepared for the MIT Computation Center explains,

> Either zero may be obtained as a result of arithmetic computations. The usual rule of signs holds for results obtained by multiplication or division, but a zero obtained by addition or subtraction has the same sign…as the original contents of the accumulator. The reader should also note that the computer considers +0 to be larger than -0 whenever the question arises.

In addition to the thirty-six bits (thirty-five plus the sign bit), the accumulator had two additional bits available: the "register overflow positions," which usually flagged arithmetic results that wouldn't fit into the confines of the accumulator but could also be utilized in other operations. They are represented by Q and P in the diagram below.

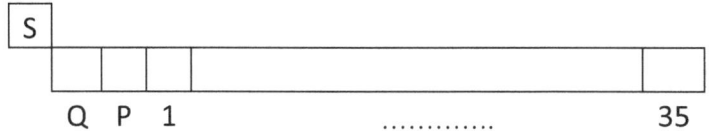

As explained in the 704 manual,

> In some operations (for instance, addition, shifting left) it is possible that the contents of the accumulator will overflow positions 1-35. When an overflow occurs, with the exception of overflow caused by the ACL instruction, the AC OVERFLOW indicator is turned on. Certain instructions permit the program to sense the condition of the overflow indicator while the program is being performed. The programmer may preserve some of the overflow information if he wishes. For this purpose, two extra bit positions, or overflow positions, are provided.

In FORTRAN, the **IF ACCUMULATOR OVERFLOW** statement would transfer control to one of two statements, depending on the status of the "Accumulator Overflow trigger," be it on or off. A light on 704's console also indicated if there was accumulator overflow. Since the **IF** statement could test logical conditions (< 0, $= 0$, or > 0) based on a quantity (or the calculation of a quantity), the possibility of an overflow always loomed.

A second 36-bit register in the Electronic Analytical Control Unit, called the multiplier-quotient register (MQ), worked with the accumulator to perform arithmetic operations, including, of course, multiplication and division. A diagram of the multiplier-quotient register is shown below.

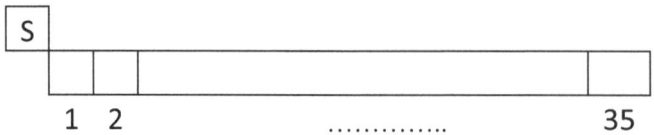

The multiplier-quotient register also assisted the accumulator with floating-point operations, for which there was no dedicated register. The MIT Computation Center manual summarizes the difference between how fixed- and floating-point numbers are handled by the machine:

> The other major category of words used in the 704 is that of words used to represent arithmetic quantities. There are two major types, those for fixed-point numbers and those for floating-point numbers. Again it should be emphasized that these conventions are only useful because there are explicit 704 instructions that manipulate words according to these conventions. In fixed-point words, the first bit is used to describe the sign (0 is positive, 1 is negative) and the remaining 35 bits give the magnitude of the significant figures. Inasmuch as the binary point is not a tangible thing inside the computer, a fixed-point number can either be an integer or a fraction depending on whether one interprets the binary point as being at the left-hand end or the right-hand end of the magnitude.
>
> In a similar way, floating-point numbers, that is, numbers which are represented by a fraction multiplied by 2 raised to a power [2^N], are represented in the following way: The first bit is the sign of the fraction, the next 8 bits are the always-positive characteristic (by definition, the exponent plus 128), and the remaining 27 bits are the magnitude of the fraction.

The statement **IF QUOTIENT OVERFLOW** transferred control of the program based on whether the "Multiplier-Quotient Overflow trigger" was on or off. A light on the 704's console indicated if there was multiplier-quotient overflow. Also, there was a divide check light on the console, which could light up with any division by zero attempt. Likewise, the **IF DIVIDE CHECK** statement shuttled control based on division by zero status. Besides the accumulator and the multiplier-quotient register, the 704 had three additional index registers, each fifteen bits in length.

In addition to the fifteen control statements, FORTRAN had thirteen input-output statements available to the programmer. The multiplier-quotient register was used as a buffer for input and output. Unsurprisingly, there were yet more lights on the front panel of the 704, these functioning as input/output flags. As the MIT manual describes it, "The word passes through the MQ [multiplier-quotient register], which is used as a buffer for IO [input-output]. If no unit is currently selected, the 704 stops with the Read-Write Check Light on." There was a great deal of complexity with I/O, because input and output could take a variety of forms: drums, tapes, card punch (along with the card reader), and line printer. The output mediums had the following restrictions: a line printed on paper could contain at most 120 characters, as could a BCD (Binary-Coded Decimal) tape record; and a punched card could have a maximum of seventy-two characters.

Before considering the transmission of data from one medium to another, however, the notion of "lists" must be considered. Lists are collections of quantities (fixed- or floating point) that are read and written in a sequential, ordered fashion. Careful attention had to be paid to the transmission of arrays (which were lists of data) from one medium to another; if one didn't set aside the memory for it with a proper **DIMENSION** specification statement, only the quantity stored in one index might be transmitted, rather than the entire array.

Notice how many of the following input-output statements are machine-dependent, to one degree or another. The upshot is that FORTRAN would have been a very different language had it been first implemented on a computer other than the 704.

- **FORMAT**, which is a non-executed statement that supplies field specifications for how, precisely, the data is to be output (Hollerith punch, decimal print, or BCD code) onto some external storage medium (paper, punched card, or tape). A number of other statements referenced the **FORMAT** statement for these specifications, which were grouped into three kinds: the type of conversion (E = transmission from internal to external storage, or vice versa, for floating-point values; F = same as E, but for fixed-point; and I = transmission from fixed-point internal storage to decimal integer in external storage); the field width W, which could be defined larger than necessary to ensure adequate blank space between the quantities; and the number of digits after the decimal to be rounded. There are many possible field specifications, and the *Manual* offers a number of examples that the reader should feel free to consult if curious. To take just one: the statement **FORMAT (I2, E12.4, F10.4)** would produce a line of three numbers formatted this way:

    27 -0.9331E 02   -0.0076

    Repetition of groups of field specifications was possible, simply by grouping the specifications within parentheses along with placing an integer outside the parentheses in the **FORMAT** statement, like so: **2(E12.4)**. Scale factors, which either increased or decreased numbers by factors of ten (e.g., turning money into units of thousands of dollars), were facilitated by using the letter P in the field specification.

    Notice that this first implementation FORTRAN offered no dedicated variable types for string or character data, as would become common in most HLLs only a handful of years later (future implementations of FORTRAN would, eventually, render these Hollerith fields obsolete, although SHARE and General Electric in particular had a number of ideas in the pipeline early on to simplify things); only numeric variable types were available. In order to output non-numeric data, the **FORMAT** statement permitted the printing of English characters in what were termed Hollerith fields (alternatively called Hollerith strings or Hollerith constants). The string length followed by the letter H would signal to the compiler that English text was to be produced. For instance, **FORMAT (4HXYZ=F9.2)** might output something like **XYZ=23.69**. Despite the compiler ignoring spaces in program statements, if spaces were inserted in a Hollerith field, they would be honored.

Nothing like a **FORMAT** statement was ever mentioned in the Preliminary Report. As Donald Knuth opined, "This feature [formats], due to Roy Nutt, was a major innovation in programming languages; it probably had a significant effect in making FORTRAN popular since input/output conversions were otherwise very awkward to express on the 704." Rather unusually, **FORMAT** statements were not compiled—they were interpreted. Nutt later explained that, although they wanted to compile **FORMAT** statements along with everything else, "we just couldn't get it done in time."

- **READ** directs FORTRAN to read punched cards placed into the card reader; the statement works hand in hand with **FORMAT**.
- **READ INPUT TAPE** causes FORTRAN to read data from BCD tapes, according to the field specifications set by the associated **FORMAT** statement.
- **PUNCH** directs the card punch to start punching cards according to the field specifications of **FORMAT**.
- **PRINT** acts like the **PUNCH** statement, but it directs the output to the line printer instead of to punched cards.
- **WRITE OUTPUT TAPE** acts like **PUNCH** and **PRINT**, but writes data to BCD tapes.

In a paper presented at the public release of FORTRAN, the development team partially illustrated the functionality of the **PRINT** statement with an example program; several germane lines from that program are reprinted below.

```
        DIMENSION ALPHA(25), RHO(25)
1       FORMAT (5F12.4)
2       READ 1, ALPHA, RHO, ARG
        ...
        PRINT 1, ARG, SUM, VALUE
```

Fifty-one data points are read in from cards once the **READ** statement is executed: the first twenty-five are stored in the **ALPHA** array, the next twenty-five are stored in the **RHO** array, and the final data point is stored into a floating-point variable called **ARG**. Statement number 1, of course, sets the formatting of the data points read from the card reader: each number is granted a field width of twelve columns, with the decimal four digits from the right; five numbers will be printed on each row. Finally, the **PRINT** statement outputs the quantities stored in the three variables. Notice that both the **READ** and **PRINT** statements directly reference the **FORMAT** statement.

Unlike the formatted I/O statements above, the following I/O statements were unformatted (meaning they didn't rely on field specifications set by **FORMAT**).

- **READ TAPE** reads in binary data from BCD tapes, with certain restrictions; in addition, there is an error check: the program halts if a record fails twice. In addition, the object program halts at the end of the file.

- **READ DRUM** does the same thing, more or less, as **READ TAPE**, only from magnetic drums, although there are some limitations on the list of data. And unlike **READ TAPE**, there is no error checking—the object program will not halt.
- **WRITE TAPE** writes binary information to BCD tapes, with certain restrictions; there is no error checking, and the object program will not halt.
- **WRITE DRUM** writes binary information to magnetic drum storage, subject to the same limitations as **READ DRUM**; there is no error checking, and the object program will not halt.

The final set of I/O statements were useful for additional machine-level control.

- **END FILE**, when called, would result in the object program writing "End of File" on the BCD tape.
- **REWIND** describes precisely what it does: it rewinds the tape.
- **BACKSPACE** moves the tape backward by one item.

The remaining statements were specification statements, of which there were three: **DIMENSION**, which we discussed earlier; **EQUIVALENCE**, permitting the programmer an additional level of control over data storage (e.g., if several variables all reference the same quantity, they can be made to reference the same location in memory as well); and **FREQUENCY**, which would optimize a program via frequency estimates provided by the programmer on the number of times **GO TO**, **IF**, and **DO** statements would likely execute during runtime (with **IF** and **GO TO** statements, the estimated frequencies for each "branch-point," or control-transfer opportunity, needed to be specified). Using **EQUIVALENCE** or **FREQUENCY** statements was always optional; using **DIMENSION** was not.

When it came to data storage, any variables pointed to by **DIMENSION** or **EQUIVALENCE** statements received top billing: at the topmost portion of data storage. Moving downward, after variables referenced by **DIMENSION** or **EQUIVALENCE** came variables with no connection to those two statements. In general, data and necessary-for-operation items were placed at the top of memory (and extending downward), while instructions and constants from the program were placed at the bottom of memory (and extending upward). The top memory location's address was labeled 77777_8, an octal representation of the decimal number $2^{15}-1 = 32,767$. (Recall that octal is base 8. Storage naming conventions were easier to work with using octal than with binary or decimal.) The 32,768th data storage location was, of course, 00000_8.

To stop the machine dead in its tracks, albeit temporarily, a **PAUSE** statement was available; provide **PAUSE** with a numeric parameter, in the form of an unsigned octal fixed-point constant—e.g., **PAUSE 77777**—and this five-digit octal number would appear, clear as day, on the 704 console's storage register's address field—a feature of FORTRAN that Donald Knuth termed an innovation. Depress the START button, and

FORTRAN resumes program execution where it left off. For a slightly different result than **PAUSE**, use its cousin, **STOP**—the machine will halt, but pressing the START button won't bring it back to life. Write a **STOP 77777** statement, and the machine will halt with a 77777_8 displaying in the address field.

In addition to running through the thirty-two statements, the *Manual* also details how to structure arithmetic formulas; recall from the Preliminary Report that arithmetic formulas are simply the modern equivalent of assignment statements like

$$C = A + B(K)$$

where the equals sign means "is to be replaced by."

The Preliminary Report also proposed functions, such as sine and cosine, but did not specify their syntax. The *Manual*, however, offers examples. The name of any function can be between four to seven alphanumeric characters, but the first character must be alphabetic and the last character must be the letter **F**. If the function will always result in a fixed-point value, then an **X** must be the first letter of its name. Here is an example function, taking a single argument, which calculates the sine of the sum of a quantity:

$$SINF(X+Y)$$

And here is another example function, taking two arguments:

$$AFUNF(X, Y)$$

Functions could be arguments of other functions. Take a look at the following line of FORTRAN code, for example:

$$D = AFUNF(SINF(X+Y), B(2))$$

There were fourteen built-in functions—what the *Manual* calls "open subroutines," automatically compiled in the object program—available in FORTRAN: absolute value for fixed- and floating-point values, which found the distance between a number and zero on the number line; truncation for fixed- and floating-point values, which chopped off all digits after the decimal; modular arithmetic, for fixed- and floating-point values, which found the remainder of a quotient; and calculation of the largest or smallest number between two passed fixed- and/or floating-point values. Additional functions could be imported via a "master tape," or simply hardcoded into an object program.

Interestingly, nowhere in the *Manual* are there instructions on how, precisely, to create a new function; all that is shown is how to use functions previously defined. Indeed, there was *no way* to do so during the time that Sayre was writing the *Manual* in 1956. The "function assignment" feature was added a short time before FORTRAN's distribution in early 1957. An *Addenda* to the *Manual* describing function assignment (among a number of other additions, changes, and deletions) was sent in February 1957 to John

Greenstadt, an IBMer who worked in the Applied Science Division responsible for distributing materials to SHARE. Here is how function assignment appeared in the *Addenda*:

> Page 14, line 3. Add paragraph.
>
> <u>Function Statements</u>. A function may also be defined in the source program itself by means of a function statement, and the definition will then persist throughout that one program. Thus it is possible to have the convenience of the function notation even for functions which are not important enough to deserve a place on the master FORTRAN tape.
>
> General Form
> "a=b" where a is a function name followed by parentheses enclosing its arguments (which must be distinct non-subscripted variables) separated by commas, and b is an expression (see next section) which does not involve subscripted variables. Any functions appearing in b must be built-in, or available on the master tape, or already defined by preceding function statements.
>
> Examples
> FIRSTF(X) = A*X+B
> SECONDF(X, B) = A*X+B
> THIRDF(D) = FIRSTF(E)/D
> FOURTHF(F, G) = SECONDF(F, THIRDF(G))
> FIFTHF(I, A) = 3.0*A**I
> SIXTHF(J) = J+K
> XSIXTHF(J) = J+K

There were several more *Addenda* pages explaining function use.

Recall that in addition to detailing functions in the Preliminary Report, expressions (sequences of constants and/or variables combined together by operation symbols and parentheses) were discussed—and, specifically, mixed expressions, or expressions involving a combination of fixed- and floating-point arithmetic. The *Manual* backtracks on the mixed expressions idea, though, restricting expressions to either fixed- or floating-point, but not both, with several exceptions: integers could appear in floating-point expressions as arguments of functions, as subscripts of variables, or as exponents. In an arithmetic formula, if the result of a floating-point expression had to be stored into an integer variable, the floating-point quantity would be truncated, not rounded, before being stored.

The *Manual* makes a slight change with the multiplication character: instead of using × to multiply two quantities (as described in the Preliminary Report), an * (asterisk) must be employed. As expected, a double asterisk denotes exponentiation, as in $X**Y$, although the following form of double exponentiation couldn't be processed by the compiler: $X**Y**Z$. Instead, $X**(Y**Z)$ had to be used. Also note that $J**(Y**Z)$, a mixed expression (since J is a different variable type than Y and Z by design), wouldn't compile. Even a mixed expression in an arithmetic formula like $X=4*Y$ would not compile; the arithmetic formula would have to be rewritten as $X=4.0*Y$ in order to execute properly. Although Backus later acknowledged that ruling out mixed expressions was a "debatable design choice," he said that the team members were "doubtful of the usefulness of the rules in our Report for evaluating mixed expressions"; plus, they wanted to ensure that the programmer was aware of the manner in which the compiler evaluated such expressions, leading them to the inevitable conclusion that the best way to guarantee this awareness "was to ask him to specify" the types (fixed- or floating-point) of quantities outright.

Following through on a promise in the Preliminary Report, enclosing repeated expressions (called "common expressions" in the *Manual*) in parentheses helped to optimize the object program. Thus, an arithmetic formula like this:

$$X=A*B*C*(A*B*C+COSF(A))+SQRTF(A*B+Z*COSF(A))$$

could be rewritten using additional parentheses to avoid any duplicate calculations like this:

$$X=(A*B)*C*((A*B)*C+COSF(A))+SQRTF((A*B)+Z*COSF(A))$$

Thus, since $A*B$ has to be calculated more than once in order to evaluate the entire arithmetic formula above, $A*B$ is enclosed in parentheses: $(A*B)$. Even if no parentheses were used, the compiler optimized the calculation of any arithmetic expression by reordering the terms, thereby minimizing the frequency of memory calls during execution.

There were many size limits that the programmer needed to be cognizant of as he translated a source program into an object program. These size limits were kept track of in over twenty tables, mostly created by Harlan Herrick, that FORTRAN generated to correspond to each source program. For instance, the TDO table kept track of the DO statements: there couldn't be more than 150 of them in a single program. The DIM tables monitored the subscripted variables, while the TRAD table limited the use of certain types of GO TO statements. A series of complicated expressions put limits on the use of arithmetic formulas, too (in the LAMBDA and BETA tables). Violate any table's absolute limits, and the program would halt.

David Sayre's *Programmer's Reference Manual* wrapped up with two example programs: one that spit out the largest number in a single-dimensional array, and the other that scanned a square matrix for a specific type of symmetry. The first program, in particular, is a startling display of efficiency for its time: only twelve lines long (not including two lines of comments), the equivalent program written in Roy Nutt's SAP would have been many, many lines longer. The program's compactness and simplicity drove home FORTRAN's *raison d'etre*: user-friendliness and accessibility in exchange for a small measure of computational speed. Here's how the program works: After dimensioning a one-dimensional array of floating-point values called A (setting space aside for a maximum of 999 elements, subscripted with indexes 1 to 999), the data filling the array is imported via the card reader (using the READ statement). Then, a new floating-point variable, called BIGA, is declared and immediately assigned to the first element of the array A: namely, A(1). Then, a clever loop, which sequentially traverses the array, takes center stage:

```
          DO 20 I = 2, N
          IF (BIGA − A(I)) 10,20,20
10        BIGA = A(I)
20        CONTINUE
```

Thus, if the difference between BIGA and A(I) is less than zero, this implies that the Ith element of the A array is larger than the previously largest element stored in BIGA, thereby transferring control to line 10, where BIGA is assigned the value of this new largest element. Otherwise, the loop iterates until it finally compares the last element of the A array to BIGA. Next, a PRINT statement references a FORMAT statement (complete with Hollerith fields for outputting alphanumeric characters) in order to output the values of N and BIGA with an appropriate description. Suppose, for instance, that the array A contains fifty numbers, with the largest of these being 67.09. Finally, then, the output would show

$$\text{THE LARGEST OF THESE} \quad 50 \quad \text{NUMBERS IS} \quad 67.09$$

and the machine would halt, displaying 77777_8 in the address field of the console.

Although this biggest-value algorithm is easy enough for a first-year computer science major to write in her sleep, don't let its simplicity fool you: what we take for granted now was a revelation then. Consider that the algorithm's simplicity is only visibly obvious *because* the code could be written in a manner that abstracted away most of the particularities of machine and assembly language, if not the overall spirit.

Now that we've examined the (nearly) finished product, we need to backtrack to late 1954 and explore how the development team built the FORTRAN compiler. In order to garner a full appreciation of the team's breakthrough, however, we must first take a brief detour in order to examine one of Roy Nutt's greatest creations: SAP, the Symbolic/SHARE Assembly Program.

CHAPTER 13

◊◊◊

The Symbolic/SHARE Assembly Program

SAP made writing machine language instructions more manageable, but it did little to break the stranglehold of the priesthood: programming still remained the near-exclusive province of computer experts.

In 1953, when Nutt was offered a job by United Aircraft after graduating from Trinity College, he was reticent to show his father, Charles, the first paystub. At $450 a month, quite a tidy sum for the time, his starting salary was sizably more than his father had ever earned at once—Charles, a World War I veteran, had graduated from Harvard with a fine arts degree, but struggled to find work as a professional artist during the Great Depression, instead resorting to industrial and commercial work—but it was enough money for Nutt to put on hold any further academic work, at least for the time being.

Around the same time Nutt was hired by UA, the company secured delivery of the ninth of nineteen 701s that were constructed. He was put to work on the machine, writing mathematical utility functions, adding to the ever-growing UA electronic library of programs available for engineers at the company. Nutt would work odd hours, sometimes toiling through nights, which typically resulted in him missing morning meetings. To counteract that, Stu Crossman, a boss of Nutt's, picked him up at home on the way to work, which resulted in them both arriving late. No good deed goes unpunished.

In addition to expanding UA's programming libraries, Nutt dabbled in Backus's Speedcoding, writing utility tools for the 701 that assisted with program loading, debugging, and a number of hardware-related tasks. "A set of Speedcode input/output routines would bring Nutt to the attention of John Backus at IBM who would put together a team to design a new language," according to Nutt's son Micah, who wrote a biography of his father to mark the 2012 dedication of the Roy Nutt Mathematics, Engineering, & Computer Science Center at Trinity.

Well before he met Backus, though, Nutt was busy at work at UA creating SAP, the Symbolic Assembly Program, expressly written for the 701. SAP was a solo effort, born of a single programmer's need to supplement Speedcoding. Even though Speedcoding offered user-friendly improvements to the 701, writing code in machine language was still the order of the day. SAP turned the unreadable numeric values of machine code into understandable three-letter mnemonics, or symbolic representations of numerical operation codes (opcodes). Using these mnemonics, coupled with the operands of machine code, IBM 701 instructions now presented themselves as easier to read, manage, and program by human beings.

But programming in SAP was nearly the equivalent of programming in native machine language, despite the dressed-up, English-style SAP instructions. In fairness, there were some additional, pseudo-operations (meaning the operations were not native to the machine) that Nutt created for the 701 to increase the programmer's productivity, such as EQU to help manage expressions symbolically. Later, Nutt rewrote the Symbolic Assembly Program for the 704, renaming it the SHARE Assembly Program.

Let us get a sense of how challenging SAP for the 704 was to program in, despite the assembly language abstracting away some of the machine language coding particulars of the machine. The three key operations of any assembly language (or machine language) are the ability to load data, store data, and perform arithmetic. The following example, adapted from the MIT Computation Center's user's manual for the 704, demonstrates all three.

Suppose that memory locations A, B, C, and D in turn store the floating-point numbers a, b, c, and d, respectively. Furthermore, let's say we wished to compute the expression (a/b)(c/d), storing the result in memory location R.

The SAP program, complete with comments, might look something like the generalized code shown below. Recall that AC refers to the 704's accumulator, and MQ references the multiplier-quotient register. Also observe that the comments below have been written in English sentences rather than in symbolic representations like C(A) → C(AC), where the C(Φ) references the contents (C) of either the Φ register or the storage location Φ.

```
CLA    A     CLEAR THE AC, THEN ADD A TO THE AC
FDP    B     FLOATING-POINT DIVISION OF A BY B; STORE
             IN MQ
STQ    R     STORE RESULT OF MQ TO MEMORY LOCATION R
CLA    C     CLEAR THE AC, THEN ADD C TO THE AC
FDP    D     FLOATING-POINT DIVISION OF C BY D; STORE
             IN MQ
FMP    R     FLOATING-POINT MULTIPLICATION OF R BY
             VALUE IN MQ; STORE RESULT IN MQ
STO    R     STORE RESULT OF MQ IN MEMORY LOCATION R
HPR          HALT THE MACHINE, AND PROCEED
```

There's too much inside-baseball knowledge required to perform even the simplest of tasks in SAP; most scientists and mathematicians didn't want to worry about dealing with memory management involving the accumulator and the registers in order to obtain a single computed value from the machine, let alone learn how to program the 704 to perform more complex operations. They had enough to do.

By the way, to perform the effectively equivalent calculation of the above SAP program in FORTRAN, only a single statement—once the variables A, B, C, and D were assigned initial values—was necessary:

$$R = (A/B)*(C/D)$$

Once people came to trust the system, it is obvious why FORTRAN caught on. Backus wasn't the only programmer who was lazy, but he was one of only a few who used that laziness as a springboard to innovation.

Please realize that the SAP program above presents only a *very small* sampling of possible SAP instructions, since each mnemonic had to correspond to a native 704 machine language numeric opcode (notwithstanding pseudo-operations like `EQU`). There were many others, such as the three-letter mnemonics `ADD` (arithmetic addition), `LDQ` (load a word into the MQ), `STQ` (store a word into the MQ), and `CPY` (copy and skip, for I/O operations); logical operations, which operate on the level of individual bits, like `ANS` (AND A, storing the result to a memory location) and `ANA` (AND A, storing the result to the AC); control instructions such as `TIX` (transfer on an index), `TXI` (transfer with an index incremented), `TNX` (transfer on no index), `TRA` (unconditional transfer), and `TZE` (transfer on zero); and bit shifts, which translated binary representations of numbers left or right, effectively equivalent to multiplying or dividing the binary values by a factor of two and then substituting in zeros or ones for any "missing" digits to keep a constant number of digits in the register, like `LLS` (logical left shift) and `ALS` (accumulator left shift). And there were fixed-point arithmetic instructions, indexing operations, and I/O operations. All told, there were well over eighty unique SAP instructions—nearly three times the number of FORTRAN statements (of course, such a comparison is apples to oranges, since SAP very closely corresponded to 704 machine language, whereas FORTRAN mostly did not). Plus, there were many ways to arrange the instructions.

Moreover, the instructions were classified by type. There were five Type A instructions, all of which were of the control variety (`TIX`, `TNX`, and so on); all other instructions were Type B, although there were subclassifications, replete with special properties, to contend with (for instance, the shift instructions and so-called sense-type instructions, like `SLN`, or sense light number, used to turn on a sense light on the front panel of the 704).

The key difference between Type A and Type B instructions was rooted in the way in which they made use of the index registers. Type A instructions divided up the 36-bit words into four fields—a prefix (bits S to 2), decrement (bits 3 to 17), tag (bits 18 to 20), and address (bits 21 to 35)—as diagrammed below.

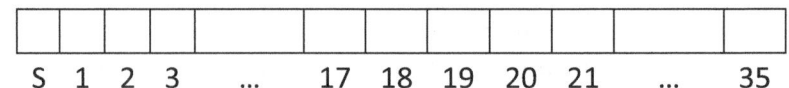

Unlike Type B instructions, Type A instructions employed the 15-bit decrement field for storing constants. Furthermore, in Type A instructions bits 1 and 2 could never both be zero. The tag indicated the index register utilized in tandem with the instruction, while the address field represented a particular memory location (in core storage).

Let's take a moment to understand the purpose of a decrement and a tag. First, in general, a SAP instruction took this form:

<instruction mnemonic> address, index, decrement

Note that, depending on the instruction, some or even all three of the operands might not be used.

Now, suppose we have the following instruction:

```
TXI A,2,100
```

The `TXI` refers to a transfer with the index incremented. Unlike the SAP program listed earlier, in which each instruction had but a single operand—the address—the `TXI` instruction above has three operands: the A represents the address; the 2 refers to the tag; and the `100` is the decrement.

As the authors of the MIT 704 user's manual explain it,

> In the decrement of such an instruction, we can store any integer that could be stored in an address; that is, any of 0,1,2,...; 32767. The decrement is used to change or test the value contained in an index register, and does not normally refer to a storage location.

Most SAP instructions had one or two operands, dispensing with the decrement (which, when omitted, was assumed to be zero). But what of the tag? Essentially, a tag permitted the programmer to modify an address by utilizing at least one of the three index registers. "Every 704 instruction may be tagged," the MIT manual reads, "and by this we mean that it may have appended to it, as a sort of second address, the number of one of the three index registers." The 704's individual index registers A, B, and C were referenced in SAP instructions by the octal (base 8) numbers 1, 2, and 4, respectively. So, for instance, an instruction such as

```
CLA A,4
```

allowed the programmer to kill two birds with one stone: first, the contents of register 4 are subtracted from address A (this is called an effective address modification); only then is the `CLA A` instruction is performed.

Cleverly, the tag permitted more than one index register to be referenced simultaneously. The tag fields translated to the index registers as follows:

Binary	Octal	INDEX REGISTER(S)
000	0	None
001	1	A
010	2	B
100	4	C
011	3	A OR B
101	5	A OR C
110	6	B OR C
111	7	A OR B OR C

When multiple registers were referenced this way, the binary quantities present in the registers were operated on by a logical OR—that is, when operating at the level of the individual bit positions, all 0's = 0; at least one 1 = 1—resulting in a single binary number.

That covers Type A instructions. Now let's examine Type B instructions, which divide up 36-bit words as follows:

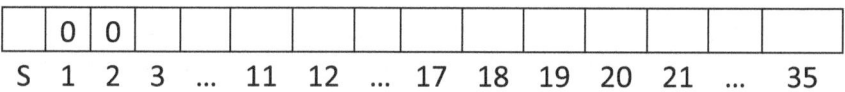

Although the tag and address fields work the same way for Type A and Type B instructions, bits 1 and 2 must each be set to zero for any Type B instruction. In addition, the address field was much smaller for Type B: although bits 21 to 35 still represented an address, bits 21 to 27 were ignored. Bits 12 to 17 weren't used in Type B instructions, either. Taken together, the sign position (bit S) and the decrement field (bits 1 to 11) correspond to the opcode, or the 704 machine language equivalent for the mnemonic in SAP. For example, the mnemonic ALS translated to 000 111 110 111 in binary; if the first twelve bits of the 36-bit word were 000 111 110 111, then the opcode signaled to the 704 to prepare the accumulator for a left shift of the bits contained therein. The machine language code could also present in octal; the ALS instruction equated to +0767 in base 8.

And it gets even more complicated. Some instructions were "non-indexable," while others were deemed "indexable"; these classifications cut across Type A and B lines. Any mnemonics with an X—like TIX and SXD (store index in decrement)—were non-indexable, used to test and alter the contents of the register in the tag field. Instructions that were indexable were readily identified by the presence of at least one zero in bit positions 8 and 9. Any instructions with an X or a Q in the mnemonic invariably referred to the MQ register, and thus cut across Type A and B lines, too.

✧✧✧

Bob Hughes, an outside contractor who helped the development team build FORTRAN, ran into a problem with the MQ register when working on a 704. One night, while running a Monte Carlo simulation for a physics problem, he was given free rein on the machine: midnight to five o'clock in the morning. After submitting his program, he received a call from the engineers: the program had stopped mid-execution. Investigating, Hughes found that *both* the green "Run" light and the red "Stop" lights were lit: "This implied that the machine was both running and stopped at the same time," he said. But his program was running just fine, and producing results as he expected, so he let it be. That decision proved to cause him trouble.

> I was called the next morning about 7 o'clock by a vice-president from IBM saying, "We have a problem here with your usage." I don't know how much they were charging me an hour maybe $100 or $200 an hour. But, anyway, I had used about $6000 for computer time. And they were wondering why this program showed it was hung from 3:00 AM and now who was going to pay for this three or four hours of computer time? I said, "Well my program worked. What's the problem?" They said, "We don't know yet, our engineers are working on it." It turned out that a problem in the IBM 704 logic design, under certain conditions, if they failed to clear the MQ (multiply-quotient) register, the accumulator got bad data. If the MQ is not cleared, then you would end up with the machine stopping, and the red light on saying "I'm stopped" and green light on saying, "I'm running."

So, Hughes challenged the vice president: "Have you been able to find anyplace in your documentation where it says that MQ has to be cleared?" The vice presented admitted he hadn't. And Hughes wasn't charged a dime.

As a reminder of how resistant to change the programmers of the time were, even though they recognized the obvious benefits of abstracting away some of their work, consider: despite the widespread distribution of SAP, "most programmers continued their heroic absolute binary programming," according to Richard Hamming.

> At the time SAP first appeared I would guess about 1% of the older programmers were interested in it—using SAP was "sissy stuff", and a real programmer would not stoop to wasting machine capacity to do the assembly. Yes! Programmers wanted no part of it, though when pressed they had to admit their old methods used more machine time in locating and fixing up errors than the SAP program ever used.

So why were programmers reluctant to use SAP? Because they were very uncomfortable with not knowing the locations of items in storage when using a symbolic system.

Before we continue get bogged down in even more historical and technical details about SAP and the IBM 704—and, to be sure, there are many, many more details—let's shift our focus back to the development of the FORTRAN compiler.

CHAPTER 14

◊◊◊

Building the First FORTRAN Compiler

In late 1954, with the language specs set and the development team fully assembled, there was only one small thing left to do: write a compiler that would set the standard for the next twenty years.

In order to successfully write a FORTRAN program, the programmer not only needed to keep the end goal in his sights, but he also needed to be able to explicitly describe *how* the computer could get there. That the step-by-step instructions could not be abstracted away (though FORTRAN certainly abstracted away the machine and assembly code) made FORTRAN the prototypical example of an HLL that conformed to what would later be termed an *imperative programming* paradigm: precisely instructing the computer in how to complete a task, thereby changing the state of the computer in the process. Even though the language was built for mathematicians and scientists, not for a privileged priesthood of computer experts, FORTRAN statements and structures couldn't help but mimic the functionality of the hardware—whether with the most low-level, machine-dependent commands, or with high-level subroutines, such as loops—since whether the programmer was pasting the ends of paper tape together to implement a loop (as Backus did when operating the SSEC) or looping through code via assembly commands or FORTRAN, loops were loops: a means of human beings adapting to the idiosyncratic manner in which computers processed information, rather than the other way around. The same went for conditional statements. To successfully communicate with the machine, the programmer had to meet the computer more than halfway.

So, to summarize, when a programmer writes code using an imperative paradigm like FORTRAN, the focus is on the how, rather than on the what. Most of the HLLs that proliferated in the decades after FORTRAN's birth would copy FORTRAN's imperative structure. When a programmer engages in *declarative programming*, on the other hand, the imperative parts—the how-to steps—are themselves treated as an abstraction layer, while the end-goal of the exercise assumes center stage. If you go to a restaurant to order dinner, you don't deliver a recipe to the chef (well, presumably you don't); instead, you ask the waiter to bring you the meal. The recipe has been abstracted away. Likewise, a declarative language permits the programmer to focus on the what, rather than the how. Implementing a declarative paradigm was well beyond the scope of the development team, despite the fact that someone had already successfully done it: in the mid-1950s, Edward K. Blum, working at the U.S. Naval Ordinance Laboratory, developed the Automatic Digital Encoding System (ADES); the language was programmed using Polish notation (i.e., sans parentheses). Rather, the goal of Backus's team was to translate the proposals set forth in the Preliminary Report into an imperative operational language, where the programmer had to specify the explicit operations and relationships between the variables.

"We did not regard language design as a difficult problem, merely a simple prelude to the real problem: designing a compiler which could produce efficient programs," said Backus. "We didn't know what we wanted and how to do it. It just sort of grew." In a paper written nearly a decade after FORTRAN's release, Backus retrospectively fingered the development team's key consideration prior to writing the language: "[E]xtreme emphasis [was] not on orderly and quick translation techniques, nor on elaborate source language features, but rather on the efficiency of the object programs themselves." Efficiency was king.

Backus hadn't built a compiler before, but he had programmed an interpreter: Speedcoding. The major problem with an interpreted language like Speedcoding was, rather ironically, speed: any source program written in an interpreted language could only run while the interpreter was running as well, bogging down the computer by hogging valuable resources. A compiler offered a solution to these problems: it would translate source code into a computer's native machine language, producing a standalone executable program able to run independently of the compiler that generated it. Plus, a compiled program didn't take up as much memory as an equivalent interpreted program and typically ran much faster to boot.

In early 1955, when the team starting building their FORTRAN compiler—or, as they usually referred to it back then, their "translator" or "executive routine"—in earnest, much so-called trial programming (early testing) had already begun by the fall of 1954. Harlan Herrick had tested the language, running the first FORTRAN program in September of that year, despite lacking a functional compiler. Backus and Irving Ziller had sketched out how to translate arithmetic expressions into machine code. The team had even mapped out the machine language routines that would be generated when the compiler encountered FORTRAN statements.

Up front, they knew that their compiler would run through the object program source code only once. Indeed, their FORTRAN compiler can be considered a *one-pass* or *single-pass compiler*, since it traversed the source code only a single time. (Backus himself called it "one pass"; a technical paper the development team published called it "single scan.") In the modern sense of the term, a single-pass compiler contrasts with a *multi-pass compiler*, which typically breaks up the compilation work into several passes through the source code. Generally, a single-pass compiler is faster than a multi-pass compiler and uses less memory, but may not produce as optimized machine code.

They divided work on the compiler into six sections. Tackling all six necessitated the team splitting up into semi-autonomous groups of one to three people each, with each group focusing their attention on one section of the compiler. As Bob Hughes remembered it, "Each person was assigned to a major section of the compiler and each person had his own set of tables to work with. And I would put the pieces together and then, somewhere along the line, there was what we call a 'Semantics Synthesizer,' where it all comes together into a machine language code that would run on the machine."

As the groups found their footing, common I/O specifications were established as well. "I think history has shown that we divided up the problem pretty much right because a lot of people have kind of followed that same pattern in general," Backus later said. "We started to do it as one unit and then we saw that, uh oh, that isn't going to work, so we had to subdivide the problem into two things, and then that kind of went on like that. It was a pretty natural process." When considering the team's circuitous path to a functional compiler, one is reminded of Hermann von Helmholtz's description of a "royal road" in *On Thought in Medicine* (1938):

> I am fain to compare myself with a wanderer on the mountains who, not knowing the path, climbs slowly and painfully upwards and often has to retrace his steps because he can go no further—then, whether by taking thought or from luck, discovers a new track that leads him on a little till at length when he reaches the summit he finds to his shame that there is a royal road by which he might have ascended, had he only the wits to find the right approach to it.

February 1954 found the team beginning their ascent, hard at work on sections 1 and 2. Harlan Herrick, Roy Nutt, and Peter Sheridan devoted their time to solving the problems presented in section 1: namely, having the compiler run through the entire source program once, translating any instructions immediately recognizable, and then organizing everything else from the source program into the tables that Herrick created (e.g., the TDO table, which kept track of the frequency of DO statements). Output instructions would be produced for arithmetic formulas, but nonarithmetic statements would receive the partial compilation treatment, where noncompiled portions were transferred to the aforementioned tables; hence the "one pass" of the FORTRAN compiler: a single scan through the source code, translating some of the instructions but transferring other information to tables.

Bob Hughes, who joined the team on loan from the Lawrence Livermore National Laboratory (LLNL), a nuclear research and weapons design facility near San Francisco, explained how much the compiler relied on Herrick's tables, especially initially:

> FORTRAN was a table-driven scheme.... TEIFNO was a typical table of IF and GOTO entries. "TEIFNO" stood for the Table of External Form of the IF Number versus its internal form. There were also "close-up" tables to close everything when finished. There were just tables, tables, tables. Later on, they discovered that the way to compile really fast was to collect everything and assemble it in a single symbol table. But, in those days, we were still learning how to walk and so, initially, it was a table-driven scheme.

Livermore Labs had been at the cutting edge of computing throughout the 1950s, procuring a UNIVAC I, an IBM CPC, an IBM 701, and two IBM 650s, all before Backus's team began developing FORTRAN. Livermore was interested in FORTRAN right away, which is why Hughes' supervisor, Sidney Fernbach, sent Hughes on an information-gathering mission to IBM to help with the development of FORTRAN. "In those early days," Hughes recalled, "[Livermore Labs] was one of the few organizations that used computers and was aware of the Fortran project."

A file called "COMPAIL" housed all instructions resulting from compilation in this first section; such compiled instructions were comprised of the generalized SAP four-part form:

<instruction mnemonic> address, index, decrement

As the compiler generated each successive machine language instruction, the correct order of these instructions was preserved through a process of automatic sequential numbering.

Nutt handled the I/O in section 1, sorting source code into two types: instructions that could be compiled easily, and those that had to be filed away to be dealt with later in section 6 (the assembler). The I/O instructions translating to read or write select—RDS or WRS in SAP—could be easily evaluated; likewise, the copy instructions, or CPY, and instructions that would convert between decimal and binary. He then turned what Backus called "lists of quantities," or repetitive I/O statements, into table entries indexed via nested DO loops—something the compiler could also handle with relative ease.

Peter Sheridan certainly had his work cut out for him in section 1, having to write the code for translating the arithmetic expressions of the source programs into assembly code. Solving the problem required accounting for many things we take for granted when evaluating mathematical expressions, as the development team explained in a technical paper:

> The difficulty in carrying out [the translation of an arithmetic formula] is one of *level*; there is implicit in every arithmetic formula an order of computation [i.e., PEMDAS, the order of operations], which arises from the control over ordering assigned by convention to the various symbols (parentheses, +, –, *, /, etc.) which can appear, and this implicit ordering must be made explicit before compilation of the instructions can be done.

Sheridan would transform these implicit computations into explicit ones, courtesy of assigning each arithmetic operation a "level number," or an explicit ordering of arithmetic instructions. He explained this byzantine process of "level analysis," replete with isomorphisms, that he utilized in a dense 1959 paper called "The Arithmetic Translator-Compiler of the IBM FORTRAN Automatic Coding System." A somewhat simplified version of level analysis is relayed below.

Sheridan turned each algorithmic formula into a set of "triples": (1) the operation to be performed; (2) the operand; and (3) the "time" at which the operation must be performed, called a "*C*-number." The number of "times" was dependent upon the number of subexpressions within each expression, where subexpressions would be designated by being enclosed in parentheses. Sheridan proffers this example arithmetic expression:

$$(((A + B) - C)/((D * (E + F)/G) - H + J))$$

Since there are six distinct pairs of parentheses, there are six distinct subexpressions that must be evaluated, he writes. A possible valid order for the evaluation of these subexpressions is shown below.

1. $(A + B)$
2. $((A + B) - C)$
3. $(E + F)$
4. $(D * (E + F)/G)$
5. $(D * (E + F)/G) - H + J$
6. $(((A + B) - C)/((D * (E + F)/G) - H + J))$

"The triples representing this computation would break up into six subsets, called *segments* according to their *C*-number (first member of a triple)," Sheridan explains. "In each segment (corresponding to a subexpression) there are as many triples as there are terms in the subexpression." So, in triples notation (with the numbers itemizing the subexpressions above doubling as names for the subexpressions—e.g., "1" represents the quantity A + B), he offers the following conversion of the steps of evaluation:

(1, +, A)(1, +, B)(2, +, 1)(2, –, C)
(3, +, E)(3, +, F)(4, *, D)
(4, *, 3)(4, /, G)(5, +, 4)(5, –, H)
(5, +, J)(6, *, 2)(6, /, 5)

Given that division is the equivalent of multiplication by the inverse (e.g., six divided by three is the same as six multiplied by one-third), some reordering of the triples was possible, thus permitting the greatest possible level of arithmetic optimization.

Sheridan had the compiler rewrite the steps of the evaluation of arithmetic subexpressions in reverse numerical order, where the largest segment number would represent the first subexpression to be evaluated (in the example above: number 1, the quantity A + B) whereas the smallest segment number would represent the last subexpression—namely, the entire expression (in the example above: number 6, the original arithmetic expression). Then, the compiler would generate the triples off of the subexpressions. Next, to keep things as uniform as possible, simple variables would be inserted to replace constants and subscripted variables. Then parentheses would be automatically added to every subexpression, making sure that the order of operations—i.e., PEMDAS—was followed to the letter. Three sets of parentheses were added around low priority operations, such as addition and subtraction; two sets were added around medium priority operations; and only one set of parentheses was added around high priority operations, such as exponentiation. So, for instance, the expression

$$A + B ** C/D$$

with parentheses added by the compiler would now read as

$$(((A))) + (((B) ** (C))/((D)))$$

Notice that the plus sign is surrounded by three sets of parentheses:))) + (((. Notice also that the division sign is surrounded by two sets of parentheses, while the exponentiation is surrounded by only one set.

Beyond the operations specified by PEMDAS, another level of precedence was considered: that of the comma character (,). The comma, of course, separates the arguments of FORTRAN functions such as the following:

$$AFUNF(X, Y)$$

In addition to additional sets of parentheses, operation signs which "tagged" the parentheses with its "strength"—for instance, like this: $+(*(**(A)))$—resulted in what were termed "normal form arithmetic expressions," ready for the compiler to chop up into triples.

Once the triples were generated, extraneous triples were purged via sorting and other techniques, saving memory and compilation time later on. The remaining triples were rearranged in a manner designed to optimize the number of times the computer would have to either retrieve a value from memory storage to copy into a register, or vice versa, when evaluating the arithmetic expressions. Next, the triples were turned into a string of triples, and were tidied up as much as possible, before the compiler converted the string into SAP code via a complex series of search-and-replace methods that relied on lists of possible forms. ("In today's terminology, this optimization was equivalent to applying, at the expression level, *copy propagation* followed by *dead-code elimination*," explained David Padua in an article for *Computing in Science & Engineering*.) Sheridan's method of processing arithmetic expressions was so powerful that he extended it to handle Boolean expressions as well.

Boolean expressions were the brainchild of George Boole, born in England in 1815 and rising to prominence in the mid-nineteenth century as a mathematics professor in Ireland. In his most famous work, *Laws of Thought* (1854), Boole systematized logic using mathematics, rather than natural language, even believing that his methods could shed some light into how the human brain functioned. Boolean algebra can be effectively pared down to two operands: 0 (off/false) and 1 (on/true) along with the operations AND, OR, and NOT. Although George Boole didn't predict the rise of computers, the mathematics he discovered came to fit digital computing hand in glove.

Sheridan realized that by treating + as union (AND), * as intersection (OR), and − as complementation (NOT/inverse), he could have the compiler to translate Boolean sentences to SAP code, which already had a grab-bag of logical instructions available, instead of arithmetic ones.

Late in the process, R. J. Beeber and Harold Stern helped the team complete section 1, but the bulk of the work was done by Herrick, Nutt, and Sheridan. Despite their successes, Backus later reflected that "the first struggle was over what the language would look like. Then how to parse expressions—it was a big problem and what we did looks astonishingly clumsy now...." (For a compiler to *parse* a source code statement, it must successfully decompose and translate the statement into object code.)

The challenges of successfully implementing section 2 were correspondingly enormous. After scanning through the entire source code and dumping information about subscripted variables into detailed tables back in section 1, the purpose of section 2 was to generate optimal machine code for the **DO** statements and subscripted variable references (which could be manipulated by **DO** statements as well as in arithmetic formulas like **J = M + 2**) documented in those tables. Each instruction which referenced a *unique* combination of subscripted variables was tagged with a symbolic index register—in essence, a fingerprint, temporarily employed until section 5. For example, the subscript combination **(I, J)** was given a different symbolic index register, a different fingerprint, than the subscript combination **(J, I)**. Section 2 had to monitor and test, line by line, precisely what contents were contained in each of the symbolic index registers as the subscripts underwent various manipulations within the source program itself. No easy task, since a change in one subscript could have a domino effect, altering the values of variables and arithmetic formulas in a number of other locations throughout the program.

The trick in section 2 was for the compiler to avoid behind-the-scenes subscript multiplication in favor of how hand-coded (i.e., machine or assembly) programs did it: by adding constants to the addresses themselves, which required the compiler to recognize when the source code itself was changing the subscripts in a linear manner. Despite the simplification, implementing this scheme was still terribly complex, since the compiler had to differentiate between when existing addresses could be incremented versus when entirely new address calculations had to be created.

So the development team drastically pared down the possibilities: rather than having the compiler analyze the source code for *any* instance of linear changes of the subscripts, only subscripts controlled by **DO** loops were considered: "every time one of the variables in a subscript combination is incremented under the control of a **DO**, the corresponding quantity is incremented by the appropriate amount," explained the development team. In other words, the **DO** loop's purpose was to block code in which the values of addresses of variables that needed changing were recalculated, typically by using address-incrementing techniques; references to arrays outside of **DO** loops would usually be found by calculating new addresses.

The team also had to be cognizant of nested **DO**s, or **DO** loops contained within other **DO** loops; inside a nest of **DO** loops, each **DO** was assigned a level number, as if the nest were one of Peter Sheridan's arithmetic expressions. From there, the level numbers of each subscripted variable were examined, resulting in a "group number," which set the order of compilation. In order to optimize the object program, as much of the code as possible was tied to the outermost **DO** loops (lowest level numbers), rather than the inner ones (highest level numbers).

True, by only considering **DO** loops, the number of search possibilities for optimization had now likely shrunk considerably, but the compiler still had to wade through a great number of them; worse yet, with each additional subscript in an array, the permutations grew exponentially. Thus, to keep the number of permutations under control, three subscripts per subscripted variable—e.g., A(I, J, K)—was the decided limit. That the IBM 704 had three index registers was a coincidence that had nothing to do with the development team's decision to go with a maximum of three subscripts.

There were several other restrictions that resulted from the team's newfound experience with looping structures. They decided that control could never be transferred from outside a DO statement directly into a block of statements within a DO. Furthermore, index variables of DO statements were only permitted to change by a constant amount—and it could only be a positive increment due to hardware restrictions. Finally, only linear expressions were allowed as index variable subscripts.

The development team couldn't just ignore subscripts that weren't associated with DO statements, however; they had to be accounted for as well. To that end, mini-subroutines were "generated at executive time," explained the development team, to efficiently handle these non-DO instances: the "computational paths" needed to be worked backwards, noting which such paths had constant changes to subscript quantities and could thus be accounted for by simply incrementing existing addresses. Also, so-called mixed cases, or situations in which single FORTRAN statements contained some, but not all, subscripts controlled by DO loops, were processed by taking a "snapshot" of the initial values of the subscripts before the outermost loop commenced. (David Padua, a professor of computer science at the University of Illinois, wrote that "[t]oday's compilers apply *removal of loop invariants, induction-variable detection, and strength reduction* to accomplish similar results" when dealing with loops and arrays.)

Once all of the compiling decisions were made, the instructions generated from the compilation in section 2 were stored in a file called "COMPDO." The machine code in the COMPDO file was so clean, so efficient, so optimal, that "its output would startle the programmers who studied it," remembered Backus.

> It moved code out of loops where that was possible; it took advantage of the differences between rowwise and columnwise scans; it took note of special cases to optimize even the exits from loops. The degree of optimization performed by section 2 in its treatment of indexing, array references, and loops was not equaled again until optimizing compilers began to appear in the middle and late 1960s.

Frances Allen, longtime employee of IBM and one of those programmers who studied FORTRAN, was indeed "startled"—she used that exact word in describing her reaction to the assembly language translation of a simple FORTRAN program that copied the contents of array B to array A. Take a look at the source code of the program:

```
        DIMENSION A(10, 10)
        DIMENSION B(10, 10)
        ...
        DO 1 J = 1, 10
        DO 1 I = 1, 10
    1   A(1, J) = B(I, J)
        ...
```

The program snippet above clearly has two loops: one loop within another. But now examine the FORTRAN compiler's translation of it into assembly:

```
        LXD  ONE,1
LOOP    CLA  B+1,1
        STO  A+1,1
        TXI  *+1,1,1
        TXL  LOOP,1,100
        ...
ONE          ,,1
A       BES  100
B       BES  100
```

There is only *one* corresponding LOOP instruction (to the left of the CLA mnemonic), not two, as in the source code. The other embedded LOOP is an operand of the TXL mnemonic (which refers to a conditional transfer instruction). To those not expecting this level of optimization, it was nothing short of startling. Some observers dismissively thought the translation was incorrect. (In terms of compiler design, Frances Allen, along with John Cocke, would eventually surpass the levels of optimization achieved in section 2 of the FORTRAN compiler—but they would take a decade to manage the feat.)

Section 2 was the responsibility of Robert Nelson and Irv Ziller, who developed and programmed the optimization techniques all on their own, with a notable exception. Although they wanted to factor the 704's three index registers into their optimization plan as well, they found the hurdle too high to overcome. So, Backus offered a suggestion: Why not write a program that assumed an *infinite* number of index registers? From there, using a Monte Carlo simulation, the source code would "execute," and the simulation would tally the frequency of transfers between the infinite registers during runtime. Then, leaning on that frequency distribution, the compiler would ensure that the actual 704 register assignments were as logical and optimal as possible. Thus, the symbolic registers—what Backus called a "mythical 704" with an "unlimited number of index registers"—would be transformed into real ones.

The modern form of Monte Carlo simulation, a mathematical technique utilizing repeated random sampling, was developed in the late 1940s by the mathematician Stanislaw Ulam; he intended the name "Monte Carlo" to bring to mind random numbers and "the element of chance." The probabilistic idea came into being during a long car ride. Ulam and John von Neumann were in the car, chatting incessantly throughout a trip between Los Alamos and Lamy, New Mexico. "Johnny saw at once its great scope even though in the first hour of our discussion he evinced a great skepticism," said Ulam. (Recall that von Neumann was initially skeptical of Backus's FORTRAN proposal as well.) "But when I became more persuasive, quoting statistical estimates of how many computations were needed to obtain rough results with this or that probability, he agreed, eventually becoming quite inventive in finding marvelous technical tricks to facilitate or speed up these techniques."

At the time of their conversation, though, computers were still what Ulam called *statu nascendi*, or in a nascent state. So, wrapped in a culturally offensive joke, Ulam offered the following suggestion to turn Monte Carlo into manual labor:

> As a joke I proposed to make Monte Carlo calculations by hiring several hundred Chinese from Taiwan and gather them on a boat, have each one sit with an abacus, or even just pencil and paper, and make them produce the random numbers by some actual physical process like throwing dice. Then someone would collect the results, and total the statistics into single answers.

Ten years removed from Ulam's flippant suggestion, computers were ready to tackle Monte Carlo calculations with ease by using "tricks" to internally generate pseudorandom numbers (such as with von Neumann's *middle-square method*)—and the development team leveraged the 704's power to do so.

Recall that Backus said of the FORTRAN compiler, "We didn't know what we wanted and how to do it. It just sort of grew." This was never more apparent than after his Monte Carlo compile-time suggestion, which spawned sections 4 and 5. Section 3 would come later, after 4 and 5 were finalized; it was designed to convert the output of the first two sections to a digestible form for sections 4 and 5.

Therefore, next up was section 4, and Lois Haibt took the reins. Section 4 processed information about the source code that was generated by sections 1 and 2 and turned the data into "basic blocks" ("a basic block is a stretch of program which has a single entry point and a single exit point") that would be run through a Monte Carlo simulation for frequency analysis, tallying the times each particular block was used. This section would permit the compiler a wide-scope view of the object program, capturing its ebb and flow. In addition, any **FREQUENCY** statements in the source code were employed in section 4 for additional optimization tweaks. The development team detailed the techniques germane to the section as follows:

> The fundamental unit of [a] program is the basic block; a basic block is a stretch of program which has one entry point and one exit point. The purpose of section 4 is to prepare for section 5 a table of predecessors (PRED table) which enumerates the basic blocks and lists for every basic block each of the basic blocks which can be its immediate predecessor in flow, together with the absolute frequency of each such basic block link. This table is obtained by running the program once in Monte-Carlo fashion, in which the outcome of conditional transfers arising out of **IF**-type statements and computed **GO TO**'s is determined by a random number generator suitably weighted according to whatever **FREQUENCY** statements have been provided.

Section 5, which performed a "tag analysis"—drastically reducing the number of symbolic index registers from a simulated infinite quantity to the three actual registers installed in the 704 by using information obtained via the "flow analysis" (later called a *control-flow graph*) of section 4—was programmed by Sheldon Best; recall that he was a temporary IBM employee on loan from MIT. Section 5 was split into four parts. Part 1, the most important, makes the decisions about the index registers, recording these decisions in two tables: the PRED table and the STAG table, with the tagged instructions. Part 2 organized these tables, part 3 added some flourishes to segments of code terminated by GO TOs, and part 4 compiled the program in accordance with the directions in the PRED and STAG tables.

Part 1 also assigned an index cell (a storage cell) for every symbolic index register; from there, through a complex series of actions involving simulation of the source program, among other techniques—while simultaneously loading index register from index cell instructions, or LXDs, and storing index register from index cell instructions, or SXDs—all the basic blocks were accounted for in as little computing time as possible.

Among the six sections of the compiler, section 5 was perhaps the best-written (in both senses of the term). Backus, humbled and delighted by what Best had achieved, called it "very difficult to improve." Best's "replacement policy" in his code bore much resemblance to that of Hungarian computer scientist Laszlo A. Belady's OPT (MIN) Page Replacement algorithm (commonly called Belady's algorithm), a type of caching/replacement routine that discards information based on least-likely use into the future. Belady arrived at IBM at a fortuitous time, briefly interacting with the FORTRAN team. "IBM hired me into their brand-new, but empty, Yorktown research facility as a 'building filler,'" he said. "I was lucky to land among an incredibly smart group, John Backus' people, who just finished their work on Fortran and its compilers."

Although not mathematically optimal (unlike Belady's algorithm, which was proved to be so in 1965), in real-world use Best's approach proved itself to be practically airtight. For that reason, Backus called section 5 the most influential part of the entire FORTRAN compiler—since other non-FORTRAN compilers would steal from, but never quite equal, the register allocation algorithm programmed by Best. (It would be decades before a new approach of assigning registers, using a graph coloring algorithm, would prove to be a more effective approach.)

Sheldon Best successfully managed to get the index register problem under control, but he wouldn't be able to stay at IBM forever. "He would do a flow chart that started out on a piece of paper, and he would just add to it, he just kept gluing pieces of paper together into this whole enormous flow chart," Backus recalled. He devised "some very beautiful but complex methods for optimizing the use of index registers…." Once the Monte Carlo phase was completed, Best's section involved a "complicated treatment, in order of frequency, which assigned index registers to index quantities within larger and larger 'regions' of the program," Backus later wrote. There were tradeoffs to this approach, however; because the development team was so focused on writing a translator that would eliminate inefficiencies in the resultant object programs, the compilation time was greatly increased—oftentimes for frivolous reasons. For example, the "region formation" portion of the translation, at least at first, began spitting out object code with index quantities nowhere to be found. Which would have been acceptable, if not for the fact that this "region formation" took up nearly half of the compile time but didn't affect the object program in the slightest. Backus said, "When [Sheldon Best] went back to MIT, it took [us] months to figure out what it all meant and how it worked." Best left IBM in late 1956, well before debugging of the compiler was complete.

There is a postscript to the team's Monte Carlo work. Bob Hughes had experience writing a Monte Carlo simulation for a physics problem on the IBM 701 at Livermore—it was one of his first assignments after being hired by the lab. Yet, strangely, when on the development team he was only tasked with writing FORTRAN documentation. He could have contributed much more to the development effort.

By the end of 1955, the team realized they had a new problem: the compiler had no means in which to translate the output generated by sections 1 and 2 into a form understandable by sections 4 and 5. Enter Richard Goldberg, who took charge of completing section 3, which would serve as a bridge between the sections by merging the COMPAIL file (from section 1) and the COMPDO file (from section 2); section 3 would also compile the uncompiled nonarithmetic statements of section 1, which had been trapped in Harlan Herrick's tables. After Sheldon Best returned to MIT, Goldberg, along with David Sayre, took over section 5 during the debugging phase—after spending much time studying and diagramming what Best had done.

Roy Nutt was placed in charge of section 6—the "backend"—which assembled a relocatable binary program of the source code into 704 machine language, making sure to include appropriate library programs (such as those for I/O). Nutt had modified SAP for this last section, supercharging it by "[t]aking advantage of the special features of the programs it assembled," Backus wrote; with this optimization in play, section 6 performed its magic ten times as quickly as SAP could alone. Unsurprisingly, Nutt also gave the user the option to turn the source code into SAP, which was output on tape. The appeal of FORTRAN source code translated into SAP was simple: if a programmer needed to optimize portions of the source code beyond what the compiler could muster, or simply wanted to get lost in the weeds of assembly language instructions, he had that option. (SAP code was so appealing that IBM employee Geoffrey Gordon used it several years later to write another 704-exclusive language called GPSS, or General Purpose Simulation System, for simulation studies.)

Nutt took some of the compiler—specifically, sections 1, 2, 3, and 6—back to his employer, United Aircraft, thus allowing the FORTRAN compiler (or at least an algebraic subsystem of it) to undergo a primitive sort of alpha test. In 1957, UA received the full version of FORTRAN.

The spring of 1956 to early 1957 found the development team frantically debugging the compiler, readying FORTRAN for its close-up. They would sometimes decamp and sequester themselves to sleep during the day at the Langdon Hotel on 56th Street so they could debug at the IBM headquarters annex on 57th Street mostly uninterrupted during the nightshift. As the days and nights passed, the robustness of their creation became more and more apparent. Though the development team could usually explain the compiler's decision-making after the fact, the compiler optimized object programs in nonobvious and novel ways that the team found quite surprising. Occasionally an object program would confound even its creators, containing a "large number of instructions which are not attributable to any particular statement in the original FORTRAN program," including even control statements like **GO TO**, **IF**, and **DO**. For instance, sometimes a **DO** statement would translate to many associated machine language instructions; yet other times, amazingly, it would lead to none at all. The FORTRAN system had truly taken on a life of its own.

◊◊◊

Two and a half years had passed since Backus was given the go-ahead to assemble the FORTRAN team. Backus later estimated that the entire compiler was 30,000 instructions in length—as compact as they could possibly make it at the time. In reality, the compiler was more like 24,000 instructions: section 1 had 5,500 instructions, section 2 had 6,000, section 3 contained 2,500, section 4 had 3,000, section 5 contained 5,000, and section 6 had 2,000. To put these numbers into perspective, modern compilers are bigger, in terms of the number of instructions, by at least a hundredfold. "Well, people were writing these things [instructions] one by one," he remembered. It took a total of eighteen man-years to complete. After all, "[y]ou didn't have these programs that could slosh out thousands of instructions from one little piece of writing." Those programs would come much later.

In a year 2000 issue of the journal *Computing in Science & Engineering*, author David Padua ranked the "Fortran I translator [as] the 20th century's top compiler algorithm." Moreover, he claimed, the consequences of the breakthrough were far-reaching.

> [I]t is almost universally agreed that the most important event of the 20th century in compiling—and computing—was the development of the first Fortran compiler between 1954 and 1957. By demonstrating that it is possible to automatically generate quality machine code from high-level descriptions, the IBM team led by John Backus opened the door to the Information Age.

The basic blocks of section 4 and the symbolic-to-real register assignments of section 5 are still ideas that enjoy currency in compiler design today.

The novelist Richard Powers observed, "[H]istory is the long process of outsourcing human ability in order to leverage more of it." FORTRAN outsourced many of the considerations of coding with an assembler to a world-class compiler, opening up the field of programming to individuals beyond a cloistered priesthood. With that opening, though, came a whole new set of unintended consequences.

CHAPTER 15

◊◊◊

FORTRAN I, Accidently Distributed

After David Sayre wrote the *Programmer's Reference Manual* (and also after the *Addenda* to the *Manual* was distributed), the development team penned a technical paper about the compiler. FORTRAN was almost already ready for prime time, but there were still a few bugs to iron out.

The FORTRAN system was formally presented to the public at the Western Joint Computer Conference on February 26 to 28, 1957, in Los Angeles, California. The development team hurriedly debugged at night, this time on a 704 at North American Aviation, right up until the final hour. The theme of the conference was "techniques for reliability"; the technical paper, entitled "The FORTRAN Automatic Coding System," was presented by the development team. Included in its pages were example programs, such as for computing the quadratic formula and multiplying matrices, as well as detailed descriptions of how, precisely, each section of the translator (compiler) performed its magic.

The development team boasted about FORTRAN's user-friendliness, telling the story of a programmer, unfamiliar with the new language, who had a "rather simple but sizable job" that required completion. After attending a single-day course in FORTRAN, and repeatedly referring to the *Manual*, he managed to squeeze out a full program in a scant four hours, start to finish. His program contained forty-seven statements, and when he fed the source deck into the hopper for translation, six minutes later the IBM 704 spit out a binary deck of around one thousand machine language instructions (or a binary tape; although it wasn't specified in this example, punched cards were the more likely output since this was still early in the life of the 704. The team warns readers in the technical paper that "[s]ome of these outputs may be unavailable at the time of publication"). But when he ran the program, the output wasn't what he expected, so he carefully pored through the source program, discovering a single statement that was causing all the grief. Recompiling the source deck and then rerunning the program resolved the issue. "[I]t might have taken three days to code this job by hand," he relayed to the development team, "plus an unknown [amount of] time to debug it." Hence, forgoing FORTRAN in favor of SAP to land gains in execution speed on the 704 would likely have been offset by losses in time spent (1) writing the program on such a low level and (2) debugging much longer, harder-to-parse source code. FORTRAN was easier to use and, when all was said and done, almost as fast as SAP.

Recall that the Preliminary Report had a sentence which began as follows: "Since FORTRAN should virtually eliminate coding and debugging...." True, the FORTRAN translator would flag *syntax errors*, or errors involving grammatically incorrect statements (employing too many arguments in an IF statement, for example), during compile time—and the source code would not be compiled. Once an error was encountered, the machine would typically halt and display an error code on the console (although sometimes error codes would print but the machine would continue processing the source code). By matching the error code number with its associated error description in the *FORTRAN Operator's Manual*, released in April 1957, the programmer would not only be informed of what type of error occurred, but also be given advice on how to fix the code. There were a great many "machine errors," or errors involving the hardware (such as problems reading from or writing to various media). There were also numerous "source program" errors, or errors in the way that the FORTRAN program was written. For example, consider error code 147; to resolve the issue, the programmer should

> Remove the unread cards from the hopper, run out the cards remaining in the feed and inspect the third card from the end for non-Hollerith characters. When the error has been corrected, ready the corrected card and the remaining unread cards in the card reader and press the START button.

Furthermore, underneath the "Details of Error" column, the following is stated: "Impossible character punched on input card." Another example of a source program error: error code 6431, in which FORTRAN complained of too many DO statements. Yet another: error code 706, a flag for unreachable code in a program—described rather equivocally in the *Operator's Manual* as "probably part of a program that can't be reached."

Putting aside syntax errors, to debug FORTRAN programs of *logic errors*, or errors resulting from a program running differently than intended, the development team suggested writing a series of PRINT statements which could relay "snapshots" of the values of variables or other information at critical points in the source code; these PRINT statements, one on each punched card, could be inserted in appropriate locations in the source deck, with the deck then recompiled. Furthermore, the use of the six sense switches on the 704's front panel, along with IF (SENSE SWITCH) statements for testing certain intermediate conditions during runtime, was recommended. Once the program was run, the output "snapshots" could be compared with what the programmer expected, permitting the programmer to make the appropriate changes to the source deck, after which he or she could remove the PRINT cards and recompile.

Clearly the logistics of finding program errors this way were tricky and thus hardly eliminated the chore of debugging.

The development team's boasting extended to possible applications of the FORTRAN system: nuclear reactor shielding computations, numerical integration, weather prediction, graphing and finding the solutions to a quartic (fourth degree) equation, and other scientific and mathematical programs. Even a functional game of Nim, which involves removing objects from a pile until none remain, could be fashioned using FORTRAN statements, the team claimed.

But such verbal descriptions of FORTRAN's early successes and tremendous potential meant little in the face of actually demonstrating the breakthrough. The hype had to match the reality; the object code had to be efficient, the translation speed had to pass muster with the skeptics. So, the FORTRAN system itself was unveiled in an impressive public demo organized and run by IBM. "Shortly before the conference, IBM had asked a few of its customers to come up with real-world computing chores, like calculating airflows for the design of a jet wing," the technology writer Steve Lohr explained.

> The problems would be given to assembly programmers to code, but also written in Fortran. When the Fortran-compiled programs ran on the computer, they matched the hand-coded programs in terms of running time on the machine. Fortran saved a lot of labor, enabling professionals to program a problem about five times faster than before; it also opened up programming to new practitioners. "It was a revelation to people," Mr. Ziller said, recalling the 1957 demo. "At that point, we knew we had something special."

Fairly quickly, the IBM 704 acquired more than quadruple the users of the 701, at eighty, with some repeat customers, such as General Electric and the Lockheed Aircraft Company. (Eventually there would be nearly twice that, at 150 machines; its appeal began at the level of the hardware, since, recall, the 704 was the first machine to come with floating-point arithmetic built-in.) Unsurprisingly, after lending out Roy Nutt to help build FORTRAN, United Aircraft also procured a model. The National Aeronautics and Space Administration (NASA) had a 704 installation, and used the machine to process heat transfer problems, orbital trajectories (along with launch and reentry), and aeronautical calculations, among other technical work. The U.S. Army Redstone Arsenal, a ballistic missile testing and development site, also had a 704 on hand for labor-intensive calculations. The U.S. Air Force had several 704s, installed at air force bases around the country, which were utilized for nuclear weapons calculations and the evaluation of the Semi-Automatic Ground Environment (SAGE) system for the tracking of ballistic missiles. Government use of the 704 extended beyond the military, with the Tennessee Valley Authority (TVA) procuring a machine to create electric generation schedules as well as for a variety of other purposes. In the commercial sector, 704s were most used by the aviation business, with the aforementioned North American Aviation, along with Chance Vought, being among the earliest adopters. Multiple 704s were delivered to the Los Alamos Scientific Laboratory (LASL); more than simply write and run programs, LASL coded a proto-operating system for the machine, called SLAM, which automated the running of programs, freeing the computer operator to do other work.

◊◊◊

Westinghouse-Bettis, a nuclear power reactor development lab in Maryland, was also a 704 customer and, accidently, became the first commercial user of the language.

IBM was supposed to ship FORTRAN with every 704, in the form of a box of binary punched cards, when the language was bug-free and finalized. In early April of 1957, Backus and company made a critical decision: FORTRAN was ready to be distributed to 704 users. To make that happen, binary card decks of the FORTRAN system had to be punched. David Sayre and Grace "Libby" Mitchell, who was a new recruit to the development team that spring, took charge of the mind-numbing work. (Mitchell would later write the *Programmer's Primer for FORTRAN*, released first as a preliminary version called the "FORTRAN Introductory Programmer's Manual" in early 1957—"distributed in this form to permit its early use for teaching purposes," reads the cover page—then again in late 1957 by IBM, and finally for a third time as a revised version published in March 1958. The *Primer* was, in effect, a much more detailed *Manual* stocked full of example programs. Backus believed that the *Primer* was integral to the early adoption of FORTRAN since it would be several years before textbooks on the language, like computer scientist Daniel D. McCracken's famous 1961 effort, *A Guide to FORTRAN Programming*, were released.) Each binary deck consisted of around 2,000 cards; between thirty and forty of these decks were needed for the mass distribution. But after only a single night, Sayre and Mitchell found themselves in over their heads, with errors in the deck-punching spinning wildly out of control. At most, they finished two decks, packaging in them in boxes that were not meant to be sent out. One SHARE member later recalled that "IBM was going to distribute on binary cards, but when they tried to punch the cards, the machine could not handle all the punching; therefore, they had to go back to [magnetic] tape for distribution."

But, that month, one of those boxes of Sayre and Mitchell's punched cards was shipped to the Westinghouse-Bettis nuclear power plant. The company received the card deck contained the FORTRAN compiler in the mail. "They figured that this must be the deck for FORTRAN," Backus said. But Westinghouse hadn't received the finalized version of the language, since the finalized system was supposed to be distributed via magnetic tapes, not card decks. Rather, the binary card deck they received contained the "late 1956" version. A group at the company headed by Herbert S. Bright "actually ran it, loaded it and then executed this program and finally had a compiler, which they then had a little test FORTRAN program which they compiled, and it ran," according to Backus. In another interview, Backus offered a little more detail: "[Westinghouse] got [FORTRAN] to run without any instructions. They were doing hydrodynamics—calculating stresses of wing structure and stuff like that to design airplanes. Before that, they would have used desk calculators and wind tunnels."

Here is the full story. It was mid-April 1957, a late Friday afternoon, when a handful of Westinghouse engineers, "flying blind," made history by writing and running a short FORTRAN program. Most of these engineers—specifically, Herb Bright, Ollie Swift, and Lew Ondis—were standing around the 704 room, filling the time by talking (as they were wont to do) about when, finally, they would dispose of the IBM 650 that was taking up so much space, when a mail carrier delivered a box of IBM cards. Bright was curious what was inside; there were no identifying markings on the outside of the box. There were no instructions included. So, Bright lifted it open, only to find the box nearly full, containing about two thousand binary punched cards.

This must be IBM's new FORTRAN system, Ondis suggested. He came to this conclusion by doing a back-of-the-envelope calculation: the size of the deck was right, the timing was right, and, of course, the company, IBM, was right. Furthermore, Ondis realized that the deck must contain the "late 1956" version of the language.

"It occurred to me that, if we could make it work, this fact would making interesting news at SHARE," Bright understatedly recollected in 1971. A SHARE meeting was scheduled for the next Monday, and Bright was the representative for Westinghouse set to attend. "Our head CE [computer engineer] came by and agreed to let us have some maintenance time on the 704 free, if we wanted to try to make FORTRAN go."

Using a report penned by Swift along with a FORTRAN *Programmer's Manual* for reference, engineer Jim Callaghan proceeded to write a "small test program" in FORTRAN. The program would calculate, in the report's words, "Gamma of Tau for the InHour Formula," a formula used for depletion calculations of nuclear reactor cores. ("The independent variable was the amount of time each material was in the reactor core under neutron bombardment. The result was used to calculate the behavior of each point in a geometric array of material as a function of time," explained Bright.) If Callaghan had written the same program using SAP, it would have taken him weeks to code and debug. Yet Callaghan had accomplished the same feat in FORTRAN in a single afternoon. A scheduled carpool then picked him up, however, so he unfortunately missed witnessing computing history.

"[I]f the FORTRAN group had its smarts," Ondis said to the remaining group members, then "the [FORTRAN] compiler deck should be self-loading; why not try it and see?"

But how could we tell? they asked.

Swift immediately piped up. "[H]ang a full set of blank tapes (ten) and try to go in through the on-line reader."

"Of course," remembered Bright, "our 704 had the SHARE Standard Reader, Printer, and Punch Boards (remember [those pieces of hardware]?). IBM had started to use these and the SHARE Standard RPQ's." An RPQ was a "request price quotation," essentially an add-on specialty product that IBM would create and sell for an additional fee. Bright continued: "Incredible though it might seem today to those who were weaned on Systems [later IBM mainframe computers' operating system], it just might be that we could fly the new compiler blind!"

They loaded a portion of cards into the hopper, pushed the commencer, and the "reader stuttered and a couple of tapes moved. We kept carding the hopper until all the cards had been put in." Lights on the 704 panel began to flick on, such as the DRUM WRITE light. By the time the final card had been digested by the machine, and the tapes rewound, there was silence: and then the READY light turned on.

Next, they loaded Callaghan's Gamma of Tau source program, pushing the READ CARDS button. Tapes spun, lights on the console started blinking, and the line printer spit this out:

```
25       GO TO (200,210,220,230,240,250,260,270,280,290,300,310,320,330)M
05065    SOURCE PROGRAM ERROR.
         THIS IS A TYPE – GO TO (), I
         – BUT THE RIGHT PARENTHESIS IS NOT FOLLOWED BY A COMMA
         END OF DIAGNOSTIC PROGRAM RESULTS
```

They examined statement 25—indeed, the diagnostic proved correct. They fixed the source code—

```
25       GO TO (200,210,220,230,240,250,260,270,280,290,300,310,320,330),M
```

—and re-compiled. An object program in the form of a binary deck was produced; they inserted this new deck into the on-line reader. Minutes later, the tapes rewound and the READY light appeared. Next, the binary deck was fed into the machine, the READY light flicked on again, and, finally, the program ran outputting correct results—around twenty-eight pages in all, but with several **FORMAT** issues, such as no space below the column headings—for nearly a half hour. Essentially, they had produced a twenty-eight-page pamphlet of (correct, to six digits after the decimal point) precomputed tables for the Gamma of Tau function on the fly; the program "was some jerky little nothing," remembered Backus. Yet despite the program's triviality, it was the first time a FORTRAN program had been successfully run outside of the aegis of the development team. "[I]t was our hands, our machine, our language!" Bright later wrote.

Over the weekend, slides were made of the program and the output, and Bright presented the full story to SHARE that Monday. "It created quite a stir. No one arose to claim precedence," Bright said. Yet Bright was sure that other 704 installations, such as United Aircraft and the University of California Radiation Laboratory, which had "participated in the creation of the first distributable FORTRAN compiler," predated Westinghouse's success. Bright was especially quick to deflect any personal credit for the success of that first program. In a 1978 letter he wrote, "[M]y only participation was as a kibitzer. It was Jim Callahan's program, Lew Ondis's idea to fly the binary deck blind, and Ollie Swift's virtuosity with the 704 (with the SHARE hardware RPQ's) that did the deed. I was just the addressee for the unmarked deck and the guy they reported to."

"Of course, that was the only time [FORTRAN] worked for [Westinghouse] for a long time thereafter," joked Backus. That's because, in due time, Westinghouse, and later other users, discovered many errors in the FORTRAN system; Backus would receive "error reports, and we kept correcting the errors." And the problems continued piling up. As Macbeth said, "We still have judgement here, that we but teach/Bloody instructions which, being taught, return/To plague th'inventor." (Tellingly, Shakespeare's quotation appeared on the title page of a university's early FORTRAN I manual as a kind of warning to students.) Harold Stern, who helped complete section 1 of the FORTRAN compiler, was now directing traffic: he would distribute the information obtained from phone calls, letters, and telegrams to the right people, and then turn around and create detailed "correction cards" that he sent to the 704 installations.

For example, Lockheed Aircraft in Marietta, Georgia, home to IBM 704 serial number 13, encountered an issue that resulted in the compiler printing out "Machine error" on an IBM 716 line printer—which was designed to work with the 700 series of computers—in the machine room and then halting. John Van Gardner, an IBM customer engineer who helped install the 704 (and, with it, FORTRAN) at the site, said to the operator, "I wonder which machine it's referring to."

"To solve this problem we needed a source listing of the compiler," Van Gardner thought, although no such listing was readily available, since IBM wanted to make sure it wasn't easy for a competitor to copy the code. (Each 704 site eventually received a "TOME": a large binder containing the symbolic listing of the FORTRAN I compiler in addition to other diagnostic tools.) "It took the Branch Manager several days to get one for us and it was on a roll of 35 mm microfilm," he recalled. "This had to be under IBM control at all times and when we finished [with] the bug it was sent back to the Branch Office." The bug, found after hours working with the Applied Science Representatives in the field, was a logical error in the source program: one of the Lockheed programmers had "coded a routine with no name and a GO TO statement prior to the routine"—and there was no way to exit out, which resulted in the error message. The "Machine error" was, by the most charitable interpretation, a misdirection, since there was in fact nothing wrong with the hardware. Van Gardner would encounter the same error message six more times, but, like the first time, the machine itself was never the issue.

When the hardware *was* the issue, the problems were harder to resolve. A number of complaints began trickling in: although nothing was wrong with the source program, the object program wasn't running correctly—until the same source code was recompiled, at which point the program ran perfectly. Why was this happening? Van Gardner traced the problem to the punched cards themselves, using an IBM 519 to compare the object decks. They weren't the same, meaning that the compiler wasn't outputting the same object program despite being input the same source code. Investigating further, he discovered that these discrepancies were rooted in the way the compiler was stored in memory. Because of its size, the compiler couldn't entirely fit in core memory all at once; instead, each section of the compiler was loaded using a loader program from tape storage as it was needed, then removed from memory to make way for the next section, and so forth, until the complete object program was generated. The 704 simply didn't have enough memory—with its two 737 magnetic core storage units (4,096 36-bit words each) and its 733 drum unit—to swallow the compiler in its entirety.

Van Gardner got ahold of a source deck that exhibited the strange behavior: not compiling correctly on the first run through, but then compiling with no errors on the second attempt. "I added some code to the loader that would add up all the words in memory except the loader locations and write each total out on a tape," he recalled. "After several runs I got a compile that the object deck checked good in the 519. I now had a tape that had a correct check sum for memory at the end of each section of the compile for that particular program." (A *checksum* is a method or algorithm which, when implemented, results in some value; checksums are typically used to detect errors in data.)

Next, he rewrote the loader instructions to not only compute a checksum at the end of each section, but to compare these calculated checksums with the set of "good" checksums that were stored on tape. Compiling the source code again resulted in an error—and a checksum mismatch. Van Gardner had used his checksums to narrow down which section had the error; he then reprogrammed the loader to write the memory location immediately to a tape unit after computing each checksum. Finally, he compared the readouts of the memory: an error-free compilation of the program versus a compilation resulting in an error. Four words in the memory were different—these four words were all zeros.

Van Gardner met with a Lockheed programmer and the IBM Applied Service Representative, showing them the fruits of his labor. The four words turned out to be "a buffer where data had been read from the 733 Drum. The drum did not have…parity checking circuits but the software used a check sum for each block of data," Van Gardner said. "We suspected the drum had read from the wrong drum address and got into an unused area containing all zeros." It was a hardware issue; they changed the vacuum tubes in the drum counter.

Van Gardner was in contact with IBM during this time, even formally submitting his ideas to the IBM Suggestion Department. In 1961, he was awarded one hundred dollars for his efforts. Several years later, he resolved a similar FORTRAN compilation problem on the IBM 7090 and was duly rewarded—this time with $375. IBM packaged together the compiler fix, calling it Project Intercept, and released it to 7090 installations across the country.

In the early summer of 1957, B. G. Oldfield, a manager at the New York Data Processing Center—which had "more experience using the FORTRAN System [thus far] than any other group in the country," according to a cover letter written by Oldfield and addressed to Backus—presented a paper at a SHARE meeting documenting the "FORTRAN experience" at the site. The paper describes the many issues the Data Processing Center had with FORTRAN, through April 1957; they had initially obtained a preliminary version of the language, missing the output system and error-detecting features, but later received the complete FORTRAN system. At the site,

- They tabulated the number of FORTRAN statements needed to compute certain specialized types of mathematical problems. For example, a projectile flow simulation they programmed needed 133 statements to work, whereas a calculus integration problem required 140 statements.
- They found that 3,163 FORTRAN instructions resulted in roughly 22,000 machine language instructions.
- They timed the number of FORTRAN statements written per hour by experienced programmers, finding it to vary between four and twelve with a mean of seven.
- On average, the system was able to compile about fifteen FORTRAN statements per minute.

- Among their experienced machine language programmers, they discovered approximately one FORTRAN coding error per twenty-four FORTRAN statements, averaging to about one machine error every 168 machine language instructions. "The reduction in programming errors is a very attractive feature of the FORTRAN language," Oldfield wrote.
- "[O]ur programmers indicated that many errors were caught" by the FORTRAN system, according to Oldfield. "Our experience to date indicates that the error detection features built into the FORTRAN system are excellent and will greatly reduce the number of programming errors which must be found in the debugging stages of a problem."

Oldfield concluded his paper on an optimistic note, recognizing that FORTRAN is easy to learn and quicker to code than machine language, reduces the cost of programming overall, and will be able to "handle at least 75 per cent of our problems."

Outside of aviation, General Motors gained experience with FORTRAN several years before it was publicly released. George Ryckman, an electrical engineer who was hired at GM in 1952, was on the front lines of computer science at the company: he was supervisor of computer operations when FORTRAN began to secure a foothold.

In 1954, Ryckman was busy programming on the 701, but also laying the groundwork for its successor, the 704. In 1955, with the 704 installed, GM was offered several opportunities to put early versions of the FORTRAN translator through its paces. That March, Ryckman recorded, in a logbook, some very minor FORTRAN milestones at GM Research Laboratories, which employed around twenty programmers: "Received proposed additions to the FORTRAN: incorporated new symbols and formulas" and "FORTRAN code plates ordered for the keypunch machines." More significant were the suggestions Ryckman and others at the GM Research Labs made to Backus's team, such as adding **IF SENSE LIGHT** and **IF SENSE SWITCH** statements so programmers could station themselves at the computer console to monitor the goings-on during program execution.

They liked FORTRAN at GM. "From the standpoint of the engineer or scientist," Ryckman explained, the algebra-like "language was closer to his thought processes, required fewer pencil marks to program an algorithm, was easier to learn and retain, easier to read and change, and lent itself to more accuracy." They knew of what they spoke, having used Speedcoding as well as a variety of assembly languages for years; if FORTRAN's promise matched the reality, then the "programming bottleneck" would be dramatically eased, with programmers freed up to complete higher-level tasks. But, in 1956, whether FORTRAN would prove to be a revolution was still very much an open question.

GM Research received the FORTRAN system at their 704 installation in April 1957. Before it arrived, trainings had been conducted and preliminary programs (mathematics- and engineering-related) had been written. Once they put some miles on the system, their first takeaway was how opaque the translator's diagnostic messages were. What, precisely, was a "nonzero level reduction," and why did the error message always pop up if a program statement was missing a parenthesis? They, by turns, "marvel[ed] at the Translator or question[ed] its sanity!"

But FORTRAN quickly proved to be a hit at GM Research. By the end of the calendar year, through conversions from SAP and other sources, about forty percent of the computer workload was in FORTRAN; plus, with FORTRAN now the order of the day (instead of SAP), computer use had more than tripled. Better yet, they found that time and effort programming in FORTRAN was reduced as much as tenfold compared to assembly language. Programming and debugging costs declined dramatically as well. Part of the reason for that was the homegrown monitor they built for FORTRAN, which functioned as a very primitive sort of operating system (recall that the 704 shipped with no operating system; FORTRAN, when it ran, assumed control of the entire machine). But, as Ryckman is quick to caution, such performance comparisons between FORTRAN and assembly language are questionable at best, since by using the FORTRAN system, the programs themselves could be much bigger and more complicated than those built with SAP.

Yet FORTRAN, though indeed revolutionary, fell short of perfection. Besides the quirky diagnostic messages, "The greatest single design weakness of FORTRAN I was the lack of a full subroutine facility with load-time linking, because this generally limited the size of programs," Ryckman recalled. Programs beyond about three to four hundred statements in length were logistically a nightmare to test. In the years to follow, FORTRAN II would address this limitation, eventually leading to FORTRAN's near-total adoption at GM Research.

At Livermore Labs, where Bob Hughes worked, a FORTRAN I compiler arrived soon after its public release in mid-1957. Employees at the site had experience with a compiler of their own creation: the algebraic Kompiler for the 701, which was, as Hughes described it, a "Spruce Goose," since "[i]t taxied well, but it never took off." There were two such 701 Kompilers: the K1 and the K2. Then came the K3 for the 704, named for "Kent Ellsworth [a Livermore Labs employee, who had led the development of the Kompiler] and the world's third compiler," which was "designed to maintain the integrity of conventional mathematical notation," recalled Hughes. "It required three cards per statement, the first and third being used for exponents and subscripts.... It then became the world's second Spruce Goose in the wake of Fortran's growing popularity."

Before FORTRAN arrived, Livermore translated a program that "Kompiled" correctly to the equivalent FORTRAN code; this test program, about three thousand punched cards long, "took longer to compile, however, than the mean time between errors on the 704 which, we learned, was several hours," recalled Norm Hardy, who also worked at Livermore.

> The compiler especially stressed the magnetic drums. We heard similar stories from other Fortran users regarding large programs. We manually transcribed the large Fortran code to assembler and proceeded with production.
>
> Gradually developers of smaller programs who migrated to Fortran were well satisfied with it. Users would encounter occasional compiler bugs but most of these could be worked around. Periodically IBM would mail out patches in the form of decks of binary cards. Such a mailing might include 100 or 200 binary cards. The bugs receded as a

practical matter and the compiler grew more efficient. The 704s became more reliable as well. The Fortran compiler was the most demanding application at most sites.

Fortran's optimization was far ahead of its time. Indeed other much smaller and faster Fortrans were soon written for other machines, but I recall observing that it was about 10 years before any compiler optimized as well as the original.

Though sometimes startling in their efficiency, the optimizations during the translation process didn't always work perfectly. As professor of computer science David Padua notes, "The compiler seemingly generated very good code for regular computations; however, irregular computations, including sparse and symbolic computations, [were] generally more difficult to transform"—and FORTRAN "did not do as well on these types of computations." To that end, subscripted subscripts—for example, A(K(I,J))—were not permitted in FORTRAN I programs.

As more reports and critical feedback from the many installation sites filtered back to IBM, the development team refocused their energies, spending the next half-year ironing out the bugs. Several hundred compiler fixes ended up being needed. (By 1959, IBM released a comprehensive manual—the FORTRAN I, II, and 709 *Customer Engineering Manual of Instruction*—to help users tackle the many issues that still arose.) Donald Knuth, in describing FORTRAN's debut, quotes the computer scientist Saul Rosen, who describes the scene:

> Like most of the early hardware and software systems, Fortran was late in delivery, and didn't really work when it was delivered. At first people thought it would never be done. Then when it was in field test, with many bugs, and with some of the most important parts unfinished, many thought it would never work. It gradually got to the point where a program in Fortran had a reasonable expectancy of compiling all the way through and maybe even of running.

There was another issue that caused some initial resistance to FORTRAN or, for that matter, any language that would automate the work of a members-only club like the programming priesthood. As Backus wrote a decade removed from FORTRAN's creation:

> At that time [in the early 1950s], most programmers wrote symbolic machine instructions exclusively (some even used absolute octal or decimal machine instructions). Almost to a man, they firmly believed that any mechanical coding method would fail to apply that versatile ingenuity which each programmer felt he possessed and constantly needed in his work.

The team feared that the skeptics of automatic coding would win out early on, through a process of confirmation bias, squashing any hope of FORTRAN's widespread adoption. Perhaps an application seemingly well-suited to FORTRAN would pop up. Further, suppose that a programmer wrote a clean FORTRAN program that handled that application with grace. What if the FORTRAN object program, though, ran at only half the speed of an equivalent machine language program coded by hand? "It was felt that such an occurrence, or several of them, would almost completely block acceptance of the new system," Backus recalled. And influential computer scientists such as Virginia Polytechnic Institute's J.A.N. Lee resisted using FORTRAN for years; back then, Lee thought of Backus as a "very lazy programmer who feels that he wants to make everything much easier for everybody else." Of course, Lee was right.

Yet, Donald Knuth writes, "in spite of these difficulties, it is clear that FORTRAN I was worth waiting for; it soon was accepted even more enthusiastically than its proponents had dreamed." In the fall of 1958, a survey of twenty-six 704 users was taken; more than half of them reported using FORTRAN for over half of their programming needs, with some users employing the new language at least eighty percent of the time. In addition, IBM SHARE records indicate that sixty 704 installations were equipped to run FORTRAN. But there were notable early skeptics, as Knuth observes, including the authors of a popular textbook on programming called *The Preparation of Programs for an Electronic Digital Computer* by Wilkes, Wheeler, and Gill, who cautioned their readers that despite the great promises of automatic programming with

> formulas written in ordinary mathematical notation…promising to reduce greatly the labor of programming…on examination they are found to be of more limited utility than might have been hoped. Even in favorable cases, experienced programmers will be able to obtain greater efficiency by using more conventional methods of programming.

"Users just found it hard to believe that a machine could write an efficient program," said Backus. Richard Hamming, employed at Bell Labs at the time of FORTRAN's release, agreed. FORTRAN was "opposed by almost all programmers," he remembered. "First, it was said it could not be done. Second, if it could be done, it would be too wasteful of machine time and capacity. Third, even if it did work, no respectable programmer would use it—it was only for sissies!"

But why? Hamming compares the opposition of programmers to FORTRAN with doctors not following their own advice, or lawyers not drawing up effective wills for themselves. As the old proverb warns, the shoemaker's children go barefoot.

Over time, FORTRAN silenced the critics and was adopted by the professional class of programmers, since no one could deny the results: roughly one thousand machine instructions was the equivalent of a mere forty-seven FORTRAN statements; around a thousand FORTRAN statements might equate to around 7,500 machine language instructions. Generally, the ratio of input FORTRAN statements to output machine language instructions, called the "expansion ratio," was between four and twenty (the New York Data Processing Center found the ratio to be between five and twenty-one, with an average of seven); the time reduction ratio was similar, with the highest ratios involving FORTRAN programs with many loops and subscripted variables. According to Backus, by late 1958, more than half of all 704 machine language instructions were being written not by human beings, but automatically by FORTRAN compilers. And at around the same time, SHARE officially adopted a second language: FORTRAN. SAP, of course, was still their first official language.

Helping to sell the FORTRAN effort was Frances "Fran" Elizabeth Allen. Born in 1932 in New York, a math teacher inspired in her a lifelong love of mathematics. After earning a degree in math from the New York State College for Teachers (which has since changed its name), she returned to her high school to teach for several years before going back to school—this time at the University of Michigan, where she obtained an MA in mathematics. Her intention was to return to teaching high school, but it was at Michigan that she was first exposed to computers, gaining experience on an IBM 650 by taking several computing courses offered by Bernard Galler, a computer scientist who helped to create the MAD (Michigan Algorithm Decoder) programming language for the 704. Compared to MAD, which took ALGOL 58 (ALGOrithmic Language; originally called the International Algebraic Language, or IAL) as its base, making errors while writing FORTRAN code was no fun at all. If there were a critical mass of compile-time errors in a program, several versions of MAD would output, on a line printer, a full-page ASCII picture of Alfred E. Neuman from *Mad Magazine*.

Frances Allen's career path as a high school teacher took a permanent detour when IBM representatives arrived on Michigan's campus to interview students for open positions. She was offered a research job at the company, which she accepted. Figuring she would work at Big Blue for a couple of years to pay down her student debt, Allen instead remained at the company for the next half century.

Right when she arrived at IBM—on July 15, 1957—she had to take a crash course in FORTRAN, which had just been released. She read through the FORTRAN compiler's source code. And then, just as quickly, she was given an assignment: teach the language to IBM's research scientists. Reflecting on the experience years later, she said, "It set my interest in compiling, and it also set the way I thought about compilers, because it was organized in a way that has a direct heritage to modern compilers."

Allen turned her attention to compiler design, working on the 704's Monitored Automatic Debugging operating system, built by Roy Nutt, as well as the IBM Stretch supercomputer and the Harvest coprocessor, which was specially designed for codebreaking at the NSA. In the early 1960s, Allen would help write a compiler framework for Stretch/Harvest that could integrate easily with three computer languages, including FORTRAN.

Even by the time of Allen's arrival at IBM, FORTRAN was beginning to migrate beyond the hardware of the 704. John Backus said that "FORTRAN was a great boon to [IBM's] competitors, because with their programs tied up in machine language, IBM customers weren't about to re-program for another computer. But if a competitor could come up with a program that would translate a FORTRAN program into the language of his machine, he had a selling point." As Frances Allen noted, in a paper written two decades after FORTRAN I's release, FORTRAN was a "language and system which established the foundations of compiler technology, set standards rarely achieved today, and, as a result, dramatically accelerated compiler development."

Eventually, as described by Stephen H. Kaisler in *First Generation Mainframes: The IBM 700 Series* (2018), IBM ironed out the bugs.

A Master Tape [of FORTRAN] was issued [to the 704 installations], but was not used directly for compilation. Rather, a system editing program could [use] as input "modification cards" which made alterations—both additions and deletions of code—to the code base extracted from the Master tape. The output of the system editing process was a working system tape which was used for compilation and execution of FORTRAN programs.

Such a system was found to reduce the logistical issues inherent with the distribution of alterations to FORTRAN, in the form of modification decks, to the many 704 installations.

"The system editing process allowed organizations to make non-standard additions without modifying the [FORTRAN] Master Tape," added Kaisler. In other words, even in the days of punched cards, IBM still had to have some way to mass distribute software updates to its users. A systematic means of keeping track of the "system level" of the language took hold. Each new batch of modification decks distributed to the 704 installations had a system level incremented by one; eventually, when the number of modification decks became unwieldly, a new Master Tape was made with a version number incremented by one.

Once distribution kicked into high gear, all 704 installations with FORTRAN were also sent the "TOME," an approximately five-inch thick, eleven-by-fifteen-inch volume containing a printed-out symbolic listing of the entire compiler as well as system and diagnostic information. Harold Stern, who had worked on section 1 of the compiler, helped to assemble the "TOME" at IBM in 1957.

Despite its wide distribution, by the end of the 1950s most people who had gained experience with FORTRAN hadn't done so on an IBM 704, but on an earlier IBM model using a stripped-down version of the language.

CHAPTER 16

◊◊◊

The (Short) History of FOR TRANSIT

At first, FORTRAN was for the privileged few granted access to IBM 704 installations; everyone else had to get their FORTRAN fix elsewhere.

IBM, concurrent with the distribution of FORTRAN (in 1957), released a pared down version of the FORTRAN language for a prior IBM model. Not the 701, as might be suspected, but the magnetic-drum, decimal-based IBM 650. Called FOR TRANSIT (sometimes concatenated to read simply as FORTRANSIT), and also, like FORTRAN, billed as an automatic coding system, FOR TRANSIT was not entirely a product of IBM; rather, it was an offshoot of a compiler, called the Internal Translator (IT), created at Purdue University by Alan Perlis, who worked at the Carnegie Institute of Technology. IBM "superimposed" its own translator on top of the IT—hence the "IT" of FOR TRANS*IT*—resulting in a partial emulation of the 704's architecture. IT did not assume operator precedence when evaluating expressions—that is, IT didn't follow the rules of PEMDAS. Which was "the most frequent single cause of errors by users" of IT, according to Donald Knuth.

In fairness, however, errors were discovered with the way that the 704 FORTRAN compiler evaluated the order of operations. Consider the following expression:

$$n * (n-1)/2$$

If n is equal to 10, then the expression should evaluate to 45, since when considering PEMDAS, multiplication and division have equal precedence so should be computed left to right. But when Bernard Galler, who worked at the University of Michigan, used FORTRAN to compute the expression, the output was 40. "Then I discovered that, in fact, the optimizer was doing things so that the right thing was in the register at the right time and the division came first," he recalled. "Thus $n-1$ being 9 divided by 2 using integer arithmetic comes out 4. That is why the answer was 40." He notified IBM, and was told that changing the compiler was too complex, so instead the issue would be addressed in the next version of the *Manual*. "Please be warned that mathematical equivalence is not the same as computational equivalence," the *Manual* now warned; apparently, Peter Sheridan, who had programmed PEMDAS into the FORTRAN compiler, had a hand in writing the warning.

Not all thirty-two FORTRAN I statements were available on IBM 650 FOR TRANSIT, and some other features of FORTRAN were excluded as well. Yet all programs written in FOR TRANSIT were compatible with FORTRAN I, as long as certain restrictions were met. According to the FOR TRANSIT *Reference Manual* (originally published in 1957, with a revised version distributed in 1959),

> For example, whereas FORTRAN variables may consist of from one to six characters in the FORTRAN system, FOR TRANSIT requires that variables consist of from one to five characters. It should be noted that in a few instances FORTRAN restrictions have been relaxed to take advantage of certain features of the 650....

Key FORTRAN statements including **READ, DIMENSION, EQUIVALENCE, DO, GO TO, IF, READ, PAUSE, STOP,** and **END** were available in FOR TRANSIT, with little or no alteration. Arithmetic formulas could be evaluated similarly, and there were some built-in subroutines (such as for handling non-routine types of arithmetic operations) as well; these subroutines were included in a Package Deck of machine language instructions which were loaded into the 650 before a FOR TRANSIT object program was executed. Although FOR TRANSIT programs were punched on standard FORTRAN punched cards, there were a number of restrictions on column usage, depending on the version of FOR TRANSIT (although no matter the version, fewer punched card columns could be utilized in FOR TRANSIT). Several versions of FOR TRANSIT were released over a two-year period: FOR TRANSIT I (S) and FOR TRANSIT II, which adjusted to the more advanced 650 hardware of index registers and floating-point arithmetic.

Unlike the single-pass compiler of FORTRAN, compiling a program in FOR TRANSIT required multiple passes: translating the source code to IT; compiling the IT code into the symbolic SOAP (Symbolic Optimal Assembly Program) assembly language, one of the first assemblers ever written, which was developed by Stan Poley in 1955 at IBM Watson Labs; and then punching an object program onto cards, which had to be fed into a hopper to run the program. SOAP instructions, which were usually two address codes (with an instruction part and an address), accounted for the drum memory of the 650. As Frances Allen explained, "By storing data and instructions on the 650 drum so that the drum was in the right position when data or the next instruction was required, a program might run as much as six or seven times faster." This type of coding—where the next instruction would be available right away, and which could be implemented on drum machines or mercury delay lines, among other storage media—was called *minimum latency coding*. In those days, gaining every last ounce of speed was critical, and this clever use of drum memory reduced processing delays as much as possible.

SOAP was an example of a self-compiling system, explained Richard Hamming, who worked at Bell Labs. Hamming asks us to imagine a "program A," loaded into the 650 as both a program and as data. Suppose we compile and run program A—we'll call the output produced "program B." Next, load program B into the 650, with program A kept as stored data in the machine. Then compile and run program B. "The difference between the two running times to produce program B indicated how much the optimization of the SOAP program (by SOAP itself) produced," Hamming explained.

Bob Bemer directed the development of FOR TRANSIT. Born in Michigan in 1920, Robert "Bob" William Bemer arrived at IBM while Backus and his team were assembling FORTRAN. Bemer had once been a movie set designer; he then went to Marquardt, which had a CPC on hand, where he ran trajectory simulations. A simulation once took so long to run that he stayed awake for more than twenty-four hours waiting for the calculations, and he forgot to shave—leading his boss to criticize him for his disheveled appearance.

Later in his career, Bemer played a critical role in the development of COBOL, helped to create the ASCII codeset (contributing several new characters, including Escape, the backslash, and the curly brackets; he is thus often called the "Father of ASCII"), facilitated standardizing the eight-bits-per-byte measurement, and is probably the first person to conceive of *timesharing*, the simultaneous use of a single computer system by multiple users, even from remote locations. (In 1940, Bell Labs mathematician George Stibitz successfully operated a relay computer using a teletype terminal from a remote location, demonstrating that reliable communication with computers was possible at long distances; this led to SAGE, which was used by the U.S. government for coordinating radar and airspace defenses). Bemer first saw the term "timesharing" in a 1957 paper on the MIT Lincoln Laboratory TX-2 computer; the very next month, he wrote a paper on how timesharing might work in practice. Top brass at IBM were not pleased with Bemer's proposed timesharing system, since it was not "in line with their policy"—and he was almost fired for crafting the proposal.

When Bemer showed up at IBM in late 1955 by way of Lockheed (even though IBM didn't typically poach talent from their customers), he was put to work on the 705 Data Processing System, a commercial machine designed for business data processing, with an assignment: write a simple language that will enable scientific-type computation on the 705. By the middle of 1956, about a year before FORTRAN's release, the PRINT I—"PRe-edited INTerpretive" Routine—was born. The opcodes of PRINT I had variable fields, with up to four variables possible for some instructions. PRINT I was a semi-interpreter, since the system would pass through the source code prior to execution, processing, modifying, and optimizing it; this altered source code was then run through the PRINT I interpreter. In addition, PRINT I also introduced *load-and-go*: the program would only need to be loaded a single time prior to execution of the original source code. (It would be years before IBM would follow suit with FORTRAN: on the "inexpensive" IBM 1620, which was released in 1959, the load-and-go GOTRAN was a one-step version of the language that automatically ran the source code after initial compilation.) Bemer presented a paper about PRINT I at the Western Joint Computer Conference the year before the FORTRAN development team presented theirs. As Bemer remembered it, "In general PRINT I was a great success with IBM's commercial customers. Studies from a few firms that had both 704 FORTRAN and 705 PRINT I showed a remarkably good comparison in overall efficiency."

But PRINT I is tangential to our story. "When I started the PRINT I project I had no thoughts of universal or standard programming languages," Bemer said.

> But that project was done in the same room with the original FORTRAN effort (not the Langdon Hotel of later stories, but a large room in an annex south of the main IBM building at 590 Madison). While not working on my own assignment I got the best outsider's view of that work that anyone ever had. And I could see that it was a big advance over what I was doing. It should have been, with about 10 times the effort.
>
> Then those thoughts started to come. Because of my great familiarity with the IBM 650s (3 of them) at Lockheed Missiles and Space Division, I started to feel that it deserved a similar capability. Especially because there were so many of them out there, due in large part to IBM's generous discount to schools and universities.

Through his connections at IBM, Bemer became aware of an algebraic compiler—the IT—being constructed by Alan Perlis at Carnegie. And because of his familiarity with the 650, Bemer also knew that Stan Poley's SOAP was "the assembler of choice for almost every 650 user." In fact, top computing minds such as Donald Knuth's were taken by the "sheer beauty" of SOAP.

By the end of 1956, PRINT I was complete. On a snowy day in December of that year, he met up with Perlis at Carnegie. Could I have permission to use the IT compiler in order to build FORTRAN for the 650? he asked him. Yes, Perlis answered, and IBM offered Bemer the manpower to help turn FORTRAN for the underpowered 650, having fewer index registers than the 704, into a reality.

Bemer saw four possible paths forward. First, dispense with the programming language altogether, and, for every new 704 FORTRAN application, write the equivalent program on the 650 using whatever resources were available. Of course, this first path was not an option, since it wouldn't translate FORTRAN to the 650 in general. Writing an interpretive emulator for the 704 on the 650 was the second path he could take; such an emulator could, at least in theory, run any 704 software put to it, including FORTRAN. The problem with this approach was speed, with 650 emulation running anywhere from one hundred to one thousand times slower than the emulated machine. The third possible path involved using the source language of the interpreter to write an equivalent interpreter for another machine. Which would have been fine, except for the fact that FORTRAN was not written by Backus's team as an interpreter, but as a compiler. The fourth path, involving writing compilers from the ground up for different machines, was the approach taken by Bemer and his team with FOR TRANSIT.

Bemer was especially fond of wordplay and puns. He would coin the acronym CODASYL, the Conference/Committee on Data Systems Languages, which resulted in COBOL (also his term); CODASYL purposely sounded like the word "codicil," an addendum to a will. He did not create the acronym FOR TRANSIT, however; through Bemer's conversations with Florence "Flo" Pessin about the project, she arrived at the name. Pessin also enjoyed words. "We agreed that it meant either 1) FORTRAN-

S(oap)-IT, or 2) FOR TRANSIT(ion), or 3) FORTRAN's IT (in the verb sense of FORTRANning the IT Compiler)," Bemer recalled.

FOR TRANSIT, in those early months of release (late 1957), was used more often than FORTRAN, because there were so many 650s in circulation as a result of educational discounts and the like. In fact, according to Bemer, around ten times as many people were introduced to the FORTRAN language on the relatively primitive 650—an old low-cost decimal-based vacuum-tube-logic machine with rotating magnetic drum memory that served as a short step up from calculating punches to punched-card computers; the 650 *looked* powerful, though, with its front panel containing many lights—than on the more advanced 704. Of course, the fact that Bemer and his IBM team had recreated FORTRAN, even if it was a stripped-down version, on an entirely different machine, was significant: "Certainly not the least accomplishment was proving that the same source language could be used, whether the hardware was decimal or binary in nature! It had never been done before." FORTRAN could be made platform independent.

In those days, Bemer reported to Backus, "but never felt the slightest pressure. I looked upon him as a friend, not a menace." Yet Bemer was partial to the accomplishments of Grace Hopper, claiming that the "rudimentary" compilers she helped develop pre-FORTRAN "might have gone faster further if she had had the type of support given to Backus and his group."

Bemer always felt enthusiasm at writing software, which didn't have to conform to any sort of dominant programming paradigms, for a group of dynamic leaders—at least until the end of the 1950s, when the Peter Principle, in which employees rise to their highest level of incompetence, took hold. "Software before FORTRAN could be considered quite medieval, even primitive, but there were certain graces," he recalled.

FOR TRANSIT faded away by the end of the decade, along with the 650. But Bemer brought one more key innovation to IBM: recognized authorship over IBM technical manuals and programs. IBM's stance, heading into the 1950s, was that such authorship should always be shrouded in anonymity. Bemer had the opposite take, and, to evade company rules when developing PRINT I, named a committee of individuals who worked on the project—including some outside contractors—and printed the committee's membership inside the PRINT I manual. "With this precedent, IBM folded," said Bemer. "Both the FORTRAN and the FOR TRANSIT manuals named names. John Backus was very pleased that this could be done."

Now all those who contributed, who shed their blood, sweat, and tears for a labor of love, would not soon be forgotten.

CHAPTER 17

◊◊◊

FORTRAN, the Sequel

The second implementation of FORTRAN was a bold attempt by the development team to solve the problems generated by the first.

John Backus sat down with Bob Hughes, who was on loan from the Lawrence Livermore Laboratory. What do you think of the FORTRAN project so far? Backus asked him.

"Well, there's one thing that I worry about," Hughes began. "[Y]ou're only putting out a main program. There are no user-defined subprograms." Hughes offered the example of Livermore: there, he claimed, they were using programs with numerous associated subprograms in the background. "You're allowing for system functions like square roots and science and trigonometric functions, and so on," Hughes added, "but we use lots of user defined subprograms, and also, you're assuming that the program can be memory contained but, we almost never get the memory contained with the big problems at Livermore, so we use a program design that can be chewed up into modules. Actually, we almost never get the memory contained with the big problems at Livermore."

Backus took in what Hughes was saying. "Well, I understand that," Backus responded, "but, in this particular case, I want to prove first that a computer can generate good code, and that a compiler can be written to generate a good program that rivals the efficiency that the hand programmer can produce.

"That's going to be the important thing, I think you can lay it right there," Backus added. "Then we can get together later on and add all the other factors that need to be added in to make it even more convenient. But, I've got to get over that first hurdle to demonstrate that the compiler can generate good code."

By 1957, Backus had succeeded in overcoming that first hurdle. FORTRAN was ready for a makeover. Now, "all the other factors," as Backus put it, could be added in.

◊◊◊

The development team was well aware that there were "shortcomings" with FORTRAN I that were hard to ignore—especially when they began receiving error reports from installations. It was time for them to rethink the FORTRAN system.

First, there was a logistical issue to consider: changing a program in FORTRAN I was like steering the *Titanic*, since if even the smallest change needed to be made in the source code, usually the entire program—and these FORTRAN programs could be massive—needed to be recompiled. Every program was its own self-contained entity.

Second, if a programmer wished to write an application program, he had no choice but to write it all in FORTRAN—no mixing and matching of FORTRAN with, let's say, SAP was permitted. It was FORTRAN or bust.

Taking into account the many FORTRAN I criticisms, reports from the field, and logistical issues, Irv Ziller wrote out three similar documents with the same name, "Proposed Specifications for FORTRAN II for the 704," but released on different dates: August 28, September 25, and November 18, 1957. (Slight clarification: Ziller *likely* wrote the first document, but certainly wrote the other two. Going forward, we will assume he wrote all three.) The latter two are much longer than the first. All three documents begin with the same expansive mission statement:

> FORTRAN has now had some use at a large number of installations and has been used heavily for some time at at least six installations. A large number plan to use the system for the majority of their programming work. Difficulties in using FORTRAN have fallen into two categories (1) Difficulties arising in the initial period of putting the system into use, and (2) Difficulties arising from the properties of the system. Problems in the first category are being solved by on-the-spot expert assistance to those installations experiencing an undue amount of difficulty. The consensus opinion concerning difficulties in category (2) is that the principal areas needing improvement are (a) facilities for debugging source programs and (b) facilities for creating and using subroutines. FORTRAN II will contain improved facilities in both these areas along the lines described below.

All the documents also contain a short discussion of "Debugging Facilities," detailing an expanded diagnostic routine that not only captures and prints out every error in a source program (in as concise and clear a manner as possible; Backus didn't want the compiler offering "very cryptic" explanations) but also greatly reduces the number of times the translator halts compilation.

The majority of all three documents, though, focus on subroutines—what Hughes, in his conversation with Backus, had called "user-defined subprograms." In the first document, from late August, Ziller writes in a generalized manner, but his promises are bold. "The FORTRAN II translator will accept an unlimited number of different statements," the subroutine section begins. That statement is nowhere to be found in the other two documents.

The August document goes on to specify how subroutines, such as the NAME subroutine below, should be declared:

$$\text{NAME}\,(\,A,\,B,\,C,\,I,\,X\,)$$

with the parameters being the names of variables (fixed- or floating-point) and/or arrays. Subroutine calls could reference SAP-coded subroutines or subroutines written in FORTRAN. Ziller promises that "[a]ll routines produced by FORTRAN II, both master routines and subroutines, will be loadable by the proposed Binary Symbolic Subroutine [BSS] Loader. This BSS Loader will enable assembled programs in relocatable binary [form] to retain <u>symbolic</u> references to subroutines at lower levels," meaning that subroutines and the main routine could be compiled, recompiled, or assembled in an independent manner, with the stacks of cards for each loaded into the hopper in any order. The BSS Loader replaces the symbolic name of subroutine B "within the routine A by a transfer to the proper entry point in B after B has been assigned a location." The upshot was that instead of each FORTRAN program being, in effect, one bloated file, a program could assume a modular form; even subroutines which hadn't been written yet could still be referenced as placeholders in routines, and those routines could be compiled independently of the subroutines referenced (ALGOL couldn't do that, nor could COBOL). Better yet, the subroutines themselves didn't have to be written in FORTRAN; they could be in SAP. The consequences of programming in this newly modular and flexible format were far-reaching: with the ability to write subprograms, big programming jobs could now be divvied up among a programming team (person A writes one subprogram, person B writes another, and so on). And there was still a job for the assembly programmers, since routines for which FORTRAN was not especially suited could now be written in SAP instead, and integrated relatively seamlessly within a modular FORTRAN program as a whole.

Ziller concludes the August document by briefly describing how to use two new proposed FORTRAN statements: SUB DEF, to define a subroutine, and RETURN, to pass control back to the calling routine. He offers an example of a subroutine called "ZERO 15,"

$$\text{SUB DEF} \quad \text{ZERO 15 (A, N)}$$

which was designed to zero-out a portion of the entries of a matrix whose dimensions were 15 by 15. A RETURN statement rounded out the subroutine. Compile the subroutine ZERO 15 by itself, and the 704 would spit out a relocatable binary deck. A calling statement might take this form, for instance:

$$\text{ZERO 15 (X, 15)}$$

The second document Ziller drew up, in September of 1957, goes into more detail than the first. The longest section, called "Subroutine Facilities," presents a different subroutine definition statement than before:

$$\text{SUBROUTINE DEFINITION, NAME(X, Y, I, ...)}$$

where NAME can be up to six alphanumeric characters, as long as the first character is an alphabetic letter. A RETURN statement in the subroutine transfers control back to the calling routine.

The UPPER statement was introduced to handle memory management. Taking the form UPPER, A, B, ..., Ziller explains the purpose of the new statement as follows:

> In FORTRAN II, data storage will be moved down in memory so that a gap no longer exists between program and data. The arrangement of such data will be in a normal manner. However, data can be located at the top of memory by listing such data in an UPPER statement. The ordering of the storage will be that of the UPPER list, except as it is modified by the EQUIVALENCE statements.

Essentially, the UPPER statement would offer a way for different parts of a modular FORTRAN program to share data.

Other statements mentioned in this second document include the END statement, which terminates a subroutine file ("permitting the stacking of source programs when compiling," Ziller notes), and the IF TAPE CHECK n_1, n_2, which was a statement transferring control of the program depending upon whether the tape check indicator on the 704 was read as on or off.

The third and final proposal document, from November of 1957, is similar to the second, but there are several notable changes. Instead of the UPPER statement, the **COMMON** statement is introduced—with the exact same functionality. Also, once a user wished to call a subroutine in a program, the subroutine's name had to be prefixed with **CALL**. For example,

CALL NAME(A, B, C)

The **RETURN, END,** and **SUBROUTINE** statements were retained, although the **END** statement now mandated five arguments (each being 0, 1, or 2) relating to the 704's sense switches (0 = ignore sense switch, and assume it is up; 1 = ignore, and assume it's down; 2 = interrogate the sense switch); for example:

END (1, 2, 2, 0, 1)

Each combination of **END** arguments had a special, machine-dependent meaning relating to the loading and compiling of programs.

Several example programs, including a matrix multiplication program (with a subroutine called **MATMPY** preceding the main routine which called it) and a program comparing Hollerith data that illustrated subroutines being called from within other subroutines, rounded out Ziller's third document.

That November, Backus distributed a brief memorandum laying out his vision for FORTRAN II—which also included a few tantalizing bits about the IBM 709. (In the following chapter, we will detail how the 709 interfaced with FORTRAN II.) Backus noted that

> The added flexibility of FORTRAN II stems from the ability to add virtually any procedure as a new statement in the language. It is therefore difficult to summarize the features which will be added. Some examples undoubtedly are: matrix, complex and double precision arithmetic; monitor routines for manipulating the arrangement of

subroutines in the store; routines for handling BCD information; special input-output operations.

With the exception of some format and spelling changes proposed for FORTRAN for the 709, FORTRAN II specs go considerably beyond any previous specs for the 709 system, in ways which we have discussed (independent subroutines; substitution of argument variables in calling statement for dummy variables in subroutine).

In an interview conducted decades later, Backus was asked what led to FORTRAN II. "Well, it was—" he paused. Then he plainly admitted to a problem with the first implementation of the language, saying, "You couldn't—there weren't any subroutines in Fortran 1. You just—it was one big mess. So Fortran 2 added the ability to have subroutines." Backus acknowledged that he was influenced by the work of the British computer scientist Maurice Wilkes, who was partly responsible for the ideas of subroutines and macros, even though he never had any direct interactions with him (recall that Backus knew of Wilkes's ideas from the book *The Preparation of Programs for an Electronic Digital Computer*). FORTRAN II would have subroutines, of course; better still, if a programmer needed to make minor modifications to FORTRAN II source code, all parts of the program typically did not need recompiling—only the portions that had been modified.

The "tag analysis" of section 5 of FORTRAN I's compiler, designed by Sheldon Best to allocate index registers, was left more or less intact for FORTRAN II. "Part of the index register optimization fell into disuse quite early, but much of it was carried along into Fortran II and is still in use on the 704/9/90" nearly a decade later, computer scientist Saul Rosen wrote at the time. "In many programs it still contributes to the production of better code than can be achieved on the new Fortran IV compiler."

Not mentioned by either Backus or Ziller was the **FUNCTION** statement, new to FORTRAN II. But didn't FORTRAN I also allow user-defined functions? "As in the original FORTRAN, library tape functions and built-in functions may be used in any FORTRAN II program," read the FORTRAN II *Reference Manual*, published in 1958, and "[t]he library tape functions may be supplemented as desired." Nonetheless,

> The most flexible and powerful means of function definition in FORTRAN II is, however, the subprogram headed by a **FUNCTION** statement.... This new facility enables the programmer to define functions in source language in a sub-program which can be compiled from alphanumeric cards or tape in the same way as a main program. Function subprograms may use other subprograms to any depth desired. A subprogram headed by a **FUNCTION** statement is logically terminated by a RETURN statement(s) in the same manner as a **SUBROUTINE** subprogram. Subprograms of the function type may also be written in SAP code, or in any other language reducible to machine language.

In a recent interview, the software architect Dennis Hamilton, who began his career in 1958, spoke of the importance of subroutines. "In Fortran I, programs were one giant file and there was no modularization structure. That small change in Fortran II was earthshaking in terms of software development and, I think, the endurance of Fortran as a technical-software programming tool."

The *Reference Manual* is also much clearer than Ziller's documents with respect to the functionality of the **COMMON** statement. In the abstract the statement allowed for programmer control over data allocation. But the power of **COMMON** was apparent when writing a subprogram that needed access to variables in the calling program, since the statement "define[d] the storage areas to be shared by several programs." So, a line of code like the following:

COMMON X, ANGLE, MATA, MATB

would assign the variables and/or arrays (listed above) to "upper storage," a separate location from program instructions and other data. (The first memory location of upper storage, in octal, was 77462_8.) This "common" storage area could be accessed and shared by a program and its subprograms as needed. In effect, such "common" variables and arrays were "global" in nature, accessible anywhere.

FORTRAN II was designed primarily by three people: Backus, Ziller, and Robert Nelson. Grace "Libby" Mitchell, who joined Backus's team at the tail end of the development of FORTRAN I, programmed most of the code for FORTRAN II—and delivered the completed product ahead of schedule. "She was a very good programmer and she did it accurately and quick," remembered Backus. (She also had a little help from Bernyce Brady and LeRoy May.) Peter Sheridan and Roy Nutt also helped out, the former modifying section 1 of the compiler and the latter section 6. All told, FORTRAN II, released in 1958, took about fifty man-years to complete and contained roughly double the number of lines of code as its predecessor. "Acceptance of FORTRAN II," Backus recalled, "was immediate." There was no putting the genie back in the bottle. Automatic programming, and FORTRAN in particular, was here to stay.

Despite its revolutionary improvements, FORTRAN II was only the first of many FORTRAN sequels (and spinoff dialects) to come.

CHAPTER 18

◊◊◊

Great Optimism and Little Discipline

Several new FORTRAN implementations paralleled the proliferation of new hardware at Big Blue.

Backus once remarked that in 1957 "the [FORTRAN] system was viewed as applying to just one machine, the IBM 704. For, although the FORTRAN group hoped to radically change the economics of scientific computing on that machine (by making programming much cheaper), it never gave very much thought to the implications of machine-independent source languages applied to a variety of machines."

Frances Allen called the period from 1957, when the IBM 709 was first announced, to 1964, with the announcement of the IBM family of computers called System/360—standardized and compatible across a product line of five models (with nineteen hardware combinations of memory capacity, ranging from 8,192 to eight million bytes, and speed, with a difference of a factor of one hundred between the extremes), complete with many peripherals—as a time of "great optimism and little discipline," with "[n]ew languages, computers, systems, and ideas appear[ing] at an astonishing rate." Indeed, FORTRAN itself was not immune to this groundswell, independent of whether Backus's development team had considered the implications of the language on a variety of platforms or not.

Although FORTRAN II was built with the 704 in mind, IBM was beginning to move on with more advanced hardware. In the book *First Generation Mainframes: The IBM 700 Series*, author Stephen Kaisler writes that Backus realized "the mean free error time for the 704 prohibited compiling and running large programs." Plus,

> Typically, a program was 300-500 statements long. When FORTRAN II allowed a program to be broken up into pieces, the restriction of program length was somewhat alleviated.

FORTRAN I did not come with or under control of an operating system. Rather, it took over the whole machine. A programmer prepared the machine with four tape units, a printer, a card reader, and a card punch. When the compiler ran, it read source cards from the card reader, printed listings on the line printer, and punched an object deck on the card punch. The object deck was then loaded into the card reader and the "GO" button was pushed. As Backus notes, the programmer then hoped it worked. After the process was completed, usually in 10-15 minutes, the programmer retrieved the cards and output for further analysis.

Besides the incompatibility of the 704 with the 701, one of the key limitations of the 704 hardware was that input/output operations and arithmetic could not be performed simultaneously by the machine's registers. That led to an IBM hardware fix: uniquely tailored processors complete with specially designated registers for I/O. It also led to a new name: the IBM 709. Like the 704, the 709, released the same year as FORTRAN II, still relied on vacuum tube logic, still stored data and instructions in 36-bit words, and still used magnetic core storage.

But transistors were the future. The company issued a catchy directive leading the way: "Solid State in '58." Finally, in 1960, IBM introduced the 7090, a so-called 7000-series computer that was around five times faster than the 709 thanks to a switch in architecture: from vacuum tubes to transistors—more than 50,000 of them. Moreover, the 7090 was compatible with the 709. The machine would be employed in powerful ways, including as the muscle behind American Airlines' SABRE reservation system, an outgrowth of the U.S. government's SAGE system. Several years later, IBM released the 7094, an upgraded 7090.

The FORTRAN Assembly Program, or FAP, translated symbolic assembly language into machine code for the 709 and 7000 series of machines. The FAP assembler, an evolution of Roy Nutt's SAP, was written by David E. Ferguson and Donald P. Moore at the Western Processing Center at UCLA. The FAP assembler permitted symbolic machine language instructions (mnemonics with a one-to-one correspondence with machine code, like ADD), macro routines (sets of instructions grouped into one instruction for convenience), and pseudo-operations (instructions that didn't correspond directly to machine language instructions, like COMMON, which had a similar function to the **COMMON** statement in FORTRAN II). As an IBM document prepared by Moore reads,

> FAP was created to provide a compromise between the convenience of a compiler and the flexibility of an assembler. Using FAP in conjunction with 709 FORTRAN in the IBM FORTRAN Monitor, a programmer may code the major part of his program in FORTRAN, and code FAP subroutines to accomplish those parts of the programming task for which FORTRAN is not suitable. Alternatively, the programmer may code the major part of the program in FAP, using FORTRAN subroutines for certain computational and input/output operations. For those tasks which must be coded entirely in symbolic language, FAP may be used to produce an "absolute" program which will operate independently of the Monitor.

The FORTRAN Monitor System (FMS), which arrived on the scene in 1958, functioned as a limited sort of proto-operating system. The post-704 FORTRAN II, which had been revised to accommodate the new hardware by a different IBM department (no longer the original Programming Research Department, and no longer the original development team), had a symbiotic relationship with FAP and FMS, as one modern observer explained:

> Fortran II was a strange beast; it ran under the Fortran Monitor System (FMS). FMS could either run the machine stand-alone, or it could run under IBSYS. Fortran II was link-compatible with the FAP assembler, the IBM product which superseded UA-SAP.... I'm not sure the compiler itself [is] of any use without the FMS monitor and the FAP assembler.

With the advent of the 7000 series of transistorized logic machines, IBM released the IBM Basic Monitor (IBSYS) operating system. "The 7090/7094 FORTRAN II Processor is composed of the FORTRAN II Compiler, the FAP (FORTRAN Assembly Program) Assembler, and the FORTRAN II Monitor," began the FORTRAN II *Manual*.

> The FORTRAN II Monitor coordinates compilations and assemblies, and permits binary object programs from previous compilations or assemblies to be executed together as parts of a single job. The FORTRAN II Processor operates under the control of the FORTRAN II Monitor which may, in turn, operate under the control of the IBM Basic Monitor (IBSYS). When operating under IBSYS, jobs for the FORTRAN II Monitor may be stacked as input along with jobs for other processors that operate under IBSYS....

The FMS could take input from object program cards, data cards, FORTRAN Monitor control cards, and FAP symbolic cards. Job control cards controlled the operation of the FMS, directing the system to read a source deck of FAP, or of FORTRAN, or of data; the binary output format of a FAP program was also dependent on the control card instructions. The object programs generated by FAP could be run on a 704 (as well as a 709, 7090, and 7094), even though FAP programs themselves had to be assembled on a 709.

Despite the more advanced hardware available, Irv Ziller wanted to squeeze out at least one more implementation of FORTRAN on the 704. Not content with juggling just one project, he was busy designing the next generation of the language while also working on FORTRAN II. Ziller called this new FORTRAN implementation FORTRAN III. It was mostly his baby, although Nelson and Nutt lent him a hand. When asked what was so "novel" about FORTRAN III in an interview conducted decades later, Backus shot back, "Well, [FORTRAN] 3 was mainly again Irv's thing, where you could sort of combine symbolic programming and Fortran programming." Ziller saw an opportunity to "intermix" assembly and FORTRAN, with the 704 assembly instructions even able to process FORTRAN variables. Such a "intermixing" feature resulted in FORTRAN III, with its machine-dependent commands, having a short half-life, since its fate was tied to the continued use of the 704. (Users of the 709 were also able to run FORTRAN III by way of a backward-compatibility feature.) Concurrent to FORTRAN III's development, SHARE members debated whether FORTRAN should allow symbolic instructions in the midst of FORTRAN programs, with the consensus declaring it to be a bad idea.

But there were other notable additions to FORTRAN III that made their way into future FORTRAN implementations—namely, the ability to pass as arguments subroutines and function names, utilize Boolean expressions, and access new FORMAT options.

Starting in the winter of 1958-59, and ending around a year later, FORTRAN III was distributed to only around twenty 704 installations. It was never released to the general public.

By early 1959, other than occasional debugging of FORTRAN II, most of the original FORTRAN group had moved on to other non-FORTRAN-related pursuits, some within IBM, some not. John Backus, for his part, developed an obsession with the four color map theorem, a centuries-old mathematical problem stating that no more than four colors are necessary to color countries on a map such that countries adjacent to each other don't share the same color. "It was just some crazy ego thing that I was totally ill equipped to deal with, but I had some idea that I was going to generalize it and thereby make it easier to solve, or something like that," remembered Backus, who didn't consider himself a mathematician regardless. "I messed with that for ages and ages and ages and never got [it]—I had all these nutty little theorems that I proved, but never really did it." The four color map theorem was proved in 1976 by Kenneth Appel and Wolfgang Haken using a computer algorithm, making the theorem among the first in mathematics to be proved this way—but Backus had nothing to do with it. (Though perhaps he was subconsciously drawn to the problem because of its inherently algorithmic nature.)

Backus was relatively isolated as the end of the decade neared, with IBM leaving him alone to pursue whatever projects he wished. "[T]hey just left me to stew in my own juices," he said. "I was pretty much a loner doing that, huddled in my office in Yorktown and later out—when I moved to the West Coast." In 1963, the company designated Backus an IBM Fellow. Also that year, he became a visiting professor at Berkeley, continuing work for Big Blue at their San Jose research laboratory.

It was, to paraphrase Churchill, not the end of the FORTRAN story, and not even the beginning of the end. But, perhaps, it was the end of the beginning. The "First Age of FORTRAN"—as Michael Metcalf, the author of a number of textbooks on modern Fortran, called it in his seminal article "The Seven Ages of Fortran"—had reached its conclusion.

CHAPTER 19

◊◊◊

The Need for Some Standards

The proliferation of incompatible FORTRAN implementations underscored the need for formal FORTRAN standards.

Announced publicly on October 5, 1959, during a closed-circuit television broadcast, the IBM 1401 Data Processing System was a small, entirely transistor-based machine which proved to be wildly popular, easy to program, inexpensive to rent (about $2,500 per month, much less than the $10,000 per month that was typical for stored-program computers of that era), and taking up little space (relatively speaking—the machine still filled up a small room). Thousands of orders poured in for the 1401 after being on the market for only a month; by the middle 1960s, over 10,000 units were in use, much more than IBM had anticipated and vastly more than the combined number of other computer models to date, which had hovered perhaps around one thousand by the late 1950s. Now there could be more than one computer at a large company; even smaller companies could have their own computer.

The 1401 came about as a response to a rival company in France called Machines Bull. Their Gamma computers, lithe and compact, were a "competitive threat," recalled the leader of the 1401 design team, Charles Branscomb. An IBM conference was set up in Germany to help formulate an accounting machine—the so-called Worldwide Accounting Machine (WWAM)—in response. But, at the end of the nearly two-month conference, there was no agreed-upon plan for the WWAM. Thomas Watson, Jr., was not happy.

No matter. The project was approved. And Branscomb took the reins, with Francis O. Underwood, a technical engineer, serving as architect of the project. WWAM became SPACE (Stored Program Accounting and Calculating Equipment), which evolved into the 1401. The 1401 would be a stored-program computer with a CPU, a card reader/punch, and a line printer; the machine had to be easy enough for people not too familiar with computers to use. The CCTV broadcast announcing the 1401 used a mockup computer in the background (unbeknownst to the 50,000-person audience), with engineers hiding behind the fake machine and hastily spinning the tapes and controlling the battery-operated flashing lights because the working prototype couldn't be moved from the test lab. The 1401 was exposed to an even larger audience at the 1964 Winter Olympics, when a working model calculated the athletes' scores.

In the early 1960s, a special version of FORTRAN was developed for the new machine. But Gary Mokotoff, who was on the 1401 FORTRAN programming group, didn't have "the vaguest idea why IBM chose to develop a FORTRAN compiler for an IBM 1401 Card-only computer."

David Macklin, the "administrator" of the programming group, had been asked by Arnie Wolf, whom he worked under, if his group could produce a FORTRAN compiler. Was Wolf joking? After all, he had asked Macklin "smilingly." But despite having assembled a cadre of young programmers he had discovered at the Bronx High School of Science—namely, Mokotoff, John Wertheim, and Stan Smillie—and despite already having written the fixed-form assembler 1401 SPS and the free-form Autocoder, Macklin reflexively answered Wolf with a "no": the 1401 was too small for FORTRAN. Then he spoke to Leonard Haines, who was familiar with a paper on serial compilation and suggested that FORTRAN could indeed work on the 1401.

Mokotoff recalled that "[t]he fact that it [a compiler for the 1401] was doable was the brainchild of Leonard Haines who worked in the Applied Programming Department for only one summer," probably in 1960. The 1401 FORTRAN project took roughly a year to complete. Haines quickly realized the impracticality of building a compiler for a paper tape-only machine like the 1401 that first produced assembly language output and then used the output to create a machine language build: multiple passes would be required. Instead, Haines looked to a version of FORTRAN for the short-lived IBM 1620 as a model. His key insight, recalled Mokotoff, was as follows: "All previous compilers passed the source program against the compiler. Haines proposed passing the compiler against the source program [and] slowly transforming it into machine language." A deck of cards, consisting of more than sixty programs, called "phases," acting sequentially, proceeded apace with the conversion. As Haines himself explained it in a paper,

> The IBM 1401 FORTRAN compiler was designed as a set of phases that operate sequentially on the source program. The source program having been placed in core storage, the compiler phases enter core one at a time. Each phase overlays its predecessor, operates on the source program and, in turn, is overlaid by the next phase of the sequence. Thus, in contrast to the customary technique of passing the source program against the compiler in core, the compiler is passed against the source program which resides in core. It is assumed that the source program is more concise than the object program, and that an object program of interest can be accommodated in core.

The FORTRAN compiler was set to operate on 8,000 core storage positions (characters), with optional tape usage. The first two of sixty-four phases—phases 00 (Snapshot) and 01 (System Monitor)—were loaded before phase 02 (Loader), which stored the entire program "backwards in order to use the 1401 machine instructions that cause address registers to decrement when processing data," Haines wrote. Phase 13 (Variables I) was one of several phases that scanned the source program for variables. Phase

33 (Arith I) was one of a number of phases that dealt with arithmetic expressions. Phase 46 (Do) analyzed DO statements in the source program. Phase 63 (Arithmetic Package) made use of an arithmetic routine loaded in the previous phase (Geaux II—pronounced "go two"). Once compiled, the program could be executed from memory.

Final compiler testing was completed at Endicott; all phases were locked, loaded, and seemingly working. "What should be the first program we should try to execute?" Mokotoff asked the group. He then went ahead and suggested something simple, like this:

```
A = 1
B = 1
C = A + B
WRITE [to printer] C
STOP
END
```

The program terminated on an Arith phase. With the bug discovered, the phase was reassembled, and the job rerun. Another error in a later phase was also dispensed with. But a third time through,

> The job got to the final phase Geaux II and the compiler indicated to press Start to execute the program. I pressed the Start button and shortly therefore there was a tiny sound from the printer. We all huddled over the printer. I pressed Stop and the Carriage Restore buttons on the printer, and there before us was a "2"!!!! We all went crazy with joy. We had been working on the project for nearly a year.

That would not be the last implementation of FORTRAN on the 1401, however.

IBM later released a version of FORTRAN IV for the 1400 series of computers, which included the 1401, 1440, and 1460. Unlike FORTRAN II, though, which was tailored for the 704 (even when it ran on the 7090, it was still, internally, very much a product of a previous generation), IBM decided to rebuild the compiler from the ground up for FORTRAN IV, designing it specifically for the architecture of the 7090. This rewrite opened the door for many improvements in the original FORTRAN system.

Irv Ziller was still involved with FORTRAN development, but he wasn't in charge of the FORTRAN IV project. The FORTRAN coordinator was an employee at IBM named Richard K. Ridgway who, in 1953, had co-written the *A-2 Compiler System Operations Manual* at Remington-Rand under the direction of Grace Hopper. But Backus, who had long since let go of the FORTRAN reins, retrospectively criticized the thought process behind FORTRAN IV, which was first released in 1962 after its announcement about a year earlier. Seeing compile times as the biggest drawback to FORTRAN II, Backus "repeatedly suggested to those who were in charge of FORTRAN that they should now develop a fast compiler and/or interpreter without any optimizing at all for use during debugging and for short-run jobs." Essentially, he proposed building two compilers, each geared toward different situations. But they didn't take his advice, instead deciding to build one compiler—spurred on by IBM's desire to include this new FORTRAN in the IBSYS operating system of the 7090.

It was Bill Heising's responsibility to transfer work on the FORTRAN project from under Backus's leadership in the Programming Research Department to the newly formed Applied Programming Department. William P. "Bill" Heising, born in 1923 in New Jersey, had earned degrees from Cornell and Columbia, landing a job at IBM in 1950. "When I became involved with the Applied Programming Department, there were approximately 10 people to take over the work of Backus's Programming Research Group," recalled Heising.

> Most of these people were capable but junior in experience in programming. Our first responsibility was to learn the structure of the compiler. Backus's group had an informal management style, and there were some things that bothered us a little. For example, the different sections were written in two different assembly languages—certain sections in one and certain in the other. When we finally got Section 2, the Programming Research Group had lost the symbolic code so it came over to us in absolute.

The most pressing need in the new Applied Programming Department was finishing development of a FORTRAN II compiler for the soon-to-be-released 709, due in 1958. Applied Programming didn't have their sea legs quite yet, so they were conservative with the FORTRAN II port: adjusting to the new I/O and supporting 8K of drum main memory instead of 4K were the only significant alterations. Plus, Applied Programming was at an inherent disadvantage right from the start, since (as Heising described it above) an original symbolic deck for one of the six compiler sections had been lost before they took over the project of maintaining FORTRAN, leaving them with only the absolute code. That missing portion needed to be reconstructed first before anything new could be attempted.

There had been more ambitious plans in the works for 709 FORTRAN beyond mere tweaks: the compiler was originally set to be integrated with the SHARE 709 System (SOS) operating system; experienced users at SHARE would build SOS while the 709 version of FORTRAN II would be developed in tandem for the new machine. Scheduling conflicts, along with technical issues—specifically, the modular programming approach of FORTRAN II on the 704—stymied any sort of easy integration between operating system and compiler. When FORTRAN II was released for the 709, it was a standalone product.

Heising's recollection of the user base of FORTRAN II, for both the 704 and 709, is telling: the least experienced computer users tended to make up a much higher proportion of FORTRAN II users than the most experienced individuals, simply because the latter were more likely to continue programming in assembly. Nonetheless, the Applied Programming Department was inundated with hundreds of improvement suggestions: "it was as if there were hundreds of people working on improving Fortran," they realized. Applied Programming was very receptive to this proto-crowdsourcing effort.

Simultaneously, Applied Programming was attempting to develop an experimental ALGOL compiler. SHARE had even urged IBM to go in that direction. But by the early 1960s it became increasingly clear that ALGOL was not catching on, certainly not enough to replace FORTRAN. "We decided to clean up Fortran II; this was the basis for the transition from Fortran II to Fortran IV," Heising wrote.

Indeed, Applied Programming's approach to FORTRAN IV involved cleaning up some machine-dependent commands from the prior implementation while also introducing a number of new features into the mix. These features, although a bit cumbersome to use by modern standards, brought some much needed functionality to FORTRAN. Besides the usual **REAL** (floating-point) and **INTEGER** types of variables defined implicitly (by the first character of the variable name: recall that I to N signified an integer), there were now **COMPLEX, LOGICAL,** and **DOUBLE PRECISION** data types available as well. The **COMPLEX** data type had an associated real part and an imaginary part, perfect for the application problems of engineers and scientists. The **LOGICAL** data type, which was Boolean in nature, could take either true or false as values, keyed in as .TRUE. or .FALSE. And the **DOUBLE PRECISION** data type was a subset of the **REAL** data type.

Explicit type specifications were now possible, for both variables and arrays; providing initial values in declaration statements were optional (the new **DATA** statement could be used to initialize variables and elements of arrays to particular values). If an integer or real variable was not explicitly declared, then the implicit first-letter naming rules of variables held. When using arrays, dimensions could be specified without the need for a **DIMENSION** statement. Here is sample code illustrating some of these new features:

```
REAL A, B, C
INTEGER X(20), Y(30)
LOGICAL R, Q
...
R = .TRUE.
Q = .FALSE.
```

Logical operators were also available, all preceded and followed by periods:

```
.NOT.
.AND.
.OR.
```

There were *relational operators* too, accounting for greater than; greater than or equal to; less than; less than or equal to; equal to; and not equal to. But inequality symbols still couldn't be used directly, like they were in the Preliminary Report; instead, the following two-letter abbreviations were employed:

```
.GT.
.GE.
.LT.
.LE.
.EQ.
.NE.
```

In addition to retaining the arithmetic **IF** statement (the traditional **IF**, introduced in FORTRAN I), in FORTRAN IV the logical **IF** statement was introduced; this new **IF** statement could process logical expressions and is therefore much more in line with the conditional statements used in modern HLLs. The general form of a logical **IF** statement was as follows:

IF (A) S

where *A* is a logical expression and *S* is any executable statement (except a **DO** or another logical **IF**). The *A* is evaluated as either true or false. For instance, all the following statements are valid uses of the logical **IF**:

IF (A .GT. B) GO TO 30
IF (C .NE. D) ANS = 3.0 * D/C
IF (P .OR. .NOT. Q) Y = Z

The logical **IF** achieved a very small measure of fame in a January 2015 episode of *The Simpsons* called "The Man Who Came to Be Dinner." In the episode, the Simpson family is transported to the planet Rigel VII, home of the many-tentacled aliens Kang and Kodos. Before imprisoning them in a zoo, one of these intellectual aliens tells the family, "As young thinglings, we are schooled in the wisdom of the universe. Physics, mathematics, FORTRAN—the greatest of the programming languages!" As the alien's speaking, we see an over-the-shoulder shot of a green thingling typing on a circa-1990s computer, with the following statement keyed in on the monitor:

IF X .EQ. Y GOTO 70

Of course, the thingling's code wouldn't work without parentheses, like this:

IF (X .EQ. Y) GOTO 70

And, although spaces were (mostly) ignored, the convention at the time of FORTRAN IV was to break up the **GO TO**:

IF (X .EQ. Y) GO TO 70

The evaluation of logical expressions was aided by a built-in feature termed "anchor-point optimization," which was what we would now call *short-circuit evaluation*. For example, consider the following statement:

IF(A .AND. B .AND. C) GO TO 700

For the logical expression above to be true—and for control to transfer to statement 700—all three variables, A, B, and C, had to be .TRUE. Suppose, though, that A was .FALSE.—in that case, there would be no need to test the values of the variables

B and C, since the logical expression would be false. Logical expressions involving .OR. would also be handled similarly, saving time. (By the time the programming language appeared on *The Simpsons*, FORTRAN had made some modest cultural waves. For example, there was the FORTRAN board game, developed at Bar-Ilan University in Israel a little more than a decade after FORTRAN I's release; containing dice, counters, a game board, and program cards featuring colorful flowcharts, the game offered a memorable tagline: "Input: Reason. Output: Pleasure." FORTRAN can also be spotted in a video game based on the animated series *Futurama*; called *Futurama: The Game*, FORTRAN is featured as a malt liquor brand called Olde Fortran, a spoof of Olde English. Olde Fortran has since evolved into a meme, "tak[ing] on a life of its own in the computer programming community. You can find the tongue-in-cheek reference on buttons, stickers, t-shirts, mugs and even pet apparel," explains an IBM website celebrating the history of the language.)

In FORTRAN IV, functions could finally be defined as originally envisioned in the Preliminary Report—without an F as the last character of their names:

$$SUM(A, B, C) = A + B + C$$
$$TEST(A, B) = .NOT. A .OR. B$$

But function definitions that were *recursive*—i.e., functions that called themselves—were not allowed. So, for example, the following function wouldn't compile:

$$FACT(N) = FACT(N) * FACT(N - 1)$$

As in FORTRAN III, subprograms (subroutines) and functions could be passed as arguments of other subprograms or functions. But an **EXTERNAL** statement had to precede a subprogram argument in a calling program. For instance, here is the calling program:

```
          EXTERNAL MULT
          ...
          ...
          CALL SUB(J, MULT, C)
```

And here is the subprogram:

```
          SUBROUTINE SUB(K, M, Z)
          IF (K) 4, 6, 6
    4     D = M(K, Z**2)
          ...
          ...
    6     RETURN
          END
```

The new **ASSIGN** statement could be used in tandem with **GOTO**, causing a transfer of control:

>   ASSIGN 750 TO ABC
>   ...
> 1000 GOTO ABC, (650, 750, 850)

Most of the machine-dependent features of previous FORTRAN implementations were excised for FORTRAN IV. Consequently, the **READ** and **WRITE** statements were now much more functional, being able to take numerous forms accounting for different methods of I/O. Error messages like "QUOTIENT OVERFLOW" were retired. More conveniently, character string literals in **FORMAT** statements weren't restricted to cumbersome Hollerith specifications; literals could be enclosed in single quotation marks instead. For example, consider two equivalent specifications for the string literal "2019 INVENTORY REPORT":

> 22   FORMAT (22H 2019 INVENTORY REPORT)
> 22   FORMAT (' 2019 INVENTORY REPORT')

The **COMMON** statement also received an upgrade, containing even more **COMMON** areas of memory, appropriately labeled, with which to share data among subprograms. A team of programmers working on the same application simply had to be careful when coordinating these shared data areas.

Although the **FREQUENCY** statement, from FORTRAN I onward, still functioned—"allow[ing] the programmer to specify which path on a branch he thought was most likely"—"people usually did not have the correct data about the best branch and often used it in circumstances that made little difference," explained Jean Sammet. In 1962, when FORTRAN IV was first released for the IBM 7030 Stretch, a transistorized supercomputer, the **FREQUENCY** statement remained part of the language. Later versions of FORTRAN IV released for the System/360 and System/370 eliminated **FREQUENCY** but included important extensions to the language like the **IMPLICIT** statement, which enabled the programmer to "Specify the type (including length) of all variables, arrays, and user-supplied functions whose names begin with a particular letter," according to the FORTRAN IV System/360 *Manual*. Stated differently, **IMPLICIT** overrode the explicit, predefined naming conventions of FORTRAN. In the following example,

> IMPLICIT INTEGER(A–H), REAL(I–K), LOGICAL(L, M, N)

any variables beginning with the characters A to H are of type **INTEGER**, I to K of type **REAL**, and L, M, and N of type **LOGICAL**. The language extensions for the System/360 also allowed the user to specify space allocations for each type of variable. The FORTRAN statement below works in the same way as the previous one, except that each of the **INTERGER** variables have two storage locations allocated, and each of the **REAL** variables have eight storage locations allocated.

> IMPLICIT INTEGER*2(A–H), REAL*8(I–K), LOGICAL(L, M, N)

A statement like

$$\text{IMPLICIT COMPLEX*16(C-F)}$$

would reserve eight storage locations for the real part of the **COMPLEX** variable (beginning with the characters C to F) and eight for the imaginary part.

Although the Applied Programming Group had initially set out, when building FORTRAN IV, to ensure that all FORTRAN II programs could run on the new implementation, for a number of reasons it didn't prove possible. For example, recall that the machine-dependent commands of FORTRAN II were excised. In addition, FORTRAN IV managed arrays in memory differently than FORTRAN I and II. In the early FORTRANs, arrays were stored starting at the highest addresses, and continuing in descending order; programs began their storage at the lowest addresses and continued in ascending order. Conflicts would arise if overlap occurred. FORTRAN IV, however, stored arrays in ascending order.

In brief, in order to ensure the smoothest possible transition from FORTRAN II to IV, a translator to convert early-FORTRAN programs was needed. SHARE took on that responsibility. The story of how that came to be begins at a SHARE meeting in February 1960 in Los Angeles, California. Members gathered to settle a debate: Should assembly code be permitted within FORTRAN programs? Those in favor argued that it promised increased efficiency. Those opposed said that there was an immediate loss of compatibility, since different machines had dissimilar assembly languages. A long floor argument ensued, and the motion was voted down; SHARE members spoke as one to say: FORTRAN III's inclusion of the assembly coding feature was a mistake, and it should not be repeated.

By this time SHARE felt that FORTRAN couldn't remain in stasis forever—it had to be rethought. "We are rapidly reaching the point at which only very minor improvements can be made within the existing framework," complained Sperry Rand's George Mealy in a letter sent to SHARE's FORTRAN chairman. "How do IBM people feel about spending their lives patching things up rather than being free to do more creative work? In short, I think we should stop trying to kid Fortran into working better and completely rewrite it." That fall, SHARE designated a "czar" to coordinate the testing of the ever-growing number of FORTRAN extensions in circulation.

In January 1961 in New York, the IBM FORTRAN Planning Group presented a report to the SHARE FORTRAN group; according to Elliott C. Nohr, a SHARE member from North American Aviation Corporation, "The ideas generated at this meeting resulted in a preliminary specification of Fortran IV."

At another SHARE meeting two months later in San Francisco, FORTRAN IV preliminary specifications were disseminated; this also marked the start of the development of FORTRAN IV for the IBM 7090. But, Nohr writes, at the time "SHARE members felt that they were having some difficulty with IBM." Nohr quotes an urgent SHARE proposal from 1961:

> The SHARE/Fortran Standards and Evaluation subcommittee wishes to report to the executive board that its ability to communicate with IBM applied programming is rapidly deteriorating. This is essentially true in the area of language modification. Decisions in this area are filtered through a group that placed undue emphasis upon compatibility with systems for non-SHARE machines and is consequently unsympathetic to our needs.

Nohr recalls that "[a]t that meeting it was obvious that the new Fortran IV that was being discussed was going to be significantly different from Fortran II and that a program would be needed" for conversion. To that end, a committee was established. Three SHARE members—IBM's Jay Allan, UCLA's Don Moore, and Aerospace Corporation's Paul Rogoway—began writing a program in FORTRAN, called the SHARE Internal Fortran Translator (SIFT), that translated FORTRAN II programs to FORTRAN IV. SIFT was scheduled for completion in January 1962, but it took until September of that year to finalize. IBM gave SIFT its stamp of approval.

There were other FORTRAN projects in the works at Big Blue. For instance, different FORTRAN compilers for the System/360 operating system were available, depending on memory requirements: FORTRAN E, for the smallest memory; FORTRAN G if more memory was available; and FORTRAN H, tailored for the largest memory. But the H compiler was one of a kind.

Edward S. Lowry and C. W. Medlock of IBM built FORTRAN H, an "optimizer" of FORTRAN IV for the System/360. FORTRAN H object program optimization techniques were described by Lowry and Medlock as follows:

> The compilation process basically converts programs from a form which is flexible to a form which is efficient in a given computing environment….

> A major novel technique used is the computation of "dominance" relationships indicating which statements are necessarily executed before others. This computation facilitates the elimination of common expressions across the whole program and the identification of the loop structure (not depending on DO statements). No distinction is made between address calculations resulting from subscripts and other expressions. Another important technique is the tracing of data flow for unsubscripted variables.

In the authors' view, their FORTRAN H compiler "performs the most thorough analysis of source code and produces the most efficient object code of any compiler presently known…" (those words were written in 1969). In fact, "For small loops of a few statements, it very often produces perfect code." First, loops are searched for "common expressions"—and then these are eliminated. Also eliminated are expressions that are independent of any of the loops. Then statements of the form A=B are substituted with references to A with B. Multiplications within any loop are replaced with repeated additions. Computations within loops are carefully run through, seeing if any can be removed in favor of constant expressions instead. All these optimizations are performed in the direction pointing from the inner loops to the outer loops.

FORTRAN H also optimized a program's control flow by using techniques that mapped out the "dominance relations" of basic blocks of code, looking for "predominators," or code that had to be executed prior to the dependent blocks. Other optimizations with subexpressions were performed as well.

Frances Allen concurred with Lowry and Medlock's sentiments about FORTRAN H, writing in 1981, "The efficacy of these optimizations is demonstrated by the fact that fifteen years after its release, it is still one of the best product-compilers in terms of object code efficiency," although she noted that others at IBM, such as Randolph G. Scarborough, were beginning to improve on the design (e.g., in better optimizing register allocations).

In general, the FORTRAN IV "standard" proliferated, both within IBM and outside of it. The language would eventually be found on machines released by Digital Equipment Corporation, Scientific Data Systems, Hewlett-Packard, and other companies. "In 1963, a number of FORTRAN IV compilers appeared on computers produced by various manufacturers," Backus wrote in 1964. "The use of FORTRAN IV has been growing steadily although FORTRAN usage is still probably preponderantly FORTRAN II."

FORTRAN was gaining significant traction at universities as well. As IBM's Bob Bemer explained, in the early 1950s, "When you were hired as a programmer then, you didn't ask about a degree in computer science; there weren't any." Recall the rather esoteric questions that were lobbed at Backus during his employment interview at IBM. "A lot of us had our own pet questions," Bemer continued, "for we were taking them [prospective employees] off the street." (Later, IBM used an in-house "Programmer's Aptitude Test" that achieved a qualified level of success at screening.) There was no pipeline churning out computer scientists, so computer programmers had a variety of backgrounds. Bemer, after all, had once worked as a movie set designer. Once, when Bemer was in urgent need of programmers, he put out an advertisement for chess players.

Things at the university level, though, were changing, with summer sessions at MIT and Michigan being curated for the programming experts, and self-contained courses—if not entire degree programs—being offered at other universities like Carnegie, Case, Penn, Purdue, and UCLA.

FORTRAN's use at the university level stretches back to the 1950s. In fact, the history of operating systems at the University of Michigan was bootstrapped by the FORTRAN I compiler, according to Bernard Galler. One of the first operating systems in the world, called the I/O System, was developed in 1955 at General Motors Research Laboratories. I/O was a three-phase batch system: batched for input formats, then execution, and finally output. When the FORTRAN I compiler was released on magnetic tape, it didn't come with any source code listings, but it did arrive with a "short bootstrap record on the tape, followed by many short records, each fully aware of the position of every other record on the tape," that could easily be understood without any source code listings, Galler recalled. Jim Fishman of GM decompiled the bootstrap record by performing an octal dump and examining it, paving the way for the new F system: an assembler preceding the original bootstrap loader. A relocatable loader followed, along with the other proper trims and trappings of a full-fledged operating system. A short time later, Galler and others at the University of Michigan adapted the GM operating system for their particular set of requirements at the school.

FORTRAN had been written for scientists and mathematicians, not students. To account for the different needs of students, who were first learning the language (and perhaps were new to programming in general), in the early 1960s schools like Purdue and the University of Wisconsin developed specialized FORTRAN compilers more tailored to error checking and quick programming compile-link-execute turnaround times. Wisconsin's system was called FORGO and was built for the IBM 1620 strictly as a means of teaching the language to neophytes.

In the mid-1960s, undergraduates at the University of Waterloo in Ontario, Canada, banded together to write a FORTRAN compiler that would greatly streamline the compilation of programs. The impetus came from one of those undergrads, James G. Mitchell, who sketched out a design on paper for a FORTRAN system that could compile, link, and execute a program rapidly and with a minimum of fuss. A computer science professor at the university named J. Wesley Graham supervised the effort; Wes Graham had previously worked at IBM, heading their Applied Science Division, before arriving at Waterloo in 1959.

The FORTRAN system they designed was called WATFOR, and it ran on the IBM 1620. The 1620 was not the first computer available for use on the campus; that distinction goes to the digital Bendix G-15, which arrived at Waterloo in 1960. An IBM 610 followed before making way for the 1620 in 1961; the computer's monthly rental fee was a paltry $672—after the educational discounts were applied. Two years later, the university purchased the machine, and by the mid-1960s Waterloo's 1620 served only one purpose: student computing.

In 1964, Ralph Stanton, who was head of the Waterloo mathematics department, along with Graham and an undergraduate named Gus German visited the University of Wisconsin. There, they procured a copy of FORGO and began using it on campus. As it had at Wisconsin, FORGO drastically reduced the compile and execution time at Waterloo: a program that took an hour to run on a conventional FORTRAN compiler now took around a minute.

In 1965, undergraduates at Waterloo began putting the computers on campus to clever use. That June, Gus German, Robert Zarnke, and Hugh Williams employed the IBM 1620 and an IBM 7040 to calculate a 200,000-digit solution to the two thousand-year-old heretofore unsolved Archimedes Cattle Problem:

> The sun god had a herd of cattle consisting of bulls and cows, one part of which was white, a second black, a third spotted, and a fourth brown. Among the bulls, the number of white ones was one half plus one third the number of the black greater than the brown; the number of the black, one quarter plus one fifth the number of the spotted greater than the brown; the number of the spotted, one sixth and one seventh the number of the white greater than the brown. Among the cows, the number of white ones was one third plus one quarter of the total black cattle; the number of the black, one quarter plus one fifth the total of the spotted cattle; the number of spotted, one fifth plus one sixth the total of the brown cattle; the number of the brown, one sixth plus one seventh the total of the white cattle. What was the composition of the herd?

Finding the answer required solving numerous simultaneous equations. Graham, out of a sense of loyalty, made sure to reach out to newspapers to publicize the student team's results.

That very same summer, Gus German and Bob Zarnke reunited, bringing along with them Richard Shirley and Jim Mitchell. Together, they wrote the WATFOR compiler for the 1620, which took FORTRAN IV as its model. Within months, nearly three thousand students at Waterloo were using it. Word of the compiler spread like wildfire, with requests for copies pouring in from dozens of American, Canadian, and international sites over the next several months. The appeal of WATFOR was immediately obvious. As the Waterloo computer science website summarizes it,

> The original WATFOR compiler for the FORTRAN IV computer language for the IBM 7040 computer had diagnostic capabilities superior to most of its contemporary counterparts so that users could find and correct errors. The program greatly expanded the potential for using computers in undergraduate instruction and it put the fledgling university on the map internationally.

Over the next decade, Computer Science Days were held at the university for visiting Ontario high school students; more than 10,000 students per year would make the pilgrimage, and they wouldn't be disappointed. A special in-house simple language called TUTOR—which was an amalgamation of FORTRAN and BASIC—was on hand for demos.

In 1966, with the arrival of a new IBM 360/75 on campus imminent—the 360 was nearly a dozen times faster than the 7040—work was begun on the next version of WATFOR, called WATFOR 360, by two lecturers at Waterloo, Paul Dirksen and Paul Cress, along with a number of other team members. Eventually awarded the Grace Murray Hopper Award for their work, WATFOR 360—which was rebranded two years later as WATFIV (resolving to "Waterloo FORTRAN IV") and modified to take into account FORTRAN language extensions courtesy of SHARE—offered yet another leap in job-execution speed and functionality for education. There would be more implementations, such as WATFOR-77, which came on the heels of FORTRAN 77's release in the late 1970s.

Besides at universities like Waterloo, another means by which users had access to FORTRAN was via a timesharing system called Quiktran, constituted in 1961 by a John Morrissey-led IBM team and finally rolled out in 1963. (By then IBM had warmed to the concept, overcoming an initial reluctance that almost cost Bob Bemer his job after broaching the idea with management.) As Jean Sammet explained, the team didn't set out to build a timesharing system: "While their original objective was to improve user debugging facilities, this eventually took the form of a dedicated system which was essentially FORTRAN but with powerful debugging and terminal control facilities added." Quiktran could support forty users at a time on 7040/44 computers using the IBM 1050 Data Communications System terminal. Once logged on, a computer user would interact with the system using a FORTRAN interpreter with attendant advantages like immediate feedback when debugging, the ability to change a program while it was running, and access to a desk calculator (called "desk calculator" mode, or "COMMAND" mode, in which each statement entered by the user was run immediately,

"COMMAND" mode contrasted with "PROGRAM" mode where statements were saved and run as a batch of commands; Quiktran was one of the first, if not the first, such dual-purposed system). The flexibility of debugging and the compatibility of the interpreter with the compiler led most people to use the system as intended: to debug a program on Quiktran for later compilation using a FORTRAN compiler.

All told, the domination of FORTRAN by the mid-1960s in the realm of scientific applications, as well as in programming in general, "has been sometimes been supposed...the result of a conscious plan by IBM to dominate the computer scene, but there is no real evidence for this," wrote Campbell-Kelly and Aspray in *Computer: A History of the Information Machine*. "What actually happened was that FORTRAN was the first effective high-level language to achieve widespread use." Thanks to popular FORTRAN textbooks like Daniel McCracken's, universities now had a primer with which to offer undergraduate courses in the language. Programmers on the job market typically had experience in FORTRAN, and they were growing in number thanks to university offerings. Competing languages like ALGOL 60, which was positioned to replace it, simply couldn't keep up with the FORTRAN juggernaut. And even though numerous dialects of the language made some machine-to-machine translations not one-to-one because of machine-dependent commands, these dialects were by and large relatively close to what had become the de facto standard: FORTRAN IV.

But not close enough. By 1963, FORTRAN IV had spread far beyond the machines of Big Blue. In 1964, Backus complained, "The existence of many FORTRAN compilers, all handling similar but slightly different FORTRAN languages has become increasingly troublesome as the range and size of application work written in FORTRAN has grown, and users frequently wish to transfer work from one computer to another of a different type." There could only ever be one solution to this logistical nightmare: standardization.

Although it had never been done with any programming language before, standardization was indeed the next step in FORTRAN's evolution. But accomplishing it would prove to be anything but easy.

CHAPTER 20

◊◊◊

Knocking Down the Tower of Babel

As the differences between the many dialects of FORTRAN piled up, successful standardization of the language would increase its popularity even more.

By 1962, there were thousands of FORTRAN programmers, but no one FORTRAN to hang their hat on. Although FORTRAN was the language of choice for scientific, engineering, technical, and mathematical problems—even the structured language ALGOL, which many academics were partial to, couldn't dethrone it, because of programmers' inherent familiarity with FORTRAN and the language's unmatched ability to produce efficient code—there were dozens of dialects floating around, as companies scrambled to tack on new marketable features to the language. Examples include EGTRAN (EGdon forTRAN, for the English Electric multiprogramming KDF9 system), ALTAC (for the Philco 2000), Automath-800 (for the H-800), FORTRAN (for the CDC 1604, H-290, and B5000), FORTRAN I (for the UNIVAC), FORTRAN II (for the LARC and the RCA 301), and AFIT FORTRAN, UT FORTRAN, FORGO, and GOTRAN (for the IBM 1620). This proliferation of dialects continued unabated, and without any controls; IBM had not even published all of the FORTRAN language specs, though the company also made little effort to stop the spread of a language they had first developed in-house years before.

Why didn't IBM patent FORTRAN in order to monetize, or at least protect, their intellectual property? A clue can be found in the company's behavior toward a roughly contemporaneous computing-related innovation: the fast Fourier transform (FFT) algorithm, which was developed in the mid-1960s by mathematicians John Tukey and James Cooley and used for applications like digital signal processing (DSP). In 1962, Cooley was hired at the IBM Watson Research Center in Yorktown Heights, New York. Tukey, who worked at both Princeton University and Bell Labs, developed the FFT algorithm on paper, while Cooley translated Tukey's ideas into code, writing a radix-2 algorithm that recursively generated fast Fourier transforms in multiple dimensions. Although Cooley initially freely shared the FFT algorithm upon request, questions of ownership rights arose after he presented the algorithm at a weekly numerical analysis seminar held at the IBM Research Department of Mathematical Sciences. A patent attorney, who was at the meeting, first raised the issue: "This has patent possibilities," the lawyer chimed in. Thereafter Big Blue went to work, researching the antecedent mathematical ideas of the algorithm. Yet despite agreeing on the uniqueness—and thus patentability—of Tukey and Cooley's work, the IBM legal team decided against filing a patent. Instead, they instructed Tukey and Cooley to write an academic paper detailing the FFT. "And eventually IBM kicked Jim [Cooley] into publication because they decided they didn't want to try to patent it and they didn't want anybody else to," explained Tukey. Cooley's take on the events was similar; he added that IBM "put it in the public domain so we protect the right of IBM to use the idea, before someone else patents it" and "to publicize it and [thus] protect the right of IBM to use it." This was typical behavior of IBM during this time period, said Cooley. IBM generally avoided patenting software (then still a nebulous concept regardless; recall that the term only came into circulation several years prior), since they preferred software be freely distributable to "help sell [their] computers," Cooley said.

So, with IBM not in the habit of either patenting software or enforcing strict usage controls, the task of standardization was left to others. In an effort to knock down what had become a FORTRAN Tower of Babel, the American Standards Association (ASA)—organized more than four decades earlier as the American Engineering Standards Committee (AESC), a consortium of engineering societies and government agencies which, by the end of the decade, became the American National Standards Institute (ANSI)—formed a committee, which employed ASA standards but was sponsored by the Business Equipment Manufacturers Association (BEMA). In 1960, the ASA Sectional Committee X3 for Computers and Information Processing was founded. From there, later that year, a subcommittee was established with the express purpose of examining languages; the X3.4 Sectional Subcommittee settled on three procedure-oriented languages for standardization: ALGOL, COBOL, and FORTRAN.

On May 17, 1962, a resolution established the first FORTRAN standards working group: X3.4.3-FORTRAN. With the participation of computer user groups and various American companies, the mission was to develop proposed standards for FORTRAN, initially termed "American Standard FORTRAN" or "ASA Standard FORTRAN." Bill Heising, who earlier had the responsibility of shifting the FORTRAN project from Backus's Programming Research Department to the Applied Programming Department at IBM, was appointed chairman of X3.4.3. He would serve in that leadership role for the life of the standards committee, which took four years to complete its work.

In June, Bill Heising began his tenure by sending out invitations for an upcoming organizational meeting; the invites were distributed to "manufacturers and user groups who might be interested in participating in the development of FORTRAN standards," he explained. Inside the invitation was an initial draft for the standardization, written by Heising along with Richard K. "Dick" Ridgeway, who also worked at IBM. The draft took FORTRAN IV, due for an imminent public release, as a starting point.

The first meeting of working group X3.4.3 was held on August 13 to 14, 1962, at BEMA Headquarters in New York City. There, because a "sufficiently wide representation of interested persons was participating," the FORTRAN standardization work was given the green light. In a resolution approved on August 14, the working group agreed that any future published set of FORTRAN standards must satisfy the following general criteria:

a. Ease of use by humans,
b. Compatibility with past FORTRAN use,
c. Scope of application,
d. Potential for extension,
e. Facility of implementation, i.e. compilation and execution efficiency.

Furthermore, the goal was that any "FORTRAN standard will facilitate machine-to-machine transfer of programs written in ASA Standard FORTRAN. The Standard will serve as a reference document both for users who wish to achieve this objective and for manufacturers whose programming products will make it possible," wrote Bill Heising in a contemporaneous published document designed to "elicit comment, criticism and general public reaction with the understanding that such working documents are intermediate results in the standardization process and are subject to change, modification or withdrawal in part or in whole."

X3.4.3 began with around fifty members, including representatives of the important hardware vendors, user groups (such as SHARE, the Honeywell Users Association, and IBM 1620 Users), higher education (such as the University of Wisconsin and Penn State), software companies (such as Computer Sciences Corporation). X3.4.3 then assumed a supervisory role—meeting only twice per year—over two technical subcommittees, which performed the yeoman's work of the standardization. By group consensus, one of the subcommittees, X3.4.3-IV, was to base a standard off of FORTRAN IV, and the other subcommittee, X3.4.3-II, would use FORTRAN II as its base. Heising described the reasoning behind the FORTRAN II standard this way: "there was interest in developing for small and intermediate computers a FORTRAN standard near the power of FORTRAN II, however suitably modified to be compatible with the associated FORTRAN IV." Thus, FORTRAN IV would be the gold standard, with FORTRAN II functioning as a subset—or at least that was the plan early on.

Despite the technical work being farmed out, the "parent" X3.4.3 committee was responsible for the final decision-making; the parent committee had to navigate some tricky paths. Martin Greenfield, chairman of the X3.4.3-IV, describes a situation calling for the parent committee to intervene. A proposal involving character-accessible hardware, which was new on the scene, raised a controversial question: Should the subcommittee employ this new technology to vary the space allocated to different data types (variable allocation), or should there be no such preset storage relationship (fixed allocation)? If the parent committee went with variable allocation, then the language standard would, in effect, be "hardware biased." A fixed allocation would not tie the language standard to any particular model of hardware. Throughout the debate, the members of X3.4.3 kept one central tenet in mind: that the key appeal of the FORTRAN language, and the primary reason why ALGOL couldn't knock it from its dominant perch, was its ability to produce very efficient object code. Therefore, "After some impassioned discussions the heavy dependence of FORTRAN on storage association for efficiency and the dominance of word-addressable processors won," Greenfield recalled.

Along with Greenfield, who worked at Honeywell, X3.4.3-IV had only nine members, including Dick Ridgeway, representing IBM, as well as representatives from Control Data Corporation, Computer Sciences Corporation, UNIVAC, Westinghouse, and SHARE. With such few members, the subcommittee could work quickly and efficiently, with everyone readily participating and staying informed about any goings-on. Committee chairman Bill Heising, though not officially part of X3.4.3-IV, pulled double duty, frequently contributing to the subcommittee's efforts.

Two years would pass before the X3.4.3-IV subcommittee brought their project to completion. The subcommittee's meetings took place primarily at one of two locations: the IBM program development center, located in the Time-Life building, or BEMA headquarters—both of which were in New York City. Because FORTRAN IV was still busily in development when the subcommittee was established, and since there were open lines of communication between the developers at IBM and members of the subcommittee, what one group did affected the other. "It was a unique situation," Greenfield remembered, "where language changes adopted by the subcommittee were incorporated into the compilers almost immediately. I have always felt that the actual standardization of FORTRAN stemmed from the discussions, understandings, and agreements of X3.4.3-IV rather than from formal text that followed some years later."

Of course, since the starting point for the X3.4.3-IV subcommittee was the (at the time) proposed FORTRAN IV language, the completed draft standards, released in mid-1964, hewed closely to IBM's implementation of FORTRAN IV. Greenfield was quick to point out, however, that the draft was far from a "slavish copy," since IBM themselves had never set rigorous standards for the language—they only published informal specs. Implementations of FORTRAN IV, which began proliferating in the midst of the subcommittee's technical deliberations, weren't all the same. For one thing, fitting the language to different hardware layouts (at IBM and elsewhere) demanded heterogeneous approaches. Furthermore, vendors were adapting the language and adding features to serve their needs—and that included IBM, which, to safeguard customers' investments, was intent on keeping a commonality between FORTRAN II's and FORTRAN IV's I/O routines.

Greenfield notes that IBM's implementation of FORTRAN II contained a number of "objectional shortcuts" that subcommittee members didn't want migrating to any FORTRAN standard. One such shortcut permitted users to substitute a multiplication calculation like 6*M with just 6M. That "feature" had to go, and IBM agreed.

Standardizing a language in the early 1960s was novel; FORTRAN was the first HLL to undergo standardization. When X3.4.3-IV began its work, one of their first debates centered on if there should even be a set of language standards at all. Answering this existential question had far-reaching implications, because such standards could, over time, suppress a language's innovation—since conforming to a published set of standards (written in the past) becomes an impediment in the future. Adding language extensions could be difficult or impossible. A waiting game might ensure, where developers would withhold or not even bother building next-generation implementations until new sets of standards, which took into account the latest advancements, were drafted. It gets worse. A feature that was worked into any set of standards would have a long half-life, even if including that feature was later determined to be a serious misstep—and those who draft language standards, knowing the high cost of missteps, would be more apt to play defense and operate conservatively, limiting what was included to the tried-and-true.

But the pressing needs for standardizing FORTRAN—the very reason why X3.4.3 was established in the first place—shot down those arguments. Members of X3.4.3-IV would draft its published standards as "permissive," meaning that any features *beyond* the set listed in the standards could be included in an implementation of FORTRAN, provided that the specifications were adhered to and that programs written to conform to the standards could be run without a hitch. As the American National Standard FORTRAN document's "Purpose" section read,

> This standard establishes the form for and the interpretation of programs expressed in the FORTRAN language for the purpose of promoting a high degree of interchangeability of such programs for use on a variety of automatic data processing systems. A processor shall conform to this standard provided it accepts, and interprets as specified, at least those forms and relationships described herein.

In addition, precisely *how* the standards are to be implemented by a processor aren't specified; for this, developers were given carte blanche. In the words of the ANS FORTRAN document, while the "standard establishes…[t]he form of a program written in the FORTRAN language,"

> This standard does not prescribe:
>
> (1) The mechanism by which programs are transformed for use on a data processing system (the combination of this mechanism and data processing system is called a processor).
> (2) The method of transcription of such programs or their input or output data to or from a data processing medium.

The X3.4.3-IV subcommittee drafted their standards in plain English, rather than using some sort of "metalanguage," pseudocode, or mathematical/symbolic language. As Greenfield described it, "This was in the belief that the description of the semantics was the difficult problem." Why should readers have to learn a new language in order to understand the standards? Yet Greenfield laments that the subcommittee didn't inject a bit of metalinguistic precision into their description of the **FORMAT** statement, since the published standards contained a **FORMAT** specification error.

By sticking to English and avoiding the use of a metalanguage, Greenfield said that X3.4.3-IV was faced with "many challenges to our ability to describe." For example, the **IF** statement came under scrutiny: How should the new logical **IF** be handled? Should it be treated like the arithmetic **IF**? Ultimately, certain restrictions with logical **IF**s were put in place; for instance, they were not permitted as terminal statements of **DO** loops.

But the biggest headache for the subcommittee members revolved around defining **DO** loops. "All the implementations of FORTRAN IV being developed [at the time] allowed a more liberal extended range than the one appearing in the standard," according to Greenfield. The subcommittee was willing to loosen up the reins and go with a less restrictive standard, but they were unable to fashion a definition of **DO** loops that would open the door to greater flexibility; Greenfield recalled that everyone in the committee "tried at least twice," but simply couldn't do it. "Any definition that included statements about the sanctity of the contents of index registers," he said, "although reflecting a real concern, was inappropriate." Take a look at the following paragraph from the ANS FORTRAN document to see the convoluted nature of the **DO** loop wording:

> A completely nested nest is a set of **DO** statements and their ranges, and any **DO** statements contained within their ranges, such that the first occurring terminal statement of any of those **DO** statements physically follows the last occurring **DO** statement and the first occurring **DO** statement of the set is not in the range of any **DO** statement.

That was only a single sentence.

To those who didn't like the labyrinthine definition of **DO** statements in American Standard FORTRAN, Greenfield has a message for you: deal with it. You simply don't understand the hardships that the subcommittee encountered, and the number of descriptions they wrote which ended up tossed in the wastepaper basket, to simultaneously maintain their descriptive cogency while also comprehensively relaying the technical aspects. The devil was in the details.

Though they struggled translating some of the more technical concepts to plain English, the subcommittee members were proud of the paucity of new terms they had to fashion. Rather than coin neologisms, they first pored through extant manuals, carefully searching to see what, if any, terminology overlapped; from there, they put these terms, already in circulation, on firmer footing. Examples include *executable program*, *main program*, *subprogram*, *procedure subprogram*, *statement*, *comment*, and *continuation line*. They also ended up using the following words in new ways: *definition*, *undefinition*, *defined*, *undefined*, *reference*, and *intrinsic function*. (According to one observer, the concept of an "undefinition" was an attempt to bridge "two worlds" so they could "coexist": the world of multi-processing environments that "saved the last-used-state of a subprogram" and those that loaded the "initial-state without preserving the last-used state and therefore all local values were lost.") Lou Gatt, a member of the subcommittee who worked at Computer Sciences Corporation, coined "intrinsic function," which navigated a path in between in-line code and internal procedures.

The publication of FORTRAN standards would not only quell the proliferation of dialects, but it would also dramatically tamp down on the spread of multiple or fuzzy terms for concepts—people came to accept and use the more rigorously defined and grounded terms of the X3.4.3 subcommittee. But, in retrospect, both of these consequences of standards publication—the former intended, the latter unintended—were lucky to come about at all, and certainly did not come to pass because of any enforcement authority in position to employ "acceptance procedures" to ensure compliance. The subcommittee disbanded post-publication (although it was reconstituted; more on that below); there was no vested power granted to any "Central Organization of Programmers" to enforce the standards, censuring those who disobeyed. And the X3.4.3 committee didn't have the time, money, or resources to create or manage a system of acceptance testing; they "hoped that market pressures would lead to some accepted verification means," but the standards emerging from their work could have been completely ignored.

Recall that there were two subcommittees: X3.4.3-IV, building standards off of FORTRAN IV, and X3.4.3-II, which started with FORTRAN II as its base. X3.4.3-II had fewer members than X3.4.3-IV; Jack Palmer, a Harvard educated IBMer who served in the Navy during the Second World War, was the chairman of X3.4.3-II. Since FORTRAN II was well established by this point, the subcommittee worked quickly, finishing their draft in May 1963—almost a year before X3.4.3-IV wrapped up. The X3.4.3-II subcommittee, therefore, produced the first-ever complete HLL standard.

Yet once the X3.4.3-IV subcommittee finalized their draft in April 1964, and the two subcommittees' drafts were compared, the stark differences between the implementations precluded interchangeability or even some sort of merge between them. There were "stylistic, terminological, and content differences and conflicts," Bill Heising recalled. X3.4.3 wanted two standards: a full language standard and a proper subset. By June of 1964, it was clear that X3.4.3-II couldn't serve as the subset. FORTRAN IV had features with "no counterpart," as stated in the ANS FORTRAN document: the **DATA** statement, logical types, labeled **COMMON** statements, and the logical **IF**. Furthermore, in FORTRAN II, the library functions; naming rules of functions; operations with decimals; and machine-dependent I/O were incompatible and not interchangeable with FORTRAN IV, precluding any sort of seamless integration of the two committees' sets of standards. At first, X3.4.3 tried to, in the words of Heising, "recast...the X3.4.3-II document to reflect the style of the X3.4.3-IV document while retaining the original content." And, that fall, both draft standards were printed in *Communications of the ACM*.

But, in the several years it took to gain final approval of the FORTRAN standards, the work of X3.4.3-II had to be thrown away. The proper subset, instead of being built from FORTRAN II, instead turned out to be a stripped-down version of the standards written by X3.4.3-IV. (For instance, the subset had no logical type or logical **IF** available; had a maximum of five characters for naming, rather than six; had no three-dimensional arrays; had no assigned **GO TO**; and had many other deletions and limitations.) The superset was given the name USA Standard FORTRAN (ASA X3.9-1966), while the subset was called USA Standard Basic FORTRAN (ASA X3.10-1966). Both were approved in the spring of 1966. Despite the process of standardization being, in the words of Michael Metcalf, an "all-American affair," the standardized language was recognized internationally by the Geneva-based International Standards Organization (ISO), with a third subset, a submission by the European Computer Manufacturers Association (ECMA), added to the mix. And with that, FORTRAN 66—as it became known—was born. (One qualification is necessary here: As explained by Jeanne C. Adams, who later chaired a standards committee, the "66" was added later, to distinguish this first standardization effort from the next one, FORTRAN 77. Thus, the name FORTRAN 66 is a retronym.)

With standards now in place, the language was finally portable, at least in theory. "Essentially, [FORTRAN 66] was a common subset of the dialects, so that each dialect could be regarded as an extension of the standard," explain Michael Metcalf and John Reid in their article "Whither Fortran?" "Users wishing to write portable code had to be careful to avoid extensions."

In practice, however, new dialects still proliferated—many vendors produced compilers that didn't even bother to conform to the standards, or had features that the standards didn't address, such as methods of file handling—and the standards had to be reviewed and set anew. "Given the wide range of environments in which a program may have to operate, portability is more a skill than a science," one observer declared, despite the standards committees "promot[ing] a high degree of interchangeability of Fortran programs for use on a variety of systems."

As another Towel of Babel was slowly being built, the education of a first generation of students in FORTRAN was already well underway.

CHAPTER 21

Coloring Outside the Lines

At the same time that some were hard at work making FORTRAN easier than ever to learn, others were busy tearing the language apart.

In 1958, hardly a year after the first FORTRAN compiler was released, a group of 450 engineers began taking a training class on the language at United Aircraft. That same year, IBM released a short educational film on FORTRAN, made in Poughkeepsie, New York, which demonstrated how the nascent programming language could be used to tackle the so-called Indian Problem. Legend has it that Native Americans were paid twenty-four dollars (converted from sixty Dutch guilders) for the entirety of Manhattan Island; if that money had been deposited in the bank at r percent interest, compounded annually, how much would we have now (the "now," in this case, being 1958)?

The film starts with a young man, dressed in a suit and tie, flashing several FORTRAN manuals on the screen—including the FOR TRANSIT *Manual*—and then introducing the Indian Problem. At first, he lays out seven FORTRAN-like statements making up a generic computer program that could calculate the total principal after more than three hundred years of compound interest had accrued. Then, he replaces the FORTRAN-like statements with actual FORTRAN statements, such as a **DO** loop and **GO TO** statement, that make up a working program, even discussing fixed- and floating-point calculations and demonstrating proper use of the **READ**, **FORMAT**, and **PRINT** statements. The film ends with a demonstration of how to use an IBM 704 to compile and run the program, with the output coming from a line printer.

Over at the California Institute of Technology, they weren't shooting FORTRAN films—they were singing FORTRAN songs. The Caltech Stock Company—a musical ensemble of faculty, staff, students, and others associated with the school that was "best described as Caltech's own version of the Capitol Steps," according to an obituary of James K. "Jim" Knowles, a Caltech professor of applied mechanics and member of the singing group—released a parody LP called *Let's Advance on Science*, recorded sometime in the 1960s. The vinyl contains twelve science-themed songs written by J. Kent Clark, a professor of literature, and Elliott Davis, a piano-playing neighbor of Clark's. Jim Knowles lent his vocal talents to the song "The Richter Scale," while Kent Clark sang the eponymous opening tune, "Let's Advance on Science."

But it was Ward Whaling, a professor of physics, who sang the third track on the record: "Fortran." The song begins with a solo—in which the word "tutored" is rhymed with "computered"—and continues with a chorus urging you to "Know your Fortran" and asking if you'll "talk Fortran with me."

Whaling appreciated the opportunity to be involved with the Caltech Stock Company. "One of the activities that I enjoyed very much and let me make the acquaintance of many people outside of physics were the musical shows that Kent Clark and Elliot Davis put together," he said to an interviewer decades later. "Davis was…a self-taught pianist and he wrote music to Kent's lyrics and accompanied all the shows." Whaling got involved with the musical shows in 1955, once "Kent wanted a young physicist to do a take-off on [Caltech's Richard] Feynman."

The tune "Fortran" would not be the last time the world of popular music would intersect with the language. "Science [is] truth for life, in Fortran tongue the answer," sang 10,000 Maniacs in 1982's "Planned Obsolescence." Thirty years later, the independent hip hop group Death*Star released an album titled *Soldiers of FORTRAN*. But only Caltech's song artfully narrated the process of programming in the language, rather than merely employing the term "FORTRAN" because its unusual sound catches one's attention.

Comprehensively introducing college students to FORTRAN, however, would require more than a catchy tune or a short film; it would necessitate the writing of a world-class textbook.

Although it wasn't the first computer book he wrote—that would be 1957's *Digital Computer Programming*—Daniel D. McCracken's *A Guide to Fortran Programming* was his first bestseller. Published in 1961, the book and its successive editions would help a generation of students learn the ins and outs of FORTRAN. Called the "Stephen King of how-to programming books" by *The New York Times*, McCracken's books were used as textbooks at universities and translated into well over a dozen languages. All told, he sold more than one and a half million books, his FORTRAN and COBOL offerings "standards in the field," according to Steve Lohr, with them doubling as respected reference books, too.

McCracken was born in 1930 in Montana. His family moved to Washington state, where his parents' relatives lived, after the mine where his father, who was a mine engineer, worked had to shut down. After snagging two degrees from Central Washington University (in mathematics and chemistry), McCracken was hired at General Electric in their chemical engineering department, but then shifted over to their computer center, where he worked for seven years. It was at GE that the writing bug took hold. "When I saw something that I thought might be publishable, I wrote something," he recalled. "I just wanted to spread the word about good stuff." After leaving GE, he launched a computer consulting company, working for decades with government and corporate entities while churning out book after book in his spare time. Eventually, he found his way to the City College of New York, where he taught computer science courses—and was known for being an early adopter of the latest and greater in the field. For example, McCracken introduced his students to Java only shortly after its release in the mid-1990s.

McCracken also dabbled in politics, organizing the Computer Professionals Against the ABM (the U.S. Safeguard anti-ballistic missile system), "an ad hoc organization of 500 people, [which was] formed to oppose the Safeguard system on purely technical grounds," read a press release.

> In describing his group's technical case against the ABM, Mr. McCracken said, "As professionals with a wide range of experience with large scale computer systems, we are convinced that the pattern of development that must of necessity be followed with Safeguard, is highly unlikely to lead to a successful computer system."

Being a pacifist, John Backus was sympathetic to McCracken's positions, so he joined the Computer Professionals Against the ABM. In March 1972, President Nixon announced a new national award for scientists: the Presidential Prizes for Innovation, and Backus was selected as one of the recipients (the others were Edward F. Knipling, Willem Kolff, Harold A. Rosen, Samuel Ruben, and Joan Ganz Cooney and Lloyd A. Morrisett, who would share a prize). The White House privately called up each of these individuals, asking them if they were "willing" to travel to Washington to receive the prize in person. An article in *Science* magazine called "The Presidential Prize Caper," written by Deborah Shapley, tells what happened next: "Some of those who were called suspected that the White House was trying to learn if any of the winners were so disaffected with Nixon, or the [Vietnam] war, that they would publicly refuse the prize and embarrass the President. They then heard nothing." Indeed, Backus was secretly planning to use his award speech to rail against the administration and the war—he was no fan of Nixon—and he corresponded with McCracken to plot strategy. But the awards were never distributed. "I guess now my plan was not a gentlemanly scheme, but anyway I was relieved when the plan fell through," Backus recalled. (Backus would go on to oppose President Reagan's Strategic Defense Initiative, colloquially known as "Star Wars," a decade later.)

From 1951 to 1958, McCracken worked at General Electric. But once he left GE—and before he launched his computer consulting company—McCracken traveled to the AEC computing facility at NYU to pursue a doctorate in mathematics. During this time, "no recollection how this happened—but I got in contact with people at Honeywell in Wellesley, somewhere in the Boston area. I wrote a FORTRAN manual for them," he explained. But then a lightbulb went off in his head.

> Somewhere along the line, I said, "Wait a minute. This could be a published book." Went to my editors at Wiley and told them what I had in mind, and it took them no time at all to see it. They were livewire people. One of them, Walker Stone, senior editor…could see that computers were going to be a big thing and that somebody in their organization ought to know something about them. He went out and got himself a

grounding education. It took no time to convince him. He saw it instantly. It took him a while to convince management to publish a book on a subject where IBM gave away manuals.... [T]he IBM manual for FORTRAN—I'll look up the code and we'll read it on the tape—was just impenetrable....

Although Walker Stone did his part to convince Wiley's management that writing a FORTRAN primer was indeed a good idea, McCracken had difficulties writing the book for two reasons: (1) He didn't have easy access to a computer, or very much machine time, to check code, and (2) The prospective market for programming books was largely unknown. McCracken spent around four hundred hours—and just under six months—assembling *A Guide to Fortran Programming*, which clocked in at just under ninety pages. The book sold over three hundred thousand copies, but McCracken never finished his Ph.D.

As good as McCracken's FORTRAN books were at introducing the masses to the language, arguably the most effective introductory FORTRAN book was written by an esoteric MIT engineering lecturer and George Washington University professor named Roger Emanuel Kaufman. Called *A FORTRAN Coloring Book, 1st. & Last Edition* (1978)—and it was quite *literally* a coloring book, completely handwritten and -drawn by the author—the text is beautifully illustrated (with a teaching duck taking center stage throughout, along with numerous appearances by other surrealistic animals), playfully and irreverently written, and, best of all, serves well as a comprehensive introduction to the language. ("Irreverence pervades the book in everything but its commitment: to teach computer programming. That is does very well," one reviewer said at the time.) No doubt influenced by the satiric approach of publications like *Mad Magazine*, even the back cover drips with sarcasm. Seemingly offering a "Money-Back Guarantee," the prospective buyer would do well to read Kaufman's fine print first:

> *If you do all the programming problems at the end of this book and don't learn FORTRAN in the process, you deserve your money back. *Offer VOID within or without U.S.A.*

Even the "About the Author" spills over with abject silliness. Kaufman begins by relaying the biography of the humorist Erma Bombeck before negatively comparing himself to her: "On the other hand, Roger Kaufman, author of the present book, is little known to millions of Americans, from his failure to appear on the Johnny Carson Show."

Kaufman's path not only to computers, but to engineering as well, was circuitous. He was always fond of the theater, having completed technical work in summer theaters from the age of nine. By high school graduation, he didn't know which passion to pursue: drama or engineering. Learning of Yale's graduate degree in theater engineering, he first attended Tufts, earning a bachelor's degree in mechanical engineering. Kaufman then pursued the MFA at Yale, studying under professors who had made a name for themselves in the theater, such as Stanley McCandless, who was known the "Father of Modern Lighting Design." Eventually, Kaufman pursued another master's at Yale—this time in engineering—on the way to doctoral studies. Conducting his research in kinematics (physics describing the motion of objects) resulted in him spending more and more time operating IBM mainframe computers. "I would put in a run of punch cards on Monday and get them back through the glass doors on Wednesday," Kaufman recalled. "If you were lucky you could get in three runs a week so you checked very carefully for typos before submitting your boxes of cards. (I have a dozen more powerful old computers stacked in my basement junk pile even if that was a four million dollar machine!)" He also made use of the Bell Labs programming language called SNOBOL (StriNg Oriented and symBOlic Language). But that was where he ran into problems.

> I was the first person to do a really big symbolic manipulation project using the newly developed language SNOBOL4 to derive and punch out a FORTRAN program to do five position kinematic synthesis. In the midst of pages of printouts of complex arithmetic equations with thousands of terms strange errors would appear, like the time of day or my system password. I was having all sorts of problems for months trying to debug my program which seemed to be perfect.

Desperate to reach a solution, he phoned Bell Labs. They were one step ahead of him—they had found the same error the very night before. Why did it take so long for them to discover the issue? Because employees at Bell Labs hadn't put SNOBOL4 through its paces yet, preferring instead to have it print simple strings like "Merry Christmas and Happy New Year" in the pattern of a Christmas tree. "My project was the first serious mathematical manipulation problem that really taxed SNOBOL's garbage collection abilities," claimed Kaufman. He explained why:

> They asked me to send them a tape with my program and a few weeks later they sent back several big seven track tapes with a new version of the compiler and a thank you note saying my program was fine and the problem was with the SNOBOL language itself. So my kinematics program played a little role in debugging SNOBOL4, the granddaddy of modern symbolic manipulation languages!

By the late 1960s, Kaufman would develop KINSYN (KINematic SYNthesis), a computer-aided kinematic design visualization system, which he first wrote in FORTRAN on an IBM 1130. Improved versions of the program would follow for a variety of hardware. At least in mechanical engineering circles, KINSYN was what he became best known for.

But it was *A FORTRAN Coloring Book* that brought Kaufman the widest recognition. Early on in the book, the reader encounters several quotations of faux praise. "With skillful satire, Dr. Kaufman has written one of the great textbooks of our time," says the author's mother. "I would have never thought he had it in him," replies the author's mother-in-law.

The *Coloring Book*, at one point, brings algorithmic thinking to bear on, of all things, picking lint out of one's belly button. "Like most of us," Kaufman writes, "you have probably spent years in a disorganized fashion, picking lint from your belly button. See how much more efficiently this can be done when you systemize the process in a logical fashion by drawing a flowchart.... In just a few months I was able to produce a shag rug, two tweed jackets, three ties, and a tea cozy."

A number of other strange analogies pervade the text. "A computer is like your mommy's bureau drawers," writes Kaufman. "It has <u>big</u> drawers for numbers with decimal points. These are called real or <u>floating point</u> numbers…and it has <u>teeny tiny</u> drawers for <u>integer</u> numbers. Integers are numbers without decimal points or fractional parts. Integers are used for counting and things like that."

The idiosyncratic book, which was originally written to supplement classes Kaufman taught on FORTRAN at MIT, proved very popular, no doubt helped by an early *The New York Times* review in their "Paperbacks: New and Noteworthy" section. "Folks, here's a book for all these bright high-school kids and ambitious college sophomores who nowadays are more eager to learn FORTRAN, the language of computer programming, than, say, French, just to mention another popular tongue," the review begins. It continues:

> Dr. Roger Kaufman, a lecturer at a small Massachusetts college called M.I.T. …wrote it as an alternative to your stuffy textbook or technical manual. We mean *really wrote* it, the actual words, with a pen. He also drew the diagrams, flow charts, pictures and things…. He even made the pictures so you can color them if you're in the mood. Dr. K. says he classroom-tested the book on hundreds of M.I.T. students, who liked it just fine.

The *Coloring Book* was also the subject of a 1978 *The New York Times* piece called "The Scientific Comics: A New Theory in Teaching."

A review of the book in the *American Mathematical Monthly* from that same year ran but a single poetic line: "A lively approach to seduce,/In manner quite sim'lar to Seuss./Handwritten, with drawings and lots of guffawings/Disposed to make Fortran transluce." Coincidently, Ted Geisel (Dr. Seuss himself) mailed Kaufman a letter not only praising the *Coloring Book* but also lamenting that he didn't have available a similar teach-it-to-yourself book as a student at Dartmouth.

The *Coloring Book* was translated into a number of languages, like Hungarian; it was also plagiarized into some as well, like German. The book shared the stage with a number of other similar cartoon-style offerings, such as *The Cartoon Guide to the Computer* and *The Cartoon History of the Universe*, both by Larry Gonick, and, perhaps least surprising of all, *Illustrating FORTRAN* (1982) by Donald Alcock, which took a more serious approach to its subject matter but still offered a polished, comprehensive product featuring drawings as the central pedagogic tool. (Alcock, unlike Kaufman, penned a series of *Illustrating* books on languages besides FORTRAN, such as BASIC, C, and Pascal. It should be noted that Alcock's first *Illustrating BASIC* book arrived on shelves a year before Kaufman's *Coloring Book*.) The writer Simon Yuill, in the chapter "Bend Sinister: Monstrosity and Normative Effect in Computational Practice" found in *Fun and Software: Exploring Pleasure, Paradox, and Pain in Computing* (2014), observes that Kaufman's book was "the first published computing text to use cartoon and comic strip drawings as a pedagogic medium"; furthermore, the *Coloring Book* was the "archetype to the entire *For Dummies* series and all its numerous imitators." Indeed, as Kaufman himself admitted, "Imitation is the sincerest form of flattery."

Yuill explores the implications of Kaufman's work, contrasting it with the *For Dummies* series. Effectively, Yuill takes a Marxist approach—forgive the simplification, since we're now wading into academic territory—claiming that unlike the *For Dummies* books, which conform to the bourgeoisie values of acquiesance to the capitalist framework of materialism and the like, the *Coloring Book* is a deeply subversive work merely dressed up as a children's book:

> The *For Dummies* books primarily draw upon humour as a means to grease the wheel of cognitive capital, facilitating the ever-recurrent re-skilling (and de-skilling) of the contemporary IT worker. They represent an end-point in the transformation of the use of humour to aid production within the workplace, which has devolved from being a liberal characteristic of privileged workers such as scientists and creatives, as explored in Arthur Koestler's *The Act of Creation* (1964), to being a general form of managerial control known as 'structured fun'. Stylistically, *A FORTRAN Coloring Book* most resembles the world of Dr. Seuss, and rather than offering a series of ironic platitudes such as stalk the pages of *For Dummies* books, it engages in a scatological satire that positions the reader in a somewhat Freudian relation to its subject.

This "Freudian relation" can be seen with, for instance, the comparison between computers and "your mommy's bureau drawers."

Although aesthetically most similar to Dr. Seuss, the *Coloring Book* in overall presentation has more in common with the contemporaneous graduate school fanzine culture, explains Yuill. The *Coloring Book* in fact bore more resemblance in layout and content to genre-busting books like *Gödel, Escher, Bach: An Eternal Golden Braid* (1979) by Douglas Hofstadter than other pedagogic cartoon-laced works that may have superficially seemed akin to Kaufman's but were in fact different in kind, in that they were not "emergent" literary texts, "assembl[ing] different forms and figurations into itself."

Yuill thought the *Coloring Book* also had similarities with the computer manuals of software activist Richard Stallman. Stallman, born in 1953 in New York, had his own formative experience with FORTRAN—and it wasn't positive. As a high school senior, he "got involved with the IBM New York Scientific Center, where they actually let me start programming real computers," he said. A year later, they hired him. His first assignment was writing a FORTRAN program: "I got that program done in a few weeks, and I swore that I would never use FORTRAN again because I despised it as a language compared with other languages."

Stallman wasn't FORTRAN's most trenchant critic. That distinction unquestionably belongs to the highly influential Dutch computer programmer Edsger Wybe Dijkstra, who became well known for his pithy writing and no-nonsense attitude toward what he characterized as poor programming style. In one of his most famous essays, called "Go To Statement Considered Harmful" (1968)—but also referred to as EWD 215: "A Case Against the **GO TO** Statement"; the piece was first published as a letter to the editor of *Communications of the ACM*—Dijkstra, who was born in 1930 in the Netherlands, lays bare the problems with **GO TO** and urges the command be eliminated from use:

> For a number of years I have been familiar with the observation that the quality of programmers is a decreasing function of the density of go to statements in the pro-

grams they produce. More recently I discovered why the use of the go to statement has such disastrous effects, and I became convinced that the go to statement should be abolished from all "higher level" programming languages (i.e. everything except, perhaps, plain machine code)....

The go to statement as it stands is just too primitive; it is too much an invitation to make a mess of one's program.

Dijkstra even offered a psychological reason for why **GO TO** was a bad idea: our brains were more comfortable with "static relations" than with "processes [which are] evolving in time." Thus, "The unbridled use of the go to statement has an immediate consequence that it becomes terribly hard to find a meaningful set of coordinates in which to describe the process progress"—in other words, it's tough to trace what will happen once the program runs. The action of **GO TO** wasn't a FORTRAN original—unconditional jumps were a mainstay of assembly and machine language long before Backus arrived on the computing scene—but FORTRAN's **GO TO** brought the statement to the masses, with other high-level languages, like BASIC, following FORTRAN's example. Dijkstra's push for a shift to structured programming didn't involve merely the elimination of **GO TO**s in favor of other conditional control structures (like **IF** statements), but a rational rethinking of the way programs were structured, from tip to tail.

Dijkstra's "Considered Harmful" publication caused an uproar, with the author receiving "a torrent of abusive letters." The overwhelmingly negative response also led to a shift in ACM policy: no more publishing of explicitly controversial pieces on programming style. Although Dijkstra wasn't the first programmer to call for the elimination of **GO TO**—that distinction likely belongs to Dewey Val Schorre of UCLA, who created a subset of ALGOL for crafting compilers called META II; Peter Naur, George Forsythe, and Peter Landin followed suit—he was certainly the most impassioned.

About six years later, a *Datamation* article called "A Linguistic Contribution of **GOTO**-less Programming" by R. Lawrence Clark satirized the **GO TO** debate, which had reached a fevered pitch. The author proposed a programming construct that he believed would unite the pro- and anti-**GO TO** forces in agreement: the replacement of **GO TO** with the **COME FROM** statement. Clark illustrated the use of **COME FROM**, which came in unconditional, conditional, and computed varieties, by employing FORTRAN. Here is his unconditional **COME FROM** example:

```
10      J=1
11      COME FROM 20
12      WRITE (6,40) J STOP
13      COME FROM 10
20      J=J+2
40      FORMAT (14)
```

"Having at last put to rest to GOTO controversy, we now may enter the era of the COME FROM conundrum," Clark concluded.

Donald Knuth weighed in on the GO TO debate, taking a middle path in his 1974 article "Structured Programming with go to Statements." "I argue for the elimination of **go to**'s in certain cases, and for their introduction in others," he wrote.

> In other words, it seems that fanatical advocates of the New Programming are going overboard in their strict enforcement of morality and purity in programs. Sooner or later people are going to find that their beautifully-structured programs are running at only half the speed—or worse—of the dirty old programs they used to write, and they will mistakenly blame the structure instead of recognizing what is probably the real culprit—the system overhead caused by typical compiler implementation of Boolean variables and procedure calls. Then we'll have an unfortunate counterrevolution, something like the current rejection of the "New Mathematics" in reaction to its overzealous reforms.

The upshot was that soon, perhaps within ten years, a consensus about what a programming language should be will emerge from these battles. "I'm guessing that people will become so disenchanted with the languages they are now using—even COBOL and FORTRAN—that this new language, UTOPIA 84, will have a chance to take over." Dijkstra was unmoved by such arguments.

In another EWD manuscript of Dijkstra's—he wrote, usually longhand with a fountain pen, more than 1,300 of these concise essays on the state of mathematics and computing—he diagnoses a series of diseases that affect a programmer's thinking habits and abilities. Called EWD 498: How Do We Tell Truths that Might Hurt? (1982) he wastes no time in striking a number of targets. IBM, for example, doesn't escape criticism, with Dijkstra excoriating companies that have "made themselves dependent on IBM-equipment (and in doing so have sold their soul to the devil)," because of the labyrinthine nature of IBM's systems. As Simon Yuill notes, Dijkstra even takes an indirect swipe at educators like Roger Kaufman, who freely use anthropomorphic metaphors when teaching computer science (e.g., computers as "your mommy's bureau drawers"). Dijkstra, who had first taken a three-week computer course at Cambridge University in 1951 when he was only twenty-one years old, wrote that "[t]he use of anthropomorphic terminology when dealing with computing systems is a symptom of professional immaturity."

Note that Dijkstra, in general, was not fond of computer science education; he was a member of the priesthood generation, a cloistered group of programming experts coming of age in the 1940s and '50s who opposed most efforts to open up programming to the public, whether it be with the creation of easy-to-use and accessible high-level languages or by educating the masses in the joys of the discipline. These priests were the gatekeepers of a profession requiring a hyper-specialized knowledge of machines and machine language, inefficiencies and computer-time costs be damned. John Backus was a computing countercultural rebel, with the creation of FORTRAN serving as the ultimate rebellion.

So it should come as no surprise that Dijkstra, the high priest, saved his most virulent bile for a certain high-level language. "FORTRAN—'the infantile disorder'—, by now nearly 20 years old, is hopelessly inadequate for whatever computer application you have in mind today: it is now too clumsy, too risky, and too expensive to use." Dijkstra, whose background was in theoretical physics, pushed the argument further: "In the good old days physicists repeated each other's experiments, just to be sure. Today they stick to FORTRAN, so that they can share each other's programs, bugs included." (Dijkstra abandoned physics as a career path early on. "In '55 after three years of programming, while I was still a student, I concluded that the intellectual challenge of programming was greater than the intellectual challenge of theoretical physics, and as a result I chose programming," he said, adding that although leaving a scientific field for, what was perceived at the time, a discipline lacking a "clear scientific component" spurred him on to perhaps "be one of the people called to make it a science." With the later release of the language ALGOL 60, to which he contributed enormously—e.g., recursion and the concept of a *stack*, akin to a stack of plates at a cafeteria—programming had finally become a "topic [that was] academically respectable," he said.)

Where did this antipathy to FORTRAN come from? In EWD 340, from 1972, we are presented with at least a partial answer. After discussing his misgivings with being labeled a programmer in the profession's infancy—and offering an amusing anecdote (as mentioned earlier in this book) of how he was not permitted to write "programmer" on his marriage license by the municipal authorities in Amsterdam, so he had to settle for "theoretical physicist" instead—Dijkstra pivots to a discussion of the software scene. The birth of FORTRAN, he writes, "was a project of great temerity and the people responsible for it deserve our great admiration." But there were unintended consequences:

> It would be absolutely unfair to blame them for shortcomings that only became apparent after a decade or so of extensive usage: groups with a successful look-ahead of ten years are quite rare! In retrospect we must rate FORTRAN as a successful coding technique, but with very few effective aids to conception, aids which are now so urgently needed that time has come to consider it out of date. The sooner we can forget that FORTRAN has ever existed, the better, for as a vehicle of thought it is no longer adequate: it wastes our brainpower, is too risky and therefore too expensive to use. FORTRAN's tragic fate has been its wide acceptance, mentally chaining thousands and thousands of programmers to our past mistakes. I pray daily that more of my fellow-programmers may find the means of freeing themselves from the curse of compatibility.

An article published in *Datamation* a year after EWD 340's publication summarized the attitude of many programmers who were sympathetic to Dijkstra's concerns but couldn't conceive of a better alternative: "I tend to agree with [Dijkstra] that the right language remains to be developed. When that happy day arrives, I will endeavor to write the first textbook about it! But in the meantime…FORTRAN it is, for the technical and engineering side of the computing world." In other words, don't let the perfect be the enemy of the good.

Roger Kaufman and Daniel McCracken made learning historic FORTRAN as easy as it was ever going to be, especially in the FORTRAN II/IV/66 days when "personal computers" were inconceivable and programs had to be written on paper and run in one's mind. But Dijkstra, the self-styled "Humble Programmer"—and a product of the frontier days of computing where, as John Backus described it, "an idea was the property of anyone who could use it, and the scholarly practice of noting references to sources and related work was almost universally unknown or unpracticed" (Dijkstra freely distributed his EWD manuscripts and usually did not bother to include bibliographies)—didn't want people to learn FORTRAN; he wanted them to unlearn it in favor of a structured language like ALGOL 60. If only the programmer could disabuse himself of the bad habits of thinking resulting from too much time spent with a language like FORTRAN, as well as its kissing cousins BASIC and COBOL, Dijkstra believed, then the world would be a better place.

CHAPTER 22

◊◊◊

Setting the Standards, Again

Simply maintaining the existing FORTRAN 66 standards wasn't good enough—a new set of standards had to be written from the ground up.

In the second half of the 1960s, with FORTRAN 66 widely available and growing in popularity, especially among scientists, the language was "often pressed into service for tasks for which it had never been designed," according to FORTRAN textbook author and academic Michael Metcalf. With the advent of ALGOL, a language conforming to the structured programming paradigm that was written from the ground up by computer scientists, many people predicted that the "old fashioned" FORTRAN would be supplanted by the more modern, "'superior' concepts." Worse yet, adds Metcalf, "The permissiveness of the FORTRAN 66 standard, whereby any extensions could be implemented on a given processor so long as it still correctly processed a standard-conforming program, led again to a proliferation of dialects," like FORTRAN IV (for the RCA Spectra), DITRAN (for the CDC 1604$), FORTRAN T3 (for the Titan), and MOD8 FORTRAN (for the H-8200), among numerous others. With the requirement of the organization succeeding the ASA, called the American National Standards Institute (ANSI), that language standards be renewed, withdrawn, or rewritten every five years, FORTRAN was due for a shakeup regardless.

The X3.4.3 committee was, unsurprisingly, disbanded after the release of FORTRAN 66. But by late 1967, the National Bureau of Standards (NBS) pressed for X3.4.3 to be reconstituted. The NBS, a nonregulatory federal agency founded in the early twentieth century and tasked with providing the United States with standard weights and measures, was staffed by a legendary programmer: Betty Holberton.

Born Frances Elizabeth Snyder in Pennsylvania in 1917, Betty Holberton, despite her obvious talents at mathematics, encountered overt and repeated instances of unreconstructed sexism during her very first class in college. At the University of Pennsylvania, where she had earned a scholarship, Holberton was told by her analytic geometry professor—who, she said, was "a very well-known Russian who had no time for women"—the following: "You women should be home raising children." The mathematics class she was enrolled in consisted only of women students, and the sexist professor said variations of the inappropriate comment daily—for four straight months. Even worse, the follow-up math course was also taught by the same professor, and there were no other scheduling options available.

Even though Holberton ultimately did sit for more classes in mathematics at the university, she ended up majoring in journalism. According to Martin K. Gay, author of *Recent Advances and Issues in Computers* (2000), journalism was "one of the few fields open to women as a career in the 1940s, and it allowed her to study any subject in which she found an interest." As Holberton told an interviewer a half century later, "The only way I knew of getting an education that would get through that system up there was to go into English and journalism. This would allow me to take something in every discipline in which they would expect you to know something. I didn't know what I wanted to do."

But she wouldn't escape math so easily. Although Holberton was hired by *Farm Journal* to write about consumer spending and other economic statistics (she even diagnosed problems with the keypunch equipment the magazine was using to tabulate figures), the advent of war set her on a different path. Once the U.S. entered World War II, the U.S. Army was in dire need of computers—people, not machines—to compute the trajectories of ballistics. The work would take place at the University of Pennsylvania's Moore School of Electrical Engineering. Since men were in short supply—they were being shipped overseas at a frenetic clip—the Army recruited eighty female mathematicians, including Holberton, to perform the calculating labor. Holberton had a unique approach to solving problems. "It's taken me about 30 years to figure it out, but I think differently from most people," she explained. "I think kind of like a radar screen. On any problem I have I go around and around the problem until I have all facets of it well in my mind before I either sit down to write anything out on how it's going to be solved."

Recall that around this time, the Army Ordnance Department reached out to the Moore School; they wanted a computer—an electronic machine, not a human being—built to automate the assembly of artillery firing tables. In response, John W. Mauchly and J. Presper Eckert began building the electronic, digital ENIAC. Once the machine was finished, programmers were needed, but there were few to be found—the ENIAC was *sui generis*. Mauchly and Eckert wandered around the Moore School, asking the mathematicians: Who do you think might be able to code this thing? Asking for "programmers" wouldn't have made much sense, since the term was not in circulation yet. Coding was physical work, involving replacing vacuum tubes, flipping switches, routing pulses, fiddling with plugboards, and navigating masses of wires.

Six women from the Army-recruited computer pool, including Betty Holberton, rounded out what Martin K. Gay deemed the "First Programmers Club." Holberton and the team of women weren't permitted inside the room housing the thirty-ton ENIAC; they were deemed "subprofessionals by the government that was relying on them," wrote Gay.

They were considered security risks. They were forced to work with wiring diagrams and blueprints only. But they did learn how the machine was built, what each relay and tube could accomplish; and finally they were allowed into the room to start testing their procedures. In the early months of 1946, they completed a first run of their program for ballistic trajectories. It ran without a hitch, cutting the time for a single calculation done by hand from 20 hours to 30 seconds.

The women weren't even allowed to keep notes on anything. Despite the restrictions, Holberton found that working on the machine was akin to figuring out a puzzle—and she loved solving puzzles.

When the ENIAC was moved to the Aberdeen Proving Grounds in Maryland following the war, three of the First Programmers Club moved with it, teaching the new skill of programming to other women. Holberton and Jean Jennings Bartik, a fellow Club member who thought the world of Holberton ("Betty had an amazing logical mind, and she solved more problems in her sleep than other people did awake," she said), traveled with Mauchly and Eckert to New York as they laid the groundwork for the Electronic Control Company, which in short order became the Eckert-Mauchly Computer Corporation (EMCC). "Look like a girl, act like a lady, think like a man, and work like a dog," Holberton preached. With Mauchly, she assisted in designing the UNIVAC and created the instruction code called C-10, which permitted keyboard commands to control the machine. Holberton also wrote a UNIVAC program for sorting and merging files; in explaining the genesis of the program, she said, "I couldn't conceive of anybody having to go through the same thing that my group was going through.... I couldn't see anybody else having to do that when I knew it could be done mechanically by putting the pieces together with just the parameters that would come into play with different subroutine parts." Perhaps most notoriously, she also convinced the engineers to change the UNIVAC's black color to gray-beige, thereby inadvertently setting the standard for the exterior color of computers for decades to come.

But the culture at the company changed once it was purchased by Remington Rand in 1950, so Holberton decided to leave.

> Women, as far as I could see, had absolutely no future under Remington Rand, absolutely none. I would go out on various things to try to sell computers and what not and the salesmen would pretty soon know that I was the only woman salary coming out of Buffalo which meant you were a certain grade above the secretaries. This was so annoying that I could see the writing on the wall; I really could. I knew that since I didn't have a Ph.D. and I had nothing to go on, that it just wasn't going to work.

Before she left, though, she helped develop a FORTRAN compiler that the Computer Sciences Corporation had contracted with Remington Rand to build. To complete the project, Remington Rand teamed up with Livermore, where the former would set the specs and the latter would actually build the compiler. Once the compiler was delivered to Remington Rand, seventeen people, including Holberton, needed four months to whip it into shape.

In 1953, Holberton began work at the Navy's Applied Mathematics Laboratory in Maryland, specifically within a complex of buildings called the David Taylor Model Basin; she was supervisor of advanced programming. Holberton was first tasked with assembling insurance tables for pensions and annuities; it was a trial by fire, which afforded her opportunities to test out a number of programming theories she had formulated. Holberton said that the work "proved...my theories about how you take care of desk checking, flow charting, rerun procedures, the whole philosophy of tape labeling—everything that I had been teaching people you ought to do, I did, and it worked." Later on in her tenure, she became a member of CODASYL, which developed and released COBOL in 1959.

Herbert Bright, who intercepted the "accidently distributed" FORTRAN I card decks at the Westinghouse-Bettis nuclear reactor in 1957, made sense of a key result to come from the work of the mathematicians and programmers at the Applied Mathematics Laboratory. Large-scale computing became critical to nuclear power calculations by the 1950s, with "[s]ystems of elliptic partial differential equations...used to describe fixed-geometry nuclear-power reactors for criticality calculations," Bright explained. But digital computing didn't seem to offer any advantages with problems of order six hundred or above. But Elizabeth Cuthill, who headed a team of mathematicians at the Applied Mathematics Laboratory, developed a new mathematical technique called the "Cuthill Code" to write a program able to handle problems of order 2,500. They used a UNIVAC I computer—Holberton's specialty—to run the demo program, which took around forty hours to spit out a single solution successfully. "Without such a successful demonstration that the world's outstanding authorities could be wrong, there would have been no early large-scale nuclear codes," claimed Bright. "The demand for more and more powerful computers would not have gained a major push," setting the stage for the importance of the FORTRAN I breakthrough several years later. (Mathematicians at Westinghouse-Bettis were skeptical that FORTRAN, before it arrived on the scene, could ever match the efficiency of the tens of thousands of lines of assembly instructions required to code the depletion calculations, which simulated the life of a reactor core. They were surprised when FORTRAN proved itself equal to the task.)

While still employed at the Applied Mathematics Laboratory, Holberton was among the first to learn about FORTRAN firsthand: in 1954, when Backus took his show on the road and presented the sketchiest outlines of the future HLL to interested parties in a handful of cities around the United States. When FORTRAN I was released in 1957, the Applied Math Lab, Holberton recalled, "volunteered to be a guinea pig for trial of the system."

By 1966, Holberton had moved on again, this time to the National Bureau of Standards, where would remain for the next twenty years. Early on, she realized how important clear and concise wording and documentation is to programming and computer science in general.

> I didn't go there [NBS] to work in FORTRAN at all. I had just spent three years correcting a computer sciences compiler, and I thought I had done an excellent job of organization and documentation. I felt that human communications was our basic problem. Whenever we went anywhere people couldn't understand what we were saying; the vocabulary was bizarre (it still is). We were always making up terms...very much a parochial kind of attitude in the computer field, and I think very much today.

Even when she was designing the UNIVAC C-10 instruction code, she consciously tried to make the commands intuitive: *s* referred to subtraction, *t* to testing, and so on.

A large part of her job at NBS involved persuasion; people are generally resistant to change, after all. When working with engineers and other employees, she developed a technique to "make it look like the idea came from them": to "make them think that they are the ones, by pulling them out, who have come up with a solution even though you knew the solution was there because you pointed the right questions to them." She would admit to using this technique numerous times during her nearly two decades serving on FORTRAN standards committees.

Recall that NBS pressed for the reassembly of the X3.4.3 committee. The pressure came mostly from Betty Holberton. She hadn't been involved with writing the FORTRAN 66 standards, but only a year after they were released she had many questions and concerns about them. "I believe the most fundamental fault in the X3.9-1966 Fortran standard is the inability to retain local variables and arrays in subprograms of a standard conforming program," she said. But she had her doubts with the effectiveness of committees in general. "It is questionable whether 25 people on a standardization committee can force the rest of the world to change. The market place [*sic*] calls the shots."

Others had questions and concerns about the standards as well. As Michael Greenfield recalled, this period of revisions of the FORTRAN 66 standards—which extended from 1967 to 1970—was more difficult, mind-numbing, and arduous than the years spent writing the standards *ex nihilo*. "Because we were dealing with an approved standard, not a single comma could be altered without going through the same long approval cycle," he said. Two reports were commissioned. The first, "Clarification of Fortran Standards—Initial Progress," was published in *Communications of the ACM* in 1969. In it, issues that outside observers had with the FORTRAN 66 standards were laid bare:

> (1) exceptions to the inclusion or omission of features; (2) requests for minor extensions to the language; and (3) questions concerning the intended scope, purpose, content, and interpretation of the standards. Many editorial remarks and statements in area (1) may also be related to misunderstandings with respect to aspects of (3).

So, with the number of questions and criticisms snowballing, a dramatic course of action was taken:

> Having allowed one year for exposure to the approved standards, it was then concluded that chronic difficulties in application of the standards should be identified and suitably remedied. Accordingly, on February 23, 1967, the technical subcommittee X3.4.3 for FORTRAN standardization reconvened and established the working subcommittee X3.4.3B for dealing with questions of interpretations of, errors in, and omissions from the USA Standard FORTRAN and Basic FORTRAN specifications.

Resolving the mechanical flaws, ambiguities in language, inconsistencies, omissions, and mistakes of the original set of standards would be the primary mission of the X3.4.3B subcommittee. An index organizing the fruits of their labor would be assembled as well.

Bill Heising was the first chairman of X3.4.3B, but wouldn't remain for long in the position (although he would stay on the subcommittee). Dick Ridgeway and Dennis Hamilton (a Sperry Rand employee) took turns as chairman. In 1970, Frank Engel, who worked at the MITRE Corporation, assumed the mantle. He had earlier overseen a study to determine if the many FORTRAN 66 extensions that had proliferated should be written into the standards—the subcommittee was against it, opting instead to write a whole new set of standards. Engel would oversee, from start to finish, the development of these new draft standards, despite the process taking the better part of a decade to complete.

Frank Engel's history with FORTRAN extended all the way back to the first compiler. In 1957, Engel was an employee of Westinghouse, Pittsburgh, when the company received a copy of the compiler from IBM. Even by then, "[e]verybody knew that FORTRAN could be improved," according to J.A.N. Lee. When Engel saw the new FORTRAN system run on an IBM 704, he noticed something interesting: "watching the flashing lights and observing tape activity," Engel recalled, "it was easy to infer that there was appreciable time lost positioning the tapes, waiting for rewinds and counting down records." So, Engel thought of ways to improve the through-put, but he would have to overlap the tape operations. We could "improve performance through redistribution of program and data segments among the available tape units, prepositioning reels by anticipating rewinds," he explained. Since Engel would need the source code of the FORTRAN compiler to proceed with the improvements, he asked his system engineer, Ken Powell, for access. So Powell called up his boss, Frank Beckman, requesting the source code. Beckman's reply caught everyone off guard. "IBM does not supply source code," he told Powell. Engel, taking matters into his own hands, decided to dump the compiler code in octal, "read [the] extensive octal dumps like a novel," according to Powell, and then, using a series of mental gymnastics, decompile the compiler and improve the through-put dramatically. Powell rather quickly noticed the increased performance of the compiler. "What have you done?" he asked Engel, who proceeded to tell him. In a frenzy, Powell telephoned Beckman, who flew to Pittsburgh to see. "That is fantastic," Beckman said, "can we have a copy of that?" Frank Engel chimed in to respond: "Westinghouse does not supply object code."

IBM might not have supplied source code, but it did distribute a single copy of the "TOME"—a thick binder of the symbolic listing of the FORTRAN I compiler along with other diagnostics—to each 704 installation shortly after the release of the FORTRAN system. Decades later, Bob Hughes kicked himself for not retaining a copy of the very rare compiler listing contained in the "TOME." "I worked on what they called the 'first-level' documentation," Hughes said. "And I made the biggest mistake of my life by not bringing a copy of that home. Now you understand why I missed making my first million dollars." IBM also issued a "stop book," which helped users with diagnostic issues. "Another document that came with Fortran, which everybody got to know, was the 'stop book,'" explained Frank da Cruz of Columbia University. "The compiler did not issue diagnostics. Instead it halted. The machine operator would record the instruction counter from the console lights. The stop book told what the cause of each stop was, often very cryptically: 'trouble in the tag table, or some other cause.'" Presumably, the stop book was a repackaged version of the original *FORTRAN Operator's Manual.*

The X3.4.3B subcommittee included a number of people who were part of X3.4.3, like Martin Greenfield, for continuity's sake. But the subcommittee also included some fresh faces, such as Herbert S. Bright of Westinghouse-Bettis. Betty Holberton, of course, was also new to the standardization effort.

The level of scrutiny, analysis, and parsing of the most minor of details that X3.4.3B applied to FORTRAN 66 was staggering; the two reports issued by the subcommittee give only a taste of the many debates and tedious work that went into the Talmudic-style commentaries of the draft standards.

Let's take a look at a representative, albeit simple, example. In their discussion of the STOP statement, a question is posed: "In a STOP statement, is n accessible?" Recall that the syntax of a STOP statement could take the form STOP n, where n is an octal string digit like 77777. An interpretation is offered: "The following sentence should be appended to the last paragraph of [section] 7.1.2.7.1 [of the FORTRAN 66 standards]: 'The disposition of the octal digit string is not specified.'" Next, a rationale for the interpretation is given: "The accessibility of n in a STOP statement is intentionally not specified in the standard. By not so specifying, the standard permits the practice of terminating program execution without necessarily making n accessible." There is more detail not included here. And this was just one of many such questions posed, some with answers that go on for pages, replete with a surfeit of technical detail.

The subcommittee members tried their hardest to whip FORTRAN 66 into shape. They wrote repeatedly of the importance of "maintenance of the standards" and of offering "clarifying interpretations." But ultimately it wasn't enough; nips and tucks weren't doing the trick. FORTRAN had to be rebuilt, from the ground up, rather than attempting to patch up FORTRAN 66 by the five-year deadline, 1971. At worst, they initially believed, a FORTRAN 66 replacement could be released before New Year's Day, 1972. They missed the mark by more than six years, with "American National Standard Programming Language FORTRAN, X3.9-1978" released and officially approved in April of 1978; two years later, an international version, ISO 1539-1980, representing twenty-one countries, was approved as well.

The X3.9-1978 standards were roughly six times longer than the first set. Much of the glaring increase in length was due to a concerted effort to increase readability; to that end, the ANSI X3J3 committee employed English terms as much as possible, used a syntax resembling Backus-Naur Form (BNF is explained in detail in the following chapter), and employed cutting-edge word processing, computer graphics, and concordance (indexing) tools. The committee had to pore through hundreds of technical proposals as they compiled the new standards; multiple drafts and massive amounts of editing were the order of the day, with committee members Lloyd W. Campbell, who worked at the Ballistic Research Laboratory (BRL) at Aberdeen Proving Ground in Maryland and had experience working with FORTRAN on the BRLESC I and

BRLESC II computers, and J. C. Noll, a Bell Labs employee, serving as the long-suffering editors. By the time the X3J3 committee wrapped up their work, the cost of the standardization effort totaled over two million dollars; the committee had spent at least thirty-three man-years finalizing it.

Starting from the time she spent programming the ENAIC in 1945, "I have endeavored to make computers more accessible to a potentially wider user community," Betty Holberton said. "To this end, I hope to help make this Fortran standard a language for writing more portable programs and to bring the standard closer to the needs of the user community."

Maintain world-class efficiency; don't enlarge; modernize; and increase accessibility. These were the key goals that Holberton and the rest of the X3J3 committee kept in mind as they built the successor to FORTRAN 66. But they also wanted to ensure backward compatibility—programs written with the old standards would, they hoped, be able to work with no major modifications using the successor language, only minor tweaks. To that end, the **STOP** statement was now made optional—a main program would stop just fine without one.

But the need for greater convenience with strings led to a decision that caused a significant area of incompatibility: the implementation of a **CHARACTER** data type in place of the cumbersome Hollerith fields, which were a notoriously nonportable feature of FORTRAN 66. FORTRAN had always used integer variables to store characters. Now, **CHARACTER** strings would be enclosed in apostrophes, as the following program snippet—which concatenates (joins) two character strings together, using the concatenation operator, //, and then outputs the concatenated string—illustrates.

```
CHARACTER X*6, Y*5, Z*11
X = 'HELLO '
Y = 'WORLD'
Z = A // B
PRINT *, Z
```

There were a number of other features associated with the new **CHARACTER** data type, such as character substrings (which capture a segment of a string; for example, Z(1:3) has the value **HEL** in the program snippet above). In addition, arrays of **CHARACTER** data could be generated.

CHARACTER variables weren't an original idea of the standards committee. The variable type was first introduced at a SHARE meeting in February of 1967. "As most of you are aware," writes SHARE member Elliott Nohr, "IBM did listen and implement it, even though we had to wait 14 years."

In addition to **CHARACTER** variables, the successor to FORTRAN 66, eventually called FORTRAN 77, would also permit the zero-trip loop—meaning a **DO** loop could be written that would not iterate even once, if the conditions to execute the loop weren't met in the program. Take a look at this sample code to see an example.

```
J = 1
DO 10 I = 15, 3
```

```
10      J = J + 1
```

The issue lies with the initial and final values of the loop: since $15 > 3$, and there is no step-size specified at the tail end of the **DO** statement (a negative step-size, which was now permitted, would cycle through loops backwards), there is, quite literally, nothing to **DO**.

Although some dialects of FORTRAN in circulation allowed the zero-trip loop construction, FORTRAN 66 technically did not. "Many processors extended the [FORTRAN 66] standard by permitting this situation and executing the loop once," wrote the members of X3J3. "Some processors executed such a loop zero times. Other processors aborted after diagnosing the condition as a violation." In FORTRAN 77, the loop would be executed precisely zero times. But including this zero-trip loop caused controversy at first, since some FORTRAN 66 programs, written with the assumption of a minimum one-trip loop (and an **IF GOTO** stationed before the loop to skip it completely if necessary), would need adjustment—which would prove to be another incompatibility between FORTRAN 66 and FORTRAN 77.

The toughest features to standardize, the committee discovered, were input/output. "[T]he implementation of input/output features usually involves interfacing with an operating system, whose nature cannot be specified by a language standard," the X3J3 committee explained. FORTRAN 66 kept I/O simple—by briefly specifying the syntax for **READ** and **WRITE** statements. FORTRAN 77 would lay out more detailed I/O specs:

> The new standard allows the programmer to have direct (random) access to a file, to specify a default format, to specify a default unit, to open and close files, to inquire about the status of a file, to treat character strings as files, and to specify actions to be taken in the event of an end-of-file or error condition.

There was also much ink spilled on features of subprograms (e.g., generic functions, where a single function or method could be passed different data types), precision (specifically, computations involving real and double precision numbers), and a new control construct: **IF-THEN-ELSE**. As Michael Metcalf notes, the **IF** block construct was included as part of a "push for 'structured programming'" that had become all the rage.

In February 1976, the committee members presented the draft standards publicly at the West Coast FORTRAN Forum in Anaheim, California. A short time later, an East Coast FORTRAN Forum, at the National Bureau of Standards in Gaithersburg, Maryland, was also held. In addition to these two large gatherings, each of which several hundred people attended (and responded overwhelmingly positively to the proposed standards), smaller meetings were held by X3J3 members across the country. An initial printing of more than eight thousand copies of the two-hundred-page standards document were distributed to interested parties, with three-fourths sent to SIGPLAN (a subset of the ACM) members and the remainder to CBEMA (the Computer Business Equipment Manufacturers Association), the federal government, and the International Standards Association, among other groups. The first iteration of the committee's efforts were now open to public review and scrutiny. It would take the committee "852 meeting man days" and over one hundred thousand dollars to bring the process to fruition.

Public comments began pouring in immediately: 1,225 pages of them, submitted by nearly three hundred individuals. X3J3 spent the better part of a year sifting through the documents, assigning each a sequence number, parsing the documents to irreducible suggested items, and assigning each of these items to one of the seven working groups of the committee. Most of the comments they received were positive overall about the proposed standards; the committee incorporated suggested changes where warranted. Many letters concluded similarly to this one: "The proposed standard is such an improvement over the 1966 standard that I cannot wholeheartedly support any proposal, however, valuable, which may delay its adoption." Some comments were very negative, but also contradictory. For instance: "Fortran is an ill-structured language and should not be extended," "It fails utterly to correct any of the manifest failings of Fortran," and "The proposal does not go far enough...." Chairman Frank Engel felt that the final product "represent[ed] a good compromise between the extreme positions, between modest growth and development of the standard Fortran language and the state-of-the-art that is consistent with the criteria X3J3 established to govern [the] revision." Furthermore, he said, "X3J3 was reluctant to make any changes" beyond error corrections or improvements in clarity, since "the committee wished to avoid any drastic changes that might necessitate another extended public review and further delay" the release of the standards. To that end, in terms of the categories of public comments, only eighteen percent of the new features suggested were incorporated into the standards, but of the improvements to clarity and style, well over half were accepted.

By and large, committee members found that the most frequent public comments requested adding support for structured programming. While there were at least fifty so-called *preprocessors* that permitted programmers to write code using structured programming constructs and then automatically translate them into FORTRAN code (for example, B4tran, written by Loren Meissner, who would go on to create the *Fortran Forum* newsletter), these preprocessors weren't standardized—and there was a clear need to make them redundant by building structured programming features directly into FORTRAN itself. It gets worse: the standards-compliant FORTRAN code generated by these preprocessors oftentimes resembled gobbledygook.

There are a number of legends and lore that grew around FORTRAN, only some of which were rooted in fact. One of them centers on the latter stages of the development FORTRAN 77, mocking the silly lengths to which some might go to ensure that structured programming concepts made their way into the language. Although this story may be apocryphal—read it with a grain of salt—apparently an anonymous tongue-in-cheek proposal called "Letter O Considered Harmful" was circulated at a late 1976 committee meeting. The idea was simple: remove the letter "O" from the set of FORTRAN characters available, reducing the number back to forty-eight, which was the standard on most punch-card equipment (when the colon was added later, the number of characters increased to forty-nine). Not only would eliminating the letter

"O" avoid confusion with the number zero, but the GO TO statement wouldn't be available anymore (nor would the problematic FORMAT), thus forcing all FORTRAN programmers to heed Edgar Dijkstra's advice in "Go To Statement Considered Harmful"—and bringing them that much closer to writing structured code.

Another urban legend associated with FORTRAN gained widespread circulation in computer science books for a generation. The NASA Mariner 1 spacecraft, built in the early 1960s, was slated for a flyby of the planet Venus. Launched on July 22, 1962, within minutes the rocket didn't respond correctly to guidance instructions, so it was destroyed by a range safety officer 293 seconds into the flight. According to NASA,

> The failure was apparently caused by a combination of two factors. Improper operation of the Atlas airborne beacon equipment resulted in a loss of the rate signal from the vehicle for a prolonged period. The airborne beacon used for obtaining rate data was inoperative for four periods ranging from 1.5 to 61 seconds in duration. Additionally, the Mariner 1 Post Flight Review Board determined that the omission of a hyphen in coded computer instructions in the data-editing program allowed transmission of incorrect guidance signals to the spacecraft. During the periods the airborne beacon was inoperative the omission of the hyphen in the data-editing program caused the computer to incorrectly accept the sweep frequency of the ground receiver as it sought the vehicle beacon signal and combined this data with the tracking data sent to the remaining guidance computation. This caused the computer to swing automatically into a series of unnecessary course corrections with erroneous steering commands which finally threw the spacecraft off course.

Nowhere is FORTRAN, or any other programming language for that matter, mentioned in NASA's official account of the incident. Nevertheless, over time, like a game of telephone, the story evolved into a misplaced comma (instead of an omitted hyphen) in the specification of a DO loop. Textbooks like *Software Reliability: Principles and Practices* (1976) by Glenford J. Myers breathlessly described how a single line of FORTRAN code resulted in a "billion-dollar error" (overstating the cost of the mission by a huge margin, since the combined cost of Mariners 1 to 10 amounted to just over a half billion dollars). Myers wrote that

> In a FORTRAN program controlling the United States' first mission to Venus, a programmer coded a DO statement in a form similar to the following:
>
> DO 3 I = 1.3
>
> The mistake he made was coding a period instead of a comma. However, the compiler treated this as an acceptable assignment statement because FORTRAN has no reserved words, blanks are ignored, and variables do not have to be explicitly declared. Although the statement is obviously an invalid DO statement, the compiler interpreted it as setting a new variable DO3I equal to 1.3. This "trivial" error resulted in the failure of the mission. Of course, part of the responsibility for this billion-dollar error falls on the programmer and test personnel, but is not the design of the FORTRAN language also partially to blame?

Apparently, for want of a comma, a NASA spacecraft was lost. The story, which Myers didn't source in his book, *seemed* to be true, because it fed into so many people's longstanding biases and qualms about FORTRAN. But the story is probably a canard. In the book *Beyond the Limits: Flight Enters the Computer Age* (1989), author Paul E. Ceruzzi describes the "myth" that grew around the Mariner 1 launch:

> This event has since become part of computer folklore and has taken on a mythical dimension. Several introductory college textbooks on computer programming cite it in their first chapters. Most of these accounts wrongly state that it was a simple typographical error that caused this failure. Other accounts have the basic facts wrong: they state that it was not a missing bar, but the substitution of a period for a comma in a Fortran program that caused the failure. The example is cited to show, among other things, the need for careful typing, the computer's lack of common sense, and above all, the inadequacies of Fortran, which did not detect the error when the program was compiled.

Ceruzzi goes on to detail the typographical error that was likely made—which had nothing to do with FORTRAN.

Of course, NASA did make use of FORTRAN only shortly after its debut. The Soviet's launch of *Sputnik* in 1957—the same year FORTRAN I was released to the public—led to a dramatic uptick in the hiring of scientists, engineers, and mathematicians who coalesced around a nascent space program. As dramatized by the book *Hidden Figures: The American Dream and the Untold Story of the Black Women Mathematicians Who Helped Win the Space Race* (2016) by Margot Lee Shetterly, as well as the 2016 film by the same title, the American mathematician Dorothy Johnson Vaughan, born in 1910 in Missouri, was hired at Langley Research Center in Hampton, Virginia, during World War II and made an impact in the realm of digital computing. Jim Crow laws led to her being assigned to work in a segregated unit called West Area Computing, where she and other African American women worked as computers, performing hand calculations. Before the end of the decade, Vaughan assumed a supervisory role over her unit. The National Advisory Committee for Aeronautics (NACA), the precursor to NASA, employed the women to help with the space race, which heated up after John F. Kennedy was elected president.

Vaughan eventually saw the writing on the wall: electronic computers would replace human ones. "At fifty years old and many years into her second career, she reinvented herself as a computer programmer," writes Shetterly in *Hidden Figures*.

> Engineers still made the pilgrimage to her desk, asking for her help with computing. Now, instead of assigning the task to one of her girls, Dorothy made the date with an IBM 704 computer that occupied the better part of an entire room in the basement of Building 1268, the room cooled to polar temperatures to keep the machine's vacuum tubes from overheating.

> In the past, Dorothy would have set up the equations in a data sheet and walked one of her girls through the process of filing it out. At ACD [Analysis and Computation Division], it was her job to convert the engineers' equations into the computer's formula translation language—FORTRAN—by using a special machine....

But Project Mercury required more powerful machines, so NASA procured two IBM 7090s (one of which is featured in the film). Vaughan, who was so smart that she had "brains coming out of her ears," in the words of a colleague, not only taught herself FORTRAN, she taught it to her coworkers as well. Vaughan blazed a path for women such as Christine Darden, who, in the early 1970s, wrote a FORTRAN program calculating the minimization of sonic boom parameters for a variety of airplane types; her code lives on in programs engineers still employ today.

FORTRAN code also lives on by powering the farthest manmade object from our planet: NASA's Voyager 1 interstellar space probe, launched in 1977. Voyager 2, launched the same year but more recently interstellar, is also dependent on FORTRAN code. Both probes, which are mechanically identical, flew by multiple planets in the outer solar system—Jupiter, Saturn, Uranus, and Neptune—on a so-called Grand Tour, courtesy of gravity-assisted trajectories. The control and analysis software of the Voyagers was written in Fortran 5, a Data General Corporation variant of FORTRAN 66. Data General had successfully implemented FORTRAN on their NOVA minicomputers, rather than on mainframes. (Note that there was also a FORTRAN V, developed by the Control Data Corporation, which was based off of FORTRAN IV and arrived years before Fortran 5.) The Fortran 5 code in the spacecraft was eventually converted to FORTRAN 77; later, some, but not all, of the code was rewritten in C.

Modern Fortran code still powers some NASA software. In 2017, NASA sponsored a contest through the crowdsourcing website HeroX called the High Performance Fast Computing Challenge. Here is a portion of the contest's overview:

> Do you want to help aerospace engineers solve problems faster? Does the phrase "nonlinear partial differential equations used for unsteady computations" excite you? Do you want to try yourself with the complex computational software that NASA scientists use? This might be the challenge for you.
>
> NASA's Aeronautics Research Mission Directorate (ARMD) is responsible for developing technologies that will enable future aircraft to burn less fuel, generate fewer emissions and make less noise. Every U.S. aircraft and U.S. air traffic control tower has NASA-developed technology on board. It's why we like to say, NASA is with you when you fly!
>
> We need to increase the speed of computations on the Pleiades supercomputer, specifically for computational fluid dynamics, by orders of magnitude, and could use your help!

Specifically, NASA put out a call for "proposals for improving the performance of the NASA FUN3D software running on the NASA Pleiades supercomputer. The desired outcome is any approach that can accelerate calculations by a factor of 10-1000x without any decrease in accuracy and while utilizing the existing hardware platform." The FUN3D software was written mostly in "Modern Fortran" (specifically, the flow-analysis solver was Fortran-based; other components were in C++ and Ruby).

But NASA got more than they bargained for—within a month they were flooded with entries and didn't quite know how to fairly judge them. So NASA issued a press release calling off the competition. "The extremely high number of applicants, more than 1,800, coupled with the difficulty in satisfying the extensive vetting requirements to control the public distribution of the software made it unlikely we would achieve the challenge's original objectives in a timely manner." So, HeroX themselves decided to tap into the enthusiasm and go the retro route instead:

> After launching the High Performance Fast Computing Challenge, it came to our attention that the mere mention of the Fortran programming language really resonated with the challenge community! A lot of you started out with Fortran, back when it was still one of the go-to programming languages for calculation-intensive applications like weather prediction, fluid dynamics, and even computational chemistry.
>
> Even though NASA had to reconsider their approach for improving the access-restricted software in the High Performance Fast Computing Challenge, we thought we could still have some fun with this and crowdsource the best stories about our innovators and Fortran. For the sake of history, appreciating our community's expertise, and just hearing a good story, this challenge will offer a total of up to $1750 split amongst the top three "Fortran" reminiscers!

A one-to-three-minute video, including an introduction, background with Fortran, and answers to the questions "How are you using it now?" and "How is it a different experience than it was in the beginning?" were required to participate. HeroX accepted contest entries for roughly a month, closing the competition in late June of 2017—marking sixty years, almost to the month, since the birth of FORTRAN.

The winner of the grand prize was Jay McInvale, who told an amusing "war story," called "Oil Refinery Blues," that involved maintaining a particular FORTRAN program. A hapless engineer unknowingly placed McInvale's debugging card (with the debug flags set to print the maximum possible lines) into the input deck of the computer, resulting in a program set to output a million and a half lines. To make things even worse, the engineering department was charged based on the quantity of printed lines. McInvale laughed as he told the rest of the story. "Fortunately, the million and a half lines never came off the printer. I told him [the engineer], 'Well, you just take that debugging card out!'" The engineering department wasn't charged for the error, and McInvale received one thousand dollars for winning the HeroX contest. Stephen Chase won the second-place prize of five hundred dollars for his video "FORTRAN Over a Half Century Ago," while Terence Dowling was awarded third place along with two-hundred and fifty dollars for the video "Computer Architecture has Changed."

In 1976, the X3J3 standards committee had a critical decision to make: What structured programming features should be adopted for FORTRAN 77? Since there were a great number of such features floating in the ether at the time—including in dialects such as RATFOR, or RATional FORtran, which lifted a number of control structures from C—X3J3 was especially cautious, deciding to add only **IF-THEN-ELSE**, believing the **IF** block (where each block terminated with an **END IF**) would be sufficient; the feature could be utilized in complex ways (e.g., with nested structures). For example,

```
            IF (K .EQ. 10) THEN
                K = K + 1
            ELSE IF (K .LT. 10) THEN
                K = 100
            ELSE
                K = 200
            END IF
```

Notice also that indenting code, though not required, had become an expectation. Of course, earlier implementations of FORTRAN, which offered space independence, also permitted indenting. But employing a structured programming style made it a must.

Martin Greenfield, upon later reflection, was pleased with his committee's conservative approach toward navigating the siren song of structured programming, calling it a "good example of how a responsible committee should avoid an over reaction [*sic*] that would prematurely add features that it would shortly regret." He wasn't very happy, however, with FORTRAN 77 additions like **ENTRY** and **ALTERNATE RETURN**, both of which were parochial statements associated with subprograms.

As Michael Metcalf observes, "The new language was rather slow to spread"; inertia prevented FORTRAN 77 from replacing FORTRAN 66 overnight. IBM bears some responsibility for the unhurried switchover, too, since the company hardly tripped over itself to build a FORTRAN 77 compiler, taking a leisurely four years to release one. In less than a decade, however, FORTRAN 77 kicked into high gear, sweeping away the vestiges of prior implementations, including FORTRAN 66. With home computing ascendant, there were FORTRAN compilers released for the "Trinity" of bestselling personal computers: the Tandy TRS-80, the Apple II, and the Commodore PET. Mainframe implementations of FORTRAN continued to be developed. Supercomputers like the Cray-1, which arrived on the scene at Los Alamos in 1976, and the Cray X-MP (multiprocessor) were running the language (called CFT, or Cray FORTRAN Compiler, which translated source code into CAL, or Cray Assembly Language) as well. "Programs written in FORTRAN 77 were routinely used to perform such diverse calculations as designing the shapes of airplane fuselages, predicting the structures of organic molecules, and simulating the flow of winds over mountains," Metcalf said.

X3J3 didn't rest on their laurels, and certainly didn't disband, after language approval in April 1978. The committee started laying the groundwork for the next iteration of the language; they reached out to organizations that were eyeing FORTRAN extensions, such as CODASYL, which had developed COBOL, and IEEE, the Institute of Electrical and Electronics Engineers. The committee also reached out to international organizations, leading to unprecedented cooperation and communication. What's more, X3J3 members realized that FORTRAN was still evolving outside the confines of standards committees, and so they took note.

Take "free form" for statements (also called "free-source form"), for example. By the time FORTRAN 77 was released, most people weren't programming FORTRAN using punched cards. But there were holdovers of the punched-card era that persisted. One of these anachronisms involved the columns on the cards. Recall that the first five columns on an eighty-character line were reserved for statement numbers; column six was meant for an optional continuation character; columns seven to seventy-two had space for a single FORTRAN programming statement; and the remaining columns were designated for an identification sequence, which was optional. Regardless of whether programming using punched cards or not, FORTRAN 77 required that the first six spaces on each line of code be statement-free. Until the advent of free form, that is, in which some implementations of FORTRAN 77 permitted flexibility (called "column independence") with the starting position of statements on lines. (The retronymic option called "fixed form" retained the usual punched card formatting rules.)

There was also a larger recognition starting to come into focus. Like the brilliant nineteenth century mathematician Carl Friedrich Gauss, who was perhaps the last person on earth to understand all of mathematics—after Gauss, the discipline grew too big to be entirely comprehended by any one human being—a single committee probably no longer had enough expertise to successfully tackle all of FORTRAN. True, the X3J3 committee members "felt confident" that they could handle extensions like free form, new control structures, and expanded array and storage features, according to Greenfield. FORTRAN 77 didn't have a means of dynamic storage; once an array size was set, it couldn't be altered. Lacking both elements hurt the language with supercomputers that were then arriving on the scene.

But X3J3 members were less confident on how, precisely, to integrate databases and graphics into the FORTRAN 77 edifice they had painstaking detailed for the better part of the 1970s, especially because there were a great number of unchecked database and graphics approaches springing up. To that end, other committees arose to deal with the ever-growing extensions. The FORTRAN Data Base Language Committee (FDBLC), an offshoot of CODASYL, was established to build database structures in the language. The ISA, then known as the Instrument Society of America, along with the Purdue Workshop, formed standards relating to file management.

X3J3 had a plan for the next language revision: emphasize generality, modularity, and compactness, keeping the size commensurate with FORTRAN 77, courtesy of some much needed deletions to the language set. Since the ANSI operated under a mandatory five-year review cycle, the next language revision was due in the fall of 1982. Referred to as FORTRAN 8X for numerical consistency with draft standards due by November 1980, it took more than a decade to complete—and would prove to be the most controversial revision yet.

CHAPTER 23

◊◊◊

FORTRAN the Foil: Rise of the Competition

During the period of FORTRAN's ascendance, a number of programming languages, big and small, sprang up in opposition to FORTRAN; FORTRAN, in effect, played the foil.

Think of these "opposition languages" as resembling FORTRAN, albeit seen through a funhouse mirror. Each of these languages successfully exposed and then attacked at least one of FORTRAN's weak points.

What follows are the most notable examples—ALGOL, BASIC, C, COBOL, FORMAC, LISP, MATLAB, PL/I, and S—presented in roughly chronological order according to their initial public release dates.

ALGOL, the ALGOrithmic Language (1958)

The late 1950s found many dissatisfied with the state of computing in the wake of FORTRAN's birth, as the proliferation of machine-dependent programming languages (and not just dialects of FORTRAN) was turning the field into an archipelago of specialized fiefdoms.

John Backus, though he likely hadn't foreseen the unintended consequences, had helped to set this process in motion and wasn't happy with the state of affairs. After his time developing FORTRAN came to an end, he continued to work at IBM, floating from one project to another. For instance, like he did with the IBM 704, in the early 1960s he advised the company on building a new set of hardware: the IBM 7030 Stretch supercomputer, in which Backus suggested a different register and instruction set design. But Gene Amdahl, who led the design team, ultimately disregarded most of Backus's recommendations.

Computer scientists in Europe had, at least in part, seen the disaster on the horizon. In 1955, two years before FORTRAN I's public release, the GAMM (*Gesellschaft für an-*

gewandte Mathematik und Mechanik) in Germany began the work of specifying details of a generalized programming language by setting up a committee on programming (a *programmierungsausschus*); a subcommittee would begin building a translator.

Computer scientists in the United States took up similar work at a May 1957 conference attended by representatives of organizations such as SHARE, when a petition was delivered to the ACM (the Association of Computing Machinery, established in the late 1940s, whose name reflects a "preoccupation with the physical aspects of automatic computing" common among older computing organizations, Dijkstra noted), recommending forming a committee to examine the possibility of the creation of a universal computer language. The committee would be made up of more than just industry programmers; it would also include individuals from the government, academia, and even users. Backus joined the committee.

In the fall of 1957, GAMM sent a letter to John W. Carr, president of the ACM, suggesting cooperating on the unification project. Carr agreed to the proposal. To prepare for the project, Carr convened a committee in January 1958 representing computer manufacturers, users, and academics. The committee held three meetings, the result of which was a "language...orientated more towards problem language than towards computer language and was based on several existing programming systems," according to a later summary report.

The ACM and GAMM committees—four individuals representing each organization—met at ETH Zurich (the Swiss Federal Institute of Technology in Zurich, Switzerland) over the span of a week in late May 1958; there, the International Algebraic Language, or IAL, was born. IAL was a machine-independent language that merged two independent proposals—one from the Americans, another from the Europeans—resulting in some uneasy compromises. For example, the Europeans wanted to use a comma for decimal points; the Americans pushed for a period.

The result of this cross-continental merger can be seen in the "Preliminary Report—International Algebraic Language," disseminated after the weeklong meeting in Zurich. "The language described naturally enough represents a compromise," according to the authors of the report, Alan Perlis and Klaus Samelson, "but one based more upon differences of taste than on content or fundamental ideas. Even so, it provides a natural and simple medium for the expression of a large class of algorithms."

There was much agreement between the two groups as well. For instance, GAMM was in favor of using English words for IAL whenever they were needed. They also agreed on three objectives:

I. The new language should be as close as possible to standard mathematical notation and be readable with little further explanation.
II. It should be possible to use it for the description of computing processes in publications.
III. The new language should be mechanically translatable into machine programs.

Tellingly, the joint committee recognized that there were "certain differences between the language used in publications and a language directly usable by a computer. Indeed, there are many differences between sets of characters usable by various computers." The upshot of their realization of what we might now think of as "code-switching"—the same root language being used differently, depending on context—was the joint committee's decision to have three levels of IAL: one for reference, one for hardware, and one for publication. In an article published a year later, Backus elucidated these distinctions:

> It should be kept in mind, however, that the reference language form of IAL exists primarily for the purpose of describing the rules of construction of the language and its meanings. In actual use, a variety of symbolizations and notational conventions are envisaged, each representation being a fairly direct transliteration of the reference language and having the same rules of syntax and semantics. "Hardware representations" will generally use a smaller set of symbols than that employed in the reference language and will be suitable for mechanical translation into machine programs by a given type of machine. On the other hand, the "publication forms" of the language will employ many of the notational conventions of mathematics (e.g., exponents, subscripts, Greek letters) and will be used in human communication of IAL programs.

Mostly by using mathematical notation, the bulk of the joint committee's sixteen-page document lays out, in great detail, the reference language. However IAL is implemented on a set of hardware, as long as there is a one-to-one correspondence between the implementation and the reference language (e.g., symbol x corresponds to symbol y in IAL, operation m corresponds to operation n in IAL), the implementation is IAL compliant.

IAL was also known as ALGOL 58 (ALGOrithmic Language 58). According to Friedrich Bauer, who was one of the European representatives on the joint committee,

> The whole thing went on quite quickly. In a very short time we had some exchange of our preliminary papers. We then agreed on a meeting that we had in Zurich in May of 1958, which in about 8 days hammered out the first ALGOL report, the ALGOL 58 report. At that time, the American side called it IAL, the International Algebraic Language. We called it ALGOL. We agreed on everything except the name. Later, the name ALGOL was at least kept in Europe. In the United States, I think, the IAL is still existing in words like JOVIAL, ending with IAL.

FORTRAN, as it was in 1958, was certainly not IAL/ALGOL compliant. For one thing, FORTRAN I didn't have the block structure of IAL, which was a way of grouping statements together (twenty years later, FORTRAN 77 would include the **IF** block construct). In addition, FORTRAN didn't differentiate between its use of the equals sign: the symbol was used for both assignment and comparison. IAL offered two different symbols for these operations, with = used for comparison, whereas := was used for assignment. Furthermore, unlike FORTRAN I which was implicitly typed (based on the first letter of the variable or array name), IAL offered explicit type declarations, with real numbers serving as the default type. IAL offered the switch statement, allowing for control transfers based on labels, as well as the if-either statement, for branching conditions. For its part, "FORTRAN [was] a collection of Warts, held together by bits of Syntax," complained one programmer.

As was his wont, Backus downplayed his involvement in the reference language definition. "It was a big committee deal, and I don't think I contributed very much to it."

Backus was at his best when he took measure of the conventional wisdom, spotted the inefficiencies and errors in group thinking, and then turned everything on its head. Things were no different with IAL. Backus was very uncomfortable with the imprecision in the reference language definitions. "They would just describe stuff in English," he remembered, still incredulous. "You were hassled in these…committees enough to realize that something needed to be done. You needed to learn how to be precise." The language description was an inconsistent mess because "[t]hey were just writing English."

So Backus began the hard work of bringing his sense of precision to the syntax of IAL, which he finished in 1959. Typed up in a paper called "The Syntax and Semantics of the Proposed International Algebraic Language of the Zurich ACM-GAMM Conference," Backus laid out his metalanguage—a language to describe a language—which consisted of a context-free grammar of symbolic notation and mathematical formalism. The *production rules* of the metalanguage, which was at first called Backus Normal Form (BNF), were the linchpin; these production rules manifested themselves as a series of metalinguistic formulas, consisting of left-hand-side name (or *non-terminal symbol*) and a right-hand-side alternative or alternatives (which could be *terminal symbols* and/or *non-terminal symbols*), delimited by ORs (using the vertical bar, |), with the ::= symbol separating the left- and right-hand sides of the production rules and having the meaning "is defined as." Angle brackets, <>, are used to enclose *classes* or metalinguistic variables, which related to a set of associated symbols of a category. For instance, an integer variable implicitly defined in FORTRAN I could be explicitly defined using a modern version of BNF as

$$<\textit{integer-type}> ::= I \mid J \mid K \mid L \mid M \mid N$$

Below is a formal description for integers in IAL, as taken from Backus's 1959 paper; note the :≡ symbol and the word "or":

$$<\textit{integer}> :\equiv <\textit{digit}> \text{ or } <\textit{integer}> <\textit{digit}>$$

Backus was worried that without using a precise mathematical formalism to define IAL, "it is likely that many man-years may be invested in producing a number of translating programs which will not reliably produce equivalent machine programs."

Recounting the events that led him to develop his metalanguage, Backus gave credit for the inspiration of his ideas to Emil Post. "In a recent course on computability given by Martin Davis," Backus wrote in the late 1960s, "I had been exposed to the work of the logician Emil Post and his notion of a 'production.' As soon as the need for precise description was noted, it became obvious that Post's productions were well suited for that purpose. I hastily adapted them for use in describing the syntax of IAL." Many saw the influence of the MIT linguist Noam Chomsky in Backus's use of context-free grammar as well.

But Martin Davis hadn't taught the computability course then, despite what Backus claimed, and he wouldn't do so for some time. Thus, several decades later, with the timeline now in dispute, Backus offered another version of events. "There's a strange confusion here," he began.

I swore that the idea for studying syntax came from Emil Post because I had taken a course with Martin Davis at the Lamb Estate.... So I thought if you want to describe something, just do what Post did. Martin Davis tells me he did not teach the course until long afterward. So I don't know how to account for it.

Just as Backus had initially claimed he took inspiration from the Laning and Zierler system when devising FORTRAN I, he had to retract a claim-of-origin statement. But he put to rest the Chomsky connection with a typical self-deprecating wave of the hand: "I didn't know anything about Chomsky. I was a very ignorant person." Asked about Chomsky again near the end of his life, Backus underscored the point: "Somebody sort of proved that I was wrong about it, that I hadn't got it from Noam Chomsky, because the dates were all wrong somehow." Martin Davis believed that Backus learned of Post's and Chomsky's work from discussions with mathematician Richard Goldberg, one of the original FORTRAN team members.

The response to Backus's paper by the joint committee, however, was underwhelming. "The resulting paper was received with a silence that made it seem that precise syntax description was an idea whose time had not yet come," recalled Backus. Perhaps it was merely too little, too late: "Well, I had come to one of these meetings with this BNF description. It was a little paper and I handed it—I hand carried it because it was so late in the game, so I had these copies that I dragged to the meeting and passed out to people and nobody paid any attention to it."

But there was one exception to this silence: Peter Naur, a Danish mathematician. Born in 1928 in Denmark, Naur was a joint committee member on the European side. He read Backus's paper and was convinced: the ALGOL 58 language definition was too vague, too imprecise. Naur also saw avenues for improvement in Backus's ideas, specifically with respect to notation, with the introduction of the vertical bar (|) for "or," the change of :≡ to ::=, and the dispensing of certain symbol abbreviations in order to improve clarity. With a revision of ALGOL slated for January 1960 in Paris—this time having a larger contingent of people on the committee (thirteen, including John McCarthy, whom we'll learn more about in this chapter)—Naur incorporated these changes into BNF and edited the final document, called "Report on the Algorithmic Language ALGOL 60," released shortly thereafter.

ALGOL 60 proved the international language had finally come into its own, with significant advantages over contemporaneous FORTRAN, including recursion and local variables. In FORTRAN I, all variables were *global*, meaning that the entire program had access to any variable's contents. But it also meant that mistakes with variable naming, especially in lengthy programs, were easy to make; a programmer could accidently use the same variable name for two different representations. *Local variables* solved the problem by compartmentalizing code, making the variables only available "locally," or in a specific context. Memory allocation in ALGOL 60 occurred on a stack—with *scope* rules "by which a variable declared in a block could only be accessed in the block itself, or in blocks interior to it," explained Maurice Wilkes in the article "From Fortran and Algol to Object-Oriented Languages." Thus, a variable "A" in one part of a program couldn't been "seen" (that's the notion of scope) in another part of the same program—thus permitting the "A" to be reused as a new variable name in a different context. Direct recursion was dependent upon a programming language being able to locally define variables; thus, direct recursion was not possible in FORTRAN I. Most American programmers at the time were either unfamiliar or uncomfortable with recursion, which would, in part, help buy FORTRAN just enough time to squeak by the ALGOL threat.

In 1964, Donald Knuth suggested that Backus Normal Form be called Backus-Naur Form instead, partly in recognition of Peter Naur's contributions but also because there was no "Normal Form"—no standard way of writing the grammar of a language. Later, computer scientists, most notably Niklaus Wirth, further extended BNF.

As for ALGOL, though it served as a springboard for a number of other languages, such as Ada, C, PL/I, Simula, and Pascal (which Wirth designed for commercial, scientific, and educational applications)—collectively called ALGOL-like languages—ALGOL itself never garnered much popularity, especially in the United States; only a few companies, such as Burroughs, ever bothered to release ALGOL 60 compilers. This despite its clever design and support from SHARE, which passed a resolution urging IBM to write an ALGOL compiler. ALGOL was ahead of its time, too abstract for the average user when it arrived on the scene. Plus, because of its block structure (the language was built on a stack), any change to a program required that the program be recompiled.

FORTRAN had begun its life by fighting off its first existential threat, assembly language; several years later, it slayed ALGOL, too, though it wouldn't fare as well against ALGOL's successors. Richard Hamming attributes the failure of ALGOL to the theoreticians' failure to recognize that a logical language was not "humane"—unlike a psychological language, such as FORTRAN, which wasn't burdened by being "stated in a Boolean logical form which is not comprehensible to mere mortals...."

Regardless of the reasons, ALGOL syntax lives on in pseudocode descriptions of algorithms. The structured approach ALGOL offered (by grouping code in blocks, for instance) came to dominate the field. In addition, the creation of the language coincided with the advent of the scientific study of computer programming.

An Interlude on Recursion

Before moving on to the next programming language impacted by FORTRAN, we need to take a moment to examine the concept of recursion. In mathematics, a recursive function is a function that calls itself; past output becomes current input, perhaps ad infinitum. In computer science, the definition of a recursive function is similar: it is a function, procedure, or subroutine that calls itself. "This at first seems very baffling...somewhat like a snake swallowing its own tail," observed computer science teacher Charles E. Cook. "Would the snake eventually disappear?"

The idea of recursion is sometimes introduced to computer science students courtesy of a factorial (represented by the ! character), which is typically employed to shortcut certain mathematical counting problems. For instance, $3! = 3 \times 2 \times 1 = 6$, $6! = 6 \times 5 \times 4 \times 3 \times 2 \times 1 = 720$, etc. By definition, $0! = 1$.

A computer program in modern Fortran using iteration (loops) to calculate 5! might look something like this:

```
program factorial
implicit none

   integer :: n
   integer :: fact = 1

   do n = 1, 5
      fact = fact * n
   end do

   print*, fact

end program factorial
```

When run, the number 120 is output—because 5×4×3×2×1 = 120, which is calculated iteratively by cycling through the do loop five times. Note that the algorithm above is not recursive in nature, since at no point does a function call itself.

Although the formula for $n!$ is

$$n! = n \times (n-1) \times (n-2) \times (n-3) \times \cdots \times 1$$

We can benefit by rewriting the formula as

$$n! = n \times (n-1)!$$

We will code this re-expressed factorial formula recursively. Factorials lend themselves to recursive routines because the next output always depends on previous input. Early FORTRAN implementations did not permit recursive routines; so, instead, consider the factorial program written below in modern Fortran, which has a Factorial() function that calls itself repeatedly until the variable n winds down to zero:

```
program recursion_example

implicit none

interface
   function Factorial(n)
      integer :: Factorial
      integer :: n
   end function Factorial
end interface


print*, Factorial(5)

end program recursion_example


!----------------------------------------------
```

```
recursive function Factorial(n)   result(fact)

implicit none
integer :: fact
integer :: n

if (n == 0) then
   fact = 1
else
   fact = n * Factorial(n-1)
end if

end function Factorial
```

The recursive trick lies in the second return statement:

```
fact = n * Factorial(n-1)
```

since the function takes the "current" value of n and multiplies it by the result of the Factorial() function—after that function is passed a parameter value one less than n. In addition, the fact that the integer variable n is local, not global—with repeated instances of the variable created at each pass through the function—makes the recursive structure possible.

Note that if we rewrite the Factorial() function in the following manner, the program will quickly run out of memory and crash since it slips into an infinite loop:

```
recursive function Factorial(n)   result(fact)

implicit none
integer :: fact
integer :: n

fact = n * Factorial(n-1)

end function Factorial
```

The "limiting" return condition—what to do when n equals 0—is necessary because it prevents a down-the-rabbit-hole, forever decreasing value of n. Every recursive routine must have at least one limiting condition (which is also called a *terminating condition* or a *base case*); without it, the call stack grows infinitely large and squashes the program dead in its tracks.

Although technically any algorithm that can be written using recursion can also be written using iteration (loops) and vice versa, there are certain tasks (such as searching and sorting algorithms) that better lend themselves to one approach or the other.

FORTRAN was slow to adopt recursion. As detailed in "A Poor Man's Realization of Recursive Structured Fortran" (1981) by Masataka Sassa, programmers were crafting preprocessors of various levels of functionality to permit forms of recursion in

FORTRAN as far back as the early 1970s; Recursive Structured Fortran and Arisawa's STAR system are examples.

FORTRAN IV precluded recursion, as Doris Appleby explained in a 1992 issue of *BYTE* magazine. "FORTRAN IV provided for programs that call subroutines through a return-jump mechanism (i.e., process control jumps to the subroutine and returns to the line after the subroutine call)," she noted. "Return-jump eliminates recursion, since a recursive call returns to the first line of a recursive subroutine, rather than to the line after the call."

Even though recursion was not explicitly allowed in FORTRAN 77 either, since neither functions nor subroutines were able to call themselves, there were ways to game the compiler without resorting to a preprocessor. For instance, Andrew J. Miller of Penn State's College of Engineering explains that "one can implement recursion [in FORTRAN 77] in a round about [*sic*] way by passing the subroutine as an argument to itself. The subroutine can then call itself by calling the dummy subroutine." But standards committees would not support recursion directly until the release of FORTRAN 77's successor, which arrived in 1991. Why the delay? Perhaps part of the answer can be found in a discussion that took place in Vienna in 1982 among members of an international standards committee called the WG5. Their general topic: What should be included in the FORTRAN 8X standard?

Loren Meissner starts the conversation by asking, "Are recursive procedures needed?" The very fact that the question even needs to be asked at such a late date is a window into the thinking of the committee.

"I am still waiting for examples of the need for recursive procedures," responds Kees Ampt, representing the Netherlands. "But should there be a difference between recursive and non-recursive procedures? Recursive should be the default."

Michael Metcalf chimes in. "I found one example. In the survey we took, there was a very negative response to recursion."

"It is the only way to solve some problems," says L. G. J. ter Haar, another representative from the Netherlands.

"You should be able to declare that a routine is non-recursive for efficiency," Austria's Willy Weisz adds.

UK representative J. Lawrie Schonfelder, noting the importance of recursion, addresses the group. "There is a lot of simulation of recursion in Fortran programs. Recursion has a definite place. Once you allow a stack, it [recursion] is free."

"No, they are not needed," counters yet another Netherlands representative, Jan A. M. Snoek, since "recursive algorithms can be made cyclic."

"In Fortran 77, things are stated ambiguously," Loren Meissner says. "In a recursive environment, there is more than one possible obvious extension. Recursion can be looked at in two different ways: a copy of the text or a reentrant routine. Each view gives a different interpretation."

A straw vote is taken: *Should recursive procedures be in Fortran 8X?* Sixteen vote yes; five vote no; and five vote undecided.

Recursion was a go, but FORTRAN programmers would have to wait nine more years to get their hands on it.

◊◊◊

Edsger Dijkstra once remarked that "[t]he tools we use have a profound and devious influence on our thinking habits, and therefore on our thinking abilities." He expanded this idea with a telling anecdote.

> The devious influence was inspired by the experience with a bright student. In the oral examination we solved a problem. Together we constructed the program, decided what had to be done, but very close to the end, the kid got stuck. I was amazed because he had understood the problem perfectly. It turned out he had to write a subscripted value in a subscript position, the idea of a subscripted subscript, something that was not allowed in FORTRAN. And having been educated in FORTRAN, he couldn't think of it, although it was a construction that he had seen me using at my lectures.

The student's patterns of thought were shaped by the limitations of FORTRAN. Unsurprisingly, Dijkstra also believed that FORTRAN's lack of recursion also had a profound influence. "When young students have difficulty in understanding recursion, it is always due to the fact that they had learned programming in a programming language that did not permit it," he explained. "If you are now trained in such an operational way of thinking, at a given moment your pattern of understanding becomes visualizing what happens during the execution of the algorithm. The only way in which you can see the algorithm is as a FORTRAN program."

LISP, the LISt Processor (1958)

John McCarthy, who was born in 1927 in Massachusetts, organized the Dartmouth Summer Research Project on Artificial Intelligence in 1956—the first such conference of its kind. He was seriously thinking about simulating human intelligence using machines in the late 1940s while he was busy pursuing his doctorate in mathematics at Princeton; after attending a symposium at Cal Tech featuring a talk by John von Neumann on self-replicating automata, McCarthy scheduled a one-on-one meeting with the elder mathematician to discuss the connections between automata and human intelligence. Von Neumann liked what he heard from the Ph.D. student. "Write it up, write it up," von Neumann instructed him, but McCarthy demurred. "I didn't write it up because I didn't feel it was really good," he admitted.

Like a drop of water he couldn't dislodge from his ear canal, simulating the thinking of human beings was an idea McCarthy couldn't shake from his brain. McCarthy, who would go on to become an artificial intelligence pioneer (he coined the term AI when settling on the name of the Summer Research Project on Artificial Intelligence), wanted to make use of an IBM 704 for AI work. He was already serving as a consultant to IBM as they moved toward using the 704 to solve problems in Euclidian (plane) geometry; IBM's geometry "theorem-prover" was based on a proposal of Harvard's Marvin Minsky's, who would later move to MIT to cofound their AI Lab. In addition, IBM was busy building the New England Computation Center at MIT, which Dartmouth had access to. McCarthy would teach at Dartmouth in 1955, and be hired to teach at MIT the next year.

The ambitions of the Summer Research Project were sky-high and, as it turned out, unrealistic. McCarthy, Minsky, Nathaniel Rochester, and Claude Shannon (a Bell Labs employee whom McCarthy reached out to; Shannon is known as the "Father of Information Theory," after identifying the *bit* as a basic unit of information in a 1948 paper called "The Mathematical Theory of Communication." John Tukey coined the term bit, a contraction of "binary digit") wrote up a grant proposal to the Rockefeller Foundation, requesting a modest $7,500 for the project's expenses, including railway fare fees. The study would be conducted by ten individuals over a two-month timeframe in the summer of 1956. The purpose of the study, they wrote, was to "Proceed on the basis of the conjecture that every aspect of learning or any other feature of intelligence can in principle be so precisely described that a machine can be made to simulate it." Decades later, McCarthy would admit that the "goals that I had for that conference were entirely unrealistic. I thought that major projects could be undertaken during the course of a summer conference."

Although the Summer Research Project barely scratched the surface of the burgeoning discipline of artificial intelligence, McCarthy, as a result of the experience, had his sights set on employing some sort of algebraic list processing language to solve AI problems. "The beauty of using lists for logical reasoning is that they can grow and shrink and reform themselves as the inferences proceed," explain Dennis Shasha and Cathy Lazere in *Out of Their Minds: The Lives and Discoveries of 15 Great Computer Scientists*. "Further, one can represent both rules and data in the same form."

Perhaps McCarthy didn't have to look far for a suitable list processing language. During the Summer Research Project, three attendees—John Clifford Shaw (who developed the programming language JOSS, or JOHNNIAC Open-Shop System), Allen Newell (an expert on human cognition and AI), and Herbert Simon (economist and political scientist who would go on to be awarded a Nobel)—presented a list processing language called IPL 2 (Information Processing Language 2), which was designed for the JOHNNIAC (John von Neumann Numerical Integrator and Automatic Computer), a von Neumann architecture computer built by the RAND Corporation in Santa Monica, California. IPL 2 was merely a conduit toward building a "Logic Theorist" program designed to mimic the thinking of human beings, specifically with mathematical proofs; the Logic Theorist eventually managed to prove some theorems from Russell and Whitehead's three-volume magnum opus *Principia Mathematica*, published in the early twentieth century. But Herbert Simon wasn't happy with how their work was received. "They [Minsky and McCarthy] didn't want to hear from us," he said, "and we sure didn't want to hear from them!... In a way, it was ironic because we had already done the first example of what they were after; and second, they didn't pay much attention to it." For his part, McCarthy wrote that "There was little temptation to copy IPL, because its form was based on a JOHNNIAC loader that happened to be available to them, and because the FORTRAN idea of writing programs algebraically was attractive."

McCarthy needed to have, at his disposal, something that could represent "information about the world by sentences in a suitable formal language and a reasoning program that would decide what to do by making logical inferences." To that end, "Representing sentences by list structure seemed appropriate—it still is—and a list processing language also seemed appropriate for programming the operations involved in deduction—and still is," he wrote in 1979. But just because he settled on the structure of the hypothetical language doesn't mean he knew how to implement it on the available hardware.

> The first problem was how to do list structure in the IBM 704. This computer has a 36 bit word, and two 15 bit parts, called the address and decrement, were distinguished by special instructions for moving their contents to and from the 15 bit index registers. The address of the machine was 15 bits, so it was clear that list structure should use 15 bit pointers. Therefore, it was natural to consider the word as divided into 4 parts, the address part, the decrement part, the prefix part and the tag part. The last two were three bits each and separated from each other by the decrement so that they could not be easily combined into a single six bit part.

Several functions for decomposing lists were proposed: *car*, or contents of the address part of the register; *cdr*, or contents of the decrement part of the register; *cpr*, or contents of the prefix part of the register; *ctr*, or contents of the tag part of the register. (LISP also introduced the *eval* function, which migrated to a number of other computer languages. Writing code today in an interactive shell interface called REPL—which stands for read-eval-print-loop—derived from the first generation of LISP.) McCarthy's proto-language, at this point, wasn't even close to being implemented on an actual IBM 704, since IBM hadn't yet been supplied the New England Computation Center with its promised 704.

Around this time, McCarthy made a suggestion to Rochester, Herbert Gelernter, and Carl Gerberich at IBM: build a list processing language using FORTRAN as the base (starting with something already established seemed like the easiest path to success). They created FLPL, or FORTRAN List Processing Language, an extension of the FORTRAN language. FLPL could handle expressions and serve as Minsky's geometry theorem-prover. But there were limitations, namely, the lack of recursion and conditional expressions.

McCarthy had, when writing a chess program in the 1957-58 academic year at MIT, partially gotten around the conditional expressions issue by creating a new function. Recall how the arithmetic **IF** statement worked in FORTRAN I with this example:

$$\text{IF } (B - A) \ 10, 20, 30$$

would transfer control to statement 10 if $B - A < 0$, statement 20 if $B - A = 0$, or statement 30 if $B - A > 0$. McCarthy called the arithmetic **IF** statement "awkward to use" and therefore created the **XIF** function:

$$\text{XIF}(M, N1, N2)$$

The function would return the value $N1$ if M was zero or $N2$ if M was not zero. But the **XIF** function couldn't be used with abandon, since it slowed down the execution of programs considerably.

The summer of 1958 found McCarthy spending time at the IBM Information Research Department; Rochester had invited him. There, McCarthy attempted to use FLPL to write a program to differentiate algebraic expressions, but he quickly ran up against a wall: recursion, which wasn't possible with FORTRAN I because variables could only be global in nature. "If FORTRAN had allowed recursion, I would have gone ahead using FLPL," he admitted. "I even explored the question of how one might add recursion to FORTRAN. But it was much too kludgy."

> At this point a new language was necessary, since it was very difficult both technically and politically to tinker with Fortran, and neither conditional expressions nor recursion could be implemented with machine language Fortran functions—not even with "functions" that modify the code that calls them. Moreover, the IBM group seemed satisfied with FLPL as it was and did not want to make the vaguely stated but obviously drastic changes required to allow conditional expressions and recursive definition. As I recall, they argued that these were unnecessary.

With both FORTRAN and FLPL not meeting his needs, McCarthy invented LISP, or LISt Processor. The hard work began in the fall of 1958, when he returned to MIT, but now in the role of Assistant Professor of Communication Sciences in the Electrical Engineering department. "[LISP] was designed to facilitate experiments with a proposed system called the Advice Taker, whereby a machine could be instructed to handle declarative as well as imperative sentences and could exhibit 'common sense' in carrying out its instructions," McCarthy explained in a 1960 article with the verbose title "Recursive Functions of Symbolic Expressions and Their Computation by Machine, Part I." (There was never a Part II.) The Advice Taker, as conceived, would be able to arrive at logical deductions by manipulating expressions which represented English sentences.

With Marvin Minsky, several programmers, a secretary, and half a dozen graduate students, completing the task of repeatedly hand-compiling functions into assembly language helped to build a quasi-realized LISP environment. The lists of LISP were enclosed in parentheses; the order of the elements in the lists might or might not matter (depending on the relationships between the list elements), and further sets of parentheses could add additional structure to the lists. These early LISP programs were written using M-expressions (M = *meta*), which was an informal style that resembled FORTRAN and ALGOL. Like in FORTRAN, the go to statement was available in LISP, as were assignment statements, but, unlike in FORTRAN, conditional expressions and recursive functions were also built-in. Functions in LISP used brackets rather than parentheses, since the latter were reserved for lists. All data sets were formatted as lists; all arithmetic expressions were formatted as lists; all functions were formatted as lists. LISP was undeniably a list processing language.

As compared with M-expressions, S-expressions (S = *symbolic*) were machine-independent representations of *atomic symbols*, or sets of contiguous characters (which could be a single character), such as A, HELLO, or HOT CHICKEN SOUP (where the spaces don't disqualify the string from being atomic). The S-expressions, which are formed by using parentheses and the dot symbol, could consist of atomic symbols or simpler S-expressions. McCarthy offers these examples:

$$AB$$
$$(A \cdot B)$$
$$((AB \cdot C) \cdot D)$$

LISP didn't mimic FORTRAN when dealing with expressions of arithmetic operations. For example,

$$x + 2y + z$$

would be rewritten in Cambridge Polish notation (a prefix notation variant) as

$$(PLUS\ X\ (TIMES\ 2\ Y)\ Z)$$

Here is a second example of Cambridge Polish notation. The expression

$$(2 + 5) \times 3$$

would be rewritten as

$$(*\ (+\ 2\ 5)\ 3)$$

Among the initial adopters there was, at first, an inherent awkwardness in writing S-expressions. The S-expressions, as originally conceived, were intended as a stopgap until the language could handle M-expressions. But that never happened. "The project of defining M-expressions precisely and compiling them or at least translating them into S-expressions was neither finalized nor explicitly abandoned," McCarthy wrote. "It just receded into the indefinite future, and a new generation of programmers appeared who preferred internal notation to any FORTRAN-like or ALGOL-like notation that could be devised." The computer scientist Steve Russell translated McCarthy's ideas into LISP for the IBM 704. (Several years later, Russell would develop the early videogame *Spacewar!* for the Digital Equipment Corporation PDP-1 computer.)

Eventually, one of McCarthy's students realized that a LISP compiler could itself be written in LISP. McCarthy was surprised by the idea and asked the student to go forward with the project. Using the notion of self-compiling, the student succeeded in building the LISP LISP compiler.

Variants of LISP are still in use today; recursion works naturally with the list structure of the language. To illustrate, consider the short Lisp program below, complete with nested lists, which outputs the result of 5!

```
(defun Factorial (n) (if (= n 0) 1 (* n(Factorial (- n 1)))))
(print (Factorial 5))
```

LISP also influenced a number of programming languages including Forth, JavaScript, LOGO, Prolog, Python, Smalltalk, and Swift.

McCarthy took what he had learned when creating LISP to the ALGOL 60 committee meetings in Paris in 1960, selling the members on conditional expressions and recursion. These features were integrated into the language, as well as in many other ALGOL-like languages to follow.

COBOL, the COmmon Business-Oriented Language (1959)

The scientists, engineers, mathematicians, and academics had a language tailored to their needs: FORTRAN. But where was a language for commercial uses? Where was a language for businesses? Where was a language adept at data processing? FORTRAN I didn't fit the bill.

The U.S. government sought to solve the problem, so government representatives organized the Conference/Committee on Data Systems and Languages (CODASYL), which was held at the Pentagon in Arlington, Virginia, in 1959. There, they would develop a common data processing language. Having such a standardized language on hand would significantly reduce costs, since completely rewriting programs and utilities every time old hardware was discarded in favor of new—both in government and in industry—would no longer be necessary.

COBOL 60 (COmmon Business-Oriented Language 60), completed a year later, was the result of their efforts. Although verbose and unwieldy, COBOL code *looked* easy to understand, at least to the uninitiated—because it resembled English. Thus, technophobic bureaucrats pushed programmers to move forward with COBOL. By the late 1960s, spurred by actions of the federal government, COBOL compilers were available on most computers.

We have already touched on the development of COBOL earlier in this book. But beside the obvious point—that COBOL offered data processing tools which FORTRAN didn't—how is COBOL intertwined with FORTRAN?

Shortly after Roy Nutt finished his work on Backus's FORTRAN development team, he quit United Aircraft and cofounded the Computer Sciences Corporation (CSC) with Fletcher Jones, whom he had first met at SHARE. A third founder, General Motors computer technician Bob Patrick—who knew both Jones and Nutt from SHARE—also came aboard. A site in Los Angeles was designated as the company's headquarters.

CSC's first contract, landed in 1959, was with Honeywell, which agreed to the contract based on the strength of Nutt's reputation alone. The assignment: build a FORTRAN-like compiler for the Honeywell H-800 computer, but for business data processing rather than engineering or science applications.

Fletcher Jones proved to not work well with others, at least at first. When he incorporated the company, he gave himself seventy percent ownership, with Nutt and Patrick acquiring only fifteen percent each. So Jones was summarily ousted, with CSC conditionally retaining the Honeywell contract—as long as Nutt was still part of the development team. Nutt then caught a flight to Boston to meet with Honeywell representatives. But Jones followed him there, meeting with Nutt. They couldn't be more different: Nutt was the prototypical introvert, a man who drove around in an old Volkswagen Beetle cluttered with paper printouts and punched cards and never raised his voice, whereas Jones was the ostentatious showman, reveling in cruising around in a custom green Cadillac convertible and showing off by sailing on his forty-foot yacht.

Despite their wildly contrasting personalities, the two came to a decision: it was in fact Bob Patrick who had to go, since, with his micromanaging ways and his need to institute dress codes along with other rules and regulations in the office, *he* was the person causing the problems. A new, fairer partnership was drawn up, with the two of them buying out Patrick's stake in the company. Ironically, Patrick would land at Honeywell, where he programmed acceptance tests for the new CSC compiler.

After Patrick left, Nutt got right to work building the CSC compiler, which was first called Transdata but later named FACT: the Fully Automated Compiling Technique. By leveraging his SHARE contacts, Jones was able to bring some of the best programmers to CSC to help code the compiler.

FACT looked to be the Department of Defense's chosen language for their CODASYL project, which the Pentagon established to gauge the feasibility of building a common data processing programming language. CODASYL was comprised of multiple committees; the intermediate term committee, which Nutt and Jones met with, voted 15 to 1 to go with FACT as a template language, but the short-term committee disagreed and urged the executive committee to adopt a language design by Grace Hopper, who, recall, had not only designed one of the first compilers (the A-0 for the UNIVAC I) as well as the FLOW-MATIC data processing compiler, but was also a former officer in the Navy and thus personally knew many of the government and military players involved.

The CODASYL executive committee went with Hopper's design over CSC's. Nutt still had many suggestions for the new language, which evolved into the COmmon Business-Oriented Language, or COBOL, but Hopper disregarded most of them. Nutt, who had been friends with Hopper, was hurt by this decision, which "forever put a rift in their relationship," according to Nutt's son Micah. Moreover, he added, "FACT was in many ways superior to COBOL and many of FACT's language and database innovations were later incorporated into COBOL. David Ferguson, an early CSC systems programmer, said, 'FACT influenced COBOL more than any other language.'" Honeywell received the completed FACT compiler in 1961. But because COBOL was not built off the FACT template, FACT quickly faded from the scene.

Work at CSC shifted from developing new compilers to building previously established ones. The first FORTRAN compiler not coded by IBM was made by CSC; it was implemented for the Livermore Automatic Research Computer (LARC), a Sperry Rand transistor-based machine built in 1960 for two sites: the Lawrence Radiation Labs in Livermore, California, and the David Taylor Model Basin in Washington, D.C. (Even by 1957, the year of FORTRAN I's release, the most popular programming language at Livermore Labs was an extended FORTRAN called LRLTRAN, mostly used to compile compilers and keep software on the mainframes at the site up to date. Many of the LRLTRAN extensions eventually became part of the FORTRAN 77 standards.)

In a fitting coda to the story, the very first COBOL compiler was delivered to the electronics company Philco, based in Philadelphia. The company that built this first compiler? CSC, of course.

As for COBOL, it's still very much alive, with hundreds of billions of lines of the language still being maintained on legacy systems around the world.

PL/I, the Programming Language One (1964)

Although FORTRAN had spread far and wide by 1960, it fell far short of satisfying all customers' needs. Sure, it was great for many academic, engineering, mathematical, scientific, and technical applications, but wasn't suited for business data processing, which was in high demand. COBOL, on the other hand, was tailored for the latter. One Big Blue employee described the zeitgeist this way:

> In the early 1960's computer applications, programmers and equipment were much more clearly divided among scientific, commercial, and special-purpose lines than they are today. There were computers designed primarily for scientific applications, such as the IBM 7090 and the IBM 1620, scientific operating systems for these computers, a scientific programming language (FORTRAN), and a user's group for installations whose primary applications were scientific (SHARE). Similarly there were computers oriented toward commercial applications, such as the IBM 7080 and the IBM 1401, system facilities for these, a commercial language (COBOL), and a users' group for installations involved primarily in commercial applications (GUIDE)....
>
> Moreover, there were accepted characteristics which distinguished these categories. Scientific users needed floating point arithmetic, arrays, subroutines, fast computation, fast compilation and batch job scheduling. Commercial users needed decimal arithmetic, string handling instructions, fast and asynchronous I/O, compilation which produced efficient object code, and excellent sort programs....

But the "elegant separation," the wall that stood between different types of users, was crumbling fast. Commercial users needed to calculate advanced statistical summaries of their financial data; scientists required easy means of handling copious amounts of information, both numerical and string; and installation managers were tired of having to maintain two separate operating systems, on segregated hardware, running at cross-purposes.

Thus, a language with broad scope, complete with the power of a FORTRAN *and* a COBOL, emerged as a new goal at IBM. This unification project, begun in the fall of 1963 when a handful of people from IBM and SHARE formed the Advanced Language Development Committee of the SHARE FORTRAN project, had Standard Oil's Bruce Rosenblatt—who was knowledgeable about programming, installations, and SHARE's expectations—assume the mantle as chairman.

The SHARE delegation included Hans Berg, an employee at Lockheed with knowledge of computing installations, and Jim Cox, an employee of Union Carbide with a multitude of programming experience; importantly, Cox knew his way around COMTRAN, or COMmercial TRANslator, a pre-COBOL IBM business-oriented data processing language developed by Roy Goldfinger and Bob Bemer in 1958. COMTRAN offered scientific formulas in a business context to programmers, implemented the IF...THEN of ALGOL 58, and provided a number of convenient and innovative data options, like the "picture clause" (which was later incorporated in COBOL). COMTRAN, along with Roy Nutt's FACT and especially Grace Hopper's FLOW-MATIC, highly influenced the design of COBOL, a language that IBM's customers clamored for the company to supply.

The IBM delegation for the unification project included C. W. Medlock, a FORTRAN expert, and Bernice Weitzenhoffer, an experienced programmer of both FORTRAN and COBOL. George Radin (who is the IBMer quoted above), a scientific programming specialist, served as chairman of Big Blue's delegation.

There were several other committee members from IBM and SHARE; some of them had nearly full-time involvement in the project, which would consist of three- or four-day bimonthly informal meetings, mostly held in assorted New York hotels, that usually stretched out over weekends. SHARE members, having other full-time gigs, weren't in the privileged position of IBMers, who received time off for their efforts.

A key factor driving the unification project was the imminent release of the IBM System/360 and OS/360, representing a radical shift in IBM's design philosophy: from discrete, unrelated pieces of hardware at a variety of price points to an integrated "family" model of machines where compatibility was the order of the day.

The push for integration began around 1960. That year, IBM was producing seven completely different computer models—some of which were for scientific processing, others of which were geared toward business applications. Each of these models required its own production line, peripherals, and sales force. If action wasn't taken soon, then costs would spiral out of control, burying the company in the process.

It hadn't always been this way. When punch-card machines were at the cutting edge of the technology business, IBM produced numerous models of effectively the same machine. Decades passed, and the mainframe computer industry emerged. As Campbell-Kelly and Aspray explain, a "combinatorial explosion" of different software products required for each computer, not to mention the need to reprogram software for upgraded machines, led to a push within IBM to make their entire product line of computers, from the smallest and most underpowered to the biggest and most powerful, compatible. In early 1960, however, it was far from a given that it was even technically *possible* to fully implement this vision and, even if it were, the cost of doing so might be too great to ensure continued profitability up and down the hardware product line (to say nothing of the software). Plus, there were 1401 loyalists within IBM who thought it business malpractice to leave the incredibly successful machine by the wayside in pursuit of a fanciful, and perhaps fanatical, goal.

The "combinatorial explosion," though, was forcing IBM's hand. By the end of the year, the company would devote considerable energy to sketching out how, precisely, to make a compatible "family" of machines a reality. Thomas Watson, Jr., turned to the Harvard-educated Vincent Learson to spearhead a task group called SPREAD, designated with formulating a compatibility plan. SPREAD came to a consensus: the company must build a New Product Line (NPL). Despite the high costs associated with SPREAD's detailed proposal, Watson and top management gave the NPL a green light.

In early 1962, the company began work on five processors with purposely misleading identification numbers—101, 250, 315, 400, and 501—disguising IBM's intentions to the competition (if word got out). Secrecy was the order of the day, with research costs ultimately totaling half a billion dollars. That dwarfed the costs of development—in terms of new factory equipment (for massive semiconductor and integrated circuit production) and employee education—which rang to the tune of about five billion dollars. Big Blue selected a name "betokening all points of the compass": System/360.

IBM had planned a slow rollout of the technology: one new computer model released every year or two. But Honeywell put a wrinkle in IBM's plans by releasing the Honeywell 200—a faster and cheaper 1401-style machine that was, in an unprecedented move, mostly *compatible* with the 1401. By using the "Liberator" program, software that ran on the 1401 would also (probably) run on the 200, only faster. Sales of the 1401 flatlined, and IBM retaliated by launching the entire System/360 product line via a coordinated, nationwide publicity tour. Big Blue was consequently crushed by a cavalcade of orders that ended up taking years to fill. But companies sat up and took notice, realizing that IBM was right: hardware compatibility was the wave of the future.

So, if an integrated compatibility model ruled the hardware product line, why should customers have to employ different programming languages for scientific and business uses—shouldn't they be integrated as well? If the programming language unification project had been entirely successful, both FORTRAN and COBOL would have been rendered redundant—and probably relegated to the dustbin of history in only their first decade of life. Plus, a unified language would have given IBM a stranglehold in the HLL market for at least a generation.

Obviously, that's not how history played out. There had been bold attempts to build such a unified language before, JOVIAL being the most noteworthy. With development completed in 1960 at the System Development Corporation by a team managed by Jules Schwartz, JOVIAL was utilized primarily by the U.S. Air Force (the Strategic Air Command in Omaha was the first user). The language offered a number of data allocation features—with its "Data Definition area"—but also possessed FORTRAN-style scientific functionality. Yet JOVIAL ultimately didn't fit the bill as a true FORTRAN and COBOL replacement.

JOVIAL, an acronym for Jules' Own Version of the International Algorithmic Language, was originally set to be called OVIAL, Our Version of the International Algebraic Language—essentially, *their* (the development team's) own version of ALGOL, originally called the International Algebraic Language, which the team early on took as a blueprint for JOVIAL—but, as Jules Schwartz explained, "In the late 1950s, society wasn't quite as free thinking as it is today." He elaborated:

> The name OVIAL seemed to have a connotation relative to the birth process that did not seem acceptable to some people. So, during a meeting, held approximately January 1959, at which a number of technical issues were discussed—a meeting attended by members of the staff of the SACCS Division Management, the CUSS project, and IEC personnel—the subject of an acceptable name for the language was initiated. Someone in the group, and it's not known by me who it was, suggested the name JOVIAL. This

seemed like the easiest transition from OVIAL. The question then was the meaning of the "J". Since I was standing in front of the room conducting the meeting at the time, somebody—perhaps somebody other than the one who suggested JOVIAL—suggested it be called Jules' Own Version of the International Algebraic Language. This suggestion was met with laughter by the assembled group. The meeting ended shortly afterward without actually finalizing the discussion of the name.

Schwartz then left to take a trip. When he returned, the die had been cast: Schwartz's language was now also officially his namesake. And the joyous laughter elicited during the meeting was apropos of the acronym.

With JOVIAL out of the running, the Advanced Language Development Committee of the SHARE FORTRAN project turned its attention to FORTRAN. Perhaps, they reasoned, a new language could be built off of FORTRAN by simply extending its capabilities. Their bias toward FORTRAN was understandable—there were a number of world-class FORTRAN experts on the committee. IBM fully approved: compatibility with FORTRAN was a plus in Big Blue's eyes. Informally called FORTRAN VI, part of the language definition read as follows:

> FORTRAN VI is not intended to be compatible with any known FORTRAN IV. It includes the functional capabilities of FORTRAN as well as those capabilities normally associated with "commercial" and "algorithmic" languages. In order to embrace these capabilities in a usable and practical language, it has been found virtually impossible, and certainly undesirable, to retain FORTRAN IV as a compatible subset.

Nathaniel Rochester, the MIT-educated engineer who helped build the Whirlwind I computer, noted that full compatibility with FORTRAN IV would be an albatross, since FORTRAN IV was already suffocating under the weight of its own complexity and its adherence, more or less, to the standards set in prior versions of FORTRAN. In addition, the FORTRAN experts within IBM were pushing back against any attempt to further extend or introduce another version of the already much-too-burdened language.

A meeting involving management and language experts on the future of FORTRAN was held in February of 1963. The fate of FORTRAN VI—and a possible FORTRAN V, too—hung in the balance. Perhaps FORTRAN V could be an extension of VI, according to a report summarizing the meeting, with "field and character handling capability," thus introducing some much-needed "information processing" capabilities as opposed to moving forward with a business- or scientific-exclusive approach. But FORTRAN V would be the end of the line—FORTRAN VI would not retain compatibility with its predecessors, instead having streamlined syntax and functionality suited for both business and science applications. The committee came to realize that backward compatibility with FORTRAN IV and extensions to the language couldn't be successfully implemented simultaneously—it was either one or the other.

So they chose neither route, instead opting to start over. "By starting over," realized chairman George Radin, who was most responsible for the decision, "we were not required to live with many technical compromises, but the task was made much more difficult." The "major drawback" of employing FORTRAN's existing foundation was no longer a problem. After all, using FORTRAN IV as a base had many disadvantages: the language, which had been developed with punched cards in mind, didn't look quite right on display terminals; arrays were stored in a column format rather than a row format, which was an impediment to business-oriented programmers, who organized data using tables, not vectors and matrices; and the manner in which variable definitions were made was less than optimal, according to the committee. Plus, once an ALGOL-like block structure was built-in—certainly required for any language going forward—along with implementing the many necessary extensions, their newly fashioned language would be an altogether different animal compared with FORTRAN IV regardless.

Starting from scratch, though, meant the committee needed a new foundation, and fast, because the first generation of IBM System/360s were due to ship in 1965—and IBM expected a unified FORTRAN/COBOL replacement to be released with them. But the committee found the rigid deadlines intolerable. With only several months allotted to arrive at a finalized language definition, and an additional year afterward to complete the programming, the committee scrambled, choosing ALGOL as the base.

Of course, they couldn't call their new language FORTRAN VI. They couldn't call it APL, either, since that acronym was already taken by the hyper-concise A Programming Language, developed by Kenneth E. Iverson at Harvard University. The committee liked MPPL, standing for Multi-Purpose Programming Language. But they liked NPL, or New Programming Language, even better, since it was of a piece with IBM's New Product Line. Throughout most of the language's development, it was referred to as NPL, until England's National Physical Laboratory made a prior-use claim, requiring the name be changed. Programming Language 360, or PL/360, was considered; that would tie the language directly to the New Product Line as well. But the committee wanted their burgeoning language to live beyond the System/360 product line and be machine independent. So Programming Language One, or PL/I, was settled on.

The team developing PL/I faced significant challenges, not least of which was the ever-evolving nature of the System/360 operating system, OS/360, as well as the limitations of the new hardware. Some SHARE members on the team were especially frustrated during the early language definition stages, with at least one complaining that he had "no idea what OS[/360] was." When the initial language specs were presented at a SHARE meeting, contrasting "old" programs (FORTRAN) with "new" programs (PL/I) of the same ilk, the "new" came under considerable criticism from SHARE: Yes, PL/I is a Swiss army knife of languages, but why wasn't the kitchen sink included too? they asked. Despite their misgivings, SHARE officially endorsed NPL (as it was still called).

A second version of the PL/I language specifications was released in 1964, but in two different reports. It is here that we see interesting additions to the language, like semicolons to terminate statements, multiple storage classes and BEGIN…END blocks à la ALGOL, the addition of special characters like the | (vertical bar) to signify OR, a modified FORTRAN DO loop, and the IF…THEN…ELSE control structure. We also see the SET statement for variable assignment, as in:

SET <some variable> = <some expression>;

Stylistically, SET was of a piece with other NPL statements, since they all began with verbs. However, neither ALGOL nor FORTRAN used this structure, so SET was eliminated in favor of

$$\mathit{<some\ variable>}\ =\ \mathit{<some\ expression>};$$

Coincidently, when John Kemeny and Thomas Kurtz were sketching out Dartmouth BASIC in New Hampshire in the early 1960s, the word LET was proposed for variable assignment—because it was a command-like verb. Unlike NPL, however, LET was never excised from Dartmouth BASIC.

Responsibility for the development of NPL eventually shifted to an IBM laboratory located in Hursley, England. Even though the detail present in the documents of language specifications was exhaustive, the language definition would still go through a number of critiques and resultant upheavals. Another report, written at the tail end of this process, reads favorably of NPL's prospects. For example: "NPL should not be presented as a language that can fully replace COBOL, but it is likely that a large number of commercial shops will find it superior and eventually will want to convert to it." In comparison to ALGOL, NPL went a "long way toward incorporating ALGOL concepts, and has a much richer repertoire of extended arithmetic operations than ALGOL does." NPL was even put head-to-head against JOVIAL: "NPL has all the essential capabilities of JOVIAL…[and] should prove strongly competitive with regard to JOVIAL." But, though it compared favorably to FORTRAN, NPL was found to be "a little more prolix" (i.e., long-winded) than FORmula TRANslation. But NPL did have recursion built-in, which was years away from being included in FORTRAN.

The programmers at Hursley did the yeoman's work of whipping NPL into shape; the language definition had been rushed and needed much work to midwife it into real-world use. Meanwhile, Richard Goldberg, who was an integral member of the FORTRAN I team, was part of a new committee, established in the fall of 1964, tasked with a feasibility study: Realistically, how well will the NPL compiler work? The committee chose ASA FORTRAN IV, or standardized FORTRAN, as a baseline with which to compare NPL. They came to a consensus: due to the proposed large set of language features of NPL, both coding and compile times would be significantly longer than in equivalent FORTRAN programs. ALGOL power users were overwhelmed by the NPL specs, viewing the nascent language as nothing more than a superset of ALGOL.

NPL was rebranded PL/I by the end of 1964, and the finalized language specifications took shape. Jean Sammet notes that PL/I was the apotheosis of contemporaneous languages such as FORTRAN, ALGOL, COBOL, and JOVIAL—PL/I was, quite simply, the best option for programming available at the time; it was a general purpose language, laying claim to a number of innovations, such as the concatenation (appending together) of strings and the introduction of generic functions (where, recall, a single function or method can be passed different data types). In addition, variable typing and arrays were offered with a level of flexibility not possible in FORTRAN.

Ultimately, IBM deadlines for the System/360 framework proved too rigid. PL/I wasn't finished in time for the release of OS/360, giving COBOL a significant head start with the New Product Line that became insurmountable, although PL/I proved to be popular with IBM customers of all stripes. For instance, by 1980 at GM Research Laboratories, PL/I took a sizeable chunk out of FORTRAN's dominance—which had once been effectively one hundred percent of their computing workload.

PL/I proved robust enough that variants of the language (e.g., PL/S) are still in use to this day.

FORMAC, the FORmula MAnipulation Compiler (1964)

The basic ideas for FORMAC (FORmula MAnipulation Compiler), a FORTRAN add-on, were first conceived in 1962 at IBM's Boston Advanced Programming Department by Jean Sammet, with assistance from Robert G. Tobey. The goal was to support FORTRAN with methods for formal algebraic manipulation. As Sammet notes in discussing the origins of FORMAC, using programming languages for algebraic purposes wasn't a new idea; even as far back as 1954 there were master's theses at institutions like MIT sketching out how such a concept might work in practice, although, prior to FORMAC, there was only one attempt: ALGY, an interpreter for the Philco 2000. (There were specialized *programs* written in a variety of languages to perform algebraic tasks, but there weren't *programming languages* expressly designed to manipulate expressions algebraically.) ALGY permitted a number of algebraic manipulations, including factoring and the substitution of expressions. There were differences in the input of expressions between ALGY and FORTRAN, with exponentiation in ALGY requiring a $ instead of FORTRAN's **, for example. The ALGY programmer had to deal with great coding limitations, however, such as—rather incredibly—no access to looping mechanisms of any kind.

FORMAC needed to be much more robust than ALGY, of course, to secure anything close to widespread adoption: FORMAC had to offer the standard features of most programming languages, such as loops, I/O, and the like. So FORMAC was designed as a FORTRAN IV language extension, with sophisticated formula manipulation implemented by using subroutines accessed while a user's program was running.

In its first incarnation, FORMAC offered powerful mathematical functionality, with differentiation, expression simplification, and much more built-in; the language offered true symbolic manipulation capabilities. A second incarnation was tailored for the System/360, but it was based on PL/I rather than FORTRAN.

Simultaneous to FORMAC's development, starting in January 1963, Alan Perlis, who had developed the Internal Translator (IT) at Carnegie, was conjuring up his own version of FORMAC (initially unbeknownst to Sammet)—but as an extension of ALGOL 60, not FORTRAN. Called Formula ALGOL, and also capable of symbolic mathematical manipulation, it didn't spread beyond Carnegie.

In 1965, work at IBM began on another computer algebra system. Called SCRATCHPAD, it was not built atop FORTRAN, or any other language for that matter; SCRATCHPAD was built from, well, scratch, and it offered a number of advantages over FORMAC. Like Formula ALGOL, however, SCRATCHPAD never traveled outside its birthplace—in this case, IBM—so it didn't have a chance to gain widespread adoption. Nevertheless, a SCRATCHPAD descendant, called Axiom, lives on.

BASIC, the Beginner's All-purpose Symbolic Instruction Code (1964)

Perhaps the most significant rebuke of FORTRAN came courtesy of BASIC (Beginner's All-purpose Symbolic Instruction Code), a product of two professors from Dartmouth College. John Backus aspired to free programming from the clutches of the priesthood, making the process accessible to mathematicians and scientists. But Dartmouth professors John Kemeny and Thomas Kurtz wanted to do one better: to bring programming, and computing in general, to the masses, regardless of previous experience, although democratizing the entire field of computer science wasn't their goal at first—they were initially parochial, limiting their sights only to undergraduate students at male-only Dartmouth College, situated in Hanover, New Hampshire. The school has a storied history dating back centuries, including offering comprehensive education to the "Youth of the Indian Tribes" and "English Youth and Others" prior to the American Revolutionary War.

Kemeny, a Hungarian mathematician who had once been Albert Einstein's assistant and also worked for Richard Feynman at Los Alamos on the Manhattan Project, and Kurtz, a statistician who earned his doctorate at Princeton under John Tukey, labored on their democratizing project in fits and starts.

Before arriving at Dartmouth, Kemeny studied and then taught at Princeton, interacting frequently with the likes of von Neumann and Einstein at the Institute for Advanced Study. (Kemeny was an invaluable assistant to Einstein because the scientist "wasn't very good at math," Kemeny recalled.) Then he traveled to California, landing a job at the RAND Corporation in Santa Monica in 1953, before decamping only several months later to Dartmouth.

When Kemeny arrived on the campus, there was not a computer in sight, despite Dartmouth's history with computation—of which the most notable event was George Stibitz's 1940 demonstration of remote computing for which he employed a Teletype Model 26. Sixteen years later, John McCarthy would organize his summer artificial intelligence research project at the college, which led to LISP. That same year, IBM established the New England Regional Computer Center at MIT, with some individuals at Dartmouth permitted access to the machine, an IBM 704. By this point, Kemeny had risen to his first position of power: mathematics department chairman (he would later become Dartmouth's president). He whipped the department into shape, turning its focus toward research and hiring a number of new faculty, including Thomas Kurtz, who sported a mop of black hair, a thick mustache, and large, dark-frame glasses. Kurtz had written computer programs as a student at Princeton; once he arrived at the mathematics department, located on the top floor of Dartmouth Hall, he and Kemeny got to know one another quite well over the next several years through bonding experiences like writing computer programs for the New England Regional Computer Center's 704. But not in FORTRAN—that wasn't yet installed on the machine (it was still 1956; FORTRAN wasn't released until the following year), nor was there any operating system to speak of. Instead, they learned and programmed SAP together; Kurtz was responsible for transporting a steel box full of SAP punched cards on the train to MIT's campus every two weeks. He usually had to wait for hours before retrieving printouts from the 704, which he would lug back to Dartmouth.

Kemeny was unhappy with SAP. For one thing, how could such a complex language be taught to his colleagues, let alone to undergraduates? So he wrote DARSIMCO (DARtmouth SIMplified COde), which grouped together sets of SAP operations into "templates," such as for addition, subtraction, multiplication, division, and even simple loops. But DARSIMCO died quickly for two reasons: the faculty failed to use it, and FORTRAN was released less than a year later. But it was not for naught: "DARSIMCO reflected Dartmouth's continuing concern for simplifying the computing process and bringing computing to a wider audience," Kurtz later wrote.

Even though FORTRAN supplanted DARSIMCO, Kemeny and Kurtz didn't immediately transition to it on the 704. As Kurtz remembers, FORTRAN's "acceptance was tempered by its alleged inefficiency in comparison to assembly language." A particular incident, though, changed Kurtz's mind about FORTRAN. He had to code a tricky statistical problem that needed the 704 to pull its weight; after writing the program in assembly language to save time—after all, FORTRAN was really "inefficient" compared to assembly—Kurtz tried for *months* to get his program right, repeatedly scanning through the core dumps but struggling to find any answers. So he finally waved the white flag and turned to FORTRAN. After writing what was surely an inefficient HLL program, Kurtz ran it. Five minutes of computer time later, he had a printout of the answers to the problem. "This lesson," he said, "that programming in higher level languages could save computer time as well as person time—impressed me deeply." Kurtz realized that "[f]or klutzes like me, one had to use higher level languages."

In 1959, Kemeny and Kurtz decided to bring a computer to the college. They settled on the 4K, 30-bit word, drum-based, sixteen-instruction LGP-30 (Librascope General Precision) computer; the drum rotated at thirty times per second, hence the "30" in the name. During the summer of 1959, a handful of Honors Program undergraduates were invited to see what they could coax out of the computer. One of those undergrads, a physics major named Robert Hargraves, took only a couple weeks to write a FORTRAN-like language and compiler for the LGP-30 that he called DART. The language didn't permit the generalized arithmetic expressions allowed by FORTRAN; rather, simplified expressions enclosed in parentheses were required. But still: Kememy and Kurtz realized that a "good undergraduate student could achieve what at the time was a professional-level accomplishment, namely, the design and writing of a compiler. The observation was not overlooked," according to Kurtz.

That same summer, a Princeton student named Edgar T. Irons took hiatus at Dartmouth to work on a syntax-directed compiler, which caused Kememy, Kurtz, and the undergraduates working on the LGP-30 to investigate ALGOL 58. Kurtz and four of the undergraduates—Hargraves, Steve Garland, Jorge Llacer, and Anthony Knapp—began building an ALGOL 58 compiler for the LGP-30. Once ALGOL 60 was released, the team decided to scrap the ALGOL 58 design in favor of implementing the updated version of the language. Calling it ALGOL 30, the team shaved down ALGOL 60 features by necessity for the little machine: recursion was out, as were strings, variable array bounds, and arrays called by value. Through a bit of clever programming they called "thunks," parameters could be called by name; in addition, integer labels made the cut.

The biggest limitation of ALGOL 30 wasn't that it only offered a subset of ALGOL 60; rather, it was that the compiler took two passes to translate the source program, with the requirement that the binary code be punched on paper tape. The time between compiling and executing a program was significant, opening the door for the load-and-go SCALP (Self Contained ALgol Processor: an inappropriate acronym purposely referencing Dartmouth's long history of educating Native Americans that was of a piece with the unofficial mascot of the college, the Indian), designed by Kurtz, Garland, and Knapp. With the compiler only able to use a third of its 4K of word memory, the functionality of ALGOL's for loop had to be pared down considerably. On the other hand, the SCALP system was so fast that at least five student jobs could be completed, start to finish, in about fifteen minutes (as a comparison, recall that a single job on the IBM 704 in FORTRAN I would take, at a minimum, fifteen minutes to run through). Many Dartmouth students would use SCALP in the early 1960s.

Kemeny was also busy developing his own language. Called DOPE (Dartmouth Oversimplified Programming Experiment), the math department chairman had undergraduate student Sidney Marshall's help in the development phase. DOPE presaged early BASIC's variable-naming scheme—a single alphabetic letter or a letter followed by a single digit—as well as a number of other features, such as input formats and line numbers serving as jump labels. FORTRAN's influence could be felt in several places of DOPE as well, with the letters E to H implicitly defined to represent vectors, and, as Kurtz noted, "commands includ[ing] four functions (SQR, EXP, LOG, SIN), a jump (T), and a three-way branch (C)—shades of FORTRAN!"

At Dartmouth in the early 1960s, only about a quarter of students majored in science or engineering. Kemeny and Kurtz weren't comfortable with a scant twenty-five percent of the undergrads being exposed to computing on campus, especially since "the nonscience group produce[d] most of the decision makers of business and government." So they asked themselves, "How can sensible decisions about computing and its use be made by persons essentially ignorant of it?" The answer was obvious: everyone, regardless of major, needed to be taught computing. Not in a lecture format, where an instructor, chalk in hand, would serve as a sage on the stage while eager students lapped up the arcane details of the lesson. No, students needed to *do*—they needed to program, not merely listen to an expert describing the process. But assembly language was clearly too difficult for beginners, leaving FORTRAN and ALGOL as the only realistic alternatives. But those languages didn't sit well with Kemeny and Kurtz. "The majority [of students]," Kurtz worried, "would balk at the seemingly pointless detail" required to program using these HLLs.

Here is a bit of that "pointless detail" that Kemeny and Kurtz believed would turn off students without the requisite mathematical or scientific bent. Consider the FORTRAN I code snippet below.

```
        DO 20 I = 1, N
        X = X + ARRAY(I)
20      CONTINUE
        AMEAN = X/N
```

Will the value held by the floating-point variable AMEAN be the correct mean of the values stored in the array called ARRAY? Not necessarily. The problem involved a mixing of types: N, the loop counter, is implicitly typed as an integer, while X holds the floating-point sum of the floating-point values contained in ARRAY. To guarantee that AMEAN is calculated correctly, the loop counter needs to first be converted into a floating-point value. That means changing the program to the following:

```
       DO 20 I = 1, N
       X = X + ARRAY(I)
20     CONTINUE
       AN = N
       AMEAN = X/AN
```

The HLL that Kemeny and Kurtz drew up, called BASIC, would not be fussy about such details and thus would be much more accessible to nonprogrammers.

To address their computing needs for education, Kemeny and Kurtz devised a four-part plan. They knew that developing a user-friendly computer system first meant dispatching punched cards in favor of a timesharing system using terminals, a relatively recent innovation that John McCarthy had demonstrated to Kurtz at MIT several years earlier. "Why don't you guys do time sharing?" McCarthy asked Kurtz. (In 1961, the MIT Computation Center successfully tested timesharing with the Compatible Time-Sharing System [CTSS], run using an IBM 7090 under the direction of Fernando Corbató. CTSS had a proto-emailing system as well as a text-formatting utility called RUNOFF.) Kurtz, describing the process to Kemeny, said, "I think we ought to do time sharing," with Kemeny replying, "OK." They would use Teletype Model 33 and 35 machines and interface with ASCII code. Why the aversion to punched cards? Recall that the warning "Do not fold, spindle, or mutilate" was coopted by radical left student groups in the 1960s. Quite simply, Kemeny and Kurtz were worried that students would be "prejudiced against" the cards.

Timesharing was the first part of their four-part plan. Building a new programming language from the ground up was the second—at least, Kemeny believed so. Kurtz was resistant to the idea, figuring that a subset of FORTRAN or ALGOL could be used instead. "This belief proved wrong," Kurtz admitted later. For one thing, ALGOL's compound statements (such as with for loops) couldn't be easily simplified. FORTRAN posed its own unique set of problems.

> With FORTRAN, a subset wouldn't make much sense if it violated the IJKLMN convention [implicit typing]. But how many nonscience students could appreciate the distinction between integer and non-integer variables. Other problems included remembering the punctuation in the DO and IF statements, and the order of the three statement numbers in the IF statement. Very early, then, I agreed with Kemeny that a new language was needed to meet our requirements.

FORTRAN, with all its idiosyncrasies, wasn't built to serve the uninitiated. It was built to produce efficient object code after translating algebraic-like statements. Kemeny and Kurtz turned FORTRAN on its head: "In all cases where there is a choice between simplicity and efficiency," a 1963 memorandum describing the design goals of BASIC read, "simplicity is chosen."

Furthermore, BASIC at Dartmouth would be a compiled language, not an interpreted one. Within a decade, users were much more likely to encounter BASIC outside of Dartmouth's campus, and these implementations were typically of BASIC interpreters, not compilers; interpreted languages were thought to be more "interactive." But there was nothing about BASIC per se that lent itself to being interpreted. "[Dartmouth BASIC's] closest relative in many ways is FORTRAN, which was never thought to be interpretative," explained Kurtz.

The third part of their plan involved structuring a computing course using BASIC. Instead of a standalone course, computing would be introduced as an adjunct lab-like class for second-term calculus and finite mathematics. These labs would feature application problems coming from their associated mathematics courses, rather than a professor standing at a chalkboard, lecturing on programming. "Lecturing about computing doesn't make any sense, any more than lecturing on how to drive a car makes sense," according to Kurtz. By 1968, eighty-five percent of Dartmouth students were taking either second-term calculus, or finite mathematics, or both.

The plan's fourth part centered on open access. Just as the Dartmouth library's open-stack concept offered freely democratized access to knowledge, Kemeny and Kurtz would establish free and accessible on-campus computing to all students; they didn't want anyone having to ask for permission. Open access was facilitated by Dartmouth's faculty and administration, who mostly didn't seek government grants for research; therefore, students and faculty didn't have to compete for time on the computing system, with such competition invariably leading to the college having to charge for system use.

The conditions were ripe for the implementation of their four-part plan. Kemeny, Kurtz, and a revolving door of undergraduate programmers were supported by a mostly sympathetic administration led by Dartmouth president John S. Dickey. In February 1964, a GE-225 computer along with DATANET-30 hardware arrived on the campus; Kurtz and Kemeny had made use of National Science Foundation grants and educational discounts offered by General Electric to procure the equipment. Knowing the computer was on its way, Kemeny started work on a compiler for the new language during the previous summer. By the fall, he had employed two students, Michael Busch and John McGeachie, to complete the bulk of the work of designing and programming the timesharing operating system for DTSS: the Dartmouth Time-Sharing System.

On May 1, 1964, at approximately 4:00 AM, the first BASIC program ran successfully on the DTSS. By the fall, there were twenty terminals accessible to students and faculty alike, and the GE-225 had been upgraded to a GE-235. Then access to the system spread further, outside the campus to other universities that were nearby; even some high schools were able to join the network, all through telephone lines.

Like Quiktran, BASIC on the DTSS had a command mode and a program mode. The operating system recognized any statement beginning with a line number as being part of an ever-growing program, while statements not prefixed with line numbers were interpreted as monitor commands, ready to be executed immediately. (Unlike in FORTRAN, every BASIC statement began with a line number, "primarily to aid editing," according to Kurtz; and also unlike in FORTRAN, these line numbers were automatically sorted in ascending order.) Monitor commands consisted of friendly-sounding, nonthreatening English words like GOODBYE, HELLO, LIST, NEW, OLD, RUN, and SAVE, perfect terms for the non-expert, with no operating system jargon in sight. Better yet was the ease of use of the DTSS: simply typing RUN would compile *and* execute the user's program (assuming it was free of errors and could be successfully compiled). BASIC, due to its simplicity, permitted single-pass compilation. Within two years, BASIC would even become interactive courtesy of the INPUT statement; beforehand, only the READ statement could be used for input, albeit not interactively during runtime.

"The relation of BASIC to FORTRAN and ALGOL is apparent," Kurtz explains. He continues:

> From FORTRAN comes the order of the three loop-controlling variables—initial, final, step—thus permitting the step size to be omitted if it is unity [i.e., if the step size is equal to one]. From ALGOL come the words FOR and STEP, and the more natural testing for loop completion *before* executing the body of the loop. These and other similarities are not surprising, since we knew both languages, and we did not hesitate to borrow ideas.

To get a sense of BASIC's pidgin approach to loops, look at the following example program, which output the numbers 0 to 100 by 5's:

```
10 FOR X = 0 TO 100 STEP 5
20 PRINT X
30 NEXT X
40 END
```

Here is, more or less, the equivalent program in an implementation of ALGOL 60:

```
for x := 0 step 5 until 100 do
  begin
    print(x);
  end
```

Kemeny and Kurtz were also influenced by CORC (CORnell Compiler), developed by Richard Conway at Cornell; specifically, CORC required the LET statement for variable assignment (as would Dartmouth BASIC) and didn't require the user to specify the variable type (neither did Dartmouth BASIC). But CORC required users declare variables, which BASIC did not.

Ironically, lines of BASIC were structurally more similar to assembly language instructions than were FORTRAN I statements. Consider this BASIC instruction again:

```
20 PRINT X
```

The line number 20 is really an instruction number, the PRINT is an operation, and the X is an operand—a clear tripartite similarity to assembly and machine language code. Specifically, BASIC instructions were indebted to DARSIMCO.

BASIC, as originally designed, stitched together the best of FORTRAN, ALGOL, and several other computer languages into a coherent whole. That BASIC offered such a synthesis was itself the most unique characteristic of the language.

Kemeny and Kurtz released six implementations of Dartmouth BASIC by the end of the 1960s. BASIC the First arrived in 1964. There were fourteen statements available to users—including LET, PRINT, END, FOR, NEXT, GOTO (obviously modeled after FORTRAN's GO TO), and REM (a "remark," or comment; recall that FORTRAN had introduced computer programming comments, denoted by the letter C)—unlike the more than twice as many statements offered in FORTRAN I.

Also unlike FORTRAN, there were no distinctions made between fixed- and floating-point numbers; in explaining this decision, Kurtz waxed poetic: "A number is a number is a number." Using BASIC IF statements, numbers could be directly compared with each other using relational operators (=, <, >, <=, >=, and <> for not equal to) instead of with the trickier arithmetic **IF** of FORTRAN. Whereas producing formatted output of numbers in FORTRAN required judicious use of the **FORMAT** statement, BASIC's PRINT statement took care of the details, automatically adjusting the output based on the type of number.

But like in FORTRAN, there were some functions built-in to BASIC (mathematical functions, such as SIN, COS, SQR, and INT) and programmers could create their own as well. The first BASIC manual (from 1964) played up the language's facility with mathematics, offering example programs ranging from logarithms to quadratic equations to matrix products. In fact, BASIC the Third introduced the MAT statement, which permitted matrix operations directly—something Backus suggested be built into FORTRAN as early as 1954's Preliminary Report. BASIC the Fifth permitted subprograms, under the umbrella of a main program, where variable names could be in common—"as if in a giant **COMMON**," said Kurtz—but, with all the restrictions necessary to make it work, the innovation was eventually deemed a mistake. By 1971's BASIC the Sixth, Kemeny, Kurtz, and the student programmers—some of whom had returned to Dartmouth as professors themselves—had finally produced a product with which they were completely satisfied, at least for an extended stretch.

BASIC would eventually be standardized by the American National Standards Institute (ANSI). Similar to FORTRAN, BASIC's standardization came very late—for nine years, BASIC was left to proliferate, with many implementations appearing on a variety of computers, including microcomputers. Kemeny and Kurtz didn't approve of most of these BASIC knockoffs, which they derisively called "Street BASICs," and were fully onboard with ANSI's standardization efforts—so much so that Kurtz himself served as chairman of committee X3J2, which was tasked creating the BASIC standard.

Regardless of how they were exposed to it, by 1981 Kurtz said that while there might be more lines of FORTRAN and COBOL extant, by far more people had seen or know how to program in BASIC than in any other language, with at least five million school children having learned it. FORTRAN was designed for industry; BASIC was designed for education, with error messages that made sense, no need to worry about numerical variable types or other sorts of declarations (arrays were automatically set to a default dimension size), and English terms given preference over punctuation (such as commas and semicolons). As Kurtz concluded, "[I]f FORTRAN is the lingua franca, then certainly it must be true that BASIC is the lingua playpen."

The Bell Labs Languages (1970s)

Bell Telephone Laboratories was a birthplace of a number of groundbreaking computing technologies, such as the transistor, invented by John Bardeen, Walter Brattain, and William Shockley, and the UNIX operating system, originally implemented by Dennis Ritchie and Ken Thompson on a Digital Equipment Corporation PDP-7 computer and inspired by the Multics OS (a combined effort of MIT, GE, and Bell Labs and originally programmed in PL/I).

Dennis Ritchie was a Harvard-trained mathematician and physicist, and Ken Thompson a Berkeley-trained computer scientist. According to Ritchie, "Thompson decided that Unix—possibly it had not even been named yet—needed a system programming language. After a rapidly scuttled attempt at Fortran, he created instead a language of his own, which he called B." The B programming language was a modified form of BCPL (Basic Combined Programming Language), a procedural and *typeless* (meaning the variables weren't specified a type, such as integer or real, when initialized) language created by Martin Richards in the 1960s that was similar to FORTRAN and ALGOL 60. The PDP-7 hardware was crude, Ritchie remembered. "Although we entertained occasional thoughts about implementing one of the major languages of the time like Fortran, PL/I, or Algol 68, such a project seemed hopelessly large for our resources: much simpler and smaller tools were called for. All these languages influenced our work, but it was more fun to do things on our own."

With new hardware made available—namely, the PDP-11—Ritchie got to work extending the B language, ultimately arriving at the C programming language in 1972, which retained some similarities to FORTRAN. "Fortran influenced the syntax of declarations: B declarations begin with a specifier like `auto` or `static`, followed by a list of names, and C not only followed this style but ornamented it by placing its type keywords at the start of declarations," Ritchie explained.

FORTRAN was able to fight off early competitors like ALGOL but lost headway in the education realm to BASIC. By the 1980s, later iterations of FORTRAN couldn't fend off the ascent of UNIX and C in scientific and numerical computing. (UNIX was eventually rewritten using C.) As Michael Metcalf explains, "Only towards the end of that decade [the 1980s] did C draw increasing support from scientific programmers who had discovered the power of structures and pointers," which store memory addresses of other variables. C went on to become one of the most popular programming languages in history—and heavily influenced other general-purpose languages like C++, Java, and Python. (The Python programming language contains some obvious nods to FORTRAN: for example, the operator module's `operator.gt(a,b)` and `operator.le(a,b)` functions, with `gt` referring to greater than or equal to and `le` meaning less than or equal to, respectively.)

Just as FORTRAN didn't prove adequate to addressing Thompson and Ritchie's computing needs, at Bell Labs several years later (around 1975), some employees were growing dissatisfied with the in-house Statistical Computing Subroutines (SCS), which contained readymade libraries of FORTRAN subroutines written for data analysis. Though SCS offered statistical functionality on the computer—including large-scale Monte Carlo simulations—using the subroutines meant that evaluating even the most basic of statistical functions required line-by-line coding. Simple computations were especially tedious, remembered Bell Labs' Richard A. Becker:

> On the other hand, we did occasionally do simple computations. For example, suppose we wanted to carry out a linear regression given 20 *x,y* data points. The idea of writing a FORTRAN program that called library routines for something like this was unappealing. While the actual regression was done in a single subroutine call, the program had to do its own input and output, and time spent in I/O often dominated the actual computations. Even more importantly, the effort expended on programming was out of proportion to the size of the problem. An interactive facility could make such work much easier.

Becker added that the statisticians and scientists at Bell Labs "wanted to be able to interact with our data, using Exploratory Data Analysis [EDA] techniques" that had been developed primarily by the statistician John Tukey, who also worked at Bell. (Tukey would rarely, if ever, program in FORTRAN, preferring to write out code by hand using a wordy pseudocode that loosely resembled FORTRAN.) "It was the realization that routine data analysis should not require writing FORTRAN programs that really got [the] S [programming language] going."

So, in the spring of 1976, work was started on sketching out interactive statistical computing software. The development team included Becker and John Chambers, who had been writing a book on statistical computing to be called *Computational Methods for Data Analysis*. The S statistical programming language, which was written in FORTRAN, was the result of the team's efforts; according to Becker, "there was little other choice [but to program S in FORTRAN]. C was only beginning to get a start on the GCOS [General Comprehensive Operating System for the Honeywell 645]…and at the time, very little numerical work had been done in C." But there was a practical reason to use FORTRAN as well: linking up S with the SCS library.

The United States Bicentennial found the team members busy debating a name for the language. What about ISCS (Interactive SCS)? or SCS (revised to now stand for Statistical Computing System; but that might cause confusion)? or SAS (Statistical Analysis System; a company already laid claim to this name)? But they hesitated to use an acronym, since there were so many already floating around Bell Labs. Someone noticed that all of their suggested acronyms began with the letter "S" and—inspired by the one-letter languages, B and C, that emerged from Bell Labs—the team called their new language 'S', initially with the quotation marks; by 1979 the quotes were dispensed with.

Right off the bat, flexible interactive graphical displays were a particularly notable feature of S. Also of note: that the language's definitions were very generalized and had few constraints. "We were all tired of Fortran's seemingly capricious restrictions, on the form of subscripts, etc.," Becker realized.

S underwent a number of evolutions, eventually spawning the R programming language, which is still widely used for statistical computing. Other popular statistical software packages, such as SPSS, were also written from the ground up in FORTRAN.

MATLAB, the Matrix Laboratory Language (1970s)

In the 1970s, a mathematics professor and chairman of the computer science department at the University of New Mexico named Cleve B. Moler, who taught linear algebra and numerical analysis, was looking for a means for his "students to have easy access" to two software packages—EISPACK and LINPACK—but "without writing Fortran programs," he recalled. "By 'easy access,' I meant not going through the remote batch processing and the repeated edit-compile-link-load-execute process that was ordinarily required on the campus central mainframe computer." EISPACK, the Matrix Eigensystem Package, and LINPACK, the Linear Equation Package, were software libraries of mathematical functions involving matrices and linear algebra originating from the Argonne National Laboratory following National Science Foundation (NSF) proposals; EISPACK translated ALGOL routines into FORTRAN 66 (using TAMPR, a preprocessor which transformed unstructured FORTRAN code into a structured programming style) and was first released in 1971, while LINPACK, which Cleve Moler had a direct hand in creating, was written in FORTRAN and included more than forty subroutines. Moler described the development of LINPACK to an interviewer decades later:

> The algorithms themselves didn't have that much machine dependence, to solve systems of linear equations you don't need to know the accuracy...of the floating point arithmetic, for example, so we don't need that parameter there, and we knew about how to cope with the different kinds of FORTRAN by the time we got to LINPACK.

Moler's work at the crossroads of mathematical subroutines and FORTRAN stretched back to SHARE in the 1960s. "[T]here was a collection of software that SHARE maintained and distributed, and the FORTRAN program that's in this book for solving systems of liner equations, I also contributed that same program to SHARE," he said. That book, entitled *Computer Solution of Linear Algebraic Systems* (1967), was cowritten by Moler and his doctoral advisor at Stanford, computer science professor George Forsythe. *Computer Solution* contained matrix-computation programs written in ALGOL, FORTRAN, and PL/I.

But by the late 1970s at UNM, Moler didn't want to have to teach his mathematics students how to code in FORTRAN ("which they didn't know how to do"), along with tutorials in using a mainframe system to compile, link, load, and run a program, simply so they could employ the linear algebra numerical analysis routines in EISPACK and LINPACK. Therefore, he decided to write a new language—or at least create a technique to abstract away FORTRAN. He pored through Niklaus Wirth's book *Algorithms + Data Structures = Programs* (1976), learning the tricks of the trade when it came to parsing computer languages (Wirth creates a simple language called PL/0, based on ALGOL, in the book, using it to illustrate programming concepts like building a recursive dissent parser; PL/0 predated PASCAL). Moler recalled that "[t]he original thing about MATLAB was the language parser, and that's something you don't ordinarily write in Fortran, and that wasn't easy to do and easy to make it portable." He found the recursion piece especially challenging to code, since FORTRAN wasn't recursive and thus Moler had to build his own stack as a workaround.

From these beginnings, MATLAB was born: it was a matrix calculator, not a programming language in the conventional sense, that Moler wrote in FORTRAN. "It was not very sophisticated, you couldn't add functions to it, it didn't have any graphics," he explained. "It was simply a calculator for matrices, you could invert matrices and compute determinants, and compute their eigenvalues, and that was about all." Moler certainly had no plans to market MATLAB, let alone build a business around the product; rather, it was informal, had only a single data type (called "matrix"), and was relatively inflexible—new mathematical functions couldn't be added without writing FORTRAN statements directly into the MATLAB source code and recompiling—but it was interactive and had dozens of premade mathematical functions readily available without the need to code in FORTRAN. Operations with matrices could be performed with ease. MATLAB's PLOT function even permitted a primitive form of graphics (typically by printing asterisks on teletypes to represent ordered pairs). MATLAB computations of a diagonalized matrix were used in the background of 1979's *Star Trek: The Motion Picture*, in the form of graphical output on an *Enterprise* bridge console display at Mr. Spock's station.

MATLAB was portable, and the software was installed and run on a variety of computers, including timesharing systems, that appeared in the early 1980s. When Moler taught at Stanford as a visiting professor in the 1979-80 academic year, he noticed an interesting split in his numerical analysis course: after assigning MATLAB for homework assignments, half of his students—the math and computer science majors—were disappointed with the limited functionality of MATLAB; but the other half—the engineering majors—liked Moler's software. "They were studying subjects that I didn't know anything about, such as control analysis and signal processing," he recalled, "and the emphasis on matrices in MATLAB proved to be very useful to them."

Inspired by the booming personal computer market in general and the IBM PC in particular, an electrical engineer named John N. "Jack" Little—who was introduced to MATLAB by a student of Moler's—along with Steve Bangert, revamped Moler's software, rewriting all of it in C. In 1984, PC-MATLAB debuted, and Moler, Little, and Bangert founded MathWorks. Three decades later, the valuation of the company surpassed one billion dollars.

Parts of contemporary MATLAB are written in modern Fortran in order to efficiently handle linear algebra calculations, but, since MATLAB is tailored to technical computing in commercial applications, the software competes directly in Fortran's wheelhouse.

LINPACK today serves as a benchmark program, helping to gauge the speeds of supercomputers around the world.

Although FORTRAN, in one way or another, inspired the creation of the programming languages detailed in this chapter, and though some of those languages seriously chipped away at FORTRAN's popularity (especially in the field of education), FORTRAN was never completely replaced by any of them—at least for cutting-edge scientific and engineering work on powerful mainframe computers. Perhaps it was Honeywell's Martin N. Greenfield, detailing the history of FORTRAN's standardization, who best described the language's continuing appeal: "FORTRAN has for most of [its] life been the blue-collar worker of the programming language set. What it lacked in [*savoir faire*] and style, it returned in cost effectiveness."

Writing in *BYTE* magazine of programming languages that stood the test of time, Doris Appleby agreed with Greenfield's assessment.

> Jeanne Martin, of the ANSI FORTRAN committee X3J3, explains why FORTRAN has not been subsumed by another, more general language: PL/I is no longer viable as a portable language, since its standards committee has been disbanded; Ada has never been accepted by the scientific community; and although currently popular, C is, according to Martin, "sort of a hacker's language," with code sometimes readable only by its author. FORTRAN code looks more like the application being programmed and has superior array facilities. So much is invested in already written and optimized FORTRAN code that it will necessarily continue to be used. It is the blue-collar language of the scientific, number-crunching community.

Once FORTRAN's popularity exploded, an anonymous quotation circulated around: "FORTRAN is a language to avoid—unless you want some answers." You could always count on FORTRAN to get the job done quickly, and done well.

CHAPTER 24

◊◊◊

Implicit None

With fresh programming languages and new programming paradigms nipping on the heels of FORTRAN 77, a significant modernization effort—rather than another mere standardization—was undertaken.

In the years between the release of FORTRAN 77 and its successor, first called FORTRAN 82 but quickly transforming into the open-ended working name FORTRAN 8X, a great many programs were written in FORTRAN 77. Such software gave rise to a new term: *dusty deck*. According to the Jargon File—"a comprehensive compendium of hacker slang illuminating many aspects of hackish tradition, folklore, and humor"—a dusty deck is

> Old software (especially applications) which one is obliged to remain compatible with, or to maintain (DP [Data Processing] types call this 'legacy code', a term hackers consider smarmy and excessively reverent). The term implies that the software in question is a holdover from card-punch days. Used esp. when referring to old scientific and number-crunching software, much of which was written in FORTRAN and very poorly documented but is believed to be too expensive to replace.

Not only FORTRAN 77, but also FORTRAN 66, too, had plenty of dusty decks lying around, perhaps stored in old punched card file cabinets that resembled public library card catalogs, but the FORTRAN 66 ship had already sailed—the FORTRAN Standards Committee X3J3 could protect the compatibility of FORTRAN 77 programs in FORTRAN 8X, via retaining all of FORTRAN 77 as a subset (which ultimately ended up happening; no FORTRAN 77 features were deleted), but couldn't do much about prior implementations of the language. Moreover, X3J3 had every intention of modernizing the language as well: FORTRAN had lost a step compared to its rivals Ada, Pascal, C, and C++, even as it still led the pack in the production of efficient object code. (Though powerful and relatively simple to use, FORTRAN 77 didn't offer the protections of some of the more modern languages—it was technically possible to write a program to overwrite the contents of the program itself.)

If X3J3 wished to conform to the mandated ANSI five-year review cycle, they needed to finish their work by November 1982 (hence the initial moniker FORTRAN 82). But there was much work to do. According to Thomas M. Lahey of Lahey Computer Systems, Inc., who penned an article for the *Fortran Forum* documenting the process, right after the release of FORTRAN 77 the committee already had its eyes on many possible innovations which might be included in the next set of standards. "After the committee finished the 77 Standard, a number of the members agreed to carry on to create the next standard," he wrote. "They recognized there was much to do: array operations, block structures (**CASE**, some form of **REPEAT**), and various types (**POINTER, STRING, BIT, BYTE**) and **INCLUDE** were some of the important features that were not in FORTRAN 77. The goal was to complete the next standard by 1982."

Following such a tight schedule meant that the first set of draft standards needed to appear by no later than 1980. Frank Engel, the long-serving chairman of X3J3, had established a subcommittee on future revisions back in 1975, years before the finalized FORTRAN 77 made its public debut. By July of that year, the subcommittee held their first meeting, with the key objective of "[d]evelop[ing] suitable criteria to determine whether or not another revision of ANS X3.9 [FORTRAN 77] is necessary and desirable." Engel clearly had one eye firmly fixed toward the future, and urged his charges to be mindful of future revisions as well. "It has taken two years to change the attitude of X3J3 members from trying to get one more new feature into this revision, to focusing on the next revision as the proper time to make other needed extensions to the language," he wrote in 1977, adding, "A not insignificant contributing factor in this transition has been sponsor pressure to terminate this project that has extended over ten years." Engel saw the writing on the wall: produce and release a new FORTRAN standard in a timely manner, or watch sponsors jump ship and see FORTRAN's popularity wither on the vine—or, worse yet, see some other group (such as the federal government) adopt a set of de facto standards, stealing the thunder and authority of X3J3 from right under the committee's noses. Delay could only "encourage the proliferation of those practices that standardization is intended to avoid," Engel concluded.

Early on, X3J3 proposed what they called a "core plus modules approach." The "core" would be a general, compact, lithe, and complete version of FORTRAN, no bigger than FORTRAN 77 in size. As described in a contemporaneous report:

> The core is a complete and consistent language comprising a set of language features sufficiently rich for the implementation of most applications. The core will have at least the same functional capabilities as Fortran 77. In addition, the core should
>
> (a) be especially suitable for scientific applications,
> (b) be portable,
> (c) be safe to use, and effective for the development of reliable software,
> (d) be widely efficiently implementable,
> (e) be concise,
> (f) comprise generally accepted contemporary language technology,

(g) minimize non-automatable conversion from Fortran 77.

The compatible modules could be easily plugged into the core to extend the language. X3J3 would create a set of these "language extension modules" containing features that weren't necessarily tested or approved for standardization in the core, nor were general enough to make the cut. The justification for the introduction of modules was as follows.

> There is no way in Fortran 77 to define a global data area in one place and have all the program units in an application use that definition. In addition, the **ENTRY** statement is awkward and restrictive for implementing a related set of procedures, possibly involving common data objects. And finally there is no means in Fortran by which procedure definitions, especially interface information, may be made known locally to a program unit. All of these deficiencies, and more, are remedied by a new type of program unit that may contain any combination of data element declarations, derived data type definitions, procedure definitions, and procedure interface information. This program unit, called a MODULE, may be considered to be a generalization of and replacement for the BLOCK DATA program unit. A module may be referenced by any program unit, thereby making the module contents available to that program unit. This provides vastly improved facilities for defining global data areas and procedure packages. It also provides a convenient mechanism for encapsulating derived data type definitions (including operations defined on them), i.e., for encapsulating data abstractions.

One of these extension modules would be an "Obsolete (Transitions) Features Module" ("obsolete features module" or "obsolete module" for short), housing all FORTRAN 77 features not part of the core for compatibility's sake. Examples of obsolete features included the **COMMON** and **EQUIVALENCE** statements, along with the arithmetic **IF** statement. Going forward, features in the obsolete module would be retained for one revision, then discarded.

In addition to the language extension modules, "applications modules," which X3J3 wouldn't typically create or have control over, would be highly specialized in nature; possible examples include database or graphics modules. Taken together, this "'core plus modules' architecture [was designed to be] able to accommodate featurists and generalists, traditionalists and revisionists," according to Brian Meek, author of the definitive history of the time period called "The Fortran (Not the Foresight) Saga: The Light and the Dark" (1990). As the title of his eyewitness account makes clear, the development of FORTRAN 77's successor went anything but smoothly; political infighting was the rule, not the exception. The literary flare of his article's heading titles underscore this point—e.g., "The conscience of the rich," "The valley of bones," "Books do furnish a room," and "Hearing secret harmonies." It was the most dramatic and controversial revision of programming standards of all time. The FORTRAN saga was "a baroque a tale as any," remarked one observer.

Meek sketches out two intersecting axes on a coordinate plane that categorized individuals involved with this contentious FORTRAN revision. On the horizontal axis at one end lay the "traditionalists," who were akin to conservatives—i.e., the cautious types; at the other end of this axis were the "revisionists," who were more progressive about the whole enterprise. On the vertical axis, the "featurists," who were focused on the trees (particular features) of the language, resided on one end, while the "generalists," who took in the whole forest, were on the other.

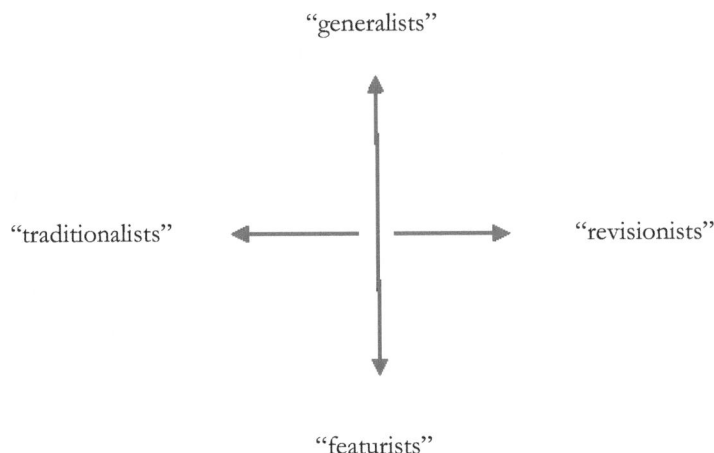

A person could find himself in the traditionalist/featurist camp with one issue but not another—so placement on the coordinate plane was fluid, depending on context, opportunism, and a host of other factors. "For example," Meek writes, "a featurist who is also a traditionalist may generally support moves to 'reduce the size of the language' (a recurrent rallying call through the [FORTRAN] saga) but will change sides if the proposal is to remove a wished-for facility." There were also differences between national (U.S.) and international approaches (note that not everyone on X3J3 was American). No one person was locked into any particular spot on the plane for every issue that arose. That, along with the ever-evolving computer technology and membership changes of the committee over time, made reaching consensus on even the most minor of issues dauntingly challenging.

"In this saga of light and dark, in the beginning there was light," Meek tells us. The core plus modules approach was laid out during the first official standards meeting, which took place in 1978 in London. At that meeting were members of the U.S. Fortran Standards Committee X3J3 and the international FORTRAN standards group, referred to generally as the ISO (International Standards Organization) but, around this time, referred to more specifically as the WG5 (the WG5's full designation was ISO/IEC JTC1/SC22/WG5), which was the international body's technical working group. (Recall the ISO approved the FORTRAN 66 and 77 standards, both of which were written in the United States.) X3J3 reported to X3, the senior committee of ANSI; X3 also functioned as the U.S. representative to ISO.

The plan was as follows: X3J3 would write the new FORTRAN standards, while WG5 would interface with the international community and also offer X3J3 advice on the work.

Things went well initially. Both X3J3 and WG5 quickly came to realize both the strengths and weaknesses with the core plus modules approach. On the one hand, any "battles"—which took place at Fortran Forum public meetings, ACM-published *Fortran Forum* newsletters, computing publications, and technical journals—over new features could be circumscribed solely to associated modules, rather than interfering with the core.

But this approach left the core as a battlefield; even worse, determining the contents of the obsolete features module, poised to contain FORTRAN 77 non-core vestigial features, caused a pitched battle that allied the revisionists/generalists against the traditionalists of all stripes along with the revisionist/featurists, who acted akin to hoarders, agreeing in principle with the core/obsolete model but strongly objecting to the fact that "cherished features" of FORTRAN 77 would be casually dumped into the obsolescence module like yesterday's garbage. Some even objected to using the term "obsolete." A debate ensued over the future of FORTRAN: What was the primary goal of the language revision? Consider a prototypical exchange between committee members that brings this existential debate into relief.

REVISIONIST/FEATURIST'S ASSERTION: "Fortran was not the greatest possible language when it was developed, but now there are many libraries and programs that depend on it. We need to improve the language, but in such a way that existing programs won't suddenly be unusable, but can gradually be upgraded and improved by making use of the new language elements and eliminating the older unreliable, unreadable elements."

REVISIONIST/GENERALIST'S RESPONSE: "The priority list for Fortran used to have 'efficiency' at the top. Now it seems to have 'compatibility with old Fortran.' There were once a lot of codes in assembly language too. Can't we move away from it? Some complain that the only resemblance between old Fortran and all the new features is the name. Is that bad?"

The resolution was a fait accompli: by 1983, the whole core plus modules approach was dumped—for lack of agreement of what the core should be. The dramatic rise and rapid fall of core plus modules was an internecine affair, taking place almost entirely between X3J3 members with little prodding either way from the international WG5. As Burroughs Corporation employee and X3J3 member Walt Brainerd caustically put it, "It appears to be the old problem that a committee simply cannot design something small and elegant; one person's frill is another's essential feature...."

Reflecting on the debacle years later, one observer wrote that the list of "obsolete features" proposed in the FORTRAN 8X standard would be "possibly removed" in the next standard, and then, finally, "possibly fade from compilers and general use around 2020. This schedule was considered too radical by many people, both on and off of X3J3, so all the features that really can make a difference in performance, such as EQUIVALENCE, were removed from the list" of features declared obsolete, only "leaving things like assigned GO TO and the PAUSE statements."

In the spring of 1984, with the goalposts receding further into the distance, the X3J3 members decided to gather public feedback. First, though, X3J3 had to inform the American public of what they had been doing since 1978; this would be accomplished via a "Fortran Information Bulletin," or FIB—not a promising acronym. The FIB would also be disseminated internationally.

But the FIB would only be published pending X3 committee approval. Which proved to be the snag, since two vendors—Digital Equipment Corporation (DEC) and IBM—voted against publication. (By paying an annual fee, any company could join X3 and be granted the right to vote on proposals. Binding votes on major issues required a two-thirds majority. Voting rights were stripped if members, or their representatives, failed to show at more than one-third of the meetings.) DEC wanted to radically alter the document—only then would they vote in favor of distributing it. IBM didn't necessarily push for any changes to the document proper, but requested that the full set of vendor objections to the FIB be published as well. Although vote turned out to be 40 to 2 in favor of FIB distribution (without publishing vendor objections), the two no votes happened to be from very powerful voices of dissent.

X3 reached out to the X3J3 committee members: Are you guys (and they were predominately men) comfortable with meeting the demands of DEC and IBM? X3J3 responded with a firm no: the FIB was meant to be a status report, not a persuasive essay. The FIB was never intended to convince readers of the positives or negatives of the work on new standards that the X3J3 had done over the last six years, and the ISO/WG5 agreed. Here is the introduction to the report that was eventually released, underscoring that point:

> This report describes the current status of the technical work of X3J3 since the adoption of X3.9-1978 (Fortran 77). This work, informally referred to as "Fortran 8x", is incomplete and tentative, and is subject (and likely) to change prior to issuing a draft proposed standard (expected to occur no earlier than 1985). The purpose of this report is to summarize the status of current work by X3J3 relative to a future revision of the current Fortran standard.

In response, the X3 held off on publication. But information wants to be free, and the text somehow found its way outside the hallowed halls of committee meeting rooms anyway, thanks to the ACM publishing it in issues of *ForTec Forum: A Quarterly Publication of the SigPlan Technical Committee on FORTRAN* (which turned into the *Fortran Forum* in 1984) as well as the *SIGNUM Newsletter* (from July 1984). None of the vendors' objections were reported in either journal.

An extensive three-page "FORTRAN 8X Survey" prefaced the technical report, querying readers about their FORTRAN opinions and usage habits. The second page of the questionnaire has an extensive checklist: a long list of features (e.g., "Loop Constructs" and "Recursion") starts each row, while columns are devoted to value judgments (from "Strongly Approve" to "Strongly Disapprove" or "Don't Care"). Page three is devoted to what were termed "DEPRECATED FEATURES," or features from FORTRAN 77 that users might wish to see deleted (e.g., "Alternate **RETURN**" and the "**PAUSE** Statement").

People sent in completed questionnaires, and the X3J3 resumed drafting FORTRAN 8X standards. They made much progress. One year later, at a meeting in Bonn, Germany, during the summer, a resolution was passed declaring that X3J3's work thus far looked poised to "broadly [meet] the needs of the Fortran community worldwide." But vendors, not only including DEC and IBM, as well as traditionalists were mounting a counterinsurgency. Vendors thought the emerging language too large; traditionalists didn't like some of the new features in addition to the fact that there were "deprecated" features at all.

Months passed, and the work continued. After an internal ballot, a draft was readied for public consumption. Internationally, at least as represented by an ISO vote, the future of the draft standards looked bright. Not so much in the United States, though, where, as Brian Meek recalled, "there was a powerful group of US objectors, complaining that the language was too large and should be cut down, and brought more into line with 'existing practice' (which, being translated, meant what the vendors already supplied)." X3J3 went into "panic mode," eviscerating large swaths of the draft standards to appease the counterinsurgency—much to the dismay of the ISO/WG5. What was left from the wreckage was a weakened, much smaller, and now inconsistent set of standards—a "compromise plan"—burdened by a large appendix of "suggestions" that had once been integrated seamlessly within the main body of the draft but were now rendered as vestigial as a human appendix. This was Meek's "the valley of bones"—the move caught most parties by surprise, and anger and confusion resulted. Featurists were unhappy since their favored features had been rendered superfluous; revisionists, which made up the majority of the WG5, were displeased because they had never subscribed to the view that the language was too large. The WG5's displeasure especially was a result of how the cuts were made: by fiat, without discussion or consent.

Criticism of the process came from within, but it also came from without. In a 1985 issue of *Computer Language* magazine, one revisionist observer disparaged "Futuretran":

> Everybody has taken FORTRAN 77 and extended it with all sorts of wonderful new features. Along comes X3J3 with all these beautiful, bold ideas and that's "Futuretran." That's where we're trying to get. The question is, how can we get there from here? The answer that X3J3 came up with is to take everything you want and concatenate it to everything you've got and you build this huge compiler. You live with this huge compiler until the 1990s. It has to handle all of FORTRAN 77 plus everything you want in that compiler of the year 2001. Then in the year 2000 these deprecated features fly away, leaving you with Futuretran. You get there, then, at the expense of having an unnecessarily large language for at least one revision cycle.

Criticism notwithstanding, the next year involved further revisions and a tidying up of the FORTRAN 8X "compromise plan," such as it was. At a 1986 meeting in Scranton, Pennsylvania, ground was ceded on deprecated features: **COMMON** and **EQUIVALENCE** were no longer deemed obsolescent, and other concessions were made to protect future standards. Because "the committee felt the language was too large," said Thomas Lahey, a number of FORTRAN 8X features were ruled out—such as arrays of arrays as well as a new statement that would appear in future standards:

FORALL—so that a draft could successfully pass an internal vote. A proposal put forth at the meeting called for a special appendix:

> There has been considerable discussion over the last few meetings about the size and complexity of Fortran 8x. It is my personal view that the language is too large and too complex. These are subjective views and hard to quantify. I propose removing several features from the language and simplifying several others. This does NOT mean that I think these features are bad, useless, inconsistent, incomplete or unnecessary. It merely means I think Fortran fills a restricted ecological niche. I believe that Fortran stands for high-performance, easy-to-use computation and that the features on my hit list have gone too far, too fast. I do believe that most of the features are of merit and I propose that they be placed in an "official" appendix to the standard.

So, deleted features were relegated to Appendix F: Removed Extensions. "Appendix F preserves the committee's work and suggests carefully thought-out approaches to implementors who wish to provide these capabilities," according to Lahey. "In the 77 Standard, Hollerith constants were described in such an appendix."

At that same April 1986 meeting, a ballot of draft standards put forth by X3J3 was voted down by a majority: 16 to 19 against. And in late 1986, at a meeting in Halifax, Nova Scotia, many X3J3 members admitted that the "compromise plan" was hardly that, since the WG5 didn't have much of a say in it. The many vested interests were further apart than ever, with a finalized standard seemingly a distant dream.

A flurry of more thoughtful revisions followed, many of which were in response to another call for public comments, of which nearly four hundred were received (and had to be responded to one by one). Many of the public comments were roundly negative and critical. In mid-1987, the standards earned a handful of no votes, including from DEC, IBM, and Boeing. By August 1987, a proposed draft standard was submitted to X3 and the ISO. The X3 vendors still weren't happy, and WG5 had their own "short shopping list" of features, including free form for statements (free-source form), which the revisionists had been unsuccessfully pushing for years, as well as granular data handling options. (The adoption of free form would have consequences—namely, blanks would become significant. So, for instance, in FORTRAN 77, **GO TO** could be written as **G   OT   O**, and the compiler would still recognize the statement. But with blanks being significant, **GO TO** could be written as **GOTO** but not as **G   OT   O** or some other strange permutation of letters and blanks.)

The traditionalists, still smarting from the "compromise plan," hatched their own counteroffensive, putting out stories and messages designed only to scare: that FORTRAN 8X would not be compatible with FORTRAN 77, for instance. This propaganda, with little to no basis in fact, perhaps caused an uptick in the membership of X3 near the end of the decade, speculates Brian Meek. These "new men," who weren't particularly aware of the technical struggles, were predominantly in the traditionalist camp—and they didn't assign much importance to how the rest of the world felt about FORTRAN. (X3J3 membership would reach its highest level—nearly fifty—at the end of the 1980s.)

The May 1988 meeting in Champagne-Urbana, Illinois, resulted in yet more internecine strife and a deadlocked committee. Voting on the proposed draft standards revealed even more pronounced fault lines. Few were pleased with what was on offer, even if their reasons for displeasure didn't line up. (Not enough features! Where's my favorite feature? How can we still keep this in the language? The language is way too big!) There was no consensus. A number of plans put forth were voted down. So, like an embattled prime minister trying to secure just enough votes in parliament to retain power, X3J3 decided to ignore any international concerns in an effort to capture a slim majority of votes to go forward.

The WG5 was summarily locked out of the process. But they were mad as hell and not going to take it anymore.

The WG5 gathered in Paris in the fall of 1988 and dismissed the three plans crafted by the X3J3 before them as inadequate. They wanted to see a fourth plan that X3J3 had withheld from the international body. The two traditionalist plans were thrown out; the other two plans, WG5 said, needed to be merged together. Within a week, WG5 had crafted the basics of a new FORTRAN 8X standard, which they called FORTRAN 88, that would carry international support (sans the United States). They also established a timetable for next steps. In addition, WG5 issued an "unprecedented in the standards world" ultimatum: "The ANSI committee was to produce a new draft document, corresponding to the WG5's wishes, within five months! Failing that, WG5 would assume responsibility and produce a new standard itself," wrote Michael Metcalf. The X3, troubled by the machinations and threats, ordered that X3J3 create a single document satisfying both the domestic needs and the needs of the international community. In other words, the U.S. committee caved.

"For the last few years, Fortran 77 has been widely (though not universally) regarded as the Living Dead of the world of major programming languages, kept in existence only by the wrangling over the nature of its successor, Fortran 8X," one observer at the time wrote in *DATALINK* magazine.

> Despite the huge bulk of its user applications, it seemed that gradually it was becoming more zombielike as various segments began to break off, and fall victim to examples of the Deadly Living, like Ada or C. However, all that seemed to have changed when the international (ISO) Fortran committee, SC22/WG5, put its foot down...in Paris [in 1988] and said, in effect, "enough is enough"...and the US committee X3J3 thereafter, if with reluctance in some cases, felt into line in the interests of international agreement....

In November 1988, at a meeting in Boston, X3J3 capitulated: voting 24 to 9, they followed the format of the WG5 in writing a public draft. IBM, looking to move forward, approved of the new draft standards. There was renewed urgency at a July 1989 meeting in Italy to wrap things up. One week after the meeting, however, a new wrinkle developed.

X3J3, by itself, met in Vienna, Austria—a nondomestic meeting place for a domestic organization, which was atypical but nonetheless permitted. There, a vendor who performed double duty, retaining membership on both X3 and X3J3, submitted a proposal to the X3 Standards Policy and Requirements Committee (SPARC): Keep FORTRAN

77 exactly as is, designating FORTRAN 8X merely a "collateral" standard. In other words, dissolve the idea of a single standard in favor of a pick-and-choose model. If such a proposal were implemented, the worldwide standards model for programming languages like FORTRAN would be effectively killed off.

Yet SPARC approved the proposal and sent it to X3, which endorsed it in September 1989. Some in the traditionalist camp, including vendors, had pushed for this result; they wanted to ensure a continued market for their FORTRAN 77 products, replete with specialized extensions. "Most compiler vendors were represented [at X3J3 meetings] as a matter of course but, for many, their main objective appeared to be to maintain the status quo and to ensure that [a new FORTRAN] never saw the light of day," according to Michael Metcalf. "One vendor's extended (and much-copied) version of Fortran 77 had virtually become an industry standard, and it saw as its mission the maintenance of this lead. A new standard would cost it its perceived precious advantage."

Moreover, as Brian Meek notes, by this point there were many people who were moving on from FORTRAN to other, more modern, languages like C. And with all those lost years spent arguing and haggling over FORTRAN 8X, who could really blame them? FORTRAN wasn't keeping up with the times, thereby permitting competitor languages to sneak in the back door. The standardization process was taking such a long time that the "X" of FORTRAN 8X was "becoming a hexadecimal digit," Metcalf joked. Further political infighting, with heated debates over the status of FORTRAN 77 as a proper subset of the new standards, bedeviled the committees as the decade closed out.

WG5 met again in London in March 1990; the international committee, which had been in an advisory role when the process began a dozen years before, had taken over the development of the standards ever since that contentious Paris meeting in 1988. The name for the draft standards had changed: from FORTRAN 8X to FORTRAN 88 to Fortran 90.

For years, the language was officially spelled with all capital letters. The upper-to-lowercase transition was slow and gradual, yet there are plenty of documents ("official" and otherwise) extant that spell the language "Fortran" prior to 1990, including on the cover of the first *Programmer's Reference Manual* from 1956 (interestingly, inside the *Manual* the language name is printed in small caps: FORTRAN. Typographically, this style assumed a middle ground between FORTRAN and Fortran). Once the Fortran 90 standards were released, however, "FORTRAN" was now, for the first time, officially standardized to "Fortran"; as the new standards read, "Note that the name of this language, Fortran, differs from that in FORTRAN 77 in that only the first letter is capitalized. Both FORTRAN 77 and FORTRAN 66 used only capital letters in the official name of the language, but Fortran 90 does not continue this tradition." In addition, around this time we start seeing a shift in the manner in which Fortran programs were being written: from using uppercase statements to lowercase statements, although program examples from the Fortran 90 standards document were still printed in uppercase.

There was an overlap in committee membership: a number of individuals who were part of the X3J3 performed some of the technical work for the WG5. It was now up to X3J3 to conform with the ISO Fortran 90 standard and implement their own ANSI version.

By November 1989, most of the new features of Fortran 90 were implemented, including pointers, vector-valued subscripts, free-source form (column independent, with blanks not ignored), new recursive procedures (allowing for both direct and indirect recursion), improved DO loop functionality, the SELECT CASE statement (for selective execution among a list of statements, as an alternative to the old-fashioned computed GO TO), inline commenting (using the exclamation point, !), and many other changes along with some deletions. After an exhausting eighteen months—filled with six-day meetings, multiple public comment phases, and "cliff-hanging votes" (in the words of Michael Metcalf)—the U.S. and international Fortran 90 standard was codified in April 1991 in Minneapolis, Minnesota.

Fortran 90 took some lessons from popular manufacturer extensions of the language. For example, the U.S. Department of Defense's FORTRAN 77 specification called MIL-STD-1753, which arrived in 1978, was built off of the ANSI FORTRAN 77 standard and was a supplement expressly "necessary to the operating needs of the DOD Departments and Agencies." The DoD supplement offered a number of features that would find their way into Fortran 90, such as bit manipulation, DO WHILE loops, the END DO statement, the CYCLE and END statements, the INCLUDE statement, and the IMPLICIT NONE statement, which switched off all of traditional FORTRAN's implicit typing rules (e.g., variables beginning with the letters I to N being integers by default). Fortran 90 variable names could be a maximum of thirty-one characters in length, greatly expanding the six-character maximum of FORTRAN 77.

Including an IMPLICIT NONE statement in a program meant that all variables required explicit type declaration before use (ironically enough, IMPLICIT NONE was itself not implicit, since the statement had to be explicitly included in a program). A joke about the language's type declarations circulated around: "GOD is REAL (unless declared INTEGER)." A less snappy but more comprehensive variant of the joke read, "God is Real (unless otherwise declared in an explicit type statement or in an implicit declaration)." Sun Microsystems was still releasing versions of their Sun Fortran 77 compiler, which included features such as IMPLICIT NONE that were nonstandard in FORTRAN 77 but became standard in Fortran 90, deep into the 1990s.

Fortran 90 also introduced a new data-parallel array language, allowing whole-array operations rather than merely element-by-element manipulation; with this, Fortran 90 took some lessons from APL and DAP FORTRAN, an implementation of the language for the ICL DAP (Distributed Array Processor) parallel computer that arrived on the scene in the early 1980s. DAP FORTRAN allowed programmers to declare arrays but omit some or all of their dimensions. Fortran 90 permitted essentially the same thing, while offering a variety new of array-handling features perfect for scientific programming, which employed mathematical vectors and matrices with regularity. Consider the following program, demonstrating several of these array operations:

```
PROGRAM ARRAY

    IMPLICIT NONE
    REAL, DIMENSION(4) :: A, B, C
    A = 2       ! All four elements equal to 2
    B = SUM(A)  ! All four elements equal
                ! to the sum of A's elements
    C = SIN(A)  ! All four elements equal
                ! to the sine of each of A's elements

    PRINT *, A, B, C

END PROGRAM ARRAY
```

The output of the program is

```
2.00000000    2.00000000    2.00000000
2.00000000    8.00000000    8.00000000
8.00000000    8.00000000    0.909297407
0.909297407   0.909297407   0.909297407
```

Whole-array operations was a feature whose time had come. Back in 1982, a paper was presented in Vienna extolling the virtues of working with arrays on a macro level; in part, it read as follows:

> The first reaction of most Fortran programmers on seeing examples coded in the array features of Fortran 8x is of incomprehension or horror and rarely of delight. This is a shame because there is no question that it is marvelous to be able to write
>
> X = 0
>
> for example, to initialize an array X to zero. Everyone likes to be able to do such things, whether working on a micro- or super-computer. Difficulties arise over expressing more complicated tasks in array form.

Relational operators, last appearing in the "FORTRAN 0" of the Preliminary Report, made a comeback in Fortran 90. Instead of using, for instance, .LT. for less than, now the inequality symbol < could be utilized. Note that tests for equality now employed two equals signs. Take a look at the following code snippet for an example:

```
IF(K == 10) THEN
    K = K + 1
ELSE IF (K < 10) THEN
    K = 100
ELSE
    K = 200
END IF
```

Derived data types, a mainstay of the C programming language (in the form of structures) and C++ (in the form of classes), were suggested for inclusion in Fortran 90 by J. Lawrie Schonfelder of Liverpool University back in mid-June of 1982 during a meeting in Vienna. "Most people want to manipulate strings and find the length after assignment, so they need a dynamic string capability," he said at the meeting. "You cannot have all the things that are wanted and a small core. The only way to go is to generalize. Complex could be a derived data type—not a part of the primitive language. It could be implemented as a special library that can be called from the small core." Here is an example program featuring these user-defined, abstract, derived data types:

```
PROGRAM main
    IMPLICIT NONE

    TYPE dog
        INTEGER :: breed;
        REAL    :: weight;
    END TYPE dog

    TYPE(dog) :: dogA;

    dogA%breed = 3; dogA%weight = 45.5

    PRINT *, "dogA = ", dogA  ! Output the values

END PROGRAM
```

Notice that the program makes use of the semicolon (;) as a separator if there are multiple statements on a line. (A continuation line could be made by inserting an ampersand, &, at the end of the line to be continued.) The output of the program is:

```
dogA =      3    45.5000000
```

Also new to Fortran 90 were modules ("[d]ata and procedure definitions...organized into nonexecutable program units," where derived data types could be encapsulated), generic interfaces, operator overloading, keyword argument passing, and local functions instead of external ones; clearly, *data abstraction*, moving the programmer further even away from the machine manipulations of the data, was now a centerpiece of the language. Plus, errors could be dealt with easier and earlier than ever by using Fortran 90's exception handling facilities. The language was safer than before; as a textbook by Jeanne C. Adams, who chaired X3J3 for a spell, and others explains,

> Prior to Fortran 90, storage association was a fundamental feature for sharing data and managing storage. Almost all large programs, as well as many small ones, made extensive use of storage association.
>
> In modern Fortran, modules and dynamic allocation provide tools for sharing data and managing storage. These tools are often more effective and have fewer subtleties and complications than storage association.

Statements such as COMMON and EQUIVALENCE were still permitted for managing storage.

Viewed with the benefit of hindsight, Fortran 90 represented a sea change in the approach toward standards. Unlike FORTRAN 66 and FORTRAN 77, "which resulted almost entirely from an effort to standardize *existing practices*, [Fortran 90] is much more a *development* of the language, introducing features which are new to Fortran, but are based on experience in other languages," according to Michael Metcalf and John Reid.

The general consensus was that fashioning a Fortran 90 compiler would be tricky, but in less than a year Malcolm Cohen of the Numerical Algorithms Group (NAG) singlehandedly wrote one. In addition, software tools were being released that scoured through old code and removed the obsolete bits, like Pacific Sierra Research's VAST90 and NA Software's LOFT90; these tools also implemented *vectorization*, operating on entire arrays at once. Reference books like *Fortran 90 Explained* by Metcalf and Reid were released in short order in a variety of (human) languages. Software was also available to convert programs from fixed-source form to free-source form.

With the drama of Fortran 90 behind them, X3J3 and WG5 members took a deep breath and began work on the next version of the language. But the world was not the same. During the nearly thirteen years it took to complete Fortran 90, John Backus had sketched out a new way of programming computers that threatened not only the continued viability of Fortran, but of most other high-level languages in circulation as well.

CHAPTER 25

◊◊◊

In the Shadow of John von Neumann

As he ambled toward the podium to deliver the ACM A.M. Turing Award lecture on October 17, 1977, in Seattle, Washington, few could have predicted the surprise he had in store for the audience: John Backus was about to completely turn on his greatest creation, FORTRAN.

Since he left the FORTRAN project, Backus had worked on the ALGOL committees, created BNF (Backus-Naur Form), and been made an IBM Fellow. He had busied himself with teaching and working on independent projects at IBM's San Jose research laboratory. But he was growing weary of having to repeatedly wade into what he called a "cesspool of complexity."

"Well, I mean, just look around at software, and you see it everywhere," Backus explained. "You see the contents of the cesspool, so to speak. Everything is so complicated. Everything comes with a manual that thick, and it's a mess." He wanted to simplify things—first and foremost, the imperative programming style FORTRAN had introduced to the masses and that was replicated by programming languages that followed. Backus derisively termed all these languages *von Neumann languages*.

"I just got sick of seeing more and more new programming languages," he complained. "They've just become so baroque and unwieldy that few of them make programming sufficiently cheaper to justify their cost." These "'von Neumann languages' create enormous, unnecessary intellectual roadblocks in thinking about programs and in creating the higher-level combining forms required in a powerful programming methodology," Backus said.

It was FORTRAN which began this trend. But what is a von Neumann language? "[H]ere's my highly simplified oversimplified analysis of the von Neumann computer," he began.

> It consists of two boxes. One is the central processing unit, where the calculations take place, and the other is the store, or memory. Traffic between them takes place, figura-

tively speaking, through a narrow passage that I call the von Neumann bottleneck. Because it is just that. You see, the purpose of a program is to make a big change in the store. But how does it do it? By huffing and puffing words...back and forth through the tiny passage between the store and CPU. *One word at a time.*

The key problem, as Backus saw it, was that "all programming languages are essentially mirrors of the von Neumann computer." They might add on extra features which increase their complexity, but that doesn't increase their power. All programs employ variables to model computer's storage cells; all programs use control statements to jump and test instructions; all programs utilize assignment statements to "imitate its fetching, storing, and arithmetic. The assignment statement is the von Neumann bottleneck of programming languages and keeps us thinking in word-at-a-time terms in much the same way the computer's bottleneck does."

Thus, FORTRAN's fiercest critic turned out to be none other than John Backus himself. "The differences between Fortran and Algol 68, although considerable, are less significant than the fact that both are based on the programming style of the von Neumann computer," a decades-old paradigm that Backus felt had run its course. He didn't blame John von Neumann. He blamed himself. "In fact, some might say that I bear some responsibility for that problem."

> Once you've written a Fortran program, you can't tell what's going on really. It takes two numbers and multiplies them and stores them here and does some other junk and then makes this test. Trying to figure out what is actually being calculated is not easy. Trying to do that calculation in a different way [is difficult] because you basically don't understand what the program is doing.

The result is programming manuals which are five-hundred to one-thousand pages in length, with new computer languages being designed to fit new hardware, and new hardware in turn being made to conform to new languages, but the basic problem remains: programmers having to mentally keep track of what Backus termed "housekeeping operations," or state changes, all in one consolidated place. Dennis Shasha and Cathy Lazere, in their book *Out of Their Minds*, succinctly explain the problem Backus wanted to solve: "Backus's goal was to enable programmers to state *what* they wanted to be done without getting involved with the *how*." Backus would introduce *functional programming languages* as the solution, where mathematical functions and function composition were the order of the day. He credited Kenneth Iverson's APL, which had programs that were not "word-at-a-time" and could handle "the use of new functional forms," as well as John McCarthy's LISP, with its lambda calculus, as inspirations for functional programming.

For illustration purposes, Backus creates a functional programming language called FP and contrasts it with a typical von Neumann language like ALGOL. Consider the ALGOL code below, which calculates the inner product of two vectors (i.e., the sum of the products of corresponding elements of two one-dimensional arrays):

```
c := 0
for i := 1 step 1 until n do
    c := c + a[i]×b[i]
```

Backus relays a number of problems with this von Neumann approach to programming. First, "[i]ts statements operate on an invisible 'state' according to complex rules"—one must mentally be able to "run" the repetitive program in order to understand the state changes. Second, "the assignment statement splits programming into two worlds," he says.

> The first world comprises the right sides of assignment statements. This is an orderly world of expressions, a world that has useful algebraic properties (except that those properties are often destroyed by side effects). It is the world in which most useful computation takes place.
>
> The second world of conventional programming languages is the world of statements. The primary statement in that world is the assignment statement itself. All the other statements of the language exist in order to make it possible to perform a computation that must be based on this primitive construct: the assignment statement.

The problem is that "[t]his world of statements is a disorderly one, with few useful mathematical properties." There are other problems as well, centering on lack of generality (the code only applying to vectors a and b with lengths n), computations taking place a-word-at-a-time (by repetition and modification of the variable i), and difficulty consolidating the "housekeeping operations" carried out by the for loop and the subscripts.

"Now, in the kinds of systems I'm trying to build, you can write a program as essentially an equation, like equations in high school algebra, and the solution of that equation will be the program you want," Backus said. The computer will take care of the optimization behind the scenes.

Contrast the ALGOL code above with Backus's FP program to find the inner product of two vectors, shown below.

Def Innerproduct ≡ (Insert +) ∘ (ApplyToAll ×) ∘ Transpose

We can abbreviate the program to read:

Def IP ≡ (/+) ∘ (α×) ∘ Trans

Backus explains that Composition (∘), Insert (/), and ApplyToAll (α) are *functional forms*: they combine together existing functions in order to form new ones. In the program above, "There are no hidden states or complex transition rules," notes Backus, and the program is completely generalized.

Backus first publicly presented FP at the lecture he delivered in honor of being elected a Turing Award laureate in 1977; the prestigious award, often referred to as the "Nobel Prize of Computing," is presented only once per year. Computer science luminaries Alan Perlis (1966), Maurice Wilkes (1967), Richard Hamming (1968), John McCarthy (1971), Edsger Dijkstra (1972), and Donald Knuth (1974) had already received the prize. Now it was John Backus's turn.

The citation for Backus's award reads as follows:

> For profound, influential, and lasting contributions to the design of practical high-level programming systems, notably through his work on FORTRAN, and for seminal publication of formal procedures for the specification of programming languages.

Jean Sammet, who was Chairman of the Awards Committee, introduced Backus and then called him up to the podium. She spoke mainly of his contributions to high-level programming, specifically with FORTRAN and BNF; there was no mention in her introductory comments of what was to come: a rejection of most HLLs in the form of FP.

In 1978, Backus's lecture was expanded and published in *Communications of the ACM* with the title "Can Programming Be Liberated from the von Neumann Style? A Functional Style and Its Algebra of Programs." The paper caused quite a stir, becoming the most cited A.M. Turing Award lecture of all time. But not everyone was onboard with functional programming as the future of the field.

Take Edsger Dijkstra, for example. In EWD 692: A Review of the 1977 Turing Award Lecture by John Backus (1978), Dijkstra lays bare the problems with Backus's presentation. For starters, too many pages—nearly a quarter—of the lecture are spent justifying functional programming by attacking conventional programming languages. Plus, Backus doesn't fully develop FP; he only "sketches an alternative, [and] matters of implementation are hardly touched upon," Dijkstra writes.

Dijkstra most objected to Backus's claim that proofs about the language, which use logic rules, are merely "axiomatic game[s]." According to Backus,

> Thus denotational and axiomatic semantics are descriptive formalisms whose foundations embody elegant and powerful concepts; but using them to describe a von Neumann language can not produce an elegant and powerful language any more than the use of elegant and modern machines to build an Edsel can produce an elegant and modern car.
>
> In any case, proofs about programs use the language of logic, not the language of programming. Proofs talk about programs but cannot involve them directly since the axioms of von Neumann languages are so unusable.

And who was a key proponent of such proofs about programs? None other than Edsger Dijkstra. Continuing the lecture, Backus observes that

> So far, proving a program correct requires knowledge of some moderately heavy topics in mathematics and logic.... These topics have been very useful for professionals who make it their business to devise proof techniques; they have published a lot of beautiful work on this subject, starting with the work of McCarthy and Floyd, and, more recently, that of Burstall, Dijkstra, Manna and his associates, Milner, Morris, Reynolds, and many others.... But its theoretical level places it beyond the scope of most amateurs who work outside of this specialized field.

Dijkstra objects to the characterization. "But whereas machines must be able to execute programs (without understanding them), people must be able to understand them (without executing them)," Dijkstra says. "These two activities are so utterly disconnected—the one can take place without the other—that I fail to see the claimed advantage of being so 'monolingual'." He adds that the problem may be that Backus simply misunderstands von Neumann programs.

In conclusion, Dijkstra admits that

> He [Backus] may be right, but where are those numerous indications? I did not get them from this article.

> In short, the article is a progress report on a valid research effort but suffers badly from aggressive overselling of its significance, long before convincing results have been reached. This is the more regrettable as it has been published by way of Turing Award Lecture.

Their public battle then turned private, with letters exchanged between them. Backus came to one inescapable conclusion about Dijkstra when all was said and done: "This guy's arrogance takes your breath away."

Like Speedcoding and FORTRAN, which Backus led the efforts to create because of an admitted "laziness," functional programming had similar roots. "That was my motivating force in most of what I did, was how to avoid work," he admitted. Backus felt that language design should always be about abstracting away even more from the programmer, not giving him or her more low-level details to worry about. "Well, I guess the question of it still seems that programming is a pretty low-level enterprise, and that somebody ought to be thinking about how to make it higher; really higher level than it is," he said. Perhaps functional programming—which he transitions to calling *function level programming*, because it "eschews" lambda expressions as well—is the answer to creating programs at these higher levels of abstraction. Or perhaps not. "It's just that that whole paradigm didn't include these other [things]. Somebody needs to find a way to include those other things in a clean way," he told an interviewer near the end of his life.

In the decades following his A.M. Turing Award lecture, a number of functional programming languages would be built, most notably Haskell, first released in 1990. Backus's functional forms are now referred to as *higher-order functions*.

As for John Backus, he would focus on making FP, which turned into FL, viable; these efforts took place in the 1980s at the IBM Almaden Research Center with the help of John Williams, Edward Wimmers, and Alexander Aiken. In 1991, he reached IBM's mandatory retirement age of 65. He would retire, leaving science completely behind. In a 1995 interview, he told computer science professor Dennis Shasha that he practiced meditation and read the "introspective writings of Krishnamurti and Eva Pierrakos." He also adopted a reflective attitude toward both science and lived experience, accusing scientists of being "afraid of life" because navigating one's way through solving scientific problems is living in an "antiseptic world." In the same interview, Backus also extolled the benefits of introspection. "It's strange that by looking into yourself you really get an appreciation of the mystery of the universe," he said. "You don't by trying to find the laws of physics."

After the death of his second wife, Backus moved to Ashland, Oregon, where one of his two daughters lived. He died there on March 17, 2007, at the age of 82.

CHAPTER 26

◊◊◊

High Performance and Beyond

Fortran is dragged kicking and screaming into the modern day, imbued with more powerful features for cutting-edge machines but possessing an increasingly specialized—and ever-dwindling—user base.

Near the end of the grueling compilation of Fortran 90 standards, Thomas Lahey of Lahey Computer Systems (which produced their own Fortran compilers, such as LF90) wrote the following: "Before the next standard is started, the committee and the Fortran programming community need to agree on a few basics: What is Fortran? What is subject to change? What isn't? Under what conditions does it get changed?" The inclusion of the FORTRAN 77 subset also came under scrutiny, with one observer noting, "Ironically, one of the biggest complaints against the Fortran 77 subset was that 'nobody implemented it.' That wasn't quite true, but apparently users clamored for the full language and interest in the subset quickly fell by the wayside." The inclusion of the FORTRAN 77 subset meant that there had been precisely zero deleted features in the shift to Fortran 90 (although there were a number of obsolescent features identified, including the arithmetic **IF**, the alternate **RETURN**, the assigned **GO TO**, and the **ASSIGN** and **PAUSE** statements; obsolete features were slated to be deleted in the next revision).

Once Fortran 90 wrapped up, rules of engagement were put in place to make sure the production of the next set of standards went as smoothly, and with as little political infighting, as possible. To that end, there was a codification of the power shift that evolved over the course of Fortran 90: the WG5, not the X3J3, would be responsible for drawing up the plan; the X3J3 would then develop it. In addition, a timetable for completion of the new standards was proposed: a modest revision due in 1995 (to resolve the hundreds of questions that were submitted after Fortran 90's release), and a major overhaul due in 2000.

The 1995 revision was to be highly circumscribed, perhaps with no improvements offered at all. But the committees working on the revision didn't expect to have to account for a new development in Fortran: the advent of the High Performance Fortran Forum (HPFF) and, with it, widely circulated extensions to the language that addressed a significant problem: the need for efficient performance from parallel computing architectures while maintaining portability from platform to platform.

HPFF was the brainchild of Ken Kennedy of Rice University in Houston, Texas. Born in 1945, Kennedy became a supercomputing pioneer, having graduated from Rice with a degree in mathematics and a doctorate from the Courant Institute at New York University. There, he studied under John Cocke, the IBM computer designer, and Jacob "Jack" Schwartz, a world-leading expert in parallel and high-performance computing, who was his doctoral advisor. Kennedy founded Rice's computer science department and "spearheaded early work on software programs known as parallelizing compilers, systems that can automatically spread workloads among a large number of processors, vastly speeding calculations," according to an article in *The New York Times*. His expertise in parallel computing "served as the foundation for successive generations of scientists and engineers who developed advanced simulations, including weather and climate prediction and [modelling] of automobile collisions." Kennedy wrote a FORTRAN 77 *automatic vectorizer*, where, by leveraging parallelism, multiple operations were performed by a supercomputer simultaneously. Vector computers like the Cray-1 made use of a technique called "pipeline parallelism" in order to operate on entire vectors (one-dimensional arrays) all at once rather than on single data elements, one at a time, as traditional *scalar processors* do.

"The Rise and Fall of High Performance Fortran: An Historical Object Lesson," a paper penned by Kennedy and several of his colleagues, presents the motivation behind the creation of High Performance Fortran (HPF). (Note: for convenience only Ken Kennedy will be attributed in all further quotations from this article.)

> By the mid-1980s, it was becoming clear that *parallel computing*, the use of multiple processors to speed up a single application, would eventually replace, or at least augment, vector computing as the way to construct leading-edge supercomputing systems. However, it was not clear what the right high-level programming model for such machines would be.

HPF turned out to be one of many parallel-programming approaches for these new machines. Specifically, HPF aligned with the *data-parallel computation model*, whereby operations on data elements were completed in parallel. The early vector computers of the 1970s worked using a basic form of data parallelism. Other parallel programming approaches include the *shared-memory asynchronous parallel model* and *distributed-memory parallelism*, each having attendant advantages and disadvantages.

HPF was strongly influenced by three data-parallel Fortran implementations: Fortran D, Vienna Fortran, and CM Fortran. Ken Kennedy's research group and Geoffrey C. Fox, a scientific computing expert who earned a doctorate from Cambridge University, developed Fortran D in the late 1980s. "Fox and the Rice group produced a specification for a new language called Fortran D that produced a two-level distribution specification similar to that later adopted into HPF," wrote Kennedy. "The basic idea was that groups of arrays would be aligned with an abstract object called a *template*, then all of these arrays would be mapped to processors by a single distribution statement that mapped the template to those processors."

Several years before Fortran D was developed, a group led by Hans Zima at Bonn University in Germany began work on a data-parallel compiler called SUPERB for a supercomputing project. SUPERB converted FORTRAN 77 code into programs tailored for a parallel-processing supercomputer. Several years later, after Zima's group moved to the University of Vienna, a new language, rather than merely a compiler, was built. Called Vienna Fortran, it offered a variety of complex array features that leveraged supercomputing hardware.

While Fortran D and Vienna Fortran were products of the academy, CM Fortran was developed for the commercial market. Guy Steele of Thinking Machines Corporation, along with David Loveman and Robert Morgan of COMPASS, Inc., led a team to create a product for advanced SIMD parallel computing architecture with the "goal of attracting science and engineering users." Taking Fortran 90 as its base, CM Fortran reimplemented a deleted feature: FORALL, which permitted quite a bit of flexibility with array assignments, letting the compiler optimize the order of the assignments rather than the processor being pigeonholed via a DO loop. For example, the compact statement

```
FORALL (I=1:N) A(I,I) = I
```

would assign numbers to the diagonal of a two-dimensional array, but it would do so in a simultaneous fashion without iterating a loop. A library of computational primitives and global operations, known as CMSSL, were available for CM Fortran as well.

The High Performance Fortran Forum was born in November 1991 when Ken Kennedy and Geoffrey Fox were attending Supercomputing '91, an ACM/IEEE conference on supercomputing, in Albuquerque, New Mexico. While there, they were "approached about the possibility of standardizing the syntax of data-parallel versions of Fortran," recalled Kennedy—that is, Fortran D, Vienna Fortran, and CM Fortran, among others. As was the case for the numerous previous Fortran standardization efforts, the proliferation of too many different implementations (this time for high-performance, parallel-architecture machines) was the impetus. Both Thinking Machines and Digital Equipment Corporation (which had developed DEC Fortran), along with several other vendors, were especially interested in these high-performance standardization efforts.

A "birds-of-a-feather session" was rapidly put together, in which Kennedy and Fox met with representatives from industry and the academy; further meetings were agreed to under the more formal auspices of the newly formed HPFF, where Kennedy would serve as chairman. Only several months later, in January 1992, a first meeting of the HPFF was held at Rice; interest was sky-high, with over one hundred participants attending, including representatives from more than twenty companies. Pressure from the parties involved resulted in a tentative agreement: produce a set of agreed-upon extensions to Fortran, called High Performance Fortran, in the span of only one year. There was a restriction, however: only features that already had a track record in at least one implementation of the language would be up for inclusion in HPF. In practice, though, "the group sometimes ignored this guideline, substituting intuition for experience," according to Kennedy, largely as a result of the compressed timeline for development.

Between thirty and forty people gathered for two days every six weeks, usually in a hotel in Dallas, Texas; they were university computer scientists (e.g., from Cornell, Rice, Vienna, Yale), representatives of various vendors (e.g., from Cray, HP, IBM, Intel, Lahey Computer, and Sun), and government users (e.g., from Los Alamos), all dedicated to the task of resolving "numerous difficult and political issues," wrote Kennedy. A debate ensued about whether to base the language on FORTRAN 77 or Fortran 90. On the one hand, FORTRAN 77 was already up and running on scalable parallel machines, but, on the other hand, Fortran 90 had new features that were already being demonstrably exploited by CM Fortran. Fortran 90 emerged as the consensus choice, in part because of its array-handling features. However, Kennedy later expressed some buyer's remorse, since the inherent complexity in Fortran 90 made the HPFF's goals much harder to complete in the tight timeframe; unfortunately, "this may have contributed to the slow development of HPF compilers and, hence, to the [ultimately] limited acceptance of the language."

The HPFF met their self-imposed deadline, rolling out HPF at the ACM/IEEE supercomputing conference in 1993. The HPF Standard 1.0 included all of Fortran 90, with the HPF extensions implemented as *directives* (detailing how arrays were to be handled in memory) embedded in Fortran 90 comments prefaced by `HPF$`—which could be ignored on regular, scalar sequential machines, or implemented on parallel computing systems. Employing a distribution directive using the keyword `DISTRIBUTE` would specify how data arrays were to be arranged in memory. HPF also offered other keywords like `ALIGN`, `BLOCK`, `CYCLIC`, and `PURE` to further optimize computations; there was an associated HPF Library with added functionality as well. As Kennedy notes, "Specification of an associated library is now standard practice in C, C++, and Java."

Although HPF was a robust alternative to MPI (Message Passing Interface, the low-level standard for programming parallel computers), and despite more than a dozen vendors selling HPF products, HPF lost steam as frustration with its complexity set in. "It became clear that it was not as easy as had been hoped to achieve high performance and portability in the language and many application developers gave up and switched to MPI," Kennedy said. They simply lacked the patience to wait for HPF to mature. At the turn of the millennium, despite further standardization efforts, HPF was effectively dead in the United States, although it retained a measure of popularity in Japan and influenced the development of other languages geared for high-performance computing, such as Sun's Fortress, purposely named to evoke Fortran though functionally bearing little resemblance to it.

Despite its failure, the legacy of HPF lives on in "official" Fortran. Recall that the X3J3 and WG5 committees were busy planning for their "minor" revision of Fortran 90, to be called Fortran 95. The committees were aware of the goings-on of the HPFF; Jerry Wagener, who chaired X3J3 and FORTEC (the Fortran Technical Committee of the Special Interest Group on Programming Languages of the ACM), shuttled between the HPFF and X3J3, simultaneously keeping both groups informed about the latest developments, and Ken Kennedy delivered a presentation to X3J3 on HPF. As a result, the FORALL and PURE keywords, along with several extensions taking the HPF Library as their inspiration, were integrated into the new Fortran 95 standards. Unlike in the transition from FORTRAN 77 to Fortran 90, in which no features were deleted, a handful of obsolescent features didn't make the cut in the shift from Fortran 90 to Fortran 95, although Fortran 95 was still able to run most FORTRAN 77 legacy code. Fortran 95 was completed in 1995, with the ISO adopting the standards in 1997.

A subset of Fortran 95, called the F programming language, was developed by The Fortran Company (originally called Imagine1) in the mid-1990s. The language was geared toward education, although its use was widespread outside the classroom; F's creators emphasized safety and portability as its key selling points, dispensing with difficult-to-use Fortran keywords such as EQUIVALENCE. All keywords in F had to written in lowercase, and all variables required declaration. Eventually, even some features of Fortran 95's successor were integrated within F.

F was not the only compiler customized for educational use. Lahey also produced Essential Lahey Fortran 90, or ELF90, which offered a subset of Fortran 90 minus some obsolete features (like the arithmetic IF and assigned GO TO); thus, FORTRAN 77 programs weren't always compatible with ELF90. And a freely available compiler called GNU Fortran (or GFortran), a Free Software Foundation (FSF) product, compliant with Fortran 95 that also included some features of later standardized Fortrans, arrived on the scene during the next decade.

With Fortran 95 completed, work continued apace on the next major revision, initially set for completion around the year 2000. The X3J3, or the US Fortran Programming Language Standards Technical Committee, around this time became informally known as "J3."

As in all previous revisions, the process allowed for public comments on drafts proposals. It is instructive to briefly examine one such set of comments on a Committee Draft (CD) of Fortran 2000. Though the vast majority of countries voted in favor of the CD, Germany was the lone dissenting voice; they did not approve of the CD, and offered suggestions to the WG5. Specifically, they relayed nontechnical criticisms such as

- The proposed Fortran language and document are TOO LARGE AND MUCH TOO COMPLEX for anyone to learn or read completely.
- The standardization process has become seriously DISCONNECTED from the Fortran user community.
- The other disastrous impression we have been getting over the past few years is that the language is collapsing under its own weight and complexity and has become UNMANAGEABLE even for the experts.
- The current revision does not focus on the PRIMARY INTERESTS and the most pressing needs of the Fortran community.

Germany also proffered a host of technical criticisms, all of which were handled quite diplomatically by the WG5. Consider their responses to the first two points, for instance:

> Fortran 2000 was agreed to be a major revision of Fortran 95. WG5 has developed the proposals for Fortran 2000, described in WG5-N1259, which were approved by its members at the meeting in February 1997. It is true of many modern programming languages that few individuals are familiar, or need to be familiar, with all aspects of the language....
>
> ...Members of the standardization committees who are employed by processor vendors are continually made aware of user requirements. Individual members of the standardization committees make frequent, usually daily, contributions to the main user forums for discussion of Fortran matters, viz *comp.lang.fortran* and comp-fortran-90, and major users are represented directly on the standardization committees.

After much discussion, proposed Fortran 2000 features such as interval arithmetic (which would certainly have been a boon to scientists and mathematicians) were discarded. There were three reasons why, according to J3 member Dan Nagle.

> One is that the proponents of interval arithmetic did not agree among themselves exactly what to propose. Two is that none of the proponents volunteered to do the work and there was a lot of work to be done. And three is that some members of J3 felt that interval arithmetic would add a great deal of cost to Fortran compilers without sufficient benefit.

As the Fortran 2000 standards neared their completion, Nagle took stock of the strengths and weaknesses of Fortran at the turn of the millennium. On the one hand, Fortran was still the king of efficiency and was eminently portable: if you were an engineer, scientist, or economist who needed processing power in the form of floating-point calculations, then Fortran was your language. But the market for numerical computing was shrinking. "The cost effectiveness of commodity components to make computers for all purposes and the now ubiquitous use of open standards for software, especially communications, has created the illusion that Fortran is old-fashioned," Nagle wrote in 2002. "Databases, office automation and the Internet are all based on integer processing, and these uses are very much more widespread than floating-point based simulations."

Debate ensued on whether the language should be called Fortran 2000 or Fortran 2002 (coinciding with when the revised draft standard was set to be published); ultimately, Fortran 2003 was settled on. In November 2004, the Fortran 2003 language standard was finalized. Fortran 2003 ushered in the era of object-oriented programming (OOP) in the language, something thought several years prior by Fortran observers to be nothing more than an ephemeral fashion that could just as well be ignored. For example, in the late 1990s, Jerry Wagener wrote, "Despite good marketing, Fortran 90 is probably destined to remain undiscovered by computer science departments, at least until the current object-oriented fad runs its course. (And then there likely will be another fad—perhaps that one can be Fortran-oriented?)" Around the same time, Michael Metcalf lamented the programming community's overemphasis on the object-oriented paradigm:

> However, during the 1980s, the concept of objects came to the fore, with methods bound to the objects on which they operate. Here, one particular language, C++, has come to dominate the field. Fortran 90 lacks a means to point to functions, but otherwise has most of the necessary features in place, and the standards committees are now faced with the dilemma of deciding whether to make the planned Fortran 2000 a fully object-oriented language. This could possibly jeopardize its powerful, and efficient, numerical capabilities by too great an increase in language complexity, so should they simply batten down the hatches and not defer to what might be only a passing storm?

But the committees were right to treat OOP, which takes *objects* possessing associated behaviors and attributes as its centerpiece, as more than just a "passing storm," although they did dial back the OOP focus before the draft standards were finalized.

The history of OOP dates back to the early 1960s. The programming language SIMULA I, a superset of the block-structured ALGOL 60 designed for simulation studies at the Norwegian Computing Center in Oslo, Norway, paved the way for the revolutionary SIMULA 67, released in 1968, which introduced objects, classes, subclasses, inheritance, and a number of other concepts that were folded into the term object-oriented programming, which was coined by the American computer scientist Alan Kay while he was still a graduate student at the University of Utah College of Engineering. Kay would join Xerox PARC (Palo Alto Research Center) in 1970 and play a leading role in developing the Smalltalk language, which codified the OOP concepts of SIMULA 67, for workstations and the way-ahead-of-its-time Dynabook, a portable computer designed for educational use. "Flat," non-block languages like FORTRAN preceded stack languages like ALGOL; object-oriented languages did one better, by dynamically allocating memory on a *heap*; now, *modularity* and *data hiding* were possible, although *garbage collecting* (memory recovery) became a must.

Like Alan Kay, Danish computer scientist Bjarne Stroustrup was also taken with SIMULA and OOP; he decided to build upon the C programming language by developing "C with Classes," which evolved into C++, "a general purpose programming language designed to make programming more enjoyable for the serious programmer." In the early 1990s, a team led by James Gosling of Sun Microsystems developed Java, with syntax similar to C++, for "interactive television"; by the mid-1990s, Java was rebranded for programming applications on the then-nascent internet, and it took off. The so-called procedural languages—FORTRAN, ALGOL, BASIC, PL/I—had ceded significant ground to a new programming paradigm, and it wasn't John Backus's functional programming. OOP was gathering momentum and, by the start of the millennium, it became unstoppable.

There were ways to program in a pseudo-object-oriented style in Fortran 90 using modules and derived data types, but these were jury-rigged approaches that missed the point. Since its birth, Fortran had already ceded significant ground in education (to languages like BASIC), business and industry (to languages like COBOL and PL/I), and, most concerningly considering its specialty, scientific and technical computing (to UNIX and C). And successor languages to ALGOL, namely Pascal and Ada, had caused Fortran partisans many sleepless nights. If Fortran was to continue to be used, it had to formally adapt to the OOP approach—or further slip into irrelevance.

Fortran 2003 offered object-oriented support in the form of inheritance, polymorphism, type extension, dynamic type allocation, and type-bound procedures, in addition to various enhancements in the realms of data manipulation, pointers, and input/output. Moreover, Fortran 2003 offered "interoperability with the C programming language," meaning that the two languages could exchange data (between types, pointers, variables, and procedures) as long as certain syntactical rules were adhered to strictly. Interoperability had been on the docket even before Fortran 95 was finalized. The same year that FORTRAN 77 was released, one observer wrote of a primitive sort of interoperability between the language and C:

> The Fortran language has just been revised, and a new standard for the language, known as Fortran 77 is about to be published. We report here [about] a compiler and run-time system for the new extended language. This is believed to be the first complete Fortran 77 system to be implemented. This compiler is designed to be portable, to be correct and complete, and to generate code compatible with calling sequences produced by C compilers. In particular, this Fortran is quite usable on UNIX systems.

By the 1990s, the committees realized that in order to allow for coexistence between Fortran and C, the following items were a must:

i. the need for a means of translating from the name of a Fortran entity to the name of a C entity, which may be complicated by the fact that C distinguishes between lower and upper case characters, whereas Fortran, outside of a character context, does not;
ii. the need for Fortran data types that are equivalent to C data types; and
iii. the need to be able to handle differences in argument calling conventions in implementations of the two languages (which is closely linked with (ii) above

To facilitate interoperability, three intrinsic modules, as well as a number of other proposals, were sketched out in 1995. Committee members realized, well before Fortran 2003 was finalized, that employing interoperability features would prove to be anything but easy for the average Fortran user; moreover, there were a number of significant limitations with the process. Concerns with the implementation of the data sharing mechanism were detailed in the technical specification document "Further Interoperability with C" (2012):

> The existing system for interoperability does not provide for interoperability of interfaces with Fortran dummy arguments that are assumed-shape arrays, have assumed character length, or have the ALLOCATABLE, POINTER, or OPTIONAL attributes. As a consequence, a significant class of Fortran subprograms is not portably accessible from C, limiting the usefulness of the facility.

It would take more than a decade to resolve these issues, but not everyone was keen to wait. Projects were underway to optimally and automatically convert old Fortran code to more widespread languages. For instance, a Fortran to C++ source-to-source conversion tool, implemented in Python, was developed in the late aughts by four scientists working at Lawrence Berkeley National Laboratory and Los Alamos National Laboratory. Called FABLE—a contraction of "Fortran ABLEitung," with *ableitung* a German word meaning "derivative"—the open-source conversion software took as its inspiration the work of David Sayre, who was a crystallographer prior to joining the original FORTRAN development team. As FABLE's authors explain,

> The work presented here grew out of the development of a software suite for the determination of macromolecular structures using crystallographic methods. Crystallographic computing has been connected to language development from the earliest days of [the] scientific software [of] David Sayre.... This early influence is still evident in a substantial amount of crystallographic software implemented in Fortran 77. At the same time, developments in computer science have led to the wide-spread use of object-oriented languages. Integrating time-tested Fortran implementations into modern object-oriented software environments is often problematic..., yet in many cases it would be prohibitively expensive to replace existing Fortran implementations with a new object-oriented implementation.

Conversion of pre-OOP Fortran code to an OOP platform was tricky due to the frequent use of global variables in old code, among a host of other issues, the FABLE authors claim. Although the source-to-source translations generally resulted in slower runtimes of the C++ code than the Fortran source code, they extolled the benefits of turning the legacy programs of a highly specialized scientific nature into a modern object-oriented implementation. Yet why they chose to convert the legacy code to C++, rather than the object-oriented Fortran 2003, is not addressed.

As the committees were gearing up for the next revision—tentatively called Fortran 2K—some fun was had at the expense of the old-timers. At a Fortran Reunion held in March 2003 in Las Vegas, Nevada, committee members played a game of "guess the geezer," run by Jerry Wagener, in which eight old photographs, circa the development of Fortran 90, were circulated. "For each of the eight photos," he explained, "there was the statement that...'You might be a Fortran old geezer if...' you could identify certain people and/or activities in the photo." Jeanne Martin, in addition to promising to build an exhaustive library of X3J3 and WG5 documents, ran a "Who said this?" session of Fortran trivia. Martin Greenfield, for his part, spoke of many "cherished memories" during his decades spent working on standards committees.

Though few vendors jumped on the Fortran 2003 bandwagon and produced viable compilers, the standards committees resumed their work, readying the next standard for publication. Fortran 2008, which arrived in 2010, added *coarrays*, which began as an extension of Fortran 95 called Co-Array Fortran (CAF, but originally known as F^{--}, pronounced "eff-minus-minus"—denoting a minor change), laid out by Robert Numrich and John Reid in the 1998 paper "Co-Array Fortran for Parallel Programming." "A Co-Array Fortran program is interpreted as if it were replicated a number of times and all copies were executed asynchronously," Numrich and Reid wrote. "Each copy has its own set of data objects and is termed an image."

A Co-Array Fortran program executes as if it were replicated a number of times, the number of replications remaining fixed during the execution of the program. Each copy is called an image and each image executes asynchronously. A particular implementation of Co-Array Fortran may permit the number of images to be chosen at compile time, at link time, or at execute time. The number of images may be the same as the number of physical processors, or it may be more, or it may be less.

Using coarrays, which employed parallel processing of arrays by distributing the work to more than one processor, required programmers to learn a new set of syntactical tricks. Declaring coarrays involved using square brackets, [ ], as in the following example:

```
real :: a[*]
```

Numrich and Reid's coarrays were implemented on Cray platforms and then, with minor tweaks, were integrated into the Fortran 2008 standards. Other programmers, such as at Rice University, have refined coarrays with their own extensions.

Besides coarrays, Fortran 2008 offered a do concurrent form of a do loop that allowed further optimization in the case of "no data dependencies between the iterations" (according to John Reid, writing for the WG5); the contiguous attribute that enabled "[c]ertain optimizations...if the compiler knows that an array occupies a contiguous memory block"; the block construct for scoping; and submodules, along with a number of other additions and modifications.

The committees met in 2012 to begin work on Fortran 2015, as they first called it (because the set of features was agreed to in 2015). Their newest revision, renamed Fortran 2018, arrived in November of 2018; thus, Fortran 2018 is the only Fortran standard matching the year of its finalized definition. Why not simply drop the appended year in favor of a version number, or even nothing at all? Because the year alerts the uninitiated that Fortran isn't merely a legacy or a dead language but continues to be updated regularly. And making sure that the year of definition matches the name of the language further helps Fortran on that PR front—hence the rebranding of Fortran 2015 to Fortran 2018.

The committees integrated the changes suggested by the 2012 "Further Interoperability with C" technical specification document within Fortran 2018. Additional parallel programming features now made their home in the language definition as well.

With the smoke of the latest Fortran cleared, WG5 and J3, as usual, had only one thing left to do: prepare for the next revision.

CHAPTER 27

◊◊◊

Too Afraid to Fail

Fortran still, no doubt, retains cachet because of its power at numerical computation. But while it once dominated the conversation and set the standard, its use grew more and more specialized, to the point where now Fortran is mostly the province of a new "priesthood"—this time of supercomputing experts. In Fortran's retirement, it has been cast off to the small island of high performance computing.

When it first arrived on the scene, waxes Richard Hamming, "FORTRAN was successful far beyond anyone's expectations because of the *psychological* fact it was just what its name implied—FORmula TRANslation of the things one had always done in school; it did not require learning a new set of ways of thinking." Martin Greenfield once said, "The one central attribute of FORTRAN is its name." Yet there is a strong argument to be made that the name itself turned into an albatross: to young programmers who don't know any better, when they hear the word "Fortran" they may reflexively think, "Historical/Legacy/Dead language."

Jean Sammet wrote, "In my own view, FORTRAN has probably had more impact on the computer field than any other single software development," because it was a proof of concept: a compiler could turn source code into optimized object code automatically. But after noting the staying power of FORTRAN and attributing it to the "soundness of many of the original ideas," Sammet acknowledged that "inertia" and prior "investment" might also be explanations for its subsequent decline.

The very first issue of the *Fortran Forum*—then called the *ForTec Forum*—was published in July 1982. Fortran had just turned twenty-five years old, and the outlook for the language was optimistic. In a chairman's letter introducing the newsletter, Jerry Wagener editorialized as follows:

> "Why", you might ask, "another newsletter? devoted, of all things, to Fortran? For 25 years", you might note, "Fortran has withstood all challenges; it will continue to predominate in scientific computing circles, without the help of the FORTEC FORUM."

Precisely! Fortran will continue to thrive, evolve, and predominate in scientific computing. No matter what.

Yet by 1984, while the standards committees were locked in a mortal struggle over what was to become Fortran 90, people were openly calling for Fortran to be put out to pasture, even for scientific and technical computing. The *Physics Today* article "A Debate: Retire Fortran?"—pitting Jim McGraw, who worked at Livermore Labs, against David Kuck and Michael Wolfe, both hailing from Kuck and Associates—garnered a fair share of attention. McGraw argued that Fortran, quickly becoming the province of the high-speed world of supercomputing, should be retired in favor of non-imperative, "applicative" languages that offer a higher degree of abstraction based on mathematical functions. With multiprocessor-driven supercomputing on the immediate horizon, Fortran, such as it was in 1984, was ill-suited to take advantage of parallelism. Kuck and Wolfe, while conceding the point, retorted that with the technology in play at the time, only Fortran offered an efficient enough "supercompiler" for large-scale scientific computing needs. In 1984, Fortran was the only game in town.

Eight years later, an article in *Communications of the ACM* reopened the debate. Called "Retire Fortran? A Debate Rekindled," the piece was written by David Cann, who worked at CONVEX Computer Corporation and the Computing Research Group at Livermore Labs. Cann argued that Fortran's time had passed. "The language must insulate the programmer from the underlying architecture," he wrote. "Deriving and expressing a parallel algorithm is difficult enough; one should not have to reprogram it for each new machine." Furthermore, "Parallelism must be implicit in the semantics of the language. The compilation system should not have to unravel the behavior of the computation." At the time Cann's article was published, Fortran 90 had not yet been finalized, and the High Performance Fortran Forum was hardly a year old. Although HPF would somewhat address these issues (and much of its functionality would be built into Fortran 95), Cann's larger point is that imperative languages like Fortran fail to integrate well with high-performance machines, since such languages were built with von Neumann computers in mind. "As such their computational model assumes that a single program counter will step through a program in the order of the statements within it," he explains. "This is not necessarily the best path. Because the programmer is responsible for defining the order, he or she must explicitly map the data to the physical resources of the machine." Multiple assignment statements, for example, might not be able to execute in parallel, depending on data sharing and a host of other complex factors.

Cann's solution? The same as John Backus's: functional programming using a functional language like FP, whereby multiple assignment statements could execute simultaneously and in parallel because no dependencies exist between the statements. Cann extolls the benefits of using SISAL (Streams and Iteration in a Single Assignment Language), a functional programming language that manages to increase the level of abstraction without significantly affecting performance—the same argument that Backus once made to push assembly language programmers to switch to FORTRAN.

Notwithstanding the debates that played themselves out in the realm of high-speed computing, larger questions remain: Why did Fortran, which started as world-class innovator, slip to merely keeping up with the Joneses? Why did Fortran cede ground to its competitors? Why were languages, sensing blood in the water, repeatedly trying to dethrone Fortran?

At least some of the answers to these questions can be found in a speech given at the two-day Fortran Futures '98: Fortran for High Performance Computing conference in London by Oxford University professor, X3J3 representative, and WG5 convenor Miles Ellis. Called "Is There a Role for Standards in the Future of Fortran?" and reprinted (but only as an abstract) in the *Fortran Forum*, the speech traces the arc of standards efforts: from a timely idea in the early 1960s (when there were more than fifty dialects all competing for oxygen) to 1980, once the ISO adopted FORTRAN 77 as an international standard. After that, however, things began to turn sour. "Standards have undoubtedly replaced the chaotic, competitive, potentially incompatible language development of the 1960s with a regular, safe, well-coordinated language development of today. But at what cost?" Ellis asked. Where there was once innovation, there is now a "reluctance to add any new significant features to compilers until they have been standardized internationally"—and "the international process can be very slow!" What's more, Ellis said, "It seems ironic that in a world in which a new language such as Java can be conceived, developed, launched, and become dominant in its field in less than five years, it takes at least twice that long for a major language such as Fortran to add a few simple features."

The technical community, unhampered by governing national and international bodies, moves quickly to innovate. But the Fortran standards committees have taken forever to come to any consensus, and only one member representative is needed to throw a wrench into the process, resulting in the gears grinding to a halt; for example, an objection from the German representative about a technical detail held up adoption of the Fortran 90 standards. Quite plainly, it is hard to get everyone, especially those who represent such a wide spectrum of interests, to agree on everything.

By the time the 1990s were in full swing, and multiple implementations of the language were standardized, Ellis said we would be wise to ask ourselves: Does anybody care anymore? Are the debates of the committees akin to rearranging deck chairs on the *Titanic*? In retrospect, should program portability really have been Fortran's *sine qua non*? Time and time again we see good ideas bandied about at committee meetings that won't see the light of day until two standards cycles have elapsed. That's not a nimble approach designed to keep Fortran alive and thriving; that's a central planning model, while once necessary to herd the proliferation of dialects early in the life of Fortran, that became more trouble than it was worth. "I am afraid that that very process may be killing the language," Ellis declared, adding that faster response times by these committees are a must. But committee members have consistently found great difficulty navigating between the Scylla of innovating the language, and the Charybdis of standardizing existing practices.

A vicious circle emerged by the 1990s: the committees would proceed at a snail's pace releasing new standards, while commercial vendors would hold back on releasing new compilers until the dust settled; furthermore, the vendors would balk at including new features for fear that they would prove to be incompatible with upcoming standards. Thus, the ever-looming threat of new standards came to stifle innovation; instead of a free market serving as a laboratory to test new ideas—"True, the users vote for standards with their purchases," one observer, who encouraged user participation in the standards committees, acknowledged—Fortran's fate mostly rested in the hands of central planning committees that were both slow to respond to imminent dangers and too concerned with playing it safe. When it came to Fortran, fortune favored the bold and didn't look kindly upon the timid. But the committees were reactive, more frequently adopting innovations that originated outside their hallowed halls rather than arriving at their own breakthroughs. That lack of risk-taking, while preserving the language's position for a time, didn't expand its user base, ultimately costing Fortran its place among the first-rank of languages. It went from industry leader to follower to afterthought.

When asked why the first FORTRAN development team succeeded, John Backus explained that they had a "willingness to fail." As the decades wore on, endless compromises found those tasked with Fortran's caretaking settling for increasingly less of the pie. Though well-intentioned, they were too afraid to fail, which ultimately sowed the seeds of Fortran's descent into hyper-specialization and redundancy for everyone but a precious few. Even if the newest Fortran implementation comes complete with the latest and greatest features, if Fortran programming amounts to nothing more than maintaining legacy code, then what's the point of further modernizing the language?

By 2017, sixty years after the birth of FORTRAN, one would be hard-pressed to find universities offering classes in the language, despite weather forecasting models and computational fluid dynamics programs still being run in modern variants of Fortran. Supercomputers are still benchmarked by using programs written in Fortran. A relatively recent article in *ACM Queue* magazine, entitled "The Ideal HPC [high productivity computing] Programming Language," presented the results of testing modern Fortran on the fastest computers. The objective of the study was to satisfy a request by the DARPA HPCS (High Productivity Computing Systems) program, which "sought a tenfold productivity improvement in trans-petaflop systems for HPC (high-performance computing)." The upshot: "Almost immediately, we were struck by what we were seeing. Of course, the rewritten code was much more compact and readable than the original, but, surprisingly, the 'ideal' programming language was basically Fortran." The language proved not only to be optimal, but remarkably intuitive—just like in the old days.

IN THE BEGINNING...

◇◇◇

The software researcher James Gray once quipped, "In the beginning, there was Fortran." Twenty-five years after that beginning, most of the people who midwifed the language gathered together to pay tribute to it.

An article from *Computerworld* magazine set the scene. "Elvis, Sputnik and 'I Love Lucy' were in the national consciousness on April 15, 1957, but something else with far-ranging reverberations crept quietly in the backdoor that week, hid in a corner and waited decades for its full influence to be felt."

The article was promoting Pioneer Day at the National Computer Conference—a celebration in honor of the twenty-fifth anniversary of the release of the first FORTRAN compiler; coincidently, the event also marked the twentieth anniversary of the earliest FORTRAN standardization efforts.

Pioneer Day was held on Wednesday, June 9, 1982, in Houston, Texas. That wasn't the location originally booked; New York City, where the first compiler was built, was slated to be the venue. Houston held no particularly significant meaning for the development of the language or for any of the pioneers themselves. Unfortunately, moving the conference meant that not everyone who was invited was able to attend, because of travel costs and prior commitments.

Pioneer Day itself wasn't new. Stretching back to 1974, previous Pioneer Days had celebrated BASIC and the DTSS (Dartmouth Time-Sharing System), the ENIAC, COBOL, SHARE, and, the previous year, the UNIVAC I. It was now FORTRAN's turn. This particular Pioneer Day, like the others, was years in the making, with planning involving multiple committees and consulting historians, all organized under the umbrella of the History of Computing Committee (HOCC) of the American Federation of Information Processing Societies (AFIPS). Identifying all the pioneers of FORTRAN was no easy task, but everyone agreed: there were eleven original ones. John Backus, Sheldon Best, Richard Goldberg, Lois Haibt, Harlan Herrick, Grace "Libby" Mitchell, Robert Nelson, Roy Nutt, David Sayre, Peter Sheridan, and Irving Ziller. They were an elite team that accomplished a legendary feat. And now nearly all would reconvene, reminisce, and celebrate.

An exhibit was arranged in the Astrohall with FORTRAN artifacts (including original output from the first successfully run FORTRAN program, which calculated a Laplace transform, as well as a Sheldon Best original: a hand-drawn flowchart of the index-register allocation map), memorabilia (t-shirts, microfiche of compiler source code, and an Infograph containing FORTRAN syntax), old textbooks and manuals (over 150 representative manuals were displayed), biographical information on the pioneers, and even foreign language programming manuals (e.g., a French manual, which repeatedly used the word "*faire*" in place of "do"). Harlan Herrick donated the only known copy of the 1958 IBM-produced short film demonstrating how FORTRAN could be used to tackle the "Indian Problem." And Roy Nutt donated microfilm containing a cache of FORTRAN documents to the IBM historical archives. Sub-exhibits illustrated FORTRAN's development and influence over computing culture, with a nonoperating 704 on display stealing the show. After Pioneer Day drew to a close, the entire exhibit was moved to the Santa Tessa Laboratory in San Jose, California, to take center stage there during "FORTRAN Week": July 12 to 16, 1982.

A FORTRAN archive was established at the special collections division of the Carol M. Newman Library of Virginia Tech. Three artifacts were earmarked for the archives: the contents of the exhibit, the materials collected during the organization of Pioneer Day, and the ANSI files relating to FORTRAN's standardization.

The morning of Pioneer Day featured a press conference with the nine attending original pioneers center stage. (Two weren't able to make it to the conference.) Backus led the session; J.A.N. Lee chaired it. At this "class reunion," "Many of them hadn't seen each other for 20 years or more," wrote Henry S. Tropp. "Twenty-five years earlier they had lived in each other's pockets trying to get a job done that no one had ever done before."

Two afternoon sessions were scheduled: "The Early Days of Fortran" and "The Institutionalization of Fortran." John Backus led the former session, which ran in the early afternoon hours. It included presentations by Bob Bemer, who described software at the time of FORTRAN's birth; Richard Goldberg, who not only delved into the nuts and bolts of the first compiler's register allocation algorithm, but also recounted the interactions among the development team; Roy Nutt, who detailed the state of compiler design circa 1954; Frances Allen, who offered a rundown of the first FORTRAN compiler, comparing it to contemporary efforts; and John McPherson, one of Backus's bosses at IBM during those heady days of creation, who talked about what computing was like before FORTRAN arrived on the scene.

Jeanne Adams, at the time the chair of the standards committee, followed up "The Early Days of Fortran" by chairing "The Institutionalization of Fortran" session in the late afternoon. Herbert Bright talked about life at the Westinghouse-Bettis Atomic Power Laboratory, both before and after receiving the first FORTRAN compiler accidently; Robert Hughes described how FORTRAN was employed to solve problems at the Lawrence Livermore National Laboratory; William Heising focused on the period of FORTRAN development between 1957 and 1964, from which FORTRAN II and FORTRAN IV emerged; Martin Greenfield chronicled the history of FORTRAN's standardization; Daniel McCracken spoke of the difficulty of writing programming textbooks without easy access to machine time; Charles Davidson sketched out the simplified variants of FORTRAN developed for educational use, such as WATFOR and GOTRAN; James Sakoda spoke of how he used FORTRAN to write the list processing language called DYSTAL (DYnamic STorage Allocation Language) in 1965; and Bruce Rosenblatt explained how FORTRAN managed to survive in the face of serious competition.

To promote the event, little yellow cards had been distributed with a schedule of Pioneer Day sessions on one side—complete with the Pioneer Day logo: a five-pointed star encircled with two lines of code: **DO 25 NYEAR=1957, 1982** and **25 CONTINUE**—and sayings about FORTRAN on the other, "not all complimentary," as J.A.N. Lee observed. "The Pioneer Day chairman believed that the FORTRAN concept was so strong that it was in fact a compliment to be the subject of 'digs' from such eminent computer scientists as Edsger W. Dijkstra." No publicity was bad publicity. Indeed, Dijkstra's infamous "infantile disorder" quotation made its home on the back of a card, while one of several anonymous sayings—"FORTRAN is a collection of Warts, held together by bits of Syntax"—appeared on the back of another. All told, there were eight cards, with one quote on the reverse side of each save one, which was blank on the back. Tony Hoare, the inventor of the QuickSort algorithm, proudly passed around "his" card on Pioneer Day to fellow attendees. Emblazoned on it was the following quotation: "I don't know what the language of the year 2000 will look like," it read, "but I know it will be called FORTRAN –Tony Hoare." But even by 1982, epitaphs for FORTRAN were in abundance.

One of the most notable epitaphs, in fact, arrived on FORTRAN's silver anniversary courtesy of the American computer scientist Alan Perlis, who dismissingly said, "You can measure a programmer's perspective by noting his attitude on the continuing vitality of FORTRAN." But Perlis's attitude toward FORTRAN wasn't positive from the start. Recall that he had led the effort to develop the Internal Translator (IT) compiler at Carnegie, which was completed at least a year ahead of FORTRAN. Once both compilers were in regular use, Perlis gave a series of talks about how FORTRAN took a quarter of a century in man-years to develop, while IT, which was mostly written by his graduate students, was assembled over the course of only a single summer. Perlis couldn't figure out why FORTRAN took so long to build. Reminiscing years later, John Backus freely admitted that Perlis's talks "really annoyed me." Backus eventually came to believe that Perlis simply hadn't wrapped his mind around the importance of optimizing object programs.

John Backus never put on airs; he was a homespun, iconoclastic, plainspoken man who eschewed needless luxuries while appreciating good humor and lifelong friends. He lived simply, and comfortably, and had little patience for nonsense. He had been very sick once, when he was young, diagnosed with a bone tumor; he knew his time on this earth was short, and he was determined not to waste any of it. When it came time for the Pioneer Day banquet, Backus insisted, unsurprisingly, that the affair be a simple one: no frivolities, no black-tie dress code, no extravagances, just a gathering that was "dignified while at the same time giving the opportunity for a little levity," J.A.N. Lee said. The editor-in-chief of the *Annals of the History of Computing*, Bernard A. Galler, served as the "master-of-ceremonies/toastmaster," regaling those in attendance with stories of FORTRAN and of lives well lived. Reproductions of the first FORTRAN

Manual were distributed. The evening was capped off by a screening of an IBM original short film featuring interviews with most of the pioneers (Grace Mitchell declined to participate), documenting their contributions on celluloid for posterity.

Twenty-five years after Pioneer Day, and shortly after John Backus's death, it was his one-time colleague and close collaborator Paul McJones who best captured the appeal of Backus's greatest creation. "He invented a language allowing one to express numeric algorithms in a way that was abstracted from irrelevant details of particular computers but that was efficiently implementable on a broad class of computers: from the vacuum tube IBM 704 of 1954 to the fastest supercomputer of 2007 and beyond." Backus and his team of brilliant collaborators had successfully abstracted away the machine, leading the way for the truly intrepid to follow. FORTRAN I was merely a canary in the coal mine for the greatest advances in computing yet to come.

Therefore, Fortran will never die, even if it fades away.

RESOURCES

What follows is a list of the key resources that were used for researching and writing this book. For online materials, in addition to associated websites, the authors, dates, and source publications are provided (if available).

Books

21 Lessons for the 21st Century (2018; Spiegel & Grau—New York) by Yuval Harari. A series of contemporary essays on urgent topics.

Advances in Computers, Vol. 8 (1967; Academic Press—New York) edited by Franz Alt and Morris Rubinoff. Contains chapters covering topics such as time sharing and the FORMAC language.

Adventures of a Mathematician (1976; Charles Scribner's Sons—New York) by Stanislaw Ulam. One of the greatest autobiographies ever written, which details Ulam's experiences working on the hydrogen bomb and his close friendship with John von Neumann.

The Art of Doing Science and Engineering: Learning to Learn (1997; Taylor & Francis—Australia) by Richard Hamming. A technical treatise that nonetheless offers a number of entertaining autobiographical nuggets centering on Hamming's work with the earliest computers and programming languages.

Beyond the Limits: Flight Enters the Computer Age (1989; MIT Press—Cambridge, Massachusetts) by Paul Ceruzzi. An important book when chronicling the story of FORTRAN, since it put to rest a long-standing FORTRAN myth.

Blue Pelican Java (2012; Virtualbookworm.com Publishing—College Station, Texas) by Charles E. Cook. One of the most readable modern computer science textbooks available.

Building IBM: Shaping an Industry and Its Technology (1995; MIT Press—Cambridge, Massachusetts) by Emerson Pugh. A comprehensive institutional history of the corporate leviathan.

Code: The Hidden Language of Computer Hardware and Software (2000; Microsoft Press—Redmond, Washington) by Charles Petzold. A fascinating examination of the history behind computer hardware and software, from the earliest relay machines to modern programming languages and operating systems.

Computer: A History of the Information Machine (1996; BasicBooks—New York) by Martin Campbell-Kelly and William Aspray. The first edition of the book, in particular, is an indispensable guide to the advent of hardware and software from a twentieth-century perspective.

First Generation Mainframes: The IBM 700 Series (2018; Cambridge Scholars—United Kingdom) by Stephen Kaisler. The most comprehensive book available on the early IBM mainframe machines, covering their historical origins and technical specifications.

The Fortran 2003 Handbook: The Complete Syntax, Features and Procedures (2009; Springer—London) by Jeanne Adams, et al. A technical guide to Fortran 2003.

A FORTRAN Coloring Book (1978; MIT Press—Cambridge, Massachusetts) by Roger Kaufman. Arguably the greatest introductory computer programming book ever written, Kaufman—who both wrote and illustrated—brings a sardonic wit to the proceedings that never fails to entertain.

Fun and Software: Exploring Pleasure, Paradox and Pain in Computing (2014; Bloomsbury—New York) by Olga Goriunova. An esoteric book of academic essays revolving around several nebulous themes.

Go To: The Story of the Math Majors, Bridge Players, Engineers, Chess Wizards, Maverick Scientists, and Iconoclasts—the Programmers Who Created the Software Revolution (2001; Basic Books—New York) by Steve Lohr. The author conducted original interviews with some of the principals of FORTRAN's development for a chapter of this book, thereby making it indispensable.

Hidden Figures: The American Dream and the Untold Story of the Black Women Mathematicians Who Helped Win the Space Race (2016; William Morrow—New York) by Margot Shetterly. A book expertly documenting the hidden histories of African American women who helped shape America's nascent space program.

A History of Computing in the Twentieth Century (1980; Academic Press—Orlando, Florida) edited by Nicholas Metropolis. A collection of a variety of essays on computing.

History of Programming Languages (ACM Monograph Series) (1981; Academic Press—New York) edited by Richard L. Wexelblat. Original interviews relay the fascinating stories of the development of a number of early computer languages, including FORTRAN and BASIC.

History of Programming Languages II (1996; ACM Press—New York) edited by Thomas Bergin and Richard Gibson. A sequel of sorts to the Wexelblat book, which covers the development of a later generation of programming languages.

Howard Aiken: Portrait of a Computer Pioneer (1999; MIT Press—Cambridge, Massachusetts) by I. Bernard Cohen. Easily the best biographical treatment available of Aiken, an individual critical to the early development of computers.

IBM and the Holocaust: The Strategic Alliance Between Nazi Germany and America's Most Powerful Corporation (2001; Dialog Press—Washington, D.C.) by Edwin Black. A disturbing portrait of IBM during the period leading up to World War II, as well as during the war itself.

Modern Fortran Explained: Incorporating Fortran 2018 (2018; Oxford University Press—Oxford, England) by Michael Metcalf, et al. The definitive textbook on modern Fortran.

Out of Their Minds: The Lives and Discoveries of 15 Great Computer Scientists (1995; Copernicus—New York) by Dennis Shasha and Cathy Lazere. A mostly biographical work, with technical asides, of some of the most underappreciated (and a few celebrated) computer scientists. The authors conducted original interviews for the book, which is endlessly fascinating—and certainly deserves an updated edition for this century.

The Practice of Data Analysis: Essays in Honor of John W. Tukey (1997; Princeton University Press—Princeton, New Jersey) by David Brillinger, et al. A treasure trove of essays celebrating one of the greatest thinkers of the past century, John Tukey, along with an original interview of the man.

Recent Advances and Issues in Computers (2000; Oryx Press—Phoenix, Arizona) by Martin Gay. An overview of computers, technology, and their place in society.

The River of Consciousness (2017; Alfred A. Knopf—New York) by Oliver Sacks. A posthumously-published book of wide-ranging essays penned by the famous neurologist.

Software Reliability: Principles and Practices (1976; Wiley—Hoboken, New Jersey) by Glenford Myers. Details the process of software development and testing from a mid-1970s perspective; the book (likely) gave birth to a famous FORTRAN myth.

Videos

Harvard Mark I Tour (2014) by Professor Harry Lewis at Harvard University

https://www.youtube.com/watch?v=4ObouwCHk8w

Oral History of John Backus (2006), an interview by Grady Booch for the Computer History Museum

https://www.youtube.com/watch?v=dDsWTyLEgbk&t=4591s

The associated transcript of the interview is available at:

https://amturing.acm.org/pdf/BackusTuringTranscript.pdf

The Beginnings of FORTRAN – A 25th Anniversary Documentary (1982) by IBM

https://www.youtube.com/watch?v=KohboWwrsXg&t=384s

"Thinking" Machines (1959) by IBM for *Horizons of Science*, Vol. 1, No. 4

https://www.youtube.com/watch?v=iT_Un3xo1qE

FORTRAN (1958) by the IBM Department of Education

http://www.softwarepreservation.org/projects/FORTRAN/index.html#Films/video

1401: The Dawn of a New Era (2014) for the Computer History Museum

https://www.youtube.com/watch?v=ZPpV8X91neQ

A Dozen Precursors of Fortran, Lecture by Don Knuth (2003) for the Computer History Museum

https://www.computerhistory.org/collections/catalog/102622137

Evolution of MATLAB (2011) by Cleve Moler for MathWorks

https://www.mathworks.com/videos/evolution-of-matlab-93125.html

History of the FFT with James Cooley and John Tukey (1992), from the Plenary Session Presentation at the International Conference on Acoustics, Speech, and Signal Processing

https://www.youtube.com/watch?v=o-UUudjFR1Y&t=1113s

Articles, Essays, and Historical Documents

"The Early Development of Programming Languages" (1976) by Donald Knuth and Luis Pardo for the Computer Science Department of Stanford University

https://apps.dtic.mil/docs/citations/ADA032123

"You're Not Very Smart After All" (1950) by John Kobler for *The Saturday Evening Post*

http://www.rfcafe.com/references/saturday-evening-post/youre-not-very-smart-after-all-february-18-1950-saturday-evening-post.htm

"A Short Account of Los Alamos Theoretical Work on Thermonuclear Weapons, 1946-1950" (1974) prepared by J. Carson Mark for the U.S. Atomic Energy Commission

https://nsarchive2.gwu.edu/nukevault/ebb507/docs/doc%2011%2074.07%20Mark%20on%20H%20bomb.pdf

"UNIVAC: The Troubled Life of America's First Computer" (2011) by Matthew Lasar for Ars Technica

https://arstechnica.com/tech-policy/2011/09/univac-the-troubled-life-of-americas-first-computer/

"The Teaching of Concrete Mathematics" (1958) by John W. Tukey for *The American Mathematical Monthly*

https://www.maa.org/sites/default/files/pdf/CUPM/first_40years/1958-65Tukey.pdf

"On Algebraic Compilers and Planetary Fly-By Orbits" (1994) by Richard H. Battin for the 45th Congress of the International Astronautical Federation

http://www.gravityassist.com/IAF-3.3%202010/Ref.%203-210.pdf

"The IBM 701 Speedcoding System" (1954) by John W. Backus for the *Journal of the ACM*

https://web.archive.org/web/20110813132221/http://www.softwarepreservation.org/projects/FORTRAN/paper/p4-backus.pdf

"Born of Frustration" (1999) by Leslie Goff for *Computerworld* magazine

https://books.google.com/books?id=j7iTIoJyNk0C&pg=PT80&lpg=PT80&dq=john+backus+cuthbert+hurd+memo+fortran&source=bl&ots=5Q_JUyLHMG&sig=9QXKn7Urk2REhpvaGPBH8TnqQtw&hl=en&sa=X&ved=2ahUKEwiTxpybjLvfAhWId98KHQCgA-84ChDoATAEegQIBRAB#v=onepage&q=john%20backus%20cuthbert%20hurd%20memo%20fortran&f=false

"The Sounds of Fighting Men, Howlin' Wolf and Comedy Icon Among 25 Named to the National Recording Registry" (2010)

https://www.loc.gov/item/prn-10-116/

"The Use of Sub-routines in Programs" (1952) by David Wheeler

https://web.archive.org/web/20150628022047/http://www.laputan.org/pub/papers/wheeler

"Programming on the Ferranti Mark 1" (2008) for the University of Manchester

http://curation.cs.manchester.ac.uk/digital60/www.digital60.org/birth/manchestercomputers/mark1/program.html#autocode

"Software Development at the Eckert-Mauchly Computer Company Between 1947 and 1955" (2003) by Arthur L. Norberg for the Charles Babbage Institute

http://www.cbi.umn.edu/iterations/norberg.pdf

"Automatic Coding for Digital Computers" (1955) presented by Grace Hopper at the High Speed Computer Conference at Louisiana State University

http://bitsavers.informatik.uni-stuttgart.de/pdf/univac/HopperAutoCodingPaper_1955.pdf

"1st Fortran Program Runs, September 20, 1954" (2012) by Suzanne Deffree for EDN Network

https://www.edn.com/electronics-blogs/edn-moments/4396778/1st-Fortran-program-runs--September-20--1954

"Fortran Born of Frustration" (1999) by Leslie Goff for CNN.com

http://www.cnn.com/TECH/computing/9905/03/1954.idg/index.html

"An Electric Tabulating System" (1889) by Herman Hollerith for Columbia University's *The Quarterly*

http://www.columbia.edu/cu/computinghistory/hh/index.html#%5B-245-%5D

"Punched Card Codes" by Douglas W. Jones for the Punched Card Collection

http://homepage.divms.uiowa.edu/~jones/cards/codes.html

"'Do Not Fold, Spindle or Mutilate': A Cultural History of the Punch Card" (1992) by Steven Lubar for *The Journal of American Culture*

http://www.cs.mun.ca/~harold/Courses/Old/CS1400.W15/Diary/Lubar1992.pdf

"Programming with Punched Cards" (2005) by Dale Fisk

http://www.columbia.edu/cu/computinghistory/fisk.pdf

"The IBM Punched Card" for IBM100

https://www.ibm.com/ibm/history/ibm100/us/en/icons/punchcard/

"1955: IBM Customers Form the First Computer User Group" (1999) by Mary Brandel for CNN.com

http://www.cnn.com/TECH/computing/9905/05/1955.idg/

"Voluntarism and the Fruits of Collaboration: The IBM User Group, Share" (2001) by Atsushi Akera for *Technology and Culture*

https://www.jstor.org/stable/25147801

"The IBM 029 Card Punch" (2018) by Sinclair Target for Two-Bit History

https://twobithistory.org/2018/06/23/ibm-029-card-punch.html

"x86 Assembly Guide" (2006, rev. 2018) by David Evans for the University of Virginia

http://www.cs.virginia.edu/~evans/cs216/guides/x86.html

"Epigrams on Programming" (1982) by Alan J. Perlis for SIGPLAN Notices

http://pu.inf.uni-tuebingen.de/users/klaeren/epigrams.html

"The Arithmetic Translator-Compiler of the IBM FORTRAN Automatic Coding System" (1959) by Peter Sheridan for *Communications of the ACM*

http://www.softwarepreservation.org/projects/FORTRAN/paper/p9-sheridan.pdf

"FORTRAN Comes to Westinghouse-Bettis, 1957" (1971), along with two letters (addressed to J.A.N. Lee and to John Backus, 1978) by Herbert Bright for *Computers and Automation*

http://www.softwarepreservation.org/projects/FORTRAN/paper/Bright-FORTRANComesToWestinghouseBettis-1971.pdf

"The FORTRAN Automatic Coding System" (1957) by John Backus et al. for the Western Joint Computer Conference

https://people.cs.umass.edu/~emery/classes/cmpsci691st/readings/PL/FORTRAN-102663113.05.01.acc.pdf

"Hal Laning: The Man You Didn't Know Saved Apollo 11" (2019) by Amy Shira Teitel for *Discover* magazine

http://blogs.discovermagazine.com/vintagespace/2019/05/23/hal-laning-the-man-you-didnt-know-saved-apollo-11/#.XTbpo5NKiqA

"PRINT I—The First Load-and-Go System" by Bob Bemer for his personal website

https://web.archive.org/web/20180402220910/http://www.bobbemer.com/PRINT-I.HTM

"FORTRANSIT—Making FORTRAN a Winner" by Bob Bemer for his personal website

https://web.archive.org/web/20180402220033/http://www.bobbemer.com/FTRANSIT.HTM

"In Search of the Original Fortran Compiler" (2017) by Paul McJones for the *IEEE Annals of the History of Computing*

https://ieeexplore.ieee.org/document/7974703

"FORTRAN Experience at the New York Data Processing Center" (1957) by B. G. Oldfield for SHARE

https://archive.computerhistory.org/resources/text/Fortran/102653975.05.01.acc.pdf

"Fortran and the Genesis of Project Intercept" (2005) by John Van Gardner

https://archive.computerhistory.org/resources/text/Fortran/102663109.05.01.acc.pdf

"Fortran at Livermore" by Norm Hardy

http://www.softwarepreservation.org/projects/FORTRAN/

"Laning and Zierler Algebraic Interpreter" for the Online Historical Encyclopaedia of Programming Languages

http://hopl.info/showlanguage.prx?exp=6

"Symbolic Assembler for IBM 701" for the Online Historical Encyclopaedia of Programming Languages

http://hopl.info/showlanguage2.prx?exp=120

"EGTRAN" for the Online Historical Encyclopaedia of Programming Languages

http://hopl.info/showlanguage.prx?exp=3778&language=EGTRAN

"FORTRAN IV" (2007) by John J. G. Savard

http://www.quadibloc.com/comp/fort03.htm

"Object Code Optimization" (1969) by Edward S. Lowry and C. W. Medlock for *Communications of the ACM*

https://ece.umd.edu/class/enee446.S2018/compiler-optimizations.pdf

"FORTRAN" (1964) by John W. Backus and William P. Heising for *IEEE Transactions on Electronic Computers*

http://www.softwarepreservation.org/projects/FORTRAN/paper/BackusHeising-FORTRAN-1964.pdf

"Computing Prior to FORTRAN" (1982) by Robert Bemer for the National Computer Conference, 1982

https://dl.acm.org/citation.cfm?id=1500876

"Archimedes' Cattle Problem" (2019) for Wolfram MathWorld

http://mathworld.wolfram.com/ArchimedesCattleProblem.html

"Hans Peter Luhn and the Birth of the Hashing Algorithm" (2018) by Hallam Stevens for *IEEE Spectrum*

https://spectrum.ieee.org/tech-history/silicon-revolution/hans-peter-luhn-and-the-birth-of-the-hashing-algorithm

"The Histories of Computing(s)" (2005) by Michael S. Mahoney for *Interdisciplinary Science Reviews*

http://thecorememory.com/THOC.pdf

"The History of Language Processor Technology in IBM" (1981) by Frances Allen for the *IBM Journal of Research and Development*

https://web.archive.org/web/20060106193227/http://www.research.ibm.com/journal/rd/255/ibmrd2505Q.pdf

A Technological Review of the FORTRAN I Compiler (1982) by Frances Allen for the *National Computer Conference*

http://www.softwarepreservation.org/projects/FORTRAN/paper/Allen-technological_review_FORTRAN-1982.pdf

"Go To Statement Considered Harmful" (1968) by Edsger W. Dijkstra for *Communications of the ACM*

http://www.u.arizona.edu/~rubinson/copyright_violations/Go_To_Considered_Harmful.html

"EWD 498: How Do We Tell Truths that Might Hurt?" (1982) by Edsger W. Dijkstra for *Selected Writings on Computing: A Personal Perspective*

https://www.cs.utexas.edu/users/EWD/ewd04xx/EWD498.PDF

"EWD 340: The Humble Programmer" (1972) by Edsger W. Dijkstra for *Communications of the ACM*

https://www.cs.utexas.edu/users/EWD/ewd03xx/EWD340.PDF

"EWD 692: A Review of the 1977 Turing Award Lecture by John Backus" (1978) by Edsger W. Dijkstra

https://www.cs.utexas.edu/users/EWD/transcriptions/EWD06xx/EWD692.html

"A Linguistic Contribution of GOTO-less Programming" (1973) by R. Lawrence Clark for *Datamation*

http://neil.franklin.ch/Jokes_and_Fun/Goto-less_Programming.html

"Structured Programming with go to Statements" (1974) by Donald Knuth for *ACM Computing Surveys (CSUR)*

https://dl.acm.org/citation.cfm?id=356640

"Fortran Examples" (2002) by Andrew J. Miller of Penn State University

https://sites.esm.psu.edu/~ajm138/fortranexamples.html

"The Development of JOVIAL" (1978) by Jules Schwartz for *ACM SIGPLAN Notices*

http://jovial.com/documents/p203-schwartz-jovial.pdf

"The Early History and Characteristics of PL/I" (1978) by George Radin for *ACM SIGPLAN Notices*

https://dl.acm.org/citation.cfm?id=808389

"History of IBM's Technical Contributions to High Level Programming Languages" (1981) by Jean E. Sammet for the *IBM Journal of Research and Development*

http://citeseerx.ist.psu.edu/viewdoc/download?doi=10.1.1.85.6810&rep=rep1&type=pdf

"ALGY" for HOPL

http://hopl.info/showlanguage.prx?exp=363&language=ALGY

"In Search of the Slashed Letter 'O'" for Circuitous Root

https://circuitousroot.com/artifice/letters/characters/slashed-o/index.html

"Preliminary Report—International Algebraic Language" (1958) by Alan Perlis and Klaus Samelson

http://www.softwarepreservation.org/projects/ALGOL/report/Algol58_preliminary_report_CACM.pdf

""The Syntax and Semantics of the Proposed International Algebraic Language of the Zurich ACM-GAMM Conference" (1959) by John Backus for IBM

http://www.softwarepreservation.org/projects/ALGOL/paper/Backus-Syntax_and_Semantics_of_Proposed_IAL.pdf

"Logic Theorist History" for the History of Computers website

https://history-computer.com/ModernComputer/Software/LogicTheorist.html

"History of Lisp" (1979) by John McCarthy

http://jmc.stanford.edu/articles/lisp/lisp.pdf

"Recursive Functions of Symbolic Expressions and Their Computation by Machine, Part I" (1960) by John McCarthy for *Communications of the ACM*

https://aiplaybook.a16z.com/reference-material/mccarthy-1960.pdf

"The Development of the C Language" (1993) by Dennis M. Ritchie for *HOPL-II The Second ACM SIGPLAN Conference on History of Programming Languages*

https://dl.acm.org/citation.cfm?id=155580

"A Brief History of S" (1996) by Richard A. Becker for AT&T Bell Laboratories

http://www.math.uwaterloo.ca/~rwoldfor/software/R-code/historyOfS.pdf

"The Origins of MATLAB" by Cleve Moler for MathWorks

https://www.mathworks.com/company/newsletters/articles/the-origins-of-matlab.html

"A Brief History of MATLAB" by Cleve Moler for MathWorks

https://www.mathworks.com/company/newsletters/articles/a-brief-history-of-matlab.html

"The Fortran I Compiler" (2000) by David Padua for *Computing in Science & Engineering*

https://dl.acm.org/citation.cfm?id=615769

"Can Programming Be Liberated From the Von Neumann Style? A Functional Style and Its Algebra of Programs" (1978) by John Backus for *Communications of the ACM*

https://www.thocp.net/biographies/papers/backus_turingaward_lecture.pdf

"From Fortran and Algol to Object-Oriented Languages" (1993) by Maurice V. Wilkes for *Communications of the ACM*

https://dl.acm.org/citation.cfm?id=159553&dl=ACM&coll=DL

"A Poor Man's Realization of Recursive Structured Fortran" (1981) by Masataka Sassa for *ACM SIGPLAN Notices*

https://dl.acm.org/citation.cfm?id=947840

"Organization of Computer Experts Calls ABM Project a Dangerous Mistake" (1971) for Computer Professionals Against ABM

https://stacks.stanford.edu/file/druid:pc764bb9418/pc764bb9418.pdf

"The Presidential Prize Caper" (1974) by Deborah Shapley for *Science*

https://science.sciencemag.org/content/183/4128/938

"History and Summary of FORTRAN Standardization Development for the ASA" (1964) by William P. Heising for *Communications of the ACM*

https://dl.acm.org/citation.cfm?id=364971

"SOFTWARE; When Few Knew the Code, They Changed the Language" (2001) by Steve Lohr for *The New York Times*

https://www.nytimes.com/2001/06/13/business/software-when-few-knew-the-code-they-changed-the-language.html

"As You Sow So Shall You Reap" (2004) by Paul McJones for Dusty Decks: Preserving Historic Software

https://mcjones.org/dustydecks/archives/category/share/

"History of FORTRAN Standardization" (1982) by Martin N. Greenfield for AFIPS '82 Proceedings of the June 7-10, 1982, National Computer Conference

https://dl.acm.org/citation.cfm?id=1500877

"Status of Work Toward Revision of Programming Language Fortran" (1984) by Jerrold L. Wagener for *ACM SIGNUM Newsletter*

https://dl.acm.org/citation.cfm?id=1040946

"The Fortran (Not the Foresight) Saga: The Light and the Dark" (1990) by Brian Meek for *ACM SIGPLAN Fortran Forum*

https://dl.acm.org/citation.cfm?doid=101363.101367

"A Brief History of FORTRAN 77" (1996) by Adam Marshall of the University of Liverpool

http://www.mrao.cam.ac.uk/~pa/f90Notes/HTMLNotesnode5.html

"Letter O Considered Harmful?" (2010) on Stack Overflow

https://stackoverflow.com/questions/3902239/letter-o-considered-harmful

"The RISKS Digest: Forum on Risks to the Public in Computers and Related Systems" (1987) for the ACM Committee on Computers and Public Policy

https://catless.ncl.ac.uk/Risks/5/66

"Mariner 1" for NASA's website

https://nssdc.gsfc.nasa.gov/nmc/spacecraft/display.action?id=MARIN1

"Interstellar 8-Track: How Voyager's Vintage Tech Keeps Running" (2013) by Adam Mann for *Wired*

https://www.wired.com/2013/09/vintage-voyager-probes/

"The Fortran 8x Standard" (1987) by Thomas M. Lahey for *ACM SIGPLAN Fortran Forum*

https://dl.acm.org/citation.cfm?id=41565

"Whither Fortran?" (1991) by Michael Metcalf and John Reid for *ACM SIGPLAN Fortran Forum*

https://dl.acm.org/citation.cfm?id=122009

"FORTRAN: First in a Six-Part Series on Languages that have Stood the Test of Time" (1991) by Doris Appleby for *BYTE* magazine

https://archive.org/details/eu_BYTE-1991-09_OCR

"Retire Fortran? A Debate Rekindled" (1991) by David Cann for Supercomputing '91: Proceedings of the 1991 ACM/IEEE Conference on Supercomputing

https://dl.acm.org/citation.cfm?id=125976

"The Rise and Fall of High Performance Fortran: An Historical Object Lesson" (2007) by Ken Kennedy, Charles Koelbel, and Hans Zima for the HOPL III Proceedings of the Third ACM SIGPLAN Conference on History of Programming Languages

https://dl.acm.org/citation.cfm?id=1238844.1238851

"Essential Lahey Fortran 90" for Lahey Computer Systems, Inc.

http://www.lahey.com/elfpage.htm

"Fortran Reflections" (1997) by Jerry Wagener for *ACM SIGPLAN Fortran Forum*

https://dl.acm.org/citation.cfm?id=274104.274105

"Is There a Role for Standards in the Future of Fortran?" (1998) by Miles Ellis for *ACM SIGPLAN Fortran Forum*

https://dl.acm.org/citation.cfm?id=570978

"Notes/Executive Summary of Fortran Futures '98" (1998) by Chuck Koelbel

https://fortran.bcs.org/1998/fortranfutures98.htm

"Co-Array Fortran for Parallel Programming" (1998) by Robert W. Numrich and John Reid for *ACM SIGPLAN Fortran Forum*

https://dl.acm.org/citation.cfm?id=289920

"Doctor Fortran in 'Eighteen is the New Fifteen'" (2017) by Steve Lionel for Intel

https://software.intel.com/en-us/blogs/2017/11/20/doctor-fortran-in-eighteen-is-the-new-fifteen

"Fortran 2000 CD Ballot and WG5's Response" (2003) by John Reid for *ACM SIGPLAN Fortran Forum*

https://dl.acm.org/citation.cfm?id=941562

"Fortran 95 and Fortran 2000" (1995) by Jerrold Wagener for *ACM SIGPLAN Fortran Forum*

https://dl.acm.org/citation.cfm?id=221291

"Whither Fortran?" (2002) by Dan Nagle for *ACM SIGPLAN Fortran Forum*

https://dl.acm.org/citation.cfm?doid=510892.510893

"Fortran Photo Archive" (2003) by Jerry Wagener for *ACM SIGPLAN Fortran Forum*

https://dl.acm.org/citation.cfm?id=941563

"Fortran Trivia Questions" (2003) by Jeanne T. Martin for *ACM SIGPLAN Fortran Forum*

https://dl.acm.org/citation.cfm?id=941564

"Automatic Fortran to C++ conversion with FABLE" (2012) by Ralf W. Grosse-Kunstleve et al. for *Source Code for Biology and Medicine*

https://www.ncbi.nlm.nih.gov/pmc/articles/PMC3448510/

"High Performance Fast Computing Challenge" (2017) for NASA

https://www.herox.com/HPFCC/updates

"The HeroX Fortran Storytelling Competition" (2017) for the HeroX website

https://www.herox.com/fortran-story

"Happy 60th Birthday, Fortran" (2017) by Ben Cotton for opensource.com

https://opensource.com/article/17/11/happy-60th-birthday-fortran

"The Ideal HPC Programming Language" (2010) by Eugene Loh for *ACM Queue*

https://queue.acm.org/detail.cfm?id=1820518

"Pioneer Day to Honor Fortran" (1982) for *Computerworld*

https://books.google.com/books?id=QghOwt8qQsEC&printsec=frontcover&dq=computerworld+may+31,+1982&hl=en&sa=X&ved=0ahUKEwjSkJKt6YXjAhVhhuAKHbDHAyEQ6AEILzAC#v=onepage&q=fortran&f=false

"Pioneer Day, 1982" (1984) by J.A.N. Lee for *Annals of the History of Computing*
"FORTRAN Anecdotes" (1984) by Henry S. Tropp for *Annals of the History of Computing*
"[SHARE] Meetings in Retrospect" (1984)

https://ieeexplore.ieee.org/xpl/tocresult.jsp?isnumber=4392944

"The Fortran Story Retold" (2016) compiled by Loren Meissner, which includes the following articles:

- "More on the SAVE Statement" (1974) by Betty Holberton
- "ANS X3.9 Fortran Revision—Final Report" (1977) by Frank Engel
- "Early Fortran User Experience" (1984) by Herbert S. Bright for the *Annals of the History of Computing*
- "The Emergence of Fortran IV from Fortran II" (1984) by William P. Heising for the *Annals*
- "Early Fortran at Livermore" (1984) by Robert A. Hughes for the *Annals*
- "Fortran Activities at SHARE Meeting" (1984) by Elliott C. Nohr for the *Annals*
- "Numerical Recipes in Fortran 90" (1996) by Michael Metcalf for *Fortran Numerical Recipes*
- "Fortran 95 Handbook" (1997) by Jeanne C. Adams et. al.
- "The Seven Ages of Fortran" (2011) by Michael Metcalf for the *Journal of Computer Science and Technology*

http://ed-thelen.org/FortranHistories/2%20The%20Fortran%20Story%20Retold.pdf

Interviews

"An Interview with Gene M. Amdahl" (1986 to 1989) conducted by Arthur L. Norberg for the Charles Babbage Institute

https://conservancy.umn.edu/bitstream/handle/11299/104341/oh107gma.pdf?sequence=1&isAllowed=y

"An Interview with Cuthbert C. Hurd" (1981) conducted by Nancy Stern for the Charles Babbage Institute

https://conservancy.umn.edu/bitstream/handle/11299/107368/oh076cch.pdf?sequence=1&isAllowed=y

"An Interview with Edsger W. Dijkstra" (2001) conducted by Philip L. Frana for the Charles Babbage Institute

https://conservancy.umn.edu/bitstream/handle/11299/107247/oh330ewd.pdf?sequence=1&isAllowed=y

"Oral History of Captain Grace Hopper" (1980) conducted by Angeline Pantages for the Computer History Museum

http://archive.computerhistory.org/resources/text/Oral_History/Hopper_Grace/102702026.05.01.pdf

"An Interview with Bob Hughes" (1997) conducted by George A. Michael for *Stories of the Development of Large Scale Scientific Computing at Lawrence Livermore National Laboratory: An Oral and Pictorial History*

http://www.computer-history.info/Page1.dir/pages/Hughes.html

"An Interview with Frances E. Holberton" (1983) conducted by James Ross for the Charles Babbage Institute

https://conservancy.umn.edu/bitstream/handle/11299/107363/oh050feh.pdf?sequence=1&isAllowed=y

"Richard Stallman: High School Misfit, Symbol of Free Software, MacArthur-Certified Genius" (1999), an interview of Richard Stallman by Michael Gross for a bonus chapter of *The More Things Change: Why the Baby Boom Won't Fade Away*

http://mgross.com/writing/books/my-generation/bonus-chapters/richard-stallman-high-school-misfit-symbol-of-free-software-macarthur-certified-genius/

"An Interview with Friedrich L. Bauer" (1987) conducted by William Aspray for the Charles Babbage Institute

https://web.archive.org/web/20120422070035/http://conservancy.umn.edu/bitstream/107106/1/oh128flb.pdf

"James W. Cooley, an Oral History" (1997) conducted by Andrew Goldstein for the IEEE History Center

http://ethw.org/Oral-History:James_W._Cooley

"An Interview with Cleve Moler" (2004) conducted by Thomas Haigh for the Society for Industrial and Applied Mathematics

http://archive.computerhistory.org/resources/access/text/2013/12/102746804-05-01-acc.pdf

"Daniel McCracken Interview" (2008) conducted by Arthur L. Norberg for the Association of Computing Machinery

http://delivery.acm.org/10.1145/1460000/1452135/a11-mccracken.pdf?ip=71.224.34.52&id=1452135&acc=OPEN&key=4D4702B0C3E38B35%2E4D4702B0C3E38B35%2E4D4702B0C3E38B35%2E6D218144511F3437&__acm__=1563212140_2b38aec493b2bc8993c10723354dbd3a

"Ward Whaling Interview" (1999) conducted by Shelley Erwin for archives of the California Institute of Technology

http://oralhistories.library.caltech.edu/122/1/Whaling_OHO.pdf

Biographies, Obituaries, and Death Notices

"John Backus Biography" (2014) for the History of Computing Project

http://www.thocp.net/biographies/backus_john.htm

"John W. Backus, 82, Fortran Developer, Dies" (2007) by Steve Lohr for *The New York Times*

https://www.nytimes.com/2007/03/20/business/20backus.html

"John W. Backus" (2007), an obituary by Rene Gabriels, Dirk Gerrits, and Peter Kooijmans

http://dirkgerrits.com/publications/john-backus.pdf

"Pathfinder" (1979) by Claire Stegmann for IBM *THINK Magazine*

http://www.softwarepreservation.org/projects/FORTRAN/paper/Backus-Think.pdf

Biography of John Presper Eckert for the History of Computers (Hardware, Software, the Internet...) website

http://history-computer.com/People/EckertBio.html

"Edmund C. Berkeley" (1995) by J.A.N. Lee for the IEEE Computer Society

http://history.computer.org/pioneers/berkeley.html

"Laszlo A. Belady" (1995) by J.A.N. Lee for the IEEE Computer Society

https://history.computer.org/pioneers/belady.html

"Peter B. Sheridan" (1995) by J.A.N. Lee for the IEEE Computer Society

https://history.computer.org/pioneers/sheridan.html

"Richard Goldberg" (1995) by J.A.N. Lee for the IEEE Computer Society

https://history.computer.org/pioneers/goldberg.html

"Frances E. Holberton, 84, Early Computer Programmer" (2001) by Steve Lohr for *The New York Times*

https://www.nytimes.com/2001/12/17/business/frances-e-holberton-84-early-computer-programmer.html

"Frances Holberton, 84; Pioneer Programmer of Early Computers" (2001) by Claudia Levy for the *Los Angeles Times*

https://www.latimes.com/archives/la-xpm-2001-dec-15-me-15190-story.html

"A.M. Turing Award Laureate: Frances ('Fran') Elizabeth Allen" (2006) by Guy Steele for the Association for Computing Machinery

https://amturing.acm.org/award_winners/allen_1012327.cfm

"Cuthbert Hurd, 85, Computer Pioneer at I.B.M." (1996) by Laurence Zuckerman for *The New York Times*

https://www.nytimes.com/1996/06/02/us/cuthbert-hurd-85-computer-pioneer-at-ibm.html

"Roy Nutt Dies at 59; Helped to Develop Computer Language" (1990) by Alfonso A. Narvaez for *The New York Times*

https://www.nytimes.com/1990/06/20/obituaries/roy-nutt-dies-at-59-helped-to-develop-computer-language.html

"Dedication of the Roy Nutt Mathematics, Engineering, & Computer Science Center at Trinity College" (2012), a biography of Roy Nutt by Micah Nutt

https://www.trincoll.edu/NewsEvents/NewsArticles/Documents/nutt-dedication-program-web.pdf

"David Sayre (1924–2012)" (2012) by Janos Kirz and Jianwei Miao for *Nature*

https://www.nature.com/articles/484038a

"Daniel D. McCracken, Expert on Computers, Dies at 81" (2011) by Steve Lohr for *The New York Times*

https://www.nytimes.com/2011/08/13/technology/daniel-d-mccracken-dies-at-81-wrote-best-sellers-on-using-computers.html

"Nathan Rochester" for the Online Historical Encyclopaedia of Programming Languages

http://hopl.info/showperson.prx?PeopleID=654

"Edsger Wybe Dijkstra" (2008) by J. J. O'Connor and E. F. Robertson for the MacTutor Archive

http://www-history.mcs.st-and.ac.uk/history/Biographies/Dijkstra.html

"William P. Heising Obituary" (2002) by *Dallas Morning News* for Legacy.com

https://obits.dallasnews.com/obituaries/dallasmorningnews/obituary.aspx?n=william-p-heising&pid=544161

"John Palmer Obituary" (2015) by *The Greater New Milford Spectrum* for Legacy.com

https://www.legacy.com/obituaries/newmilfordspectrum/obituary.aspx?pid=175304394

"Ken Kennedy, 61, a Pioneer of Computer Software, Dies" (2007) by John Markoff for *The New York Times*

https://www.nytimes.com/2007/02/09/obituaries/09kennedy.html

"James K. Knowles" (2010), an obituary for Caltech's *Engineering & Science* magazine

http://calteches.library.caltech.edu/705/2/Obituaries.pdf

Manuals, Technical Reports, and Standards

"IBM Speedcoding System for the Type 701 Electronic Data Processing Machines" (1954)

https://www.computerhistory.org/collections/catalog/102678975

"A Program for Translation of Mathematical Equations for Whirlwind I" (1954) by J. Halcombe Laning and Neil Zierler for MIT

https://archive.computerhistory.org/resources/text/Fortran/102653982.05.01.acc.pdf

"Preliminary Report: Specifications for the IBM Mathematical FORmula TRANslating System, FORTRAN" (1954)

http://archive.computerhistory.org/resources/text/Fortran/102679231.05.01.acc.pdf

"Preliminary Operator's Manual: The FORTRAN Automatic Coding System for the IBM 704 EDPM" (1957)

http://www.softwarepreservation.org/projects/FORTRAN/manual/Prelim_Oper_Man-1957_04_07.pdf

"American National Standard Hollerith Punched Card Codes" (1980)

https://archive.org/details/federalinformat1411nati_0

"Coding for the MIT-IBM 704 Computer" (1957) edited by F. Helwig for the MIT Computation Center

http://www.textfiles.com/bitsavers/pdf/mit/computer_center/Coding_for_the_MIT-IBM_704_Computer_Oct57.pdf

"704 Electronic Data-Processing Machine: Manual of Operation" (1954, 1955) by IBM

http://www.bitsavers.org/pdf/ibm/704/24-6661-2_704_Manual_1955.pdf

"FORTRAN Programmer's Reference Manual: Automatic Coding System for the IBM 704" (1956) by David Sayre at IBM

https://www.fortran.com/FortranForTheIBM704.pdf

"Addenda to the FORTRAN Programmer's Reference Manual" (1957) by the FORTRAN Development Team

http://www.softwarepreservation.org/projects/FORTRAN/manual/Addenda_to_FORTRAN_Prog_Ref_Manual.pdf

"FORTRAN Introductory Programmer's Manual" (1957) by Grace E. Mitchell for IBM

http://www.softwarepreservation.org/projects/FORTRAN/manual/Intro-Section_I.pdf

"The FORTRAN Automatic Coding System for the IBM 704 EDPM: Programmer's Primer" (1957) by Grace E. Mitchell for IBM

http://www.softwarepreservation.org/projects/FORTRAN/manual/IBM-704-FORTRAN-Primer-a-32-0306.pdf

"Reference Manual for the FOR TRANSIT Automatic Coding System for the IBM 650 Data Processing System" (1957) by IBM

http://bitsavers.informatik.uni-stuttgart.de/pdf/ibm/650/28-4028_FOR_TRANSIT.pdf

"Proposed Specifications for FORTRAN II for the 704" (August, September, and November 1957) by Irv Ziller for IBM

https://archive.computerhistory.org/resources/text/Fortran/102653976.05.01.acc.pdf
https://archive.computerhistory.org/resources/text/Fortran/102663106.05.01.acc.pdf
https://archive.computerhistory.org/resources/text/Fortran/102679263.05.01.acc.pdf

"Reference Manual: FORTRAN II for the IBM 704 Data Processing System" (1958) by IBM

http://bitsavers.org/pdf/ibm/704/C28-6000-2_704_FORTRANII.pdf

"Reference Manual: IBM 709/7090 Programming Systems: Fortran Assembly Program (FAP)" (1962) by IBM

https://archive.org/details/fortran-assembly

"FORTRAN ASSEMBLY PROGRAM (FAP) for the IBM 709/7090" (1960, 1961) by Donald Moore for IBM

http://www.softwarepreservation.org/projects/FORTRAN/J28-6098-1-709_7090_FAP.pdf

"Serial Compilation and the 1401 FORTRAN Compiler" (1965) by Leonard Haines for the *IBM Systems Journal*

http://ibm-1401.info/FortranII_1401_SerialCompiler_IBMJR&D_Haines_1965.pdf

"IBM System/360 and System/370 FORTRAN IV Language Reference Manual" (1974) for IBM

http://web.eah-jena.de/~kleine/history/languages/GC28-6515-10-FORTRAN-IV-Language.pdf

"American National Standard FORTRAN" (1966) by the American National Standards Institute

https://wg5-fortran.org/ARCHIVE/Fortran66.pdf

"ARDC Technical Report No. 5 BRLESC I/II FORTRAN" (1970) by Lloyd W. Campbell and Glenn A. Beck for the Aberdeen Research and Development Center

https://apps.dtic.mil/dtic/tr/fulltext/u2/704343.pdf

"Cray-1 & Cray X-MP Computer System – Fortran (CFT) Reference Manual" (1983)

http://www.computinghistory.org.uk/det/2402/Cray-1-Cray-X-MP-Computer-System-Fortran-(CFT)-Reference-Manual/

FORTRAN 77 Standards (1978)

https://wg5-fortran.org/ARCHIVE/Fortran77.html

Fortran 90 Standards (1991)

https://wg5-fortran.org/N001-N1100/N692.pdf

"Military Standard 1753 FORTRAN, DoD Supplement To American National Standard X3.9-1978" (1978)

https://webcache.googleusercontent.com/search?q=cache:n5fdEmpPT0EJ:https://wg5-fortran.org/ARCHIVE/mil_std_1753.html+&cd=1&hl=en&ct=clnk&gl=us

Sun Microsystems FORTRAN 77 4.0 Reference Manual (1995)

https://docs.oracle.com/cd/E19957-01/802-2998/802-2998.pdf

"TS 29113 Further Interoperability of Fortran with C" (2012)

https://wg5-fortran.org/N1901-N1950/N1917.pdf

"The New Features of Fortran 2008" (2010) by John Reid for the WG5

https://wg5-fortran.org/N1801-N1850/N1828.pdf

"The New Features of Fortran 2018" (2018) by John Reid for the WG5

https://isotc.iso.org/livelink/livelink?func=ll&objId=19441669&objAction=Open

"Minutes of the Fortran Experts Group: Meeting at Vienna, 14-17 June 1982"

https://wg5-fortran.org/N001-N1100/N055.pdf

Other Online Ephemera

Columbia University Computing History: A Chronology of Computing at Columbia University by Frank da Cruz

http://www.columbia.edu/cu/computinghistory/

IBM Archives: Valuable Resources on IBM's History

http://www-03.ibm.com/ibm/history/

History of FORTRAN and FORTRAN II by Paul McJones for the Computer History Museum's Software Preservation Group

http://www.softwarepreservation.org/projects/FORTRAN/

Timeline of Computer History: Software & Languages for the Computer History Museum

https://www.computerhistory.org/timeline/software-languages/

The IBM 1401 Demo Lab and Restoration Project: Computer History Museum

http://ibm-1401.info/

John W. Mauchly Papers at Penn Libraries of the University of Pennsylvania

http://dla.library.upenn.edu/dla/ead/detail.html?id=EAD_upenn_rbml_PUSpMsColl925

Chronological Listing of A.M. Turing Award Winners

https://amturing.acm.org/byyear.cfm

SSEC Writings (2014) by Anne Pasek, NYU doctoral candidate, on her blog *QueerFragments*

https://queerfragments.wordpress.com/tag/ssec/

Cecil F. Backus in the 1940 Census for ancestry.com

https://www.ancestry.com/1940-census/usa/Delaware/Cecil-F-Backus_1lyq

"Really Old Code" (2017) by "ReallyOld"

https://reallyoldcode.wordpress.com/

"A Chronology of Computing at The University of Waterloo" (2007) by Lawrence Folland and Daniel Heidt for the David R. Cheriton School of Computer Science at the University of Waterloo

https://cs.uwaterloo.ca/40th/Chronology/

Roger Emanuel Kaufman (Author of *A FORTRAN Coloring Book*) Faculty Website

https://www2.seas.gwu.edu/~kaufman1/

The Virtual Keypunch

https://www.masswerk.at/keypunch/

Compiler Explorer

https://godbolt.org

Fortran Online Compiler

https://rextester.com/l/fortran_online_compiler

The Jargon File – The Jargon Lexicon

http://catb.org/jargon/html/index.html

US Fortran Standards Committee

https://j3-fortran.org/

"Fortran 90 for the Fortran 77 Programmer" (1993 and 1996) by Bo Einarsson and Yurij Shokin

http://ergodic.ugr.es/cphysn/LECCIONES/FORTRAN/f77to90/index.htm

The F Programming Language Homepage

https://www.fortran.com/F/index.html

The GNU Fortran Homepage

https://gcc.gnu.org/fortran/

The "Fortran" Song (1960s), sung by the Caltech Stock Company for the LP *Let's Advance on Science*

https://www.youtube.com/watch?v=yd6FLETYZ_c
https://www.discogs.com/Caltech-Stock-Company-Lets-Advance-On-Science/release/4028442
https://archives.caltech.edu/repositories/2/accessions/1615.html

ACKNOWLEDGMENTS
◊◊◊

Although I was vaguely aware of the language as a kid, diligently pecking away at type-in listings on my Tandy Color Computer 2, I first encountered books on FORTRAN in the stacks of my university's library many years later. I recall reading through the workmanlike *FORTRAN for Humans* (1977), and, fascinated, scribbling some notes down. But that didn't inspire me like my next serendipitous find: *A FORTRAN Coloring Book* (1978) by Roger Kaufman, a true masterpiece of an introductory programming book if there ever was one.

After researching the history of BASIC for my book *Endless Loop*, I knew I had to revisit FORTRAN—this time through a historical lens. However, just as I discovered when studying BASIC, I could not find a single source that thoroughly covered the wide scope of the history and development of what is surely the most significant high-level programming language, if not programming language in general, ever devised. Instead, I encountered detailed, technical works that restricted themselves to narrow timeframes or short, wide-ranging pieces that lacked depth.

Assembling the full story was some of the hardest work I've ever done as a writer, but FORTRAN's biography was long overdue in being told. Papers by (and, in some cases, interviews of) the following central players in the drama of FORTRAN were the most helpful: John W. Backus, who offered his inimitable first-person view of the gestation and birth of FORTRAN; Frances Allen and Bob Hughes, who mostly described the early-to-middle years; and Martin Greenfield, Brian Meek, Michael Metcalf, and John Reid, who detailed the maturation and standardization of the language, nearly up to the present day.

Documents found, retained, and distributed by the Computer History Museum (CHM) were invaluable to my research. The museum—which began small at the Digital Equipment Corporation (DEC) in Marlborough, Massachusetts, then moved to Boston, and, expanded and reconstituted, is now located in Mountain View, California—is "home to the largest international collection of computing artifacts in the world"; those artifacts are both of the hardware and the software variety (along with other odds and ends). For instance, a fully working 1959 IBM 1401 Data Processing System makes its home in the museum.

In the early 2000s, an innocuous e-mail urging the preservation of "classic software products" led to an expedition by a founding member of the CHM's Software Preservation Group, Paul McJones: the gathering of original FORTRAN materials. For example, John Backus donated his copy of the 1954 FORTRAN Preliminary Report (which, on the cover page, has the words "Original Copy/Property of Jean Sammet" scrawled at the top). By 2005, McJones realized that he had enough material to create and curate a comprehensive webpage on the Computer History Museum website devoted to the history of FORTRAN I and II. Without the continued efforts of McJones as well as the entire staff of the CHM to keep the historical legacy of FORTRAN and other programming languages alive deep into the twenty-first century, this book would have been vastly more difficult to write.

The story of FORTRAN has many moving parts, I quickly came to realize; tackling a subject as expansive and complex as FORTRAN really meant attempting to write a comprehensive history of the earliest days of programming. Plus, many computing stories conflict or are incomplete, a point driven home by Henry S. Tropp's fascinating article about Pioneer Day called "FORTRAN Anecdotes"; the Rashomon effect does its part to make all oral histories suspect. Of course, I couldn't include all versions of every FORTRAN anecdote I discovered, or information detailing every FORTRAN dialect, lest this book—which runs long as it is—would have been an encyclopedic effort twice as thick. Ultimately, narrative choices dictated the final shape and form of ABSTRACTING AWAY THE MACHINE. Whether the choices made were the correct ones is, as always, a job for my readers to determine.

ABOUT THE AUTHOR
◊◊◊

Mark Jones Lorenzo, a teacher of mathematics and computer programming, is the author of *Endless Loop: The History of the BASIC Programming Language* as well as many other books. He lives in Pennsylvania with his dogs.

Made in United States
Troutdale, OR
07/16/2025